TOO
MANY
WOMEN?

TOO MANY WOMEN?

The Sex Ratio Question

Marcia Guttentag
Paul F. Secord

SAGE PUBLICATIONS
Beverly Hills / London / New Delhi

Copyright © 1983 by Sage Publications, Inc.

For information address:

SAGE Publications, Inc.
275 South Beverly Drive
Beverly Hills, California 90212

SAGE Publications India Pvt. Ltd.
C-236 Defence Colony
New Delhi 110 024, India

SAGE Publications Ltd
28 Banner Street
London EC1Y 8QE, England

Printed in the United States of America

Library of Congress Cataloging in Publication Data

Guttentag, Marcia.
  Too many women?

   1. Sex customs—History. 2. Sex ratio—Social
aspects—History. 3. Women—Social conditions.
4. Sex role—History. I. Secord, Paul F. II. Title.
HQ12.G88 1982   305.3   82-19192
ISBN 0-8039-1918-2
ISBN 0-8039-1919-0 (pbk.)

SECOND PRINTING, 1983

This book is dedicated to the memory of Marcia Guttentag.

—P.F.S.

CONTENTS

PREFACE

This book was Marcia Guttentag's "letter to the world," to use a phrase from her favorite poet, Emily Dickinson. She believed that the idea which led her to write these pages was the most creative and powerful one she had in her lifetime. When talking about this project or working on it, Marcia was aglow with the joy of discovery and creation. Although it is a tragedy that her career was cut short at the height of her powers and that she did not live to complete more than one-half of the book, much less to see it in print, I am happy to have completed it for her. No memorial could be more fitting.

This book is generated from a simple but powerful idea: that the number of opposite-sex partners potentially available to men or women has profound effects on sexual behaviors and sexual mores, on patterns of marriage and divorce, childrearing conditions and practices, family stability, and certain structural aspects of society itself. Although the importance of male-female ratios among animals and humans was recognized by Charles Darwin, no one has fully developed the idea by making a comprehensive survey of the evidence for it and pointing out its profound implications. This book attempts to do just that.

That this task has not been undertaken previously should not be surprising; only the most intrepid scholar would attempt it. Marcia's boldness in meeting the challenge is clear from a look at what is required. She reviewed anthropological studies of primitive societies, ranged all the way back in history to the ancient Greeks and Romans, examined the early and late Middle Ages, and studied the lives of Orthodox Jews and of blacks in contemporary America. Dealing adequately with the evidence and its interpretation required no less than the use of history, sociology, anthropology, psychology, and reproductive biology.

From the magnitude of the task, it should be apparent that this book is only a first attempt at developing a sex ratio thesis and weighing the evidence for it. No single historical period or line of argument combined with evidence could be treated in great detail in a work of this kind. Our hope is that the book will stimulate other scholars to pursue the many ramifications of the thesis with further studies.

Marcia worked on the book in intermittent stretches during the last three years of her life. At the time of her death, toward the end of 1977, she had drafted Chapters 1, 2, 3, 4 and 8, dealing with the topics just referred to. Only a few notes, scattered statistics, and other miscellaneous materials existed for portions of the remainder. Fortunately, I had heard her discuss the book repeatedly and at length with friends and colleagues, and she had discussed it endlessly with me. As a result, I was able to carry out her general plan for completing the book. It was the least I could do for the extraordinary woman to whom I was married for the last five years of her life.

In addition to rewriting and extending the drafts that Marcia left behind, I have written Chapters 5, 6, 7 and 9, and have replaced her first chapter with an entirely new one that takes advantage of the overall perspective provided by the finished book. Chapter 5 deals with colonial and early America. Chapter 6 develops a theoretical interpretation showing how sex ratios are linked to relationships between men and women and to the roles that they assume. Chapter 7 takes us through the modern period in the United States, and Chapter 9 concludes the book with implications for the future identity of women.

Before citing our profound indebtedness to legions of scholars, colleagues, and students, let me report an anecdote in Marcia's own words, explaining how the central idea of this book occurred to her. She had been striving to understand some recent mental health statistics on young women indicating that rates of depression, suicide attempts, and other mental health indicators had risen sharply during recent years, and she reported the following:

> I was absorbed in these issues, and struggling to find out what might account for this radical change, when my family and I attended a performance of The Magic Flute. It was the first time I had heard the opera in English. The lyrics were astounding. They gave me a sense of cultural shock. Throughout much of the opera each of the male leads, Papageno and Tamino, sings of his determination to find a wife, and his longing to make a commitment to a woman for life. Both sing of the many obstacles they are willing to overcome in order to claim their beloved. The intensity of their desire is demonstrated by their willingness to undergo severe trials in order to enter Sarastro's brotherhood and claim their respective loves.
>
> Women were depicted in Mozart's opera in a manner not too different from the way they were idealized in the popular songs of the 1930s, 1940s, and 1950s. The songs of those decades emphasized romantic love, exclusive commitment for life, marriage, and monogamy. Even if taken as a parody on romantic love (see Jacques Chailley, The Magic Flute), Mozart's lyrics are in striking contrast with attitudes toward women in the U.S. today. I asked my 16-year-old daughter whether she had noticed anything odd. She said that the lyrics were strange because the men sang about wanting to make a life-long commitment to one woman—a wife.
>
> To test our impression of dramatic change, we went home and listened to records of current popular music. All the songs were about brief liaisons and

casual relationships between men and women; the theme was "Love 'em and leave 'em." There was no sign of a male's intention to make a long-term sexual commitment, and marriage was never mentioned. Why? Why the difference between Mozart's lyrics two centuries ago and our lyrics today? Could this profound shift in attitudes and behavior toward women be related to the sharp rises in statistical indicators reflecting stress and unhappiness among young women? Was there some way in which it all fitted together, and if so, how?

One striking possibility came to mind. Are there too many unattached women? Is there actually a shortage of men? If there is, could this possibly explain *all* of these changes? What kinds of evidence would test such a hypothesis? These speculations led me on an exciting intellectual journey from the present into the past, during which I pored over census statistics, sex ratios, and numerous historical materials going all the way back to the ancient Greeks. This book is a report on that fascinating trip.

Our debt to scholars, students, and friends is enormous. A wide-ranging, interdisciplinary project like this would have been impossible without their help. Almost every time that we talked about our ideas concerning the social effects of population shortages or surpluses of women or men, someone would come up with relevant material from their own area of expertise. We are especially indebted to David and Patricia Herlihy. Not only were they warmly encouraging as Co-Masters of Harvard's Mather House, but David's work on the medieval family made our manuscript on that period possible. And Pat Herlihy brought to our attention an article in Yiddish detailing nine censuses of Jews and other ethnic groups in nineteenth-century Russia, which led us to include an important section on sex ratios at birth among Orthodox Jews.

Ernst Badian's review of Sarah Pomeroy's *Women in Classical Antiquity* led us to discuss sex ratios with him, and he brought to our attention the differences between classical Athens and Sparta. Moreover, he encouraged Jay Hayward to measure sex ratios among fourth-century B.C. Athenians. Stanford Lyman alerted us to the remarkable sex ratios found among the Chinese-Americans in the 19th century, and Robert Fogel led us to some valuable demographic data on blacks in the plantation era, provided by Richard Stekel. Mildred Dickeman sent us her unpublished papers on female infanticide.

Various scholars generously read parts of the manuscript. David and Pat Herlihy gave us valuable assistance with the chapter on the medieval period. Peter Manicas made many constructive comments on the material on Athens and Sparta. Tom Beidelman read a draft of a chapter on preliterate societies and convinced us that the demographic data available on such peoples were too unreliable for our purposes; that material is not included. Paul Glick and Noreen Goldman independently read the chapters on white and black Americans, and provided many critical and helpful comments. Robert Fogel's comments on the chapter on black Americans were most valuable. Robert Wells read the chapter on colonial and early America and made a number of helpful suggestions. Ernst Badian commented on the material on classical Greece. Constructive criticism of several parts of the manuscript was generously provided by Paul Weiss and James Weinrich.

Finally, countless colleagues and friends discussed the sex-ratio question with us informally, stimulating our thinking and providing valuable leads.

We owe much to Noreen Goldman, who obtained reams of data from the U.S. Census Bureau and other statistical sources, as well as assisted us in sorting through it and debating with us over how to interpret it. She also did much of the statistical processing of the data, calculating sex ratios and other indices. Ken Ghee, Linda Spatig, Bill Wilson, and Gila Arnoni provided further assistance in processing the data. Robert Schwarz, Genece Hudson, and Bruce Macchiaverna assisted with library research. In addition, Marcia obtained assistance from many Mather House students whose names were known mostly to her, but whose anonymous assistance is gratefully acknowledged. Ann Hoffman and Kit Wheatley were two of these students; they did an exceptionally large amount of library research for this project. Cynthia Longfellow researched the literature on reproductive biology up to about 1975, and Mark Weinstein to 1980. Janet West typed much of the final manuscript, bearing up cheerfully with revision after revision, and Gwen Hodgkins helped with the final stages.

I offer my apologies to the many others who helped but who remain unnamed because knowledge of their assistance was lost with Marcia's untimely death. And, of course, none of those named here are responsible for any errors that might be found in the manuscript; these remain my responsibility alone.

—Paul F. Secord
University of Houston

1

Introduction:
The Sex Ratio Question

A common belief is that in all populations, the number of male and female babies born is almost exactly equal, with only slightly more boys than girls. And under most circumstances, we take it for granted that the number of men and women in a population is very nearly equal. But suppose for the moment that there were some populations with more of one gender than the other. What would the social consequences be?

We might first notice that much depends upon the *ages* of the two sexes, especially at the years where they are in disproportionate numbers. If the imbalance were mainly in the number of young boys relative to the number of young girls, we would not expect any serious social consequences, at least not while they were still children. But if there were more elderly women than elderly men, we could anticipate that in a traditional society where men earn more than women and many women work only as housewives, a large number of these women would be without a husband and consequently would lack adequate means of support.

Even more serious consequences would be expected if there were a disproportionate number of women (or men) at the ages when people most commonly marry and have children. Suppose that there were more young adult women than men. Under those circumstances, many of the women would not be able to find a man to marry and would have difficulty finding casual partners. How would this affect the birth rate in a population? How would this make women feel? What kinds of actions might they take? Would their attitudes and behaviors toward men change? Would they begin to relate differently toward other women? Would women get together in protest? Would they want to become less dependent on men?

And what about the men? With an unusual number of women available, what would they do? Would their attitudes and behaviors toward women change? In what way? Would they be more promiscuous? What about men who were already married? Would a surplus of single women have any effects on their marriages? Would the presence of available single women influence a husband's attitude toward his wife? Would it be easier for him to have an affair? Would the temptations be greater? Under what circumstances, if at all? Would the persistence of this imbalanced sex ratio ultimately bring about profound changes in the relationship between men and women and in the nature of the family?

Before we look for possible answers to such questions, let's consider the reverse case, where there is a considerable excess of men at the ages when people most commonly marry and have children. Because of their scarcity, would women be more highly valued by men? Would men extend themselves to find a partner of their own? Would they do more courting or wooing under such circumstances? If the shortage of young adult women persisted, would this lead to a heightening of romantic images? Would there be more appreciation of and commitment to a wife? Would men be especially concerned about competition with other men? Would women be sheltered and protected under these conditions? Would this lead them to demand that the woman they marry be a virgin? Would they be especially concerned about their daughters' chastity?

How would women feel under these circumstances? Would they feel more valued? Would their role as wife and mother seem more important? Would they have more trust in men? Would they welcome protection, or would they resent such moves and see them as restrictions on their independence? Would they be less interested in having a career of their own in the workplace? It seems possible that the implications for relationships between men and women and for the nature of the family would be considerable if there were either a persistent shortage of young adult women or of young adult men.

Before speculating any further, let's examine some actual sex ratios. Have they ever been disproportionate enough to create social consequences such as these? The sex ratio is well known to demographers, although it usually receives less attention from them than birth or death rates. Quite simply, the sex ratio is typically reported for a given population in terms of the number of men per 100 women. So, if the ratio were 110, there would be 110 men for every 100 women in the population. Or, if it were 90, then there would be only 90 men for every 100 women. Of course, sex ratios can be computed for subgroups of a population, such as for newborns, young adults, single persons, or other categories. We will see later that a specific cohort of women in a population—of a certain age, for example—is for our purposes best matched with that age cohort of men whom they would most commonly marry, in order to arrive at a sex ratio pertaining to marital opportunities. But for the moment, let's examine some sex ratios for total populations without regard to age.

Figure 1.1 provides a historical view of sex ratios in the United States. It provides ratios for the total U.S. population, both married and unmarried, for the 185-year period from 1790 to 1975. A mere glance reveals a striking fact. The last few decades have been unique in our history: Only then has

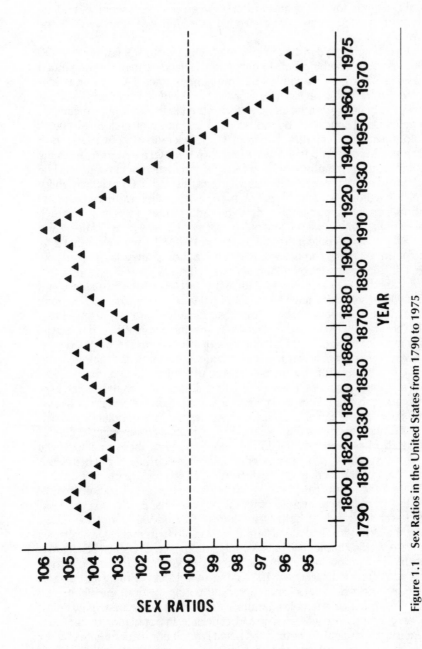

Figure 1.1   Sex Ratios in the United States from 1790 to 1975

SOURCE: U.S. Bureau of the Census, *Historical Statistics of the United States, Colonial Times to 1970,* Bicentennial ed., part I. Washington, DC: Government Printing Office.

there been a shortage of men in this country. Before World War II, there was *always* an excess of men. Is it possible that contemporary attitudes toward sexual behavior, toward relationships between men and women, and toward marriage and divorce are in part a consequence of this reversal in the sex ratio?

Before jumping to conclusions, we may ask whether sex ratios above 90 really represent anything but a negligible shortage of men. In the United States in 1970, the sex ratio for white men and women 14 years and older was 92. So 92 out of every 100 women would have a potential partner among the male cohort. Looking at this more closely, though, we can see that much is still concealed by this sex ratio, even though children 13 years and younger have been removed from it. The sex ratio of 92 in 1970 represents a surplus of over 5 million women. If we remove the married from the population, the remainder—who are single, divorced, or widowed—will be much more out of balance with respect to sex. Instead of 63 million men for 68 million women, we find 21 million men for 26 million women. There are still 5 million extra women, but now the ratio of men to women is much smaller, only 81. Now we see that one out of every five women 14 years and older did not have a potential male partner in 1970.[1] Thus it is clear that total population sex ratios can be very deceptive, although they still seem useful for making comparisons over long periods of time.

Why are there fewer men now than in the past? Are there other times and places where sex ratios have been out of balance? If it could happen in the United States, then presumably it could happen anywhere, at any time. Later in the book we will discuss sex ratios in specific populations, but a brief explanation of the factors that might raise or lower them can be given here. As every demographer knows, only three conditions can bring about change in a population: births, deaths, and migration. High birth rates, low death rates, and migration into a population all serve to increase its size. Low birth rates, high death rates, and migration out of a population reduce its size. These three factors can also affect the characteristics of a population, such as the distribution of ages or the sex ratio. Populations with very high birth rates and death rates have more younger people; reverse these rates, and the population gradually has more older people. Migration into or out of a population has similar selective effects, depending on the ages of the migrants.

These three factors can also be selective with respect to sex. Sex ratios at birth are *not* identical among different populations. Blacks, for example, have lower sex ratios at birth (see Chapter 8). And we found one ethnic group, the Orthodox Jews of eastern Europe, with extremely high sex ratios at birth. A whole chapter will be devoted to them (see Chapter 4). Sex ratios at birth also vary by socioeconomic class, approaching 110 for the highest levels and falling to barely over 100 for the lowest levels. But by far the most important effect on sex ratios among very young children, mostly in past times, is the practice of female infanticide and female neglect. At many points in history, this practice was widespread, especially in populations where subsistence was marginal. Of course, the result is adult populations with low sex ratios, that is, with a shortage of adult women. Surprisingly few historians have asked whether female infanticide or neglect and the resultant shortage of adult women have had important societal consequences. Could it be that the family is more valued and more stable when, for whatever reasons, women are scarce, and could the stability of the family help to perpetuate social tradition and the stability of society itself?

Death rates from sources other than female infanticide have also frequently been selective with respect to gender. At some periods in history, deaths of women in childbirth were an important factor creating a shortage of adult women. And populations have often been depleted of young men during prolonged wars. Pestilence and the plague have sometimes functioned selectively, especially where women and children were evacuated from towns and cities during an epidemic.

But the greatest source of imbalanced sex ratios has been selective migration. Very often migrations involve more men or more women, depending on the reasons for the migration. This is true for both migration within a country (as from rural to urban) or for immigration or emigration into or out of a country. The main reason that the United States had a surplus of men throughout almost all of its history is that more males than females have immigrated to this country. Later we will take advantage of this situation to examine the effects of the very high sex ratios in colonial and early America, when the frontier was open (see Chapter 5).

We saw earlier that the sex ratio for the unmarried white U.S. population 14 years and older was only 81 in 1970. But what are the ages of the 19 women out of every 100 who do not have a potential partner? A clue is provided by looking at another subpopulation. For unmarried white people between the ages of 15 and 44 years, we find a sex ratio of 116! Eliminating people over 44 years of age has changed the ratio from 81 to 116! What this means is that many of the women lacking a partner are over 45 years of age. This makes demographic sense. Males are more mortal than females; they die at a faster rate and do not live as long. Like most Western societies, the United States has a very large number of women over 45 years of age for whom there is no potential partner in the same age cohort.

From the ratio of 116 for men and women, it might seem that in 1970 there were plenty of suitable male partners for women between the ages of 15 and 44 years. But that is not the case at all! To see that it is not, we need to select specific cohorts of women and match each of them with a cohort of men of "marriageable" age. We will be doing this frequently in later chapters and provide only an illustration here. Of course, we must also keep in mind that other demographic characteristics of men besides age are also important for most women—education, occupation, and income, for example. But let's just look at age here.

Women typically marry men who, on the average, are two or three years older and who have an equal or better education than they do. The effect of this practice is to limit the pool of unmarried men who are of the appropriate age and educational status for women of a given age. Because of these practices, a balanced sex ratio—100 men for every 100 women—does not provide enough of the "right kind" of men. This situation prevails because there are fewer men in the higher than in the lower age and educational brackets.

But that's not all. Another circumstance has made matters even worse in the 1970s and 1980s in the United States. Demographers have coined a term for it—*the marriage squeeze*.[2] This squeeze occurs when those who were born at a time when the birth rate was rising reach adulthood and are ready to marry. The U.S. birthrate reached its lowest point in 1945 and then rose steadily for 12 years. So, for example, when women born in 1948 reached adulthood, they had to find a male partner from the smaller cohort born two or three years earlier, when the birthrate was lower. This marriage squeeze has continued well into the 1970s and 1980s, since the birthrate did not level off until 1957. When this book is published, in 1983, women who are 26 years of age or older who currently do not have a male partner will be facing a serious shortage of available males (see Chapter 7 for details).

The effect of age-selection on sex ratios combined with the marriage squeeze occurring from the late 1960s to the 1980s is illustrated in a rough way by Table 1.1. This looks at women aged 20-24, the interval when 20th-century American women most commonly marry. The method used here ignores the fact that not every young woman marries a man 2 or 3 years older, a point to which we will return later. Looking first at 1960, we see that the ratio is close to parity, with a few extra men. But this had changed drastically by 1970. By then, each 100 unmarried women aged 20-24 years had only 84 unmarried men two years older as potential marriage partners. And among men who were three years older, there were only 67 potential husbands for these women! Since the average difference between partners at first marriage has been about 2.5 years, a crude estimate of male partners available for this age group of women would be about half-way between these two figures, or only 75 men for each 100 women.

Ratios for 1980 for women 20-24 years of age are not yet available, since the single-year age tables for the 1980 Census have not yet been published. But we can anticipate that since the rise in the birth rate ended in 1957, women aged 20-23 in 1980 would not have been caught in a marriage squeeze and are apt to have more men available to them. But note that age lumps or hollows in the population do not go away with time—they last until the death of that segment of the population. Thus, in 1980 women who had been 20-24 in 1970 would be 30-34 years of age ten years later, and there still would be the same shortage of men two or three years older than they.

TABLE 1.1 Sex Ratios for Unmarried Women Aged 20-24 Years

	Year of Census	
Cohorts	1960	1970
Unmarried men 22-26 years		
Unmarried women 20-24 years	111	84
Unmarried men 23-27 years		
Unmarried women 20-24 years	93	67

NOTE: The unmarried include white, single, separated, widowed, and divorced persons. The ratios are calculated from tables of single years of age.
SOURCE: Census of the Population, U.S. Summary, Vol. 1, Tables 156 and 176. Washington, DC: Government Printing Office, 1960, 1970.

While the game of musical chairs in the form of marriage, divorce, and re-marriage may have been played in the interval, this would not eliminate the shortage of men for that segment of the population. Many women would still be left standing alone.

We can safely conclude that population changes during the decade from 1960 to 1970 resulted in a grave shortage of potential partners for young women. The shortage would be even greater if we were to reduce the male pool further by ruling out marriage of women to men with less education than they have, an adjustment that would be appropriate, given the prevailing practices.

Let's return once again to the sex ratio question, asking about the possible consequences of imbalanced sex ratios. Letting the imagination run freely, let's generate as coherent and complete a sketch as we can of how men and women would relate to each other and what the societal consequences would be under two conditions: a high sex ratio with a shortage of women, and a low sex ratio with an oversupply of women.

THE SEX RATIO QUESTION

One possible set of answers is that when the sex ratio deviates appreciably from 100 at ages when men and women most commonly marry, certain characteristic changes take place in the relationships between them that in turn have effects on the family and other aspects of society. This cluster of characteristics would be filtered through existing cultural patterns and conditions, so that at different times and in different societies the trends would be manifested differently. Throughout the variations, however, we would expect a recognizable core of characteristics with certain basic similarities. Our attempted description will mostly be in terms of Western societies, although not necessarily contemporary ones; later, we will think about others.

High Sex Ratios: An Undersupply of Women

When sex ratios are high, there are more men than women. In such societies, young adult women would be highly valued. The manner in which they would be valued would depend on the society. Most often, single women would be valued for their beauty and glamour, and married women as wives and mothers. Men would want to possess a wife and would be willing to make and keep a commitment to remain with her. But in some societies, this might be carried to an extreme, and scarce women might be valued as chattels and/or possessions.

In high sex ratio societies, women would achieve their satisfaction through traditional roles. Male and female roles would be complementary, involving a division of labor with men and women having distinctly different tasks. A woman's role would be in the family, that of homemaker and mother. High sex ratios in certain cultural contexts would give women a subjective sense of power and control over their lives. This would be particularly true when they could choose among men for a marriage partner. This sense of relative power and control would *not* be expressed by women in striving for sexual or economic independence, but would instead be reflected within traditional institutions of the society, particularly the family. Here, women would often gain economic mobility through marriage; they would marry upward in socioeconomic class. They would not have strong career ambitions, nor would they actively agitate for personal or political rights. There would be little unhappiness or despair among young women such as would be expressed in depression and suicide attempts; these would be relatively infrequent.

Both men and women would stress sexual morality rather than licentiousness, especially for women. Men would be motivated to promote morality for women so that they could maintain exclusive possession of a woman. Virginity would be prized in potential wives. These societies would often have a double standard; males would be promiscuous, while females would be expected to be chaste. In spite of various forms of illicit sexual behavior, the cultural emphasis would be on the male's commitment to a single partner for many years or for life. Occasionally, these societies would expect sexual morality and fidelity for both sexes.

There might also be an emphasis on romantic love, if women had some say in choosing the marriage partner. The concept of romantic love includes the idea of long commitment to a mate, at least throughout the childbearing years. Men would be as committed to this idea as women, and women would be valued as romantic love objects.

Low Sex Ratios: An Oversupply of Women

If young women were in relative oversupply, the social, cultural, and economic trends would, in some respects, be opposite to those of an undersupply. Women in such societies would have a subjective sense of powerlessness and would feel personally devalued by the society. They would be more likely to be valued as mere sex objects. Unlike the high sex ratio situation, women would find it difficult to achieve economic mobility through marriage. More men and women would remain single or, if they married, would be more apt to get divorced. Illegitimate births would rise sharply. The divorce rate would be high, but the remarriage rate would be high for men only. The number of single-parent families headed by women would increase markedly.

Sexual libertarianism would be the prevailing ethos, shared by men and women alike, although, because of the surplus of women, the options would be greater for men. Sexual relationships outside of marriage would be accepted. When the cultural context permitted, sexual alternatives in which men are not needed, such as lesbianism, might become more prevalent as possible sexual alternatives for women. Women would not expect to have the same man remain with them throughout their childbearing years. Brief liaisons would be usual. Women would more often share a man with other women. Adultery would be commonplace. At the same time, men would have opportunities to move successively from woman to woman or to maintain multiple relationships with different women. Because of the shortage of men, these opportunities would largely be denied women. The outstanding characteristic of times when women were in oversupply would be that men would *not* remain committed to the same woman throughout her childbearing years. The culture would not emphasize love and commitment, and a lower value would be placed on marriage and the family. Instead, transient relationships between men and women would become important.

Women would react to their situation in various ways. Some might redouble their efforts to attract or keep a man, making sacrifices and going out of their way to please him. Others would feel powerless, resentful, rejected, and angry. They might try to achieve economic and political independence for themselves and other women. We would expect various forms of feminism to be accelerated under these low sex ratio conditions. Many women would not reject men but would intensify efforts to change the balance of power between the sexes and to alter the roles that men assume. A central theme would be the attempt on the part of women to establish themselves as independent persons in their own right.

From Demography to Psychology

Before we go any further, we need to think about *how* imbalanced sex ratios could bring about changes in attitudes and behavior toward the opposite sex and ultimately in larger social structures such as the family. The path from demography to social behavior is not well marked, and some turns are uncertain. But we must try to identify the correct path. As an aid to our thinking, it is convenient to draw upon social exchange theory as developed by social scientists.[3] The essentials of one line of argument that might be laid out are as follows (for a more complete treatment, see Chapter 6):

Relationships between two persons can be thought of as a continuing series of encounters or transactions between them. Each of these transactions can be conceived of as having an outcome that is more or less satisfying to each party. But satisfaction depends not only on how pleasurable or displeasing the encounter might have been, but also on the level of satisfaction that was *expected* by each individual. This level is established by one's previous experiences in such relationships, and also by what else might have been available. The more that outcomes are consistently *above* the level that one expects, the more satisfying and attractive the relationship appears to be. But the closer the outcomes are to expectations, the less satisfying and attractive the relationship. In instances where the outcomes fall *below* one's level of expectation, the relationship is apt to be unattractive or distressing.

Two conditions that are inextricably entwined, and which are crucial to understanding couples, are dependency and power, and both of these conditions relate to the transactions. The more that one party is dependent on the other for satisfaction, the greater the power of the other party. The one with the greater dependency is in a weaker position for negotiating or obtaining satisfaction in a relationship. Conversely, the one with the lesser dependency is in a stronger position with respect to obtaining satisfaction from the relationship. One source of dependency/power is the ability of the other party to provide satisfaction. For example, a wealthy individual is able to provide more satisfaction than a poor one. But psychological characteristics are another source.

These may include physical and sexual attractiveness, a sense of humor, an ability to empathize with the partner's problems, and so forth.

For our purposes, however, a crucial feature that determines the balance of dependency and power in a relationship is the level of outcomes that is perceived to be obtainable in *alternative* relationships. In those instances where alternative relationships are not available or where alternative relationships are perceived to have low outcomes, dependency in existing relationships is high. But where high outcomes are perceived to be readily available in alternative relationships, dependency in existing relationships is low.

But it is not just that one party sees the possibility of greater satisfaction outside of the relationship. What is crucial is that the level of what is expected *within* the existing relationship is raised when alternative relationships with high outcomes are perceived to be available. The more superior the alternatives appear to be, the less one is apt to be satisfied with one's own outcomes. This rise in the level of what is expected from an existing relationship means that the outcomes obtainable within it are less satisfying, because they are no longer much above what is expected, or might even now be below what is expected, so that the relationship is now seen as unsatisfactory.

But this is not the whole story. It may not be apparent how these relationships tie in with larger structural aspects of society. One link is in terms of the satisfaction and dissatisfaction involved in or generated by the larger structure. For example, if the relationship is institutionalized, as in a marriage, the psychological costs of leaving the relationship are much greater than if the relationship were a casual one. This is because of formal constraints as well as psychological commitments. If there are children in the marriage, obvious costs would be incurred as a result of leaving. Moreover, when one is married, even in these contemporary times, one may be less ready to perceive favorable outcomes in alternative relationships.

It should be clear that the social norms of society define for individuals who have internalized these norms what the rewards or costs of various transactions between men and women *should* be. For example, if society specifies that husbands have certain obligations toward their wives, or that wives have certain obligations toward their husbands, the failure of one's spouse to meet these particular obligations is more psychologically costly than if the societal norms did not prevail or were not internalized by the parties involved. It is important to see and to be able to tease out such links between societal factors and relationships between two people, and also to see how exchange theory provides a model for organizing these interacting factors.

Now let's connect social exchange theory with the sex ratio thesis. The question here is, how does an imbalance in the numbers of men and women vis-à-vis each other affect the interpersonal relations between them, that is, the social exchanges or transactions?

We start by conceiving of an aggregate of men and women, many of whom are in some kind of relationship to one another. There is no presumption that the imbalance in the sexes will affect every pair in the same way or every unattached individual in the same way. An additional assumption probably does have to be made here, in order to link exchange theory to the imbalance in the sexes. That is the assumption that most individuals will attempt to maximize the outcomes they receive in relationships with the opposite sex. In other words, if they have a choice of more than one relationship, they will take the one that has more satisfying outcomes. Remember also that what is perceived as satisfying in these relationships depends in part on the social definitions that prevail in society with respect to such relationships.

The crucial link between sex ratios and the form that sex roles take may be stated in the following way. Each relationship is initially formed and maintained through a process of negotiation, bargaining, and compromise. This is not necessarily a fully conscious, calculating, or manipulative procedure; it may be more in terms of experiencing feelings about the partner's actions and acting accordingly. When one sex is in short supply, all relationships between opposite-sexed persons are potentially affected in a similar way: The individual member whose sex is in short supply has a stronger position and is less dependent on the partner because of the larger number of alternative relationships available to him or her. We shall call this *dyadic power.* This power is in the hands of individuals whose gender is in short supply; they are able to negotiate more favorable outcomes within the *dyad,* or two-person relationship. These outcomes, roughly parallel among large numbers of couples, eventually help to define the form that each relationship takes.

We assume that an appreciable number of the individuals with dyadic power will participate in alternative relationships or at least perceive that they are available, while at the same time a number of the other gender, with weak dyadic power, will find themselves having fewer alternatives available than they would like to have. Since we can safely assume that relationships vary in the satisfaction level of outcomes, individuals with dyadic power will more often choose to leave existing relationships in favor of other relationships perceived as having higher outcomes. Individuals lacking dyadic power who have been abandoned may occasionally find a new, satisfying relationship, but because of the short supply of the opposite sex, many of them will also have difficulty in finding a satisfactory partner, or they may enter relationships that they would otherwise not contemplate.

Those individuals with limited alternatives may, of course, move in a number of different directions in an attempt to improve their situation. Some may settle for being the weaker partner in the existing relationship and thus make sacrifices and cater to their partner. Others might go out of their way to use strategies and techniques that bring about satisfying relationships with the opposite sex. Or they might spend more time in the company of individuals of their own sex, and in such company find new satisfactions that they had not experienced before. Additionally, they may turn to other kinds of activities for satisfaction. For example, this might involve career aspirations or various other kinds of solitary activities.

If the imbalance in the relationships between the sexes continues for an extended period of time, an appreciable number of individuals from the gender lacking dyadic power may well get together and organize various types of actions to correct the situation. Thus, consciousness-raising groups might result, whose aim is to change the norms pertaining to relationships between men and women. Women are to have more freedom and independence, be on a par with men, and so on. If it is men who lack dyadic power, we might ask what kinds of organized activities they might join to remedy the situation. First, let us recognize that, like some women, some men might redouble their efforts to obtain a female partner. Thus, they might offer more, they might be more romantic, and/or they might be more likely to engage in wooing. Other men might devote more time to their careers, to athletics, to activities in the company of other men, and so forth, just as women might when circumstances are reversed.

But on the level of more organized activities, with an undersupply of women we would expect that men would push for changes in social definitions and social norms that would favor stability in existing relationships. For example, they would tend to devalue promiscuity for women so as to reduce the perceived alternatives for their female partners. Essentially, they would favor monogamy. In some societies they might prize virginity in women up to the time of marriage. These moves are all designed to place constraints on women, constraints which raise the psychological costs of alternative relationships in order to prevent women from leaving existing relationships, and also to limit their power over men. This brings us beyond dyadic power to a consideration of what we might call *structural power.*

Beyond Dyadic Power

Consider once again the differences between a high sex ratio society and a low sex ratio society in sex roles, in relationships between men and women, and in the family. Earlier, we suggested that women in a high sex ratio society would be highly valued, that they would occupy and be satisfied with traditional roles such as wife and mother, that men would be committed to their families over long periods of time, and that sexual morality would be imposed upon women. Low sex ratio societies would be sexually permissive for both men and women, women would be less valued, and men would have multiple or successive relationships with different women, either in marriage or out of it.

Why would we expect *these* two sets of societal conditions to occur under high and low sex ratio imbalances? Why not some other set? What is it about these attitudes and behaviors that make them more probable than various others? For example, when women have dyadic power because they are relatively scarce, why don't they behave just as men do when *they* are scarce? Why don't these women have multiple and successive relationships with different men? Why do they limit themselves to one man and accept it as a moral value for themselves, even when their lover or husband has an occasional affair with another woman? To understand why, we must go beyond dyadic power and look for another source of control.

One possibility is that men and women have important biological differences that enable and constrain different sets of behaviors for the two sexes. But we will put that aside for the present and consider the possibility that the constraints on women lie in certain societal controls. In order to bring out what these controlling features might be, let us consider two imaginary societies that we shall call EROS and LIBERTINIA. EROS is a low sex ratio society with a shortage of men, and LIBERTINIA is a high sex ratio society with an excess of men.

In EROS, men are treated as romantic love objects. They are idealized in song and poetry composed by women. Their manly physical attributes are much prized, and male beauty contests are popular. Women do the wooing, promising financial and emotional support and security. Women have little to do with the care of children. Typically, they take a week off to have a baby and then go back to work, leaving the baby at home with their husband. Most men covet the roles of father and homemaker, with a wife who is two or three years older and who has a high-status career. Often men marry early, terminating their education in order to take advantage of an opportunity for a desirable match and thus enabling them to move up in social class.

The male roles of father and homemaker are highly honored, almost sacred. Female politicians are especially fond of praising Fatherhood, and none would dare speak out against it, for fear that it would destroy their career. Every year, the President of EROS, who is a woman, presents a special award to the "Father of the Year." This award is based on qualities of faithful and devoted service to his family, as well as to other children, and on his special talent for raising children with high moral values. As might be expected in EROS, the divorce rates are very low, along with a low incidence of single-parent families and illegitimate births. Men are not anxious to enter the business or professional worlds and are usually happy as fathers and homemakers.

EROS has a double standard with respect to sexual morality. Men are expected to remain virgins until they marry; premarital intercourse is disastrous to their reputation, and adultery is condemned. Men are not regarded as having strong sex drives; their sexuality is muted. They are expected to behave decorously, like gentlemen. Talking, acting, or moving about in a way that is even slightly suggestive sexually is strongly disapproved. Clothes must be in good taste and must not be too revealing. Men who behave suggestively are regarded as coarse and low. The most degraded men are in brothels, patronized by women, and these men act and dress in a blatantly sexual way. They solicit on streets or in bars according to rules laid down by their female pimp. It is a well-established fact that men are better able than women to control their sexual impulses, and male brothels are necessary because the sexual needs of women are so strong. Occasionally women force themselves upon men, through the use of direct or indirect threats of various kinds. When sex is forced upon an underage male or a married one, this is a criminal act liable to prosecution. Often, however, such women escape punishment by claiming that the male victim was behaving in a provocative manner.

The other society, LIBERTINIA, is very different. In LIBERTINIA, most women are libertines. They frequently move from one brief liaison to another; at best, they practice serial monogamy. Women often have more than one man. At the same time, they have a relatively low regard for men. Generally they exploit them when they can, usually treating them as mere sex objects. In fact, sexual morality is weak for both sexes. Women in particular

see marriage as having a lot of disadvantages, and often will live with a man without marrying him if they can. Many children are born illegitimately. While most men would prefer to get married, they are not averse to having sexual relationships before marriage. What often happens, however, is that they get attached to their female partner, and she uses the attachment to exploit them.

Both men and women more often remain single, marrying only at later ages if at all. Families tend to be unstable and frequently break up in divorce after a few years. Men do not expect a wife to remain with them throughout their childrearing years, and LIBERTINIA has a large number of single-parent families headed by men. Often men make desperate attempts to hold on to the women they have a relationship with, making sacrifices in order to please their female partner and catering to her needs.

But other men respond to the situation by agitating for economic and sexual independence in an effort to achieve an adequate standard of living and a satisfactory social status without being dependent on a woman. These men have organized extensively and have developed a radical masculinist literature. Their protest takes a variety of forms, ranging from those who stress equal rights and male dignity, through those who rebel against housework and childrearing, to those who emphasize their hatred of women and praise male homosexuality.

An appreciable number of men in LIBERTINIA are unhappy, many more than in EROS. Many of these men have been exploited by women or have had other unfortunate experiences with them, such as being abandoned and left to care for the children as best they can. As a result, rates of mental depression, suicide attempts, and other indicators of stress and family instability are all high for young men in LIBERTINIA, but not for young women.

EROS and LIBERTINIA are unbelievable. But why? Perhaps the answer will give us a clue to the facilitating and constraining conditions that help to shape the social consequences of high or low sex ratios in societies with which we are familiar. Keep in mind that we have described societies with four different sets of relationships between men and women and their related institutions, such as marriage and the family. We have names for the two imaginary societies, but not for the familiar ones. Let's call the one where women have traditional roles "traditional society" and the one where they do not "sexually permissive society." What we suggest is that these four sets could be created by just two sources of power: *dyadic power,* held by that gender on the low side of the sex ratio, and *structural power,* which is associated with the political, economic, and legal structures of the society.

Structural power has many facets. Especially important in most societies is economic power, including both wealth and income. In most societies in the past, women have been economically dependent on a man, usually a husband or father, because they had no means of supporting themselves. The economic power of men is often augmented by their possession of political power and status, which in turn is related to legal power. But structural power is more than just economic, political, or legal power. These powers enable their agents to influence and shape social customs and practices, which in turn are a powerful source of control over people's lives.

In virtually all societies of the past and present, men have always been in possession of all these forms of power. Possessing these powers also means that men play the larger part in determining the moral values and practices of a society. Our traditional society and our sexually permissive society are familiar because in them, men hold the structural power. And EROS and LIBERTINIA are strange or even absurd because there, *women* hold the structural power.

The combined effects of dyadic and structural power being held by one or the other gender are illustrated in Figure 1.2. Let's consider first the two sexually permissive societies, one familiar and the other strange. From Figure 1.2, we can see that in the familiar permissive society, men hold the dyadic power *and* the structural power. In LIBERTINIA, also permissive, women hold both the dyadic power *and* the structural power. The result? In the former, men have used both powers to maximize *their* outcomes in relationships with women, and in the latter, women have done so. In both societies, the gender lacking both forms of power has the poorest outcomes in relating to the opposite sex.

At this point, many objections might be raised to the suggested line of reasoning, and at least one comes to mind that should be dealt with here. The description of the two sexually permissive societies may sound as if men (or women) obtain the best possible outcomes by remaining uncommitted to a person of the opposite sex. But it is not our intention to make this claim, nor would such a claim be consistent with social exchange theory. It is easy to lose sight of the fact that most people will probably experience more satisfaction in enduring relationships with the opposite sex and will prefer these to multiple relationships or a succession of different relationships. In fact, in spite of the very high current divorce rates, one considered estimate is that almost two out of every three first marriages in the United States will stay intact until the death of one of the partners.[4] The role of alternative relationships looms larger

Gender Holding DYADIC POWER	Gender Holding STRUCTURAL POWER	
	Males	Females
Males (Low sex ratio)	Sexually permissive society with familiar roles	Traditional society with reversed roles (EROS)
Females (High sex ratio)	Traditional society with familiar roles	Sexually permissive society with reversed roles (LIBERTINIA)

Figure 1.2   Societal Consequences of Possession of Dyadic and Structural Power

among *unmarried* individuals, and apparently alternative possibilities affect only a fraction of married people. But we do suggest that this fraction is higher when sex ratios are low and there is an abundance of women.

Let us now consider the two traditional societies. In them, structural and dyadic power are divided. In the familiar traditional society, men hold the structural power but lack dyadic power. Thus, they cannot maximize their outcomes wholly at the expense of women, but must arrive at a compromise arrangement, since women can use their dyadic power to place men in competition with one another. Because of women's power to choose among men, men are forced to make a commitment to a woman in order to have a relationship with her, and they must treat her well or run the risk of losing her to another man. But their structural power is sufficient to allow them to place constraints on women's freedoms and to impose a sexual morality on them.

In EROS, women hold the structural power but not the dyadic power, and they use these powers in exactly the same way that men do in a traditional society. In EROS, the men have roles like those of women in a traditional society. What we are suggesting, then, is that if women instead of men were to hold the structural power, the sex roles of men and women would be reversed. The two traditional societies are mirror images of each other with the sex roles reversed, as are the two sexually permissive societies.

The chain of inferences we have generated from high or low sex ratios to social effects has become quite long and could easily have weak links. If these four types of societies existed now or in the past, we could be more confident about the effects of dyadic and structural powers in high and low sex ratio societies. Of course, there are plenty of societies with high and low sex ratios where males hold the structural power. Are there any societies at all where females have considerable structural power? As a matter of fact, we have identified one such society, one with a very high sex ratio. The Bakweri, studied by anthropologists in the 1950s, lived in a cluster of villages in Cameroon, West Africa, in a plantation economy. They had a sex ratio of 236, with an extremely high divorce rate and great instability in relationships between men and women.[5] The high sex ratio was created by continual migrations of Bakweri men from other areas to work on the plantations. Bakweri women were highly valued, both as wives and for casual sex. This is illustrated by the custom of requiring the husband to pay "bride-wealth" to the family of the bride in order to obtain a wife—the reverse of a dowry— and also by the fact that casual sex was used as a lucrative source of income by Bakweri women, both married and unmarried. The large number of single men who migrated to this area made this possible. Many husbands were unhappy with their wives' extramarital activities, but their wives complained of insufficient support, the most frequent divorce complaint. Wives often changed husbands if they found a man who could pay a larger bride-wealth and repay the earlier bride-wealth. Many Bakweri women earned enough through casual sex to have an independent income, and some paid off their own bride-wealth in order to be free of a husband.

What is especially interesting about the Bakweri is the effect of the economic factor combined with the very high sex ratio. Ordinarily, we would expect a high sex ratio to produce a traditional society, with emphasis on family solidarity and a protective morality for women. But as a consequence of the combined effect of the high sex ratio and the unusual circumstances of the women having considerable economic power, the Bakweri were just the opposite. The high sex ratio gave Bakweri women an opportunity to use casual sex for economic gain, and many of them achieved considerable economic independence in this way. In contrast, Bakweri men often made only a meager living. Many found it extremely difficult to come up with the substantial bride-wealth required to obtain a bride. Without structural power matching that of the women, they were unable to impose traditional female roles on them.

Here we have a society which, in some respects at least, is like LIBERTI-NIA. Moreover, in spite of the great difference between this native society and more modern industrial nations, the situation raises the provocative idea that the more women gain economic independence through gainful, well-paid employment, the less likely it is that their society will be able to impose a different and more strict standard of sexual morality on them than on men. There are signs that this change is already taking place in the United States (see Chapter 9).

We are not aware of any populations like EROS. The universal dominance of men in all societies guarantees that if there is a society like EROS— or others besides the Bakweri that are like LIBERTINIA—they will be obscure and little known. We will reserve for the last chapter a discussion of why men have dominated society for so long and will offer there some speculations as to whether equality between the sexes in structural power will eventually be achieved. But before leaving the topic of power, we will suggest that extreme imbalances of societal and dyadic power can bring about unusual and unexpected consequences quite unlike anything we have described so far. Suppose, for example, that men have weak dyadic power because women are scarce, but that the men hold maximum structural power and use it to its utmost in order to constrain the women from effectively using their dyadic power.

Apparently something like this happened among the Chinese-Americans in the 19th century in the American West. The highest sex ratio that we know of in all history is that of the Chinese-American laborers brought to the United States in the nineteenth century to build the railroads. At one point, the ratio was 2,000—20 men for every Chinese-American woman![6] Unlike many frontier immigrants, the Chinese-Americans brought with them their traditional social structures, consisting of clans, tongs, and communal associations (see Chapter 5). Since these organizations were exclusively male, Chinese-American men had enormous structural power, while the women had virtually none. Add to this the extreme imbalance in the sex ratio, with women extremely scarce, and the result is very powerful constraints on women—their potential dyadic power is overwhelmed by the structural controls.

As a consequence, many of the women were in brothels. Those who were not were often married to wealthy Chinese-Americans who sheltered and protected them almost to the point of keeping them virtual prisoners. Moreover, in spite of the vigilance of the tongs, which controlled the brothels, it was not uncommon for a Chinese patron of a brothel to fall in love with one of these prostitutes, and if they ran off together it would sometimes lead to a war between the tong that controlled the brothel and the tong to which the laborer belonged. Such couples were often hunted down by both tongs because of their defection.

Here we have two very high sex ratio societies, the Bakweri and the Chinese-Americans, in which the roles of women couldn't be more different. While in small part this difference might be due to the much higher sex ratio among the Chinese-Americans, it seems far more likely that the differences in women's roles is to be attributed to the great structural power held by Chinese-American men vis-à-vis the possession of structural (economic) power held by the Bakweri women. This power put the very scarce Chinese-American women into brothels but left the Bakweri women free to use their scarcity to their advantage. We might add that in some preliterate societies with high sex ratios, wives who committed adultery were killed or beaten by their husbands. There, male power was based partly or even primarily on physical strength and prowess as a warrior, and women were unable to use their potential dyadic power to create favorable roles for themselves. Instead, they were often treated as chattel. This did not happen under the Bakweri because the British protectorate had brought law and order to the Cameroons by instituting a British justice system and, in the process, destroyed the old order of power among the Bakweri.

Background Conditions and the Sex Ratio Question

What we have done so far is to provide an overview of how high or low imbalanced sex ratios have different consequences for relationships between men and women and for the institutions that evolve in connection with such relationships. From our discussion, it should be clear that we are not proposing any simple sort of association between sex ratios and man-woman relationships; each situation is conditioned by a variety of other factors. Foremost among these is the possession by one or the other gender of dyadic and structural power. Dyadic power derives directly from imbalanced sex ratios, but structural power has very complex roots in the society under consideration and affects the forms that dyadic power can take. For this reason, the effects of dyadic and structural power on sex roles may be expected to vary widely from society to society.

Yet some progress can be made in discovering the sources that shape sex roles. Throughout history, almost without exception, structural power has been in the hands of men rather than women, with virtually no major exceptions. Here, rule by a queen, empress, or female dictator does not constitute an exception, for such power has always been dependent on the support of powerful men representing the aristocracy, the church, or the military. Male possession of structural power has been so unexceptional in history that historians and other scholars of civilization, virtually all of whom have been male, may have taken this for granted and underestimated the importance of this background factor in determining the course that human society on earth has taken. This is especially true in connection with the relationships between men and women and the institutions that have grown up around these relationships. This taken-for-granted, deeply buried feature of the world we live in is one reason why the fictional societies described earlier, in which women hold the balance of power, appear strange or even absurd.

This background factor pertaining to the balance of structural power cannot be separated entirely from another crucial consideration—the nature of men and women as influenced or determined by their biological makeup. For the most part, the behavioral and biological sciences have not yet been able to provide definitive answers on this issue. Of course, we do know that men are physically stronger than women and that women bear children. No doubt in early times this helped to produce differing roles for the two sexes, with men assuming the roles of hunters and warriors and women engaging in food-gathering and child care. Moreover, in hand-to-hand contests of strength between men and women, early and modern men would most often gain the upper hand. If we assume further that early societies were structured in accordance with these roles emphasizing brute strength, and that later social forms evolved from these earlier ones, it follows that at least some of the features of contemporary society are ultimately based on this difference in physical strength, which gives the balance of power to men.

But whether this is true or not, in trying to anticipate the future it is worth considering the possibility that as society advances in technology and sophistication, mere brute force becomes less and less crucial in shaping either sex roles or social institutions. This is true, for example, in any contemporary exercise of force. All humans are extremely vulnerable to modern weapons. And certainly in contemporary society we can put sheer individual strength aside as a factor in gaining economic or political power. Such power comes from much more subtle manipulations in which, in certain kinds of societies, women might well be at least as effective as men.

In essence, the power that contemporary men have over women comes primarily from their superior economic status. When women are in the work force at all, they typically occupy lower-status positions than do men. Moreover, census data from 1977 indicate that although approximately one-half of the wives in the United States work, their income on the average is less than one-third that of their husbands. In fact, another way of looking at these figures is that approximately four in five wives are financially dependent on the husband for an adequate standard of living.[7] Thus it is clear that men still have a strong grip on the purse-strings.

Nevertheless, one trend suggests that it will not always be that way. In close to one in every six marriages, the wife has an equal or greater income than the husband.[8] Since the industrial revolution, women have been entering the work force in ever-increasing numbers, and pressures for equality of status and income have been steadily increasing. More recent years have been characterized by an excess of women compared to men, a situation that increases pressures on women to enter the work force and achieve economic independence. If a time is reached in the future, even in one modern society, where women do reach equality with men in political and economic status, sex ratios will shape sex roles in directions that are very different from those of today, a point we discuss in more detail in the final chapter.

One proviso in these conclusions is that much hangs on whether there are biological differences between the sexes that relate to the roles commonly assumed by men and women. The belief that men are by nature more aggressive, competitive, and oriented toward achievement in the world outside the family, while women are more passive, less competitive, and more family- and person-oriented is widespread. Tiger and Fox, for example, have argued that such differences arise out of the evolutionary history of the species, and that males have bodies and brains that developed during the long, slow course of evolution so as to be more suited for hunting and war, while females evolved to serve more domestic functions.[9]

Compared with an evolutionary span measured in millions of years, all of history dating back to the first stone tablets containing writing is a mere instant, in which no evolutionary changes could have occurred. Thus, Tiger and Fox see contemporary humans as functioning with bodies that evolved in adaptation to such earlier circumstances. They see males as political, aggressive animals, acting out the modern equivalent of the hunter role in an arena outside of the family, and they see females as a bonding force that holds the family together. If the biological nature of the two sexes were indeed differentiated in this fashion, then we might well expect sex roles to remain much as they are at present. But the evidence is weak, both for *and* against the idea that important sex differences in behavior are brought about by divergent biological natures. We will return to this issue in the final chapter.

Feminism

Low sex ratios, signifying a shortage of men, provide impetus for feminist movements. This is not to say that low sex ratios can bring movements about by themselves, but rather that they provide some facilitating conditions. Several factors appear to be important prerequisites for the current feminist movement in the United States, and the low sex ratios that have prevailed during the emergence of feminism appear to have been overlooked.

One impetus to feminism is the extension of education to women, especially the fact that an increasing proportion of women have attained a college education and beyond in the past few decades. In the United States, as many women as men are now attending college. This has several consequences. First, it creates a pool of women who are more apt to respond to media communications concerning women's rights and women's roles, and who are more apt to be in a position to participate in or respond sympathetically to organizational efforts concerning women. Second, educated women are apt to be more aware of the alternatives that are available to them with respect to careers and lifestyles, and thus to be more ready to accept feminism. Finally, they constitute a large pool of women who can serve as leaders of the feminist movement.

At many periods in the past, women have taken feminist positions, either as individuals or as groups. Women throughout history who, as individuals, have asserted feminist views are well known. Typically, these women were quite well educated. One example is the suffragettes, and another, back in the medieval period, the Beguines, who developed a radical feminist literature (see

Chapter 3). The difference between these groups and the current women's liberation movement in the United States, however, is that these historical groups found little support among the large mass of women, most of whom were *not* educated. Further, male opposition in historical times was more extreme and far more united than it is today.

An even more important factor preparing the way for feminism today is the improved status of women with respect to employment. A much greater proportion of women than ever before are employed. While it is true that in most cases their earnings are far below those of men, and that many of them are only engaged in part-time or temporary employment, the large number of women working outside the home is bound to provide a more receptive audience for the feminist message.

Another facilitating condition for feminism in the United States is the fluidity and heterogeneity of American society. In an atmosphere of conflicting values and social norms, as well as rapid social change, it is much easier for new movements to get started, as compared with a traditional society. In view of all these considerations, it is likely that the feminist movement is here to stay and that time will see women gaining stronger and stronger positions in the marketplace, with profound changes in sex roles and identities resulting from this increased power base.

The remainder of the book will consist of two parts. Part I will examine selected societies or peoples in historical times when sex ratios were evidently very high or very low, in order to determine whether the societal characteristics—particularly those that pertain to relationships between men and women—are consistent or inconsistent with our suggested answer to the sex ratio question. We will range all the way back to classical Greece, compare the early and late Middle Ages, examine the Orthodox Jews in the shtetls of eastern Europe, and consider Colonial and early America. But Part I is *not* history; it is a highly selective search of the past, shaped by the goal of finding answers to the sex ratio question. Our focus will be on the effects of dyadic and structural powers on the relations between men and women and their related institutions, and the extent to which the consequences of these powers are tempered by other societal conditions.

Part II will expand on the idea of social exchanges as a link between demography and relations between the sexes and explore the complex interrelations between dyadic and structural powers. It will also examine sex ratios and their consequences for white and black Americans separately because of the considerable demographic differences between these populations. A final chapter will take stock of what has been learned and what still remains open, and will speculate on the future of relationships between men and women and the changing role of women in society.

I

CLUES FROM THE PAST

Part I of this volume examines selected historical periods and places where sex ratios were considerably out of balance, because of migration, repeated military campaigns, colonization, infanticide, or excessive mortality for one sex because of disease or other factors. No attempt is made at complete coverage; that would require a multivolume effort. Instead, only those societies were selected for which reasonable evidence could be obtained—reasonable in terms of the historical period under consideration—pertaining not only to population imbalances in gender, but also to the kinds of societal effects that might be anticipated from these imbalances.

By and large, this effort required that we look at populations and periods that covered considerable spans of time, and our characterization of both demographic conditions and societal effects is necessarily global rather than specific. This shortcoming is remedied in Part II, which deals with more contemporary periods where detailed census data and documentary material concerning social effects are available. In spite of this highly selective look at the past, our discussion in most instances does succeed in amassing considerable evidence on both the demographic conditions and the societal effects that prevailed at certain times and places.

Chapter Two raises the sex ratio question with respect to classical Greece. Athens and Sparta constituted high sex ratio and low sex ratio societies, respectively, and we ask whether they displayed those societal characteristics anticipated by the sex ratio question. In Chapter Three, the medieval period is examined. Roughly speaking, the early Middle Ages was characterized by a shortage of women, and was accompanied by the emergence of troubadours, knighthood, and chivalry, as well as romantic love poetry. The latter part of the medieval period featured an excess of women so large that it became a recognized problem for both secular and religious authorities. This latter period was distinguished by the appearance of various women's movements which attempted in various ways to cope with their situation.

Chapter Four takes up the high sex ratio society of Orthodox Jews, as epitomized by the eastern European shtetl culture. They constitute a virtual model of a high sex ratio society, with men and women in traditional roles and with great emphasis on fidelity to the family. Part I concludes with Chapter Five, which covers the high sex ratio periods in the British colonies in America and the frontiers in the United States, and concludes with a discussion of the plantation society of the South, the Victorian period in New England, and the feminist movements in the latter part of the nineteenth century.

Throughout the book, we emphasize that the effects of imbalanced sex ratios depend very much on other features of the society under consideration. The unequal division of political and economic power favoring men, the presence or absence of long-standing traditions, of openness and fluidity, the relative balance between religious and secular concerns, the nature of the economy, and prevailing lifestyles are some of the features that combine with sex ratio imbalances to produce effects on the relationships between men and women and the institutions associated with these relationships. At the same time, certain recognizable theses do appear repeatedly when sex ratios are high, and others when they are low. Our treatment will emphasize and highlight these consistent patterns.

2

Women's Roles in
Classical Athens and Sparta

A look at sex ratios and their social effects in at least a few societies vastly different from the contemporary United States should provide valuable clues to how sex ratios combine with various societal conditions to produce distinctively different effects on relationships between men and women and related social institutions. The present chapter focuses primarily on Athens and Sparta in classical Greece, while later chapters in Part I examine the early and late medieval period, the shtetl Jews in Eastern Europe in the 19th century, and colonial and early America.

We are not attempting to write history. Instead, we have selected a small number of historical situations where sufficient data demonstrate imbalanced sex ratios, and where documentation of customs, laws, and culture provides an adequate basis for making inferences about the effects of these imbalanced ratios on relationship between men and women. By and large, the nature of these relationships is reflected in the gender roles that characterize the period, and these in turn are reflected in personal documents and literature, and are codified in the customs and laws of the day.

Of course, our conclusions based on historical situations in this and other chapters must be very tentative. Surviving documents provide historians with only a fragmentary picture. Moreover, due to the broad scope of our thesis, for the most part it is necessary for us to use secondary sources—often sources that give little or no attention to the sex ratio question. We have tried to compensate for the limitations of data concerning the past by selecting only those times or places where sex ratio imbalances were patently obvious. Often we are able to cite historical facts that have been known for a long time but which may be seen from a new perspective when put alongside the sex ratio question.

At first it was our intention to look at sex ratios and their consequences in preliterate societies. We were attracted by anthropological reports that, particularly in those societies where subsistence was marginal, female infanticide—or alternatively, neglect of female offspring—was sometimes practiced. This practice would be likely to produce a shortage of adult women, and in the case of warlike tribes, frequent warfare would result in a shortage of adult males. Such societies would seem to constitute fertile ground for observing the social effects of imbalanced sex ratios.

We were eventually disillusioned in this effort, for many good reasons.[1] Foremost among these is that reliable demographic statistics are simply not available for the great majority of preliterate societies. Not only are population sizes often unknown, but not even the ages of people in the populations can be ascertained with certainty. Since population counts by age are crucial to obtaining sex ratios that bear on marital opportunities, the absence of such data bars these societies as sources for examining the sex ratio question. Even if such data were available, often knowledge about the culture of these societies is too sparse to enable identification of the social effects that might be expected from imbalanced sex ratios. Thus, on both of these counts, we reluctantly decided to forego examination of preliterate societies.

It is important to stress once more that we do not expect to find the same social effects of imbalanced sex ratios in all types of societies. The kinds of effects that have been proposed to accompany high or low sex ratios are apt to be associated with a wide variety of other societal conditions. For example, in a society which practices polygyny, a low sex ratio might be of little consequence if the excess women are absorbed as extra wives. It should be obvious that kinship systems that are profoundly different from those of Western society could create social effects that differ markedly from those associated with imbalanced sex ratios in contemporary Western nations. Perhaps the sex ratio question should eventually be raised for all types of societies, including preliterate ones, but that would be a vast undertaking well beyond the scope of a single volume and beyond the capacities of a pair of investigators whose primary competence lies in social psychology and social theory. Our more modest but still ambitious aim is to determine whether or not imbalanced sex ratios play a significant part in influencing gender roles and relationships between men and women in the contemporary United States. Because even that limited aim is fraught with difficulties, we have examined only a few historical situations to see whether they provide any clues to understanding how sex ratios might affect relationships between men and women. We begin our examination of selected historical periods with a discussion of Athens and Sparta in classical Greece.

CLASSICAL ATHENS AND SPARTA

Perhaps only the classical scholar can fully appreciate the enormous difficulties involved in drawing any conclusions about ancient civilizations. The historical record consists of mere fragments that are almost impossible to relate to each other with any certainty. The extent to which such fragments are representative of the original totality must remain unknown and can only be estimated in the grossest way, with only the weakest confidence. Such estimates usually depend on a variety of untested assumptions that cannot be verified and thus are subject to frequent revision.

Perhaps the foremost reason for the difficulties in obtaining reliable sex ratios, as well as information on the roles of women and their relation to men, is that historically women played only a minor role in war, politics, government, law, and commerce, and thus were apt to live and die with no surviving record of their existence. Hence, historians often refer to women as "invisible." When scraps of information on women are available, they usually pertain not to ordinary women, but to members of the upper class or to women distinguished by some unusual accomplishment.

Even rare extant documents that report family members by name are probably grossly incorrect. For example, of the families from Greece who received Milesian citizenship in 228-220 B.C., details of 79 families and their children remain. These families are reported to have had 118 sons and 28 daughters, many of them minors—an extremely improbable ratio.[2] Other scattered evidence includes the named relatives of Epicteta (c. 200 B.C.), who numbered 25 males to 7 females.[3] Of 600 families from Delphic inscriptions in the second century B.C., only 1 percent reared two daughters. Some historians cite controversial and quite limited skeletal evidence, as well as the evidence from burial plots, to support the thesis of high sex ratios.[4]

Sex ratios computed from figures such as these would almost certainly be wrong because of the numerous opportunities for biases to enter into the documentary evidence. The preparation of such documents in ancient times was relatively rare, and the reasons for their preparation are almost certain to have biased the naming or reporting of persons in them, very probably in the direction of omitting many females. For example, if they concerned disputes over property, those females who could not own or inherit property would be excluded from mention.

A further difficulty in asking the sex ratio question of classical Greece is that that region was not at all a political unity. Different communities were fiercely independent, relatively small, often geographically isolated, and self-contained in many respects. While common myths, cults, and legends provided some common culture, they by no means provided uniform values or behavior patterns for all Greeks.[5] Moreover, not all population centers in Greece were in the same stages of development, so that at no time could a cross-section of Greece be regarded as a homogeneous entity.[6]

Our solution to this particular difficulty was to look not at the whole of Greece, but rather to compare the two city-states of Athens and Sparta. This is justified by the contrasting sex ratios in the two regions, a fact supported by a pioneering study specifically assessing sex ratios in Athens.[7] As we shall see, women's roles in Athens and Sparta were also very different, in a fashion largely consistent with the corresponding high and low sex ratios.

The Homeric Poems and Archaic Greece

Before moving to Athens and Sparta in classical Greece, let us follow the customary practice and look briefly at the earlier centuries. We have no way of knowing what the sex ratios actually were in the age of Homer, yet there is one feature of Greece that is highly suggestive. Consider the following description:

> Greece is a barren land, the earth so stubborn and austere that it breaks the hearts of the men who farm the narrow valleys and the small patches of arable land at the foot of the steep-sided limestone mountains. There are few rivers, few plains, few beaches. There is a host of small craggy islands which are the fragmented eminences of mountains downed long ago, and the islands are as austere as the mainland.[8]

From this description and other sources of information, it is clear that Greece could not support more than a small, fixed number of inhabitants. Although it is possible that in the last centuries of antiquity the land was somewhat less hostile, for many Greeks life in Homeric times must have been a marginal existence at best. We shall see in the next chapter that where subsistence is marginal, female infanticide or at least neglect of female infants and young girls, is often practiced. In contrast, more settled, agrarian societies with enough arable land to support a larger population more often support children of both sexes and have sex ratios approaching a balance.

It is to be expected that infanticide and neglect—so often selective for females—were common. This practice, plus the numerous deaths of young women in childbirth, means that much of the time the population of ancient Greece would have had high sex ratios, although occasionally the balance of young adult males to females would be altered by the death of large numbers of men in wars.

Are there any clues to the roles of men and women in the epic tales of Homer? The epics were orally transmitted and thus, as history, are of dubious accuracy. But if we can view them as reflecting to some extent the social customs of the eighth century B.C., a pattern emerges. We get a picture of a society with customs and practices like those ordinarily associated with high sex ratios in subsistence-level societies. The epics depict warrior societies, with women as chattels in traditional domestic roles.

Marriage by capture or contest is frequently depicted.[9] Sagas from the later Bronze Age are replete with accounts of contests between suitors being organized by a king in order to determine which of them would prove the strongest, most valiant, most clever, and most worthy of receiving his daughter as the marriage prize.[10] Fierce competition among men, with women as the spoils of the contest, indicates the importance of women, but only as a valuable form of property. Gifts were exchanged at the time of a wedding. In the *Odyssey,* for example, Penelope was urged to accept the suitor who pressed her with the most gifts.[11] Such gifts were analogous to a bride-price. After the fall of Troy, the royal Trojan women were given to the Greek heroes as special prizes.[12]

Generations later, in preclassical Greece, marriage by capture continued to occur. Herodotus[13] remarks that the Athenian colonists did not bring women with them to Miletus, but instead seized the native Carian women and killed their male relatives outright. In revenge, the daughters of these abducted women swore that they would never eat with their husbands or call them by name. Herodotus[14] also relates a story that reflects the extremes to which suitors went in prenuptial rivalry. Cleisthenes, a tyrant of Sicyon from 600 to 570 B.C. and father of Agariste, entertained for a year the suitors of his daughter's hand. During this time they were rated by him according to their various athletic and manly virtues. The suitor who excelled in everything was chosen as Agariste's husband. However, this suitor behaved ridiculously at the betrothal feast. He was instantly replaced by the runner-up, who received Agariste as his prize and was promptly married to her.

According to our thesis, one would expect to find great role complementarity in a society where men had great power over women and where sex ratios were high. If the epics reflect social customs, then labor was indeed sharply divided between men and women. In the *Iliad,* Hector[15] tells Andromache to go back to her house and work on her loom, since war is the business of men. In epics[16] and on Mycenaean tablets,[17] the tasks of women are strictly domestic: they bathe and anoint men, weave, spin, fetch water, grind corn, and wash clothes.[18] Of course, a prime role was to bear future warriors.[19] The male supremacist complex is everywhere reflected both in Homer and other sagas: "As much as Phaiakian men were expert at driving a fast ship on the open sea, so their women are skilled in weaving and dowered with wisdom bestowed by Athene, to be expert in beautiful work, to have good character."[20]

Greek society from Homer's days had the double standard typically associated with high sex ratios. This was facilitated by the availability of slave concubines for outstanding warriors and for civilians who could afford them.[21] Women were monogamous, while men were polygamous. The sagas also depict the sex customs that reflect the importance of women as undamaged sexual possessions of men. The virginity and reputation of unmarried girls were much prized, and precautions were taken to protect them.[22]

Altogether, then, what little we know about preclassical Greece is consistent with the expected answers to the sex ratio question. But this is no more than suggestive. We turn next to Athens and Sparta.

Sex Ratios in Athens and Sparta

Of special interest for the sex ratio question are classical Athens and Sparta. Though they existed side by side, Athens had high sex ratios, while Sparta had low sex ratios. In 1976, a unique demographic study, the first of its kind ever done, provided strong evidence on what the actual sex ratios were in fourth century B.C. Athens.[23] A random sample was selected of 1500 funerary inscriptions from the fourth century B.C., and speeches were drawn from the *corpora* of three Athenian orators: Lysias, Isaeus, and Demosthenes. Speeches selected generally contained material on inheritance, abuse of guardianship, or attempts to recover dowries. An explicit set of rules was used for determining or inferring sex ratios from the inscriptions, or from the individuals mentioned in the orations, in an effort to avoid any form of bias.[24] With these independently determined and statistically reliable sex ratios from two quite different sources in the same century, only a 2-3 percent discrepancy was found. Both sources of evidence indicated that "during the 4th century the Attic population had a sex ratio of between 143 and 174."[25] The investigator points out that in spite of his efforts to avoid bias, the lesser status of Athenian women might mean that those ratios are somewhat overestimated.[26] Moreover, since funerary inscriptions and litigation both cost money, it is clear that these sex ratios apply primarily to the upper classes. But this is not serious, since our knowledge of Athenian women is mostly limited to those who belong to this class.

It should be clear that sex ratios vary in different periods. Near the end of the fifth century B.C., for example, after the Peloponnesian War, with many Athenian males lost and other expeditions yet to be mounted, Pericles exhorted married women to bear more children.[27] The problem was a lack of husbands, and there are indications that this resulted in easing the laws concerning legitimacy. In some instances, a man could have children by more than one woman, and both would be legitimate heirs. Possibly some children of non-citizen women were also recognized.[28] But this situation would be temporary until the population balance could be restored, and it would be here that female infanticide and neglect would play an important part.

In having high sex ratios, Athens was probably representative of much of Greece during the fifth and fourth centuries B.C. (always allowing for imbalances resulting from wars). The hard, marginal existence of life in Greece in those days meant that female infants would be killed or at least neglected whenever food and sustenance was a problem. But Sparta was clearly an exception to this generalization. The reason for this was connected with the fact that Sparta developed into a military state. In the latter half of the seventh century B.C., after 17 years of fighting against the revolt in Messenia and finally putting it down, Sparta underwent a thorough social and constitutional reform. The upshot was that from that time on, "the Spartan citizenbody were a professional soldiery, bred from childhood for two qualities, military skill and absolute obedience, free from (indeed, barred from) all other vocational interests and activities, living a barrack life, always ready to take the field in strength against any foe, whether helot or outsider."[29] But this preparedness was not in search of war; its function was to deter uprisings among the helots, especially those in subjugated territory, and to discourage outside enemies from interfering with Sparta or its provinces. As a result, Sparta was successful in keeping under subjugation the districts of Laconia and Messenia, which were quite fertile compared with other Greek areas, rich in iron ore, and with access to the sea.[30] In fact, the population that Sparta kept under subjugation was several times larger than Sparta itself.[31]

The emphasis on military preparedness gave the Spartan state an interest in breeding the best possible male warriors. First, Spartans recognized the importance of the mother's physical health to her offspring's well-being, and so believed that she should be well nourished during pregnancy.[32] Unlike Athenian girls, Spartan girls were as well fed as the boys.[33] Citizen women also exercised and pursued gymnastics in the interests of good health. Second, a crucial contribution to low sex ratios arose from Sparta's concern for having sturdy male warriors. In pursuit of eugenic breeding, sick infants of either sex were killed. Plutarch reported that all girls were handed over immediately after birth to the care of the women, but that newborn males were examined and were permitted to live only if it looked as though they would make strong warriors:

> And if they found him fair and well proportioned of all his limbs, and strong, they gave order that he should be brought up and appointed him one of the nine thousand parts of inheritance for his education. Contrariwise, if they found him deformed, misshapen, or lean, or pale, they sent him to be thrown in a deep pit of water.[34]

Finally, the low sex ratios in Sparta were further aggravated by the fact that Spartan couples did not live together for the first twelve years of their marriage. Although Spartan boys married at the age of 18, they went on living with their sex-segregated army group until the age of 30.[35] This practice created a de facto situation with even fewer men around than would be indicated by low population sex ratios.

Despite the limitations of our knowledge of Athens and Sparta, it seems clear that Athens had high sex ratios and Sparta low sex ratios. We can now turn to the differences in the roles of women in these two societies and see what kind of answers to the sex ratio question turn up.

Roles of Greek Women and Their Relations to Men

We should note here that the status of women in classical Greece, especially Athens, is the subject of a lively controversy among scholars.[36] While there is reasonable agreement on women's relatively impoverished political and legal status, what is not clear is their social status, especially relative to their husbands. Aristotle apparently believed them to be on a par with slaves—surely too low an estimate—and the general scholarly opinion early in the twentieth century was that Athenian men treated their women with contempt. But even before midcentury, this view of women was vigorously denied by a new group of scholars who cited evidence purporting to raise Athenian wives almost to the equivalent of the social status enjoyed by wives in modern civilizations.

These scholars were not at all sensitive to the possible limitations on the status of modern women, and with the advent of feminist views it now appears that the truth lies somewhere in between these extremes. Whatever the conclusion, it is apt to remain forever tentative. Many Greek scholars have noted that with their strong interest in the body politic, ancient Greek writers had much to say about the government, the state, and politics, but were almost silent on the psychology of the individual and on private life.[37] We must remember that conversation and oral story-telling (but not writing) were the activities of the day in classical Greece, and that Greek society must be interpreted without the sorts of personal documents that we have for examining more recent centuries—letters, diaries, biographies, and the like.

A few relevant features of classical Greece should perhaps be mentioned at the outset, since they set it off from our more familiar modern societies. Perhaps important to understand is the relative importance of "household" versus our modern notion of the nuclear family. Male Greek citizens were the absolute masters of their households and could do as they wished with their wife, servants, slaves, concubines, children, and other inhabitants of their dwelling. Athens and Sparta were class societies, with male citizens at the top and slaves at the bottom. In between were a variety of other people. Wives who were citizens enjoyed some status, though clearly less than that of their husbands. So did *hetaira,* or courtesans, whom we might expect would flourish under high sex ratio conditions. Resident foreign women, called "metics," were inferior to citizen women—they could not give birth to a citizen even if they were legally married to a male citizen. Concubines, servants, and prostitutes held various lesser statuses. Altogether, it is clear that women in classical Greece had statuses below men, but their status was vastly different depending on the class to which they belonged. And, as we shall see, of the greatest importance to us is the fact that there were important differences between Athens and Sparta in the roles that women held and in the kinds of relationships that they had with men.

Athens was in virtually all respects very much like a traditional high sex ratio society. Athenian women had domestic roles as wives and mothers, and were subservient to their husbands.[38] They were tied to the home, received little education, and did not participate in business, professional, political, or legal activities. Being a mother of legitimate offspring was considered to be the highest status a woman could achieve, and women were honored for this family role.

The family was important; Aristotle defined the family as a unit of the state, and children were the means of preserving the family.[39] Under the laws of Athens, it was only through citizen women that a man could produce children who would be his legitimate heirs. Children born of slaves, concubines, or foreigners had no rights in property and were not considered citizens. The role of female Athenian citizens as the bearers of legitimate heirs takes on added importance when consideration is given to the importance that Greeks attached to their ancestry. Family background was crucial, and the ancestral line had to be perpetuated. If a family was lacking a son, then the line was to go through the daughter. But the property and descent would go to her husband, unless she had a son as heir. And if an heiress were widowed, her nearest kin was to marry her. These practices and the ideas they represented were not private matters, but instead reflected the strong interest of the Athenian state in the perpetuation of its citizenry.[40]

Citizen girls of Athens did not receive much education and apparently were wholly outside of the active intellectual and cultural life of Athens.[41] Qualities desired in girls were opposite from those admired in boys: quietness, submissiveness, and abstinence from men's pleasures.[42] Girls were to be seen and not heard. Self-sacrifice and martyrdom was highly valued in women, while self-assertion was not. The social development of adolescent girls ended with marriage, while boys continued to develop their mental and physical skills throughout manhood.

Given the shortage of women, combined with the absolute power that men held, we would expect strong, protective controls over women. One form that this took was paternalism on the part of both fathers and husbands. The paternalism of the husband in relation to his wife was brought out in many ways.

First, while girls married at puberty, men did not marry until they were considerably older. This discrepancy in age, combined with a better education and worldly knowledge, reinforced paternalistic relationships. The disparity in the legal rights of the father/daughter and husband/wife provides further illustration. Under Athenian law a wife was a child, since she had the legal status of a minor in comparison to her husband. Males came of age at 18; females never came of age.[43] Children were the legal property of their father, not their mother, and they remained with the father in the case of divorce. An Athenian woman was always under the legal guardianship of her father, her husband, or even her son in the event of the death of her husband. Daughters' marriages were arranged by the guardian/father. A woman's husband might arrange her future marriage before his death, or if a husband died, her son might arrange the next marriage for her.[44]

The protective attitude of the father is also illustrated in the custom of the dowry. This was a way of insuring a good marriage for the daughter, and the dowry remained with her. Although her husband took charge of it, she was entitled to an income from it, and if divorce ensued, it had to be returned.[45] This paternal responsibility was taken so seriously that many female infants were badly neglected or left to die if it didn't seem that a proper marriage could be arranged when they came of age, as might be the case for a citizen of modest means with too many daughters.[46]

Although a divorce was obtainable by either spouse, if the divorce was initiated by the husband, all he had to do was expel his wife from his household.[47] On the other hand, if it was the wife who wanted the divorce, she had to have her father or some other male citizen bring her case before the archon.[48] Of the three known cases from the classical period where an Athenian divorce was initiated from the wife's side, all were negotiated exclusively among men.[49] As might be expected in such a society, all direct participation in government, such as holding public office, voting and serving as a juror, were possibilities for male citizens only.[50]

The role of the Athenian citizen woman was a domestic one, a role we have come to expect to be associated with high sex ratio societies.[51] If she was married to a wealthy man, she nevertheless served as manager of the household, which was often a considerable task involving slaves, servants, relatives, children, and concubines. Women of lesser means were occupied with the care of children, the preparation of food, and making clothing. Men, not women, did the marketing; women were largely confined to the household, reflecting in part their seclusion. Some of the poorer women did go out to work in occupations that were extensions of domestic duties such as laundering or nursing.

Athens is a good example of another feature that we have associated with high sex ratios, a strong protective morality for women. Free women were so secluded that they could never be seen by men who were not their close relatives. As part of the seclusion of respectable women in classical Athens, their clothing was designed to conceal them from men's eyes. Only prostitutes wore dresses that were provocative.[52] Virginity for unmarried girls and chastity for wives was both expected and enforced. In part this was important in determining the legitimacy of one's heirs, since a bastard had no claim to kinship rights or property, even from the maternal side. Women could be sold into slavery for unchastity. "The importance of being able to prove legitimacy had two principal results: it made adultery a public as well as a private offense, and it made the Athenians excessively preoccupied with the chastity of their women folk, with the result that they were guarded in a manner nowadays thought to be intolerable.[53]

In the sixth century B.C., Solon did away with all forms of self-sale and sale of children into slavery, except one: "the right of the male guardian to sell an unmarried woman who had lost her virginity."[54] Seduction was considered a very serious crime, as was adultery by women. Sexually, the life of the Athenian woman was restricted to the attentions of her husband. A virtuous wife was not to show any interest in sex at all, because if she did she might be led to commit adultery and her husband would become a laughingstock.[55]

The emphasis on Athenian wives as sexual property and as part of a man's household property is revealed by the fact that the penalty for rape in Athens was less than that for seduction, although both were severe. Seduction required the intrusion of a seducer into the husband's household, thus involving access to his property, and the husband had the right to kill him.[56] In both cases, the husband of a raped or adulterous woman was legally compelled to divorce her. Yet the rapist or seducer was considered the guilty party, and the woman merely a passive victim. Because of the very severe penalties, such violations apparently were not a usual course of action for either men or women.

It is tempting to close this discussion of the roles of Athenian women by moving to the later centuries of the Hellenistic period, especially since there were many changes in those roles in the direction of what might be expected of a low sex ratio society. But we have little firm knowledge of what sex ratios prevailed at those times, and instead we turn now to a discussion of the roles of Spartan women and their relationships to men.

In contrast to Athens, Sparta had low sex ratios. In at least one respect, however, they were unlike a low sex ratio society. Like Athens, Sparta placed great emphasis on women as bearers of children who could become warrior-citizens. Bachelors were ridiculed and suffered legal disabilities. This emphasis on motherhood is uncharacteristic of low sex ratio societies, and yet it is understandable given Sparta's military needs (discussed later). We should also note here that the emphasis on motherhood was not accompanied by its usual correlate, the value and sanctity of the family, as it was in Athens. After marriage at 18 years of age, the young male went off to twelve years of service in the military; hence, Sparta was largely a sex-segregated society.[57]

Sparta had a small population compared with the bigger states. The largest number of Spartans ever to engage in battle were the 5000 soldiers at Platea in 479 B.C. This number declined steadily so that by 450 B.C., Sparta could not muster 1000 men.[58] Sparta had become great only by augmenting its population through subjugation of other peoples. These included the helots, a compulsory labor force working the land for the Spartans, and other conquered people who retained their personal freedom but surrendered to Sparta their right of action in military and foreign fields.[59] Thus it is no won-der that the role of Spartan women in producing legitimate heirs was of enormous importance.

In virtually every aspect of their role other than childbearing, Spartan women contrasted with Athenian women in a fashion consistent with a low sex ratio society. We have argued that in low sex ratio societies, women are more likely to try for and actually achieve greater political, educational, and social rights. Sex practices are likely to be more libertarian, and sexual alternatives for women such as lesbianism, masturbation, and so forth will be more acceptable. Strictures against adultery are likely to be treated less seriously than they are in high sex ratio societies. Was this true for Sparta? What can be pieced together about the low sex ratio society of Sparta suggests that although it was wholly a state-controlled system, women had greater economic, educational, and sexual opportunities than in the high sex ratio society of Athens.

Unlike Athenian girls, Spartan girls received an education equal to that of Spartan boys of the same class level. They spent considerably less time in traditional women's work, such as sewing, weaving, and music, and they had the same kind of physical exercise and gymnastic training as Spartan boys. Household tasks such as cooking and making clothes were delegated to servants or slaves. The legal rights of Spartan women were especially striking. Even compared with other Dorian codes, the Spartan code was most favorable to women.[60]

When divorced, a woman took her own property and half of the produce of the household. If the husband was at fault, he paid a small fine.[61] Not only did women control their own property, but if a "father, husband, or son violated the regulations concerning the property of children, the control passed to the mother or wife."[62] A woman's work "was recognized as producing wealth which ought to be evaluated and there are stipulations in the code indicating the fraction of what she has 'woven' that a divorced or widowed woman could take with her."

Spartan women had the right to possess, control, and inherit property, including real estate. They could even dispose of real estate in their husband's absence. Daughters had the legal right to use and enjoy the property of their parents and could succeed them. As a result of these practices, fourth century B.C. Spartan women, through dowries and inheritances, controlled two-fifths of the land and property in Sparta.[63]

Also consistent in a low sex ratio society is that the Spartan legal code provided only monetary fines for adultery and rape. The code recognized homosexual relations as valid, and the penalty for raping a free person, male or female, was the same: a monetary fine.[64] Recall that in Athens the punishment for adultery was severe: The husband of an adulterous wife was compelled to divorce her, and he had the right to kill her lover if the act were a seduction rather than a rape.[65]

Not surprisingly, with more education and some economic power, Spartan women were noted for being outspoken and witty. A compendium of Spartan women's witticisms was even assembled.[66] There are many references to accomplished women in a maiden song written by the Spartan poet, Alcman,[67] a formal choral hymn sung by unmarried girls. Not one of the women poets who was praised or quoted later in classical literature came from Athens.[68]

As might be expected in a sex-segregated society like Sparta, lesbian relationships, particularly between older women and young girls, were not discouraged by the state. Lesbian relationships apparently flourished in women's choruses. The word "lesbian" comes from the isle of Lesbos, where the female Greek poet, Sappho, is sometimes depicted as surrounded by a coterie of female students. Some of her poetry vividly reflects erotic feelings about other females. In the case of Athens, there is virtually no mention of homosexuality among women.[69] Similarly, with the military life and the delay of marriage or separation from wives for men until the age of 30, male homosexuality is not surprising. But male homosexuality was apparently common in Athens as well.[70] The ancient Greeks were evidently bisexual and did not regard male homosexuality as abnormal or immoral, in contrast to many modern societies. In part, the apparent prevalence of male homosexuality among the ancient Greeks may simply reflect a lack of reasons for concealing it.

The prevalence of male homosexuality in classical Greece raises issues pertaining to sex ratios. One of the answers to the sex ratio question is that when women are scarce, as in Athens, men place protective and moral constraints on women, controlling sexual and other access to them. Of course, the presumption is that they want this sexual access for themselves. Thus, male homosexuality becomes important because of the possibility that if this were an exclusive sexual outlet, there might be be less reason for developing protective and moral constraints over women. But there are two good reasons for not accepting this reasoning. One is the importance of family and legitimate heirs, and the other is the possibility that many Greek men were bisexual and that women as well as boys or men were sexual outlets for them.

The importance to both Athenians and Spartans of family is undisputed and constitutes by itself a sufficient condition for the appearance of the anticipated social forms in a high sex ratio society. The role of wives as sexual partners is more controversial. There seems to be considerable indirect evidence that women, including wives, were important sexual partners for many Greek men who might or might not have also had homosexual relations. One scholar, for example, offers as evidence of men's sexual interest in their wives the famous "sex strike" in Aristophanes' play, Lysistrata.[71]

One cannot read Lysistrata without accquiring a strong feeling that wives were important to their husbands, both as companions and sexual partners.[72] Yet it would be unwise to let our conclusions about wives as sexual partners rest on a single play. Fortunately, the question of whether men preferred wives, boys, or other men as sexual partners is not relevant to our purposes, and we will not explore the evidence further. It is enough to know that in a high sex ratio society like Athens, the central role for women was that of household manager and mother to children who could be legitimate heirs; that women were placed in a legally and politically inferior, dependent status; that they were closely protected and guarded from contact with other men than their husbands; and that they were severely punished for any sexual transgressions. One could hardly ask for more definitive answers to the sex ratio question.

FEMALE INFANTICIDE: A PARADOX?

Female infanticide and the neglect of female infants are such ubiquitous phenomena—not only in some preliterate societies, but also in ancient Greece and Rome, in medieval times, and currently in a great many countries throughout the world—that we must pause here to examine some of the issues that these practices raise. In particular, we will examine the inferences about female infanticide that have been made by the social scientists who have studied it in various current and historical contexts.

Female infanticide or neglect has often seemed paradoxical to anthropologists, in view of the fact that women are highly valued and that wars are sometimes fought in order to capture them. Moreover, female infanticide seems inconsistent with the practice of polygyny. Why not simply raise females to maturity so that they would no longer be in short supply? At one time, "functional" explanations of various practices or customs were popular among anthropologists and some other social scientists. A functional explanation derives from the idea that some conditions or customs, such as the sex ratio, have an important function for the group, such as survival. For example, war may be seen as a form of population control. Many customs have seemed strange when such functions could not be identified, or when two practices seemed to have a contradictory function.

Some anthropologists have argued that males are favored because they are hunters and can increase the meat supply, while others have argued that they are preferred because they grow up to become warriors. While sons grow up to obtain food and to fight, daughters have to be given away to other men outside of the family. But this argument is weak in view of appreciable evidence that women's food-gathering activities often provided considerable sustenance for all—sometimes more than hunting.[73]

Does the sex ratio have a function or purpose? Functional explanations have, in more recent years, come in for considerable criticism from anthropologists themselves, as well as from other social scientists. Too often they are simply after-the-fact explanations of why what is found must be good for survival, and thus are merely circular. We do not believe that sex ratios have any function, but rather that they are unanticipated effects of various practices or conditions. But what is of great importance is that sex ratios in turn produce other conditions or consequences that help to shape the nature of relationships between men and women and the social institutions that are associated with them. Female infanticide makes young women scarce, and this in turn makes them highly valued and leads those who have power in a society to shape practices, social roles, and institutions so as to live with this scarcity condition. Thus, because of the value placed on them, women are desired for polygynous marriage as a form of conspicuous consumption, and because of their value, women are able to marry into a higher social class. High sex ratios, the high value of adult women, and the presence of female infanticide or neglect are not paradoxical. Once the sex ratio thesis is grasped, they can be seen as fitting together; as a rule, each follows the other. Moreover, this pattern occurs in traditional societies in which social customs are passed on largely unchanged throughout the generations. Women in these societies accept traditional roles that differ sharply for males and females. These institutional patterns continue to be self-perpetuating unless any one of the links in the entire chain breaks, at which point other aspects of the pattern break down as well.

The issue of female infanticide is worth examining further, in the context of other societies, particularly those which place great store in a daughter marrying up in caste or social class. One anthropologist has summarized the relationship between practices of female infanticide and marital patterns in North Indian groups, in historic China, and in Europe.[74] In India, during the late eighteenth and into the nineteenth centuries, the British were apparently astounded by the amount of female infanticide practiced among the highest ranking castes and subcastes in North India. The reason for female infanticide among the upper classes was that a high-caste daughter would have great difficulty in finding a marital partner of still higher caste. Sometimes, among the elites, all female babies were destroyed. She cites a few of these examples from North India:

> The Munhas Rajputs of Lahore Division, Punjab, were the highest ranking subcaste on the plains. An 1854 census of 50 plains villages where this group predominated discovered only 5 living Munhas females born before 1846. In the hills, however, the Munhas were at the bottom of the Rajput caste. Here, they did not practice female infanticide, but gave their daughters to the ruling Kutoch subcaste (Cave-Browne, 1957: 110-112, 189; Panigrahi, 1972: 27-28).

> In Kangra District, Punjab, the whole Hindu population had a childhood sex ratio of 119, in 1852. The Rajput ratio was 125, but that of the three leading Rajput subcastes was 302 (Cave-Browne, 1957: 185-186).

> Likewise among Sikhs, female infanticide was practiced by the Bedi Sikhs of the Punjab, highest ranking priestly subcaste and descendants of the founder Baba Nanuk. In 1846, the Commissioner of Jullundhur Division stated that there were no female children among 2000 Bedi families. Investigations in 1852 uncovered the case of one Bedi who had preserved two daughters prior to the institution of British rule. In consequence, he was outcasted and treated as a sweeper. Throughout Punjab, Bedi Sikhs were known by the epithet *Kuri-Mar* (daughter-slayer). The Sodhi Sikhs, a rival of the Bedis and the source of later religious leaders, also practiced female infanticide, as neither group would give its daughters to the other (Cave-Browne, 1957: 192-193; 283; Panigrahi, 1972: 25-28).[75]

A further consequence of the requirement that women marry up was that the lowest-caste males had great difficulty obtaining wives. Daughters were often sold to higher castes, and even poor males often paid a bride-price to obtain a wife. The intensity of competition for wives was so great that child betrothal and early marriage was practiced in an attempt to cope with the problem.

By now it will not be surprising to the readers of this book to learn that in India, despite the undersupply of females, polygyny was practiced among the wealthy. Further, high-status men often had a great many other women as concubines in their households. Women were also removed from childbearing roles by strictures against widow remarriage and by the practice of *sati,* whereby widows would throw themselves into their husband's funeral pyre.

That these social practices still persist is reflected in modern drives in India to stop child marriages and to end the practice of female infanticide. Nonetheless, these practices continue, particularly neglect of female infants. The sex ratios among young adults remain high and may be one reason why India has lower rates of depression among young women than among young men—one of the few countries in the world to show this pattern.[76]

With patterns of this type, despite the strong cultural emphasis on marriage, poor men end up with higher rates of celibacy than do poor women. This occurs because men in the lowest caste can only marry women of their own rank, while women from this caste are taken as wives by men of the higher groups. There has always been a particular scarcity of marriage mates for upper-caste women and for lowest-caste men, and this scarcity created institutionalized means of providing women.[77] Professional child thieves and middlemen once engaged in the kidnapping and sale of women and girls, particularly in North India.

Other social changes appeared as a result of the shortage of women. Male celibates were not uncommon, and it is reported that the caste of professional male prostitutes recruited members from higher-caste males who had failed in marital competition and had thus moved downward in the system.[78] Ascetics also recruited males who had failed to gain a marriage partner, giving rise to the saying: "A wifeless man takes to religion."[79]

A summary of data from traditional China also shows the prevalence of female infanticide and the expected patterns.[80] Census data from the fourteenth century onward indicate sex ratios that average 125 and go up as high as 460. Even in the 1870s, sex ratios as high as 430 for children and 194 for adults have been found.[81] In China, too, there was an emphasis on brideprices among the poor, and women marrying up was preferred. Concubinage for the wealthy created an even further upward flow of scarce females. Women were sold, and among the lowest classes males were too poor to obtain wives. Though there are differences between the Chinese and the Indian patterns, with the Chinese being a more open system, these cultures also demonstrate that the coexistence of female infanticide and polygyny is in fact a demographic-social pattern that is found consistently. A recent survey of cultural and population changes in Southern Asia indicates continued female neglect and mortality because young girls are often seen as an expense.[82]

Lest the reader think that the pattern described above characterizes only non-European societies, there is considerable evidence that female infanticide and neglect, including massive abandonment of female infants, occurred for centuries in Europe, even as recently as the nineteenth century.[83] Infanticide is often seen to be necessary in cultures where breast-feeding is the only source of nourishment for the young. When infanticide is practiced, female infanticide is usually the rule.[84]

Even historical British data[85] show sex ratios that are quite high. Langer reports that the sight of infant corpses in the streets of London was not unusual in the eighteenth century. Summaries of large amounts of evidence show that infanticide, particularly of females, increased steadily in England during the nineteenth century.

CONCLUSIONS

Classical Greek society was controlled by and structured to the advantage of men. They held the physical, political, economic, and legal power, and they used it to their benefit. As a result, women were largely an inferior class, ranging from citizen wives at the highest level to slaves at the lowest. But we have also seen that high sex ratios raised their value and often placed women in considerable demand. Under this condition, women were sometimes treated more favorably, though usually on men's terms. Their increased scarcity led men to place strict controls over women's lives, limiting their freedom of movement and imposing strict punishments for infidelity.

In contrast, when men were depleted through expeditions, warfare, and female neglect or infanticide, producing very low sex ratios, women often had more freedom. Since women were then abundant in the populations, men did not need to guard and constrain them. In addition, a shortage of men sometimes enabled women to take over some of the rights formerly granted only to men, such as owning and managing property.

Thus it is clear that a distinctive feature of classical Greece was the great power that men held, compared with women, as well as the way in which this power was used differently in high sex ratio Athens and low sex ratio Sparta. This marked imbalance of power between the sexes was characteristic of most later societies, although it was not always so extreme. We will see that when the structural power of men is less imbalanced, under high sex ratio conditions women are more favorably treated. Under low sex ratio conditions, as in Sparta, women were still greatly valued as bearers of children, but they had much more economic and legal independence than Athenian women. In the next chapter we will find that, unlike Sparta, when women were in excess in the medieval period they were much less valued, and marriage and the family were even denigrated. Like Sparta, however, under these conditions they did gain more economic independence, and a real feminist movement first appeared.

3

Love and Misogyny
in Medieval Europe

With the development of historical demography in the past few decades, new sources of data have been recovered and analyzed on the population characteristics of medieval Europe. Using these sources, we will contrast two periods that appear to have had very different sex ratios.[1] These periods convniently divide into the early Middle Ages, from 500 to 900 A.D.,which mostly had high sex ratios, and the late Middle Ages, beginning with the eleventh century and extending to about 1500 A.D. This later period mostly had low sex ratios, especially in urban areas.

A comparison of these two periods provides additional answers to our sex ratio question, as well as a useful illustration of the complex ways in which both law and social custom—particularly marriage patterns—respond to and in turn shape the oversupply or undersupply of each sex at the ages when men and women are most eligible for marriage. Statistical imbalances in sex ratios are often much aggravated by certain social conditions, which will be illustrated here.

EARLY MIDDLE AGES

In the early Middle Ages, medieval society was almost completely rural. There were almost no towns or cities,[2] and most people eked out an existence by means of subsistence agriculture.[3] Population size was stable, and the society was traditional, without great ferment—a pattern that endured for nearly 500 years.[4] Only fragmentary evidence is available on the sex ratio of this historical epoch, but this evidence is internally consistent and squares with other known conditions, such as female infanticide.

Surveys of peasant communities during this period show very high sex

ratios among young adults. In a list of peasants during the Carolingian period in Farfa, Italy, for example, the sex ratio for adults was 112, while for
children it was 136, yielding an overall ratio of 122.[5] In the polyptych of Saint
Germain-des-Pres, an extensive tax census was taken between 801 and 829
A.D. Among the adult population of Saint Germain-des-Pres, on different
estates, the sex ratios ranged from 110 to 253, while among children they
went from 116 to 156.[6]

What accounts for these high sex ratios? One minor contributing factor
might be high female mortality in the early Middle Ages and low mortality in
the late Middle Ages. In earlier history, women were believed to live shorter
lives than men.[7] This is supported by a recent study of a late Iron Age grave-
yard in Hungary that estimates that women buried there died at an average
age of 29 years, and men at 36 years.[8] In the late Middle Ages, when there
was an oversupply of women, both Averroes and Albertus Magnus offered
explanations for the greater longevity of women.[9]

Yet differences in mortality do not explain the extremely high sex ratios
among children that are found in such censuses as that of Saint Germain-
des-Pres. Was there female infanticide or differential neglect in the early
Middle Ages? Apparently there was, according to several authorities. In a
provocative set of analyses, Coleman[10] found that in Saint Germain-des-
Pres there was a relationship between the amount of arable land in a manse
and the sex ratios of the people living there. The smallest piece of land had a
sex ratio of 421 for the population living on it, while the areas with the
greatest amount of arable land had sex ratios of 97. The more arable land,
the greater the number of females relative to males. Further, the larger the
population on a farm, the more the sex ratios approached 100. Farms with
small populations had high sex ratios. In addition, Coleman found a rough
correspondence between the size of a household and the magnitude of the
sex ratio—the bigger the household, the higher the proportion of males to
females.[11] This suggests that as additional children were born to a family,
female infants were sacrificed or daughters neglected when subsistence became too difficult. Coleman also notes evidence that the nursing period until
weaning for male infants was twice as long as for females.[12]

Coleman found a similar pattern prevailing in medieval Saint Germain-
des-Pres. With more land and larger populations or multiple families, females could share labor, and higher productivity from the land was possible.
Thus, women could have some economic use, and girls as well as boys could
be fed from the larger food supply. This is consistent with the fact that in areas
with larger and more dense populations, sex ratios are lower than in rural
and sparsely populated ares. This is not limited to medieval times, but is
generally true.

In contrast to primitive societies, sons were not needed as hunters in medieval times, but were needed for hard agricultural labor. From the point of
view of medieval families at low subsistence levels, a long parental investment in daughters did not have much payoff. Daughters who did not marry
were the economic responsibility of their brothers.[13] Even if a daughter did
marry, the investment the parents made in her upbringing largely accrued to
her husband. Even the husband's bride-price went to the bride, rather than

to her family. Hence, not all female children were reared, and adult women were scarce and therefore highly valued.

Also available from the medieval period is fragmentary legal and literary evidence for the practice of infanticide. The penalty for killing an infant was reduced by more than half if the mother was a poor woman.[14] The story is told of Luidger, born in Frisia in the middle of the eighth century, that because there were other daughters in the family, she was slated to die. However, by Frisian custom she could be killed only if she had never tasted food. Her life was saved by a servant who hurriedly put some food into her mouth.[15] The Icelandic saga of "Gunnlaug Serpent-Tongue" states that if Gunnlaug's mother gave birth to a girl it must be put to death, while a boy could live. The saga says: "Those men who had few possessions, but yet they had many daughters on their land, had their children exposed."[16]

Thus we can conclude that in the early Middle Ages, where agriculture was usually at a bare subsistence level, female infanticide and/or neglect of female infants and children were common. This naturally created high sex ratios among adults. The consequences of these high sex ratios in the medieval period provide familiar answers to the sex ratio question. In the first place, historians agree that the early Middle Ages were remarkable for the high value they placed on young women of childbearing age. In fact, the exact monetary value of these women is known. The Germanic codes have been preserved, which

> offer some further inferences concerning the value attached to women in early medieval society. The codes characteristically extended a special protection over women and often assigned them a higher *wergild* than that allotted to their male counterparts. According to the laws of the Alamanni, if a person caused a pregnant woman to abort a child, and if the sex of the fetus could be discerned, the one responsible had to pay twelve solidi if the fetus was a male, and twenty-four if female. . . . In another, equally revealing provision from the laws of the Alamanni, a free man whose wife had been abducted by another man retained his paternal rights over the children she might bear, even though fathered by another. If those children died, he could claim compensation; the compensation was twice as high for a girl as for a boy. All through her life, still according to the laws of the Alamanni, women were protected with double fines for any injury done to them. "Fines are always double for their women," the Laws at one place affirm. Perhaps the most extraordinary of all these legal provisions protecting women is the imposition of a double fine even for robbing the grave of a woman. This implies that women were characteristically buried with greater treasure than men, perhaps with the jewelry they had acquired at marriage as gifts from their husbands.[17]

From one perspective, female infanticide might seem inconsistent with the double *wergild* assessed if a pregnant woman were caused to abort a female fetus. But keep in mind that the wergild was paid to the family that had lost the fetus. If, in a subsistence setting, it was more costly to rear a female, but as an adult her value was high, then the family which had lost the fetus was being justly compensated. This is a monetary indication that "valuable property should not be destroyed." Because the combination of female infanticide and a high value for adult women has seemed paradoxical to

historians, they have speculated that the high sex ratios found among children in the early Middle Ages probably indicate an underestimate of the
number of females. Many historians and demographers assume underre-
porting when confronted with very high or very low sex ratios. Yet it is difficult to account for the relationships that Coleman found between food production and sex ratios without postulating infanticide or differential neglect,
since the pattern of these relationships is consistent with findings for primitive societies at marginal subsistence levels.

It is important to realize that women themselves did not receive the
wergild for injuries done to them. Rather, their husband, father, or guardian
received the recompense. Thus, though the value of women to their families
is clearly reflected in the code, it is that of a valuable possession. How clearly
this value corresponds to the childbearing function is sharply depicted in the
laws of the Salian Franks:

> The free girl, before she was old enough to bear children, was worth a *wergild*
> of 200 solidi—the same sum which protected free men thoughout their lives.
> But after she began to bear children, her *wergild* was tripled to 600 solidi, and
> remained at that high level through all her childbearing years. During the peri-
> ods she was actually pregnant, the penalty for killing her was 700 solidi. In old
> age, her *wergild* reverted to the normal range for a free person.[18]

Two signs of the value of women in antiquity were marriage by capture
and the sale of women as slaves. Apparently, slave trade involving women
continued in the Middle Ages, because the Laws of the Alamanni imposed
double fines for selling a free woman beyond the frontiers of a province.[19]

That it was men who paid for their brides also indicates the value of
women. Tacitus, when writing about the Germans, was astonished to find
that the dowry was given by the husband to his wife and not by the wife to
her husband.[20] This dowry was often called the *Morgengabe* (gift of the
morning) and was given by the groom to his bride after the consummation
of the marriage. This practice appeared in the laws and charters of the early
Middle Ages.[21]

Such arrangements suggest competition for scarce women, thus driving
up the costs of acquiring a wife, and apparently this was the case.[22] These
reverse dowries were so extreme that they were condemned and had limits
placed on them.[23] Both the Visigoths and the Alamanni set legal limits on the
value of the gifts that the bride could receive. For example, in 458 the Em-
peror Majorian castigated the cupidity of brides and their families in exploiting young men eager to marry. In 717, King Liutprand the Lombard limited
the size of the groom's wedding gift to no more than one-fourth of his property. Among the Franks, the groom was limited to no more than one-third of
all he owned. Generally, the groom gave gifts directly to his bride, and not to
her family.

Occasionally, marriages in the early medieval period were uxorilocal.
Grooms came to live with the bride's family, a custom reminiscent of the
bride service associated with the high sex ratios of some primitive cultures.
"In a ninth century survey of the serfs belonging to the monastery of Saint

Victor of Marseilles, the number of women remaining with their families of origin after marrying so-called 'foreign men' is larger than the number of men in the household married to 'foreign women.'"[24]

With high sex ratios, one would expect role complementarity; each spouse would be thought to assume considerable responsibility for his or her own domain. In the early Middle Ages, wives had great importance in the management of the domestic economy. They commonly supervised all of the household's "inner economy."[25] This included cooking, brewing, spinning, weaving, tending the garden, and raising and caring for yard animals. Men were in charge of the "outer economy," which included work in outlying fields and tending to the herds.[26] However, what was defined as the "inner economy" was flexible, and many men spent their time in raids and wars, as the Germanic tribes spread their hegemony through invasions. Tacitus said that among the Germanic people, all functions of home management fell to the women. The Germanic warrior's only domestic function was collecting tribute from the household slaves.[27]

In the early Middle Ages, these broadly defined domestic duties meant that women of the nobility had prominent domestic roles in the management of the palace. The queen was responsible for the management of the royal household, which included paying knights their yearly gifts and supervising the royal treasury and the workshops on the royal manor, thus freeing the king to attend to affairs of state.[28] The domestic power of women was amusingly revealed when, at Vercelli, in 960 A.D., the married priests were ordered to give up their wives, and they replied "that unless they were maintained by the hands of their women they would succumb to hunger and nakedness." It was the most common excuse when other church leaders tried to introduce celibacy among the married clergy at the time.[29] Charlemagne himself may have been unwilling to give up his grown daughters in marriage because of their importance in the management of his castles and estate.[30]

As in the high sex ratio periods of classical Greece, women lived in the protective custody of males and had limited property rights. According to Lombard law, even as adults, and despite their extended domestic role, women remained under the guardianship of a male relative whose permission was required for any transaction involving their property.[31] There were, of course, exceptions: Visigothic law let the wife administer the capital she possessed before marriage, and if the husband died, the wife retained administrative control over the family property.

The culture of the early Middle Ages showed no signs of misogyny. Quite the reverse. All indications are that women were highly valued, that men wanted to marry, and that their commitment to the family was strong. Peasant life was stable, traditional, and relatively unchanging.[32] The religious opinions of Pope Gregory I (590-604) were markedly sympathetic toward women,[33] although the Church did not consider women competent to manage affairs outside of the family.[34] Within the domestic economy, however, they wielded considerable power. Hence, judging from what we have been able to glean from fragmentary evidence, societal conditions during the early medieval period were those that we would expect to find associated with high sex ratios. The later medieval period offers more abundant data, and there we will look for the social effects of low sex ratios.

LATE MIDDLE AGES

Around 1000 A.D., medieval society gradually began to change. After centuries of stagnation, the European population started to grow rapidly, particularly in the eleventh and twelfth centuries.[35] The population also spread across distant frontiers. Towns and cities began to emerge in what had previously been rural areas. Corresponding to the rise in the birth rate was a lowering of the sex ratio. With increasing urbanization and the loss of young men to the Crusades, to monasteries, and to the plague,[36] sex ratios continued to fall until, in the late Middle Ages, the oversupply of young women became so acute that it was a source of concern to philanthropic noblewomen, to religious leaders, and especially to families.

The increasingly low sex ratios of the late Middle Ages were especially related to the growth of cities. Urban life favored the longevity of women, since it relieved them of the hard physical labor of the countryside.[37] It also deprived the daughters of the middle class, at least, of a meaningful economic role in the family. In urban societies, with more adequate food supplies, the middle and higher classes expanded. Women then increased in number, since they were not neglected or overworked. Further, single and widowed women flocked to the cities. Hence, throughout history, urban areas have generally had lower sex ratios than the countryside. The loss of men in the Crusades also greatly reduced the sex ratio. St. Bernard's preaching in support of the Second Crusade (1147) supposedly helped to remove men from Europe's castles and cities.[38] During the plagues of the fourteenth and fifteenth centuries, women and children were often evacuated from the city, so the death rate was higher among men.[39]

The oversupply of young women was so great that it became the concern of clerics, among others. In the 1420s, St. Bernardine of Siena estimated that in the city of Milan alone, 20,000 girls were unable to find husbands, but chiefly blamed the reluctance of males to marry.[40] Population surveys of the late Middle Ages show a preponderance of women, especially north of the Alps:[41] "At Rheims in France in 1422, Freibourg . . . in 1944, Nuremberg in Germany in 1449, and other cities, women outnumbered men by ratios of from 109 to over 120 females per 100 males."[42] Those are sex ratios of from 92 to 83.

Along with the falling sex ratio came shifts in the economics of the marriage market.[43] First, the reverse dowry, or brideprice, became smaller and moved toward a greater equality of economic exchange at marriage. Marriage agreements made during the period from 1155 to 1164 most commonly called for equal contributions from the bride and groom.[44] Mention of a dowry given by the bride appears in early twelfth century documents. Around 1140, in the earliest surviving medieval tract on the dowry, the jurist Martin Gosia states: "In a legitimate marriage the mutual contributions of bride and groom, or their respective families had to be equal. Later . . . commentators reiterate that a dowry at least equal to the groom's gift, was essential for legitimate marriages."[45]

As the supply of marriageable girls continued to increase and the number of eligible men to shrink, the economic balance of marriage arrangements became steadily more unfavorable for women.[46] In 1143, the commune of Genoa abolished the right of a wife to claim one-third of the household property in the case of her husband's death. Many other cities (Alexandria in 1179, Volterra in 1200, Florence in 1253) imposed strict limits on the groom's contribution to the marriage.[47]

Using thousands of individual marriage agreements in Italy, one medieval historian has traced the decline of the reverse dowry until it virtually disappeared and has identified a corresponding rise in the dowry that a woman's family had to pay in order to secure a marriage partner for her. By 1200 to 1211, in Genoa[48] a bride usually brought more wealth to the marriage than did her husband. During the thirteenth and fourteenth centuries, the dowry size continued to increase. This increase continued at such a feverish pace that historians have called it "dowry inflation." It became so onerous that "in the early fourteenth century Dante remarked in his *Divine Comedy* that the size of dowries was exceeding all reasonable measure and he hearkened back to those better times, in the eleventh and twelfth centuries, when the birth of a daughter did not strike terror into her father's heart."[49]

> An example from Venice can give a sense of the trend. In a sample of fifty [mid-fourteenth century] patrician dowries, the average was about 650 ducats and the largest, about 1540 ducats. By the fifteenth century, however, it was a rare patrician dowry that fell below 1,000 ducats, and there was a strong tendency to go much higher. This tendency was alarming enough to induce the Venetian Senate in 1420 to place a limit of 1600 ducats on patrician dowries, a good indication that many dowries were larger. But such measures did no good. There are many instances of larger dowries in the years after 1420; and at the beginning of the sixteenth century the Senate passed another law reaffirming the principle of dowry restraint—but resignedly raising the ceiling to 3,000 ducats.[50]

The Senate itself called this dowry inflation "insupportable."[51]

In times when sex ratios are low, women's economic and social mobility through marriage declines, and women may even marry beneath their social class. This decline is reflected everywhere in accounts of the late Middle Ages. The life of St. Liutgardis of Tongres (Belgium) vividly portrays the plight of a young girl approaching marriageable age without a sufficient dowry. When Liutgardis was a baby, her father entrusted her small dowry to an English merchant, hoping for profit. Instead, all was lost. When she got older and wanted to marry, her mother warned her that all she could expect was a cowherd for a husband. "Her mother told her to marry Christ instead. In the *Vita*, her mother is described as *nobilis*, a noblewoman, and her father as only a *civis*, or citizen. Apparently, Liutgardis' mother knew what it was to marry beneath one's station."[52] In an analysis of marriage data among the Tuscans of Florence in 1427, a trend was found for women to marry down.[53]

Since women of the upper classes frequently had to accept socially inferior men, this created even greater competition for husbands among poor girls, many of whom had no chance whatsoever for marriage.

In the frenzy of competition for husbands in the late medieval period, the age of brides continued to drop as parents strove to assure their future in marriage. From the late twelfth century on, at least for the medieval aristocracy, many girls were in their early teens when they married. Ages at first marriage for girls at this time are revealed in the biographies of the lives of various Christian saints. St. Hildeburgis, who lived near Chartres, was probably 14 when she was married.[54] In 1114 or 1115, St. Christina of Markyate was around 18 when her parents pushed her into marriage.[55] St. Humility, born in 1226, was married in 1241 at age 15.[56] "By 1362, St. Clare of Pisa was betrothed at age 7, married at 12, and widowed at 15."[57] The parents and sister of St. Catherine of Siena tried to marry her off at age 12, and "St. Rita of Cascia, in Umbria, born in 1389, was given to a husband at age 12."[58] The lowering of the age of brides only served to intensify the over-supply of eligible women as younger and younger cohorts entered into the competition for husbands.

Two dominant characteristics of low sex ratio societies with an oversupply of young women are male reluctance to make a marital commitment and a trend toward brief, easy, sexual encounters outside marriage—licentiousness. The institution of marriage itself is challenged and disparaged by both men and women. Cultures with low sex ratios are misogynist. The value of women is low, and their easy availability makes them a glut on the market. The late medieval period illustrates all of these features. Many examples of the reluctance of males to marry young or even marry at all have been reported.[59] In the thirteenth-century poem telling of the romance of Tristan and Iseult, Mark of Cornwall refuses to take a wife until his own barons threaten to make war against him if he remains single. Another example is Hervis of Metz, the King of Spain and suitor of the fair Beatrice, who is variously represented as 60 or 80 years old. For twenty years his barons were unsuccessful in urging him to marry.[60]

During this time, sexually libertarian confirmed bachelors proliferated.

The cousin of Guibert of Nogent "refused to be bound by a layman's laws. . . . The marriage net could not hold him; he never allowed himself to be entangled in its folds." According to Guibert, no married woman was safe in his company. Bachelors crowded the towns as well as the courts. The son of St. Yvette of Huy caused great pain to his widowed mother, as he sowed his wild oats for years within the city, together with lascivious companions, presumably also unmarried. In spite of his mother's entreaties, he for long gave no thought to his soul's salvation—or to marriage.[61]

Male reluctance to marry and the disparagement of marriage became dominant literary themes in the later Middle Ages. In the allegorical twelfth-century Latin poem, *The Complaint of Nature,* by Alain of Lille, Nature complains that men are not replenishing their race in marriage. They either ignore love completely or exercise other sexual options, none of which, however, lead to procreation.[62] In the same poem Hymen, the patron of marriage, appears wearing clothes that were once decorated with ideal pictures of the event of marriage. But the clothes "are now tattered and torn from the neglect of men."[63]

An important epic poem of the thirteenth century, the *Romance of the Rose* by Jean de Meung, denounced the institution of marriage and was highly misogynist. According to de Meung, "the norms of Christian marriage were artificial and consequently ignored . . . A faithful wife was hardly to be found in the whole of France and the wise man should follow the dictates of nature and seek to perpetuate his kind at every available opportunity."[64] The poem provides a clear rationale for male promiscuity.

Misogynist attitudes were prevalent even outside the secular world. The sympathetic views that church fathers had held toward women in the early Middle Ages shifted sharply against them in the later Middle Ages. Even the late medieval church philosopher Vincent of Beauvais, supposedly enlightened and one of the least misogynous, did not escape the generally pessimistic attitude toward women of his day. According to Stuart, "his attempt to control women's impact upon society reveals the Church's growing fear of women's drives and purposes . . . The Church was only truly at ease with that totally spiritualized image of the private and domestic woman, Mary, the Mother of God."[65]

In low sex ratio societies, women themselves question the value of marriage—as well they might, when the ugliness of competition, their social and economic disadvantages in marriage and the reluctance and misogyny of men all add to its repugnance. The *Vita* of St. Christiana of Stommeln, the memoirs that she virtually dictated, reflect this anguished questioning and rejection of marriage, although in our times psychoanalytic veiwpoints allow us to read a few other feelings into what she said.

St. Christiana fled from her native village at the age of 13, apparently unmarriageable.[66] She says her parents disliked her and would not feed her. She lived by begging. She reports

> that the devil visited her with excruciating temptations. Once, he showed her a domestic scene, composed of a husband, wife, and child; the woman, playing sweetly with the baby, embraced the child and declared to Christiana: "There is no delight greater than this delight, which unites husband to his wife; there is no delight like to this delight which a woman finds in her child." For six weeks, this serene, if diabolical family group continued to appear before her, subtly tempting the lonely, abandoned girl to jealousy and despair. She resisted the temptation, but, her Vita relates, she could more easily have died.[67]

Low sex ratio societies are generally unstable. Traditional institutions of the society—not only the family, but even the church—may be questioned and attacked. In these societies, some women try, using whatever means possible within the cultural context, to gain an economic, social, and sexual existence for themselves outside the traditional roles of wife and mother. This puts them into direct competition with men, a competition which men heartily dislike, and which adds to male misogyny. As women seek to define new roles for themselves, their conflicts and struggles are reflected in speech and writing. Spokeswomen arise; women are no longer silent.

Medieval Feminism

In the late Middle Ages, what scholars have called *Die Frauenbewegung*, or women's movement, emerged. During the late twelfth and thirteenth centuries, while many women flocked into the recognized religious orders, others sought new avenues and activities. Many went into Beguine communities, which were a kind of female commune to be discussed shortly. Others helped to form and became a part of heretical groups.[68] Many women emerged as spokeswomen and sharply questioned their traditional role in a traditional society.

The upsurge in the twelfth and thirteenth centuries in the number of independent-minded, rebellious, outspoken, and distinctive women included an appreciable number who became saints. Many of these women were young widows. Their lives, some of which were carefully recorded, provide vivid testimony to their personal and social rejection of the lifestyle of their class and their insistence on a new lifestyle in which they deliberately chose to deny their noble or rich background. It was within religion, since religion was central to everyday life in the Middle Ages, that struggles for independence and self-expression were most likely to take place. The first revolutionary tack taken by these women was found in their vows of poverty and in their denial of income from communal property, but it was especially the women heretics, the Beguines, and the members of other women's organizations who constituted the counterculture of the late Middle Ages. Like modern-day feminists, the female saints and other religious leaders were independent and anti-establishment—but unlike today, the main social establishment was the Church.

Women appear prominently in the history of heresy during this time as in no earlier era.[69] The biographer of St. Dominic noted that because of poverty, many nobles of southern France did not rear their daughters, instead turning them over to heretics who educated and nourished them.[70] These heretics seem to have operated schools for young girls neglected by their families, supporting them and teaching them how to read, as well as instructing them in heresy. "'They teach little girls,' a tract of the thirteenth century says of the heretic, 'the Bible and the epistles, so that from youth they may be accustomed to embrace error.'"[71] St. Dominic founded the first Dominican convent on the grounds that the nobility had heretofore given their daughters over to the heretics.[72] Indeed, some heretical tracts were addressed only to the feminine gender, as if women were the only audience.

A common theme among heretical groups was the disparagement of marriage and hatred of the family. The Albigensians believed that *in matrimonio non salus*—in matrimony there is no salvation.[73] In the thirteenth century, a former Albigensian wrote that "physical marriage has always been a mortal sin, and that in the future life no one will be punished more severely because of adultery or incest than for legitimate matrimony."[74] "To lie with a daughter or son, to commit sodomistic acts, were no worse than, and indeed preferable to, lying with a wife."[75] The Albigensians also hated children. They believed that to marry and have children was to cause immense suffering.

The Waldensians, another heretical group, believed that marriage was sworn fornication[76] and insisted that a man was justified in abandoning wife and children if he wanted to join the ranks of the wandering *perfecti*.[77] All of the heretical movements were extremely critical of the orthodox church, and they characterized the clergy, especially the friars, as being lecherous seducers, among their other sordid qualities.[78] Many of the heretical sects allowed women to preach, and some permitted them to become priests.[79]

A natural place for many "surplus" women, it might appear, would have been the established religious orders. Yet, although there were large numbers of women who wished to join them, the nunneries remained exclusive and few in number.[80] A great many women attached themselves to charismatic religious leaders and (literally) followed them. One example was Heinrich, the first Dominican prior of Cologne, who specialized in preaching to women and who was reputed to have great success among virgins, widows, and female penitents. Women throughout the city were said to bewail his early death.[81] Another such leader was Robert of Arbrissel, who took his large female flock and settled them in a new convent at Fontevrault in the Loire Valley. Within a generation, that convent had become so aristocratic that no one other than a member of the French nobility could be a recruit.[82]

It seemed that whenever women made a major entry into a new order in large numbers, there were soon restrictions on further entrants. Among the Cistercian nuns, for example, there were many large, new female communities. These were ignored at first by the Cistercian male order, but when their rapidly growing numbers and relative freedom became too obvious to ignore, the general chapter began to discipline them. In 1228, it issued a "peremptory statute forbidding all further attachment of nunneries to the order and refusing benefit of visitation and pastoral care to existing communities."[83] There was a strong anti-female reaction in other orders against the large numbers of women who wished to join them. "It was thought that women inevitably contributed to indiscipline. . . . Women were also considered to be receptive to all forms of religious prophecy and to be completely unrestrained in relationships with their leaders or patrons."[84]

Low sex ratios, with their surplus of women, tend to create pressures for women's independence. Although the Church believed that the only possible role for women among the religious was one of attachment to existing male orders, by 1200 the women themselves began to clamor for recognition of their own separate identity.[85] Instead of giving women the opportunity to create a separate female order, however, in 1215 the Fourth Lateran Council issued a decree that there were to be no more orders and that any new religious community had to be within the rule of an approved order.[86]

Without enough convent cells, especially for the middle class and the poor, what happened to these extra women? In an apparently spontaneous movement, without a formal leader, many of them formed themselves into communal settlements, usually located in towns. A large number of these were in Northern Europe, especially in Flanders.[87] The communities were lay, rather than ecclesiastical. They were called Beguines, a name that was probably derived from their supposed Albigensian affiliations.[88] The Beguines performed occupations that were more menial than those of nuns, and they did not take vows of asceticism and chastity for life. Further, the communities were perceived as temporary resting places on the way to other things, including marriage. "The institution . . . tended to resemble a retreat for independent widows or superfluous daughters of well-to-do bur-ghers or a refuge for the dispossesed."

Because the Beguines had no real founder, no definite rule of life, and imposed no irreversible vows upon their adherents, from their inception they sought no authority from the Church hierarchy.[89] As the Beguine movement continued to grow in size and popularity, beginning in the twelfth century, the Church expressed ambivalence compounded by suspicion, distrust, tension, and concern about leaving the Beguines outside religious boundaries alto-gether.[90] In the early 1300s the Clementine decrees, which comprised the last promulgated collection of canon law in the Middle Ages, at one point defined the Beguines as an "abominable sect of women"[91] and accused them of de-ceiving the faithful with their "wrong" opinions. Religious advisers were for-bidden to help them, and their way of life was officially abolished.[92] Despite this decree, the Beguines continued to flourish. Another Clementine decree took a somewhat softer attitude toward them, considering them to be "rather foolish women who have gotten into matters far too complicated for them to handle and who, as a result, are causing much confusion and trouble."[93] De-spite these attempts to root them out of the Church completely the decrees also contain rules on housing restrictions for them.[94] These inconsistencies reflect the Church's uneasiness regarding a religious movement that was spontaneous, enduring, yet without a central administration or formal struc-ture.[95]

Some historians[96] believe that the Beguines were a natural consequence of the reluctance of the men's religious orders in the twelfth and thirteenth centu-ries to run convents for women. According to this thesis, the Beguines were not women who could not marry, but who could not get into convents. Other historians[97] point out that the various communities were different in many ways and cannot be considered a simple parallel of the men's religious move-ments. For example, large numbers of Beguines in Strasbourg were practicing in groups of two or three, with members required to do little more in common than eating. Analyses of the Strasbourg Beguines show that there were about equal numbers of women from the upper, middle, and lower classes—sug-gesting that low sex ratios characterized all classes of society.[98]

Despite (or perhaps because of) the Church's ambivalence, the Beguine movement continued to grow. In the early 1200s it gained an apologist in Jacques de Vitry, who eventually became a cardinal. In 1216 he went to Rome to secure papal approval for this new form of religious life, but the Lateran Council of 1215, which had forbidden the formation of any new religious orders, made that impossible.[99] Jacques did, however, manage to get verbal permission from the pope for women to lead a communal life in which they would exhort each other to virtue.[100]

The Council of Vienne, which met in 1311 and devoted much of its atten-tion to sources of heterodoxy, came out with a decree that essentially con-demned the Beguine status while allowing the settled communal way of life to pious women. It appears that the Church was trying to get the women off the streets where they were begging, out of individual houses and apartments and into communities, where they could be watched and controlled more easily.[101]

In Cologne, the Beguines were reported to be involved in obscene orgiastic rites associated with heretical mysticism. These reports were circulated in relation to an inquisition of 1326, perhaps related to the persecution of Meister Eckhard by Archbishop Henry of Virneburg. As a result of this inquisition, a priest by the name of Walter was defrocked by the Archbishop and burned at the stake, while another priest, a layman, and six women received life imprisonment.[102]

The Beguines also had trouble with the secular authorities. The townspeople did not want the Beguines to be too closely allied with the Church, because the Church was too powerful. As a result, the town councillors of the imperial free cities appointed secular supervisors to oversee the operations of the Beguines.[103] In the fourteenth century, that action added to the hostility of the Church authorities and led to the further persecution of the Beguines as heretics.[104] Despite the hostility from both the religious and secular authorities, the Beguines continued to grow. By the end of the fourteenth century, in Frankfurt, about 6 percent of all adult women belonged to these organizations.[105]

Sex ratios in Frankfurt provide an indication of where these women came from. In 1385, based on tax records, the sex ratio in Frankfurt was 91. The Frankfurt population in 1387 had a sex ratio of 85, not including servants; with servants, it was 83. In 1440, the sex ratio was still a low 85. Nine years later, in Nuremburg, also figured from tax records, it was 83.[106] In the 1449-50 Nuremburg population survey, there were 3853 men, 4383 women, 6173 children, 1475 servants (male), 1855 maidservants, 446 clergy and nuns, 150 Jews, and 1976 nonresidents, mercenaries, and guests, sex unspecified. The sex ratio, excluding servants, was 85; including servants, 83.[107] In Basel, in 1454, the sex ratio was 80 for persons over 14 years of age.[108]

In addition to married women and women in religious orders (who were tax exempt), a door-to-door tax survey in Frankfurt between the years 1354 and 1463 showed that independent, that is, unmarried women comprised one-sixth to one-fourth of all taxpayers.[109] How did all these women maintain themselves? Apparently, it was quite a struggle. At first, women were excluded de facto from the trade unions, the guilds. Adrian Beier, who was the editor of the oldest compendium of the rules of the guilds,[110] specified that being of the male sex was one of the fundamental prerequisites for acceptance into a guild, since there are certain kinds of work that are suitable for a man and others that are suitable for women, such as working in the kitchen, spinning, washing, and needlework. Association by young women with young men in their places of work was, according to Beier, dangerous with regard to moral principle.

Nevertheless, some women were able to enter trades surreptitiously through their own families. Widows took over their husbands' trades, and wives and daughters were often found working with their husbands or fathers.[111] Increasingly, women were hired by trades outside of their own families. They were paid, and some became independent entrepreneurs. In some cases trade unions were formed that were almost exclusively female, usually in typically female occupations such as weaving, sewing, and working with textiles.[112] Sometimes women even became *Meisterinnen* (master craftswomen). This emergence of women into the labor force, as well as their struggle toward economic parity with men, parallel contemporary times.

Then as now, employed men resisted women's struggles for economic independence. In late medieval times, women were pushed into the background, first by restricting the kinds of work that could be done by a master's wife, by limiting working hours, and later by restrictions on the amount of work that could be done by the female members of a guild member's family.[113] There was also a reaction against the independent female members of the guild. Finally, journeymen's groups refused to work with women.[114] The threat of economic competition from women increased as greater numbers of women were forced to earn a living.

While there were no legal restrictions against women who worked outside the trade unions, they were subtly discriminated against. For example, many independent women earned their living by selling in the marketplace. The police continually harassed these women. In many cities, a woman was not allowed to sell the goods of certain tradesmen unless her husband or some other man was present.[115]

Some single women, in groups of three or four, set up house together but kept their finances separate. Cooperative arrangements led to female organizations in cities like Strasbourg called *"Vereine"* or *"Samenungen"*. These secular groups, like communes, established rules for themselves that were loosely based on those of religious groups, although they were not Beguines. These institutions were strong in the mid-fourteenth century and became increasingly more secular.[116]

A few women alone, provided they were of means, could, by "leibrente," live out their lives with some protection. By purchasing a small piece of land outside a city, they also gained citizenship in and protection from the city. The leibrente was a form of life insurance for the independent woman.[117]

In fact, however, most lone women were very poor. The tax records of Frankfurt in 1410 indicate that the rate of poverty among women was over four times that among men (34 percent for women; 8 percent for men).[118] For many, begging in the streets was their only source of income. Others ran away when they could no longer pay taxes. When tax collectors went to the lodgings of taxable women, they frequently found them empty. In the tax books, the entries next to these women's names are: "Is gone" or "Has run away."[119] Of course, taxes were probably not the only reason that women ran away. The lack of opportunities for work in the city and their unbearable lives at home may have also contributed to many a flight.[120]

In the late medieval world, women's issues were the focus of the writing of a number of secular women. Around 1400, Christine de Pizan wrote at considerable length about her views on women's roles in France.[121] She wrote not only of what she saw, but also of how things might be improved. Christine was born into a cultured and well-placed family in 1364. By the age of 25 she was a widow, supporting her mother and three young children—all in considerably reduced circumstances. In a number of autobiographical works, she describes her troubles in detail. Beset by lawsuits when she tried to claim money due her husband, some of her property was seized, which she then had to sell. In her widowhood, there were few things that she could do that would earn her more than a pittance. For instance, she apparently did some menial copying work under highly distasteful conditions.

In *Epitre au Dieu d'Amour,* Christine raises the question of whether the talk of chivalry and the Courts of Love were not all hypocrisy "in a society where women really had a tenuous place, as she had learned through much bitter experience. She was willing to admit that the French might have played an honorable role in the cultivation of chivalry in the past, but insisted that times had changed to a shocking degree."[122] She became involved in the literary quarrel over the *Romance of the Rose,* possibly because of its slanderous attitude toward women. She objected to Jean de Meung's logic and to the crudity of language in his censure of women. In other literary works, she pursues the idea of the special merits of women in their historic roles.

Christine was greatly concerned with the importance of education for women. Based on her own experiences in widowhood, she insists that women should have sufficient training or education to be able to manage their affairs should they be required to do so. In *Livre des Trois Vertus,* she emphasizes that women have a serious role to play in society.[123] Yet there are constant references to women's insecurity in a system where they were almost completely lacking in civil rights. This insecurity meant that they needed to remain "in the good graces of husband, family and friends who could turn against them, and especially to avoid making enemies who could do them serious harm."[124] She admonishes women to carry out all their responsibilities well in the home and in the management of estates so that malicious tongues would not wag, and she repeats her attack on the hypocrisy and deceptions of male-female relationships. In particular, "her contention was that although chivalry might have made great lovers of men in the past, in the Paris of her day they were far more apt to be false to their fine vows and to boast in an ungallant fashion among themselves of their amorous exploits, thus endangering the reputation of any woman so foolish as to believe their fine words."[125] Several of her poems have as their major theme the deception of innocent women by knights who, after satisfying their sexual desires, deserted them.[126] At the end of her life, Christine was delighted with the advent of Jeanne d'Arc, whom she hailed as the savior of France in female form. Her last poem, *Dittie,* is about the Maid of Orleans.[127]

Christine de Pizan's themes sound amazingly modern: a call to women to prepare themselves for the exigencies of independence, a realistic appraisal of their need to be socially pliant because of their dependence on men and families when they are without civil rights, and a cynical view of men's avowals of love in relationships with women that are sexual and transient. In fact, these tend to be the attitudes of many educated women who are on their own during low sex ratio periods of history. Though muted, they are also themes of women's alienation and of the need for women to gain political and economic independence.

Prostitution

There existed traveling groups of women at this time, many of whom became camp followers. They were female travelers without honor and without rights. Those who followed along with the army often formed common-law marriages that were dissolved as quickly as they were formed.[128] Camp followers were the least tolerated and the least protected of all women. Their duties were the dirtiest and most menial. They cooked, mended, washed, attended the sick, cleaned the latrines, dug the graves and ditches, and chopped wood.[129] One nineteenth-century historian[130] used the word *Dirnen* to describe the medieval camp followers. The word has a double meaning—both "young girl" and "whore." In the last Middle Ages, when these traveling women occasionally became permanent residents of the cities through which they passed, their contemporaries accused them of contributing to the downfall of the moral standards in those cities.[131]

At a higher social level were the prostitutes. In the late Middle Ages, houses of prostitution were established in cities. Here, it would appear, was a trade that was not in economic competition with the other guilds. It might be expected that with the great oversupply of young women and with the male transients who came to the cities as commerce grew, prostitution would flourish. What is of interest is how organized houses of prostitution in some places provided women with a near-guildlike status, and even some degree of financial security, especially in sickness and old age. Eventually, the male guilds reacted successfully against this threat, and the women in these houses were reduced to inferior status. Prostitutes were allowed to practice their trade in certain parts of the city, but they were generally relegated to living outside the city in houses that had been set up expressly for them by town officials. These officials often made considerable income from such operations, and the houses were supervised by some of them. Usually, supervisors were the servants of the town masters, or the hangman, or the man in charge of the town stocks. These in turn reported to still higher officials.[132]

Houses of prostitution were protected by the city, and any misconduct that took place in them was punished with double severity. The inhabitants themselves (the prostitutes) enjoyed special business rights. For example, they were protected from the competition of individual women (called "secret women") who practiced the art in private houses. In Geneva and Paris, such houses were developed into corporations, though this happened only occasionally in Germany.[133] In Leipzig, the association of prostitutes was so well established that they elected their own head and participated in the annual Mardi Gras parade. At public ceremonies, at receptions for princes, and at any large gathering of people, the prostitutes were represented along with the other guilds.[134]

The prostitutes were so well organized that in many cities they had pension plans. Those who occupied houses maintained by the city were also required to do work. Some had to spin a certain amount of yarn daily. If they did not do this, they were required to pay a penalty for each day not worked. In return for such work, the supervisor of the house paid a certain amount into the account of each of the prostitutes on behalf of the city. This sum was used to care for those prostitutes who were sick or without bread.[135]

A number of factors were responsible for the great rise in organized prostitution, which occurred at the same time as the oversupply of young women. These included the increase in foreign trade; the presence of unmarried clerics and apprentices who were not in a financial position to marry, and of the many servants of merchants; as well as the spread of immorality from the upper classes. As expected from the low sex ratios, the prevailing ethos was sexual libertarianism, a cultural attitude shared by both men and women. Sexual cynicism, rather than an ideal of committed love, predominated. All aspects of society were touched by what has been referred to as "the decline of morals."[136]

The early fifteenth century saw a strong reaction against organized prostitution, initiated by the male guilds. The guilds, with the rationale of combating the amorality of society, helped to get laws passed against the organized prostitutes. As in the case of many socially undesirable people, the laws required that prostitutes wear a standard uniform to distinguish them from other women. They were also excluded from burial with other people.[137]

The religious community also tried to convert prostitutes back to an honest life. As early as the thirteenth century, in a Rhineland city, a priest named Rudolf applied this vow of conversion to certain of these fallen women: "Lord we are poor and weak; we are unable to nourish ourselves in any other way; give us water and bread and we will gladly obey."[138] Was this, even obliquely, an indication of the economic necessity for their adoption of this means of livelihood? Rudolf converted some of these women and took them into his house. In Strasbourg, in 1225, he set up a fund for those who were prepared to make confession. Two years later, the pope named all the women who had been thus converted to an order called the Order of the Ruing Ones, later the old Order of Magdalene. The great Reuerinnen Cloister of Strasbourg started with this group. In 1246, through a Bull of George IX, the Order of the Penitents of Saint Magdalene was established in Germany and allowed to build a cloister. Similarly, cloisters of the Penitents (*Büsserinnen*), the Ruing Ones (*Reuerinnen*), and the White Ladies (*Weisse Frauen*) quickly came into being in other cities. Here, at last, was a path into the religious life, which had been forbidden by the Church hierarchy when women had tried to gain legitimate permission to form their own order or to join existing male orders.

The large number of cloisters so quickly established via this route testifies to the number of fallen women who were there to be saved. The purpose of these cloisters was to improve their lot and to lead them back into honest, secular society. The women were required to adhere to a set of stringent, but not all that difficult rules applied to a life of prayer and work. Only those who displayed exceptional dedication were made permanent members of the order, called the "group of Saint Magdalene."[139]

In Vienna, Strasbourg, France, and Italy, other institutions sprang up aimed at restoring prostitutes to a normal life. The most colorful of these were the "Sack Beguines." In 1309, Bishop John von Dirpheim took a number of penitent fallen women under his protection and declared them free of all flaws, saying (October 8, 1309): "Slaves, when they achieve their freedom, have all the rights of free men; it would therefore be unjust if women, who have been slaves of sin, were not treated similarly as soon as they are converted to a better way of life."[140] These converted ladies (Bußschwestern) wore skirts and cloaks of sackcloth; hence their name. This order was very popular with the citizens of Strasbourg and grew to be quite large. During an attack of plague in 1315, it was changed into a hospital and the women became nurses. The citizens of Vienna founded a similar institution in 1384, which was given tax-exempt status. These facilities for women were supported by city taxes, as well as by private donations. As an incentive to get these converted women back into the marriage market (and as a further indication that incentives for men were needed), it was ordered that any man who married one of the women was to suffer no slights to his honor nor any damage to his rights as a guild member. Further, if his new wife returned to her errant ways, she was to be drowned.

These social and institutional responses to the great increase in prostitution in the late Middle Ages were only one expression of the trend toward a more sexually libertarian society. One scholar has explicitly linked the decline of sexual morality to the presence of large numbers of available, unattached women:

> It was impossible for the great number of independent women in the late Middle Ages not to have a negative effect on the relationship between the sexes. . . . There was not much left, by the 14th and 15th century, of the much-praised earlier ideals of morality and breeding—particularly in the cities. There was not much marriage fidelity among the higher classes during the entire Middle Ages, but especially in the later periods, an almost raw sensuality was the dominant factor in the relationship between sexes in all classes of the population.[141]

Woodcuts have been preserved from the end of the fifteenth and the beginning of the sixteenth centuries that frequently show women in the company of men drinking wine, gambling, feasting, and participating in wild dancing. They are seen in the celebrations of patrician and fraternal societies, at folk celebrations, at markets and fairs, in open places, and in the anterooms of churches. Women were portrayed as loose and abandoned, among companions of like morality, wherever there was something to gape at or enjoy, a chance to reel or jump. Often viewed previously as watchdogs of good societal behavior and strict morality, some were instead made ringleaders of the happy ones.[142]

There is interesting cultural evidence in a number of popular German folksongs, written in the vernacular, that date from this period. These songs tell of daughters who rebel against the drudgery of housework and who vow to flee the house and take to the country to find a nice boy. The underlying message of the songs is that these girls run away, often to their downfall, because they cannot stand the conditions at home. One song, sung on the streets in 1359, condemns the one who sent the woman away to a convent, locking her away from the excitement of the world: "May God give to him, who made me a nun, a rotten year; and the same one who gave me a black mantle with a white shirt."[143]

Courtly Love

One thesis of this book is that under certain circumstances, romantic love themes arise when there are relatively high sex ratios and women have some freedom in choosing a suitor or husband. In the eleventh century, the poetry of Muslim Spain expressed themes of the spiritualized love of women by men, emphasizing restraint, tenderness, the avoidance of gross satisfactions, and devotion to their beloved. In the twelfth and thirteenth centuries in some parts of southwestern France and southern Germany, the courtly love tradition became an important cultural theme within the upper classes. For about three generations, courtly love was the preoccupation of Provençal and German lyrical poets. Scholars have devoted thousands of pages to analyses of the origins and themes of the courtly love complex, mostly to its philosophical origins.[144]

Given the shift toward generally *low* sex ratios in much of Europe during this period, why did such an intensely romantic culture arise? According to our argument, when sex ratios are low, women are not supposed to be valued. This apparent exception needs explaining. In this instance, we will find that high sex ratios actually prevailed for limited subgroups of the population and that their effects were similar to other high sex ratio periods. The kinds of social constraints that prevail over the pairing of men and women, whether local or widespread, can determine whether an over- or undersupply of either sex exists. The development and prevalence of the courtly love complex illustrate how the relationship between the sexes may change sharply with changes in societal conditions. These changes are reflected in the culture—in song, literature, and attitude.

In the classic version of courtly love,

> the male lover presents himself as engrossed in a yearning desire for the love of an exceedingly beautiful and perfect woman whose strange emotional aloofness and high social status make her appear hopelessly distant. But the frustrated and sorrowful lover cannot overcome his fascination and renders faithful "love service" to this "high-minded" and exacting lady who reciprocates in a surprising manner: she does not grant him the amorous "reward" which he craves, but she gives him what immeasurably increases his "worth": she rewards him with approval and reassurance. The great lady accepts him as being worthy of her attention, but only at the price of behavioral restraint and refinement of manners, that is, at the price of courtois (courteous) behavior. As the contemporaries put it, *courtoisie* (courtesy) is the result of courtly love. . . . The fantasy content of the courtly love complex was not altogether pleasurable: to crave against hope the possession of an inaccessible woman, who usually was understood to be already married, to suffer agonizing fears of rejection, and to gain the coveted approval of a protecting figure only at the cost of self-denial and frustration.[145]

One of the most important influences on courtly literature was the poetry of Muslim Spain, which flourished in the eleventh century, about one hundred years before courtly poetry emerged in southern France. Using the theme of men's spiritualized love, this poetry emphasized the avoidance of gross satisfaction and the value of restraint and tenderness in a "union of souls." The tantalizing love portrayed in the lyrics had the power to ennoble and caused men to desire and seek their beloved's approval.[146]

Hispano-Arabic love poems similar to later troubadour lyrics began to appear about 820 A.D. Other poetic forms were invented in Spain at the end of the ninth century. By the eleventh century, Andalusian love poetry reached its greatest height, and around 1022 Ibn Hazm wrote *The Dove's Neck-Ring*. This provided the model for *The Art of Courtly Love*, composed a century and a half later at the court of Marie of Champagne. Love poetry in Muslim Spain did not begin to wane until the twelfth or thirteenth century.[147]

What were the social factors that achieved their greatest force in Muslim Spain in the eleventh century, and that account for the emergence of these love poems?

The heavy migrations to Spain during this period were made up mostly of young adult men and caused a chronic and severe shortage of women of marriageable age. The invasion of 711-712 brought in many Arabs and Berbers. During the ninth and early tenth centuries, mercenary soldiers and male immigrants from the Near East flocked to Muslim Spain, attracted by its economic prosperity and internal wars. Later, in the tenth and eleventh centuries, the Muslims imported large numbers of Berbers to serve as mercenaries. This was regretted later, as this mass influx eventually led to internal struggles and to the dissolution of the caliphate of Cordova in 1031. Later conquests by warlike African emigrations (1086-1106 and 1147) further swelled the number of men.

African slaves, captives of war who thus probably had high sex ratios among them, were imported for use in agriculture, private homes, and as soldiers. Ibn Hazm's *The Dove's Neck-Ring* abounds with reports of men infatuated with slave women, women who could be enfranchised and legally married. Muslim pirates were feared along the coastlines of Europe for their abductions of prisoners, especially girls.[148] Finally, harems kept by powerful Muslims further aggravated the high sex ratios.[149] We can conclude that a clear parallel may be drawn between the amorous poetry of the Muslim Spanish people and their high sex ratio, largely resulting from sex-selective immigration.[150]

In southwestern France in the twelfth century, and in southern Germany in the later twelfth and early thirteenth centuries, the chronology and geography of the spread of courtly love coincided with a unique set of social conditions that created intense competition among many men for a small group of noble women. It was one of the few times in European history when marrying up in social status was both feasible and required for men—it was, in fact, the only way they could achieve and maintain higher social status. It is important to realize that courtly love poetry was presented at social gatherings; it was a public, not a private forum. "The majority of the troubadours and minnesingers and all of the performing *jongleurs* were poor and had to cater to the tastes of the audiences; even great noblemen, however, composed love songs to win the applause of noble society."[151] Why did the themes of the courtly love poetry have such an appeal to men of the secular upper classes? A number of geographic, demographic, and social structural changes occurred which, for the higher classes in parts of southern Europe, created an insufficent supply of noblewomen for the large number of upwardly mobile men who needed to marry them.

The conditions that created this large group of men who had to marry up in class were similar in both regions. Changes occurring during the 200 years between the eleventh and thirteenth centuries created the need for a large secular class of heavily armed knights and lay administrative personnel. Because of this, the nobility was an open class, both legally and in reality.[152] In the south, a class of men known as the *ministeriales,* or persons of unknown origins, began to fill many important positions, even though they had not yet achieved noble status. Ministeriales became socially acceptable to the old nobility, and many achieved wealth and power. By marrying noblewomen, these men could achieve the only thing they still lacked: the social status of nobility.

Below the ministeriales were many aspirants to knighthood. Thousands of men became knights, even though their fathers and grandfathers had been serfs. In the south, the upper class swelled with all these new male entrants.[153] Between the eleventh and thirteenth centuries in southwestern France and southern Germany, there was also a frenzied building of castles. Each castle required guards, administrators, knights, and judges, and this led to further expansions in the still open upper class.[154] Boys of 14 to 21 years of age began as bachelor knights by serving a castle, which also had older men belonging to the lowest rank of the knights. These *baccalarii, simples, chevaliers, Knappen,* and so forth, multiplied from the latter half of the eleventh to the early thirteenth centuries. The sex ratio of this class was also raised by the migration of knights to southwestern France and southern Germany.[155]

This upward mobility in southern Germany was reflected in the increase in the proportion of Crusaders of the ministeriales class who came from this region. In the south of Germany during this period, class lines were extremely fluid. Provided that he had means, it was easy for a peasant's son to rise into the military class and lead the life of a nobleman. Moreover, the Bishop of Worms had the authority to raise any number of serfs to the status of ministeriales, and in Bavaria, the class lines between peasantry and lower nobility remained fluid well into the thirteenth century.[156]

Well into the thirteenth century, nobles and prelates were still knighting at will any person they chose. Adventurers penetrated the knightly class by serving as soldiers and assumed noble stances.[157] This entry of large numbers of men into the nobility occurred in precisely the areas where the courtly love tradition flourished. But in order to maintain this status, and to insure that their children remained in this class, these men had to marry women from the nobility. This achievement of noble status by soldiers of fortune and administrative agents, especially if they came from distant baronies, was made easier by the absence of written genealogies.[158]

Given these local opportunities for advancement, it is no surprise that there was little out-migration in the south. Northern Europe sent most of its knights into the Crusades, further lowering the sex ratios there. But there was only one noticeable contribution to the Crusades from southern France, the

large army led by Raymond of Toulouse in the First Crusade. These southerners soon returned home without sending replacements, and their state,
Tripoli, was taken over by northern Frenchmen and Italians.[159] Although
physically close to Spain, southern France did not participate in the Spanish
reconquista, while the distant northern French and the Burgundians did
make considerable efforts in that campaign.[160] Thus the sex ratios remained
high in southern France.

This continuous but contingent rise of men into the upper classes created
an extraordinarily high sex ratio in the class to which these men aspired.
Because of the consequences of marriage for status and property, the high
sex ratio created a problem for aspirants to the upper class, even affecting
the old nobility.

> It was imperative for a nobleman, or a knight, or even a young aspirant to the
> knighthood, to avoid a misalliance, lest he jeopardize his status or his chances
> for promotion and the status and inheritance of his children. . . . In this fluid
> situation, when the nobility was not yet a closed class, public opinion and
> usage insisted that a marriage to a woman of lower social status necessarily
> depressed the status of the issue from this union. A nobleman's right of inheri-
> tance could be dependent on his mother's being a nobilis.[161]

Unlike today, where class is fixed by a man's occupation, education, income, and family background, marrying down in social class was an immediate and threatening danger.[162] According to one report, a Flemish baron was
dragged to his downfall in 1127 because he unwittingly married into a family
which, though its members were well established and influential ministeriales, was below his level.[163] Abhorred misalliances were defined as marriages to women who were not high enough in social class.

> [For] social climbers it was highly desirable to marry women of higher status
> than their own, and they often succeeded in doing so. Marriage to a woman of
> superior social status . . . introduced a man to higher social circles and opened
> up greater economic opportunities; sometimes it even led to his official
> change of status. The higher up on the social ladder the people were with
> whom he associated professionally and convivially, the higher was a man's
> prestige within his own group. . . . There was no one below princely rank who
> was not aware of this. Serf-knights who married a free woman found it easier
> to gain their freedom; they could more easily bluff their way into noble society,
> if they had the funds for living a noble life. . . . In southern France, where
> daughters of noblemen were included among the heirs of landed property, . . .
> the pursuit of heiresses was a major occupation of noblemen and a fantasy
> subject for indigent knights.[164]

Girault de Bornelh, a poor troubadour of the Limousin, told in one of his
songs of a dream he had one night during the Third Crusade. It was interpreted to him to mean that

> I could not fail, if I would take great pains to gain the unemcumbered posses-
> sion of a sweetheart of superior rank, whose like no man of my family back-
> ground or of far greater merit ever loved or was loved by.

Now I am ashamed and afraid; it disturbs my sleep; I worry and sigh. I consider the dream great foolishness and I do not think that it can come true. And yet I cannot get an ambitious, proud and presumptuous hope out of my befuddled mind that after our voyage the dream will be fulfilled, just as it had been interpreted to me.[165]

The troubadour's favorite topic was the complaint about the high rank and pride of the lady, combined with the hope that "love will surmount all class differences."[166]

A poem by Aimeric de Peguilhan reflects these themes:

Lady, heed not rank and riches in your treatment of me, but your honor, for you can change it from good to better; and the profit will be mine, the glory yours. He who exalts the exalted does not do very much; but he who exalts and upholds the humble gains thereby the favor of God and friend and fair renown.[167]

There were major differences between the Hispano-Arabic poetry and its later Provençal and German counterparts—differences that reflected the changed social milieu. Muslim poetry, for example, did not have the theme that unrequited love was intrinsically ennobling. Also, the Muslim code of refined behavior did not have the social exclusiveness, a characteristic distinguishing the knightly class from the peasants.[168] Despite these differences, all three periods—Hispano-Arabic, Old Provençal, and Middle High German—had themes of "sometimes morbid interest in matters of sexual frustration and fantasied compensations."[169]

Our argument is that themes of romantic love occupy men in high sex ratio situations, whereas women can exercise some preferences, since underlying such themes is the competition among men for scarce women. In the twelfth- and thirteenth-century competition for noblewomen, men publicly embarrassed one another for being of lowly birth, or for manners that were anything less than perfectly refined and courtly. For the ambitious knight or self-conscious courtier, the "ritualized public adoration of the ladies . . . became a badge of social superiority for men."[170] Courtly lyrics were often written as direct flattery of noble ladies. Men hoped that their refinement of character, the purity of their love, and their fidelity would persuade the highborn lady to approve of them.

Comparable themes have emerged in many other historical contexts where sex ratios were high. In the literature of the American West, as we will see, one theme centered on men's willingness to renounce the cruder side of their nature in order to gain the love of a virtuous woman. This theme is reminiscent of medieval courtly love. According to Painter, the common symbolic emotional element in courtly love was an anxiety regarding acceptance, which heightened efforts at self-improvement and devoted service.[171] Men attempted to prove themselves worthy of being loved and chosen by a lady for special attention, and thus suffered the anxiety of being rejected in spite of such efforts.

What is striking about such themes is that they are found in the psychology of whichever sex is the most disadvantaged in the marriage market; that is, whichever sex is required by social custom to marry up or at least across social class, and to compete for a short supply of available partners. Some elements of this psychology—that of the one who must be chosen—are similar, regardless of sex. Emphasis is on becoming the best person possible through self-improvement, devotion—meeting the other person's needs completely and selflessly—and anxiety about acceptance. There is also the search for love, a love that will transcend the individual's competitive disadvantages and cause him or her to be chosen by the scarcer sex. Many people lose out in the competition at these times, and sadness and disillusionment with the still-prevalent idea of love become a personal theme for those who fail in the contest.

In southern France and Germany, there were large numbers of men who needed women to grant them acceptance into a privileged society and thus to establish the feelings of self-assurance and personal worth that go along with such acceptance. In modern Western societies, it is the women who are expected by social custom to marry up in social class, in spite of the scarcity of appropriate men. Popular books and magazines of the 1970s targeted for women readers emphasize themes of self-improvement in grooming and bodily appearance, how to behave so as to be attractive to a man, and how to serve his needs. In other publications, a literature providing an alternative for those disillusioned with romance has appeared, emphasizing the economic and sexual independence of women.

The courtly love complex demonstrates how radical societal changes can alter the socially available supply of men or women and either aggravate or mitigate imbalanced ratios. In much of the rest of Europe, particularly in the north, there was an oversupply of young women of the nobility because the nobility was essentially a closed class. Northern Europe was quite economically advanced during this period. The nobility was able to delegate many duties to non-nobles while retaining political power, and therefore the noble class did not grow significantly in size. In northern Germany, for example, both the nobles and the ministeriales remained a closed class. In northern France the nobility had been tending toward a closed class since the eleventh century, and the "knighting of serfs was abhorred."[172]

Generally, in northern France in the twelfth and thirteenth centuries, a rough and unbridled anti-feminism prevailed.[173] Faint versions of the courtly love theme appeared in the north only in the last third of the twelfth century, and much of it seems to have originated in the "predilections of southern princesses, especially Marie de Champagne."[174] The fact that many of the upwardly mobile southerners were able to marry highborn ladies indicates that there was probably a numerical undersupply of noblemen for women to marry, even in the south.

It may not be accidental that most of the female saints came from the north, where there was no sudden surge of marriageable men into the higher classes. The clear indications of women's suffering in the oversupply conditions that characterized many areas of Europe in the late Middle Ages[175] are not echoed among the female nobility in the parts of southern Europe where socially created high sex ratios and the courtly love tradition flourished.

CONCLUSIONS

In summary, the high sex ratios of the early Middle Ages and the low sex ratios that characterized the late medieval period both reveal the predicted patterns. In the early Middle Ages, a childbearing woman was highly valued. Men wanted to have a wife, often paying a substantial bride-price for her, and were committed to the family. These were traditional, stable societies, with role complementarity for men and women. There is no indication of massive female discontent.

The late medieval period, with its low sex ratios, provides a sharp contrast. In this more urbanized society, especially in northern Europe, women's movements both within and outside religion were notable. As their competitive position in the marriage market steadily worsened, women struggled to gain economic, religious, and social places for themselves outside the traditional roles of wife and mother. In the counterculture of the late Middle Ages, women were strongly represented. Men were reluctant to marry, and sexual libertarianism flourished. Marriage and the family were attacked from many quarters. The devaluation of women appeared in late medieval misogyny. Feminism, in its medieval version, also appeared. The quixotic occurrence of a socially induced undersupply of noblewomen in some parts of Europe was paralleled by the development and spread of the courtly love tradition, whose characteristically romantic themes reoccur at other times when men must compete for a limited number of desirable women.

Although muted by medieval societal patterns and cultural concerns very different from our own, the social, economic, and psychological concomitants expected to accompany high and low sex ratios nonetheless emerge.

4

Sex and Family Among Orthodox Jews

Throughout history, from biblical times to the modern period, Jewish societies, more than any others, typify the characteristics that we expect to be associated with a high sex ratio society. They have had a continuous history with a cultural tradition and a body of laws and customs that have been passed down through thousands of years. The traditions of ancestors are honored and preserved. Families have been highly stable, and great value has always been placed on the Jewish wife and mother. In the Jewish prayer traditionally recited by husbands to their wives on the Sabbath, she is praised for her devotion to the family as expressed in tireless work and domestic productivity, and for her strength of character and faith in God. Certain female attributes outside of the role of wife and mother are denigrated: "Charm is deceitful, and beauty is vain."[1]

The traditional role can be further detailed by looking at the laws and codes governing the family, sexual behavior, and the place of women as expressed in the Talmud and other sources. We find the bride-price and bride-service, great importance attached to virginity, emphasis on the sanctity of the family (with special attention to insuring that wives and mothers be honored and well taken care of), proscriptions against adultery, emphasis on the faithfulness of both spouses, marriage at an early age, and very low divorce and illegitimacy rates. Modern feminists have emphasized the negative side of the roles of women in Judaism, though usually to the neglect of the positive values connected with the traditional role. Women were long regarded as inferior to men with respect to such attributes as reasoned judgment, scholarship, and political affairs. Thus they were excluded from any but the most elementary education, from politics, from the more intellectual activity of the synagogue, and even there were segregated and seated at the back or in a special section.

Given our modern perspectives on women, these practices can easily be misinterpreted as misogynous. But the evidence is overwhelming that Jewish women were loved, respected, valued, admired, and cherished within the traditional role. Only our modern eyes see these Jewish women as second-class citizens. The way they were valued is precisely congruent with our argument concerning high sex ratio societies. Before moving on to examine sex ratios, we present some additional source material concerning women in Judaism.

ROLES OF JEWISH WOMEN

References to the proper role for Jewish women begin with the biblical patriarchs. Jacob, for example, in the biblical version of bride-service, worked seven years for Leah and then labored another seven for Rachel, all in their father's home.[2] In the Bible, repeated evidence of the bride-price custom is found:

> Ashor paid only 5 shekels to his father-in-law . . . while his gifts to the bride amounted to 65½ shekels in value . . . He promised to pay three times as much (200 shekels) should he at any time proceed to "drive her out of his home." It is probably an accident that this sum corresponded to the legal minimum demanded by the Mishnah (Ketubot 1,2) for each marriage contract with a virgin.

Ashor married a widow or divorcee, who was provided by later Talmudic law with a minimum of only half that amount. This woman, a well-to-do girl of the fifth century A.D., had married at least three times. "With one husband, an Egyptian, who had perhaps adopted Judaism, she concluded a marriage contract minutely safeguarding her rights."[3] The career of this woman indicates that even a woman who had been married several times had so powerful a bargaining position that she could make strong economic stipulations in the marriage contract.

Both the bride-price and sequential marriages for women are characteristic of high sex ratio societies. Later Talmudic legislation elaborated the principle of the *ketubbah*, considered in substance to be of Mosaic origin. It was a marriage contract designed to safeguard, at the time of the wedding, the rights of the wife in case of divorce or widowhood.

> The minimum sum of 200 *zuz* for a virgin and 100 for a widow or divorcee was to be provided; without it the marriage act was null and void. A woman converted to Judaism, ransomed from captivity or freed from slavery before the age of three and one day was placed on a par with a virgin; others on a par with a widow. This amount was usually doubled in priestly and aristocratic families.[4]

Virginity was given an extraordinarily high importance in the Jewish society of biblical times. A priest could marry only a virgin; widows or divorcees were explicitly forbidden to him.[5] Among the common populace, virginity was also of great significance. In *Deuteronomy*, the Mosaic law reads:

> A man marries a woman and cohabits with her. Then he takes an aversion to her and makes up charges against her and defames her, saying, "I married this woman; but when I approached her, I found that she was not a virgin." In such

a case the girl's father and mother shall produce the evidence of the girl's virginity before the elders of the town at the gate. And the girl's father shall say to the elders, "I gave this man my daughter to wife, but he has taken an aversion to her; so he has made up charges, saying, 'I did not find your daughter a virgin.' But here is evidence of my daughter's virginity!" And they shall spread out the cloth before the elders of the town. The elders of that town shall then take the man and flog him, and they shall fine him a hundred (shekels of) silver and give it to the girl's father; for the man has defamed a virgin in Israel. Moreover, she shall remain his wife; he shall never have the right to divorce her. But if the charges prove true, the girl was found not to have been a virgin, then the girl shall be brought out to the entrance of her father's house, and the men of her town shall stone her to death; for she did a shameful thing in Israel, committing fornication while under her father's authority. Thus you will sweep evil from your midst.[6]

Although conquerors were permitted to kill all men and any women who had had intercourse, they were admonished to spare virgins.[7]

Marriage and the family were not only highly valued, but were protected by moral injunctions, and even legally. A great number of specific laws in the Mosaic code emphasize strong marriage bonds and admonish the husband to respect and care for his wife. "When a man had taken a bride, he shall not go out with the army or be assigned to it for any purpose; he shall be exempt one year for the sake of his household, to give happiness to the woman he has married.[8]

The great importance attached to progeny, especially to a man having a son, is expressed in the law of the levirate from *Deuteronomy*:

When brothers dwell together and one of them dies and leaves no son, the wife of the deceased shall not be married to a stranger, outside the family. Her husband's brother shall unite with her: take her as his wife and perform the levir's duty. The first son that she bears shall be accounted to the dead brother, that his name may not be blotted out in Israel.[9]

In the Code of Maimonides, in the case of the levirate, all of the man's brothers shall be excused from war.[10]

Here is a typical tannaitic statement, "He who loves his wife as himself and honors her more than himself . . . is referred to in the verse, 'And thou shalt know that thy tent is in peace.'"[11] Later, R. Helbo explained that one ought to honor one's wife, because the home is blessed only on her account. . . Several Palestinian rabbis vied with each other in describing the psychological effects of a wife's decease. "It is as if the Temple were destroyed in one's own lifetime," declared one; "The whole world is darkened for the widower," declared another; "His steps are shortened," said a third; "He loses his counsel," stated a fourth."[12] The value of the wife is further attested to by the priority given to widows: "To insure particularly, the collection of a widow's dowry and marriage settlement from her husband's estate, rabbinic law granted priority to her claims over all other civil obligations."[13]

Within the family, women were accorded great respect in their roles as mothers. In Leviticus, the biblical injunction is: "Ye shall fear every man his

mother and his father." The mother preceding the father was taken by Talmudic scholars to mean: "to teach you that both are equal."[14] Compared
with other ancient societies, this was an unusually high value to be placed on
the mother's role. High value placed on the woman as wife and mother, and
on the piety of filial relations in the family, are characteristic where women
are in short supply. Extremes of filial piety toward mothers were praised in
the Talmud: "R. Eliezer praised . . . one Domna (who) suffered calmly when
his deranged mother threw slippers at him and spat in his face in the presence of strangers."[15]

As we noted in our introductory remarks, women were highly valued only
for their traditional role in the family. They were considered the mainstay of
the family, and the family itself was greatly valued. Women outside these
domains had little status. The law gave great protection to a woman in her
family, but little outside of it.[16] Writing in Roman times, Josephus described
the contemporary Jewish woman's position when he said: "The woman,
says the Law, is in all things inferior to the man. Let her accordingly be submissive, not for her humiliation, but that she may be directed."[17] They were
not expected to step out of the role, not to excel in what was expected of
males. Women were often derogated as easygoing, devoid of judgment,
prone to excessive talk, indulging in sorcery, and setting their hearts on trin-
kets.[18] Roles were sharply differentiated, with women assigned to household
chores and child rearing, while men became the scholars, and the actors on
the larger stages of the world.[19]

In Talmudic times, in a culture that valued learning, few women won high
repute as scholars. In every case, these few were the daughters or wives of
famed scholars and had grown up or were living in intellectual homes. These
women did not seek independent roles outside their homes. Since Jewish
society placed great emphasis on learning, there was a continuous debate
about how much education women should receive. The mother role could
include teaching children how to read and write, but it did not include any
major public roles in the synagogue or in public affairs.[20]

The proscription against adultery was important enough to be a commandment. Marital fidelity, at least on the wife's part, was taken for granted.[21]
During early Talmudic times, adultery was still a capital crime, although exe-
cutions for it were extremely rare, if not nonexistent.[22] Later tannaitic legal
and social penalties included obligatory divorce of the adulteress, regardless
of the wishes of her husband, and she was not permitted to marry her para-
mour. Offspring of adulterous relations were bastards, unable to marry a Jew
or a Jewess.[23] Both adultery and divorce, which was permitted by law, were
exceptional in Talmudic times.[24]

Evidence that divorce was rare and marriages generally long and stable
comes initially from Jewish funerary inscriptions in the Roman world. "No
divorce appears in any Roman inscription, while several inscriptions mention specifically that the deceased woman had been an *univira* (married to
only one man), or that the deceased man had enjoyed a prolonged marital
status."[25] Men were able to enjoy a long marriage because, with the aim of
"avoidance of temptation . . . the sages advised early marriages. Most boys
(in Talmudic times) seem to have been married at the age of eighteen, some

starting their marital careers at sixteen or earlier."[26] Girls also married as adolescents. "Even in metropolitan Rome, Jews seem to have married quite early and stayed married for most of their lives . . . nor was the young man Anteros exceptional when, at the age of twenty-two, he left behind a widow to whom he had been married for almost six years."[27] Early marriages among Jews continued in the Diaspora throughout the Middle Ages.[28]

In order to preserve the family, there were many laws restricting the possibility of sexual licentiousness outside marriage. Among Jews, sexual life was more regulated and sexual deviations considered egregious religious sins.[29] Priestly practitioners of religious prostitution were eliminated from the Temple. With the aim of counteracting licentiousness in the Temple, the sexes were separated with women above and men below.[30] Philo taught that "a woman should not shew herself off like a vagrant in the streets before the eyes of other men, except when she has to go to the temple and even then she should take pains to go, not when the market is full but when more people have gone home."[31] Even much later, when the Jews were surrounded by an advanced Islamic civilization, the rabbis severely frowned upon concubinage with female slaves, a common social practice among the Muslims.[32]

Although polygamy was possible in biblical times, it was apparently never widely practiced and was an occasional custom only of kings or the very wealthy.[33] In the entire Talmud, there is no mention of any relationship other than a monogamous one.[34] Following the return from the Babylonian exile in the sixth century B.C., polygamy was effectively proscribed for the people. The rabbis believed that more than one wife would create domestic dissension. The most recently discovered Dead Sea Scroll, which was written by the Essenes somewhat earlier than the New Testament, prohibits polygamy or even divorce for kings: "From his father's house (the king) shall take unto himself a wife . . . and he shall not take upon her another wife, for she alone shall be with him all the days of her life."[35] Early in the eleventh century, Rabbi Gershom officially decreed what had for centuries been an established practice—that polygamy was forbidden for Ashkenazic Jews.[36] As we will later see, monogamy, combined with the rules governing a man's sexual relationship with his wife, may have contributed to the high sex ratios at birth.

Illegitimacy rates based on population statistics have only become available in recent history. These rates for Orthodox Jewish communities were, and continue to be, quite low. In western European countries, and in the United States, "illegitimate births, which are characterized by higher infant mortality, have been more infrequent among Jews than non-Jews."[37]

This discussion of Jewish tradition leads overwhelmingly to the conclusion that Jewish society is a prototype of the high sex ratio society; it fits in every detail, with nothing out of place. Of course, in the millenia of Jewish history, many Jews became assimilated—for example, those in Hellenistic Greece, the Sephardites in Spain, and those in nineteenth-century Germany and twentieth-century America. Nevertheless, there were, and continue to be, groups of Orthodox Jews who practice the laws of conduct, sexual rules, family codes, and dietary restrictions as transmitted throughout the generations. It is they who provide the continuity throughout the ages and who perfectly fit the high sex ratio society. But now we must ask: Did Jewish populations in fact have high sex ratios?

SEX RATIOS IN JEWISH POPULATIONS

The historical and demographic literature contains intriguing, scattered, and offhand comments about unusually high sex ratios among Jews, even as far back as antiquity. Finley, for example, remarks that the Jews in antiquity had very high ratios at birth, and yet were one of the few peoples in the ancient world who never practiced infanticide.[38] The genealogies and censuses in the Bible mainly report male offspring.[39] Although occasional female children are mentioned in a "begat,"[40] there is no way to determine true population characteristics from these predominatly male genealogies. Whenever it appears that all of the living children in a single generation are reported, as in the cases of the children of the partriarchs,[41] the number of males is overwhelming. Hence we must assume that many females were not counted.

A surplus of men is often noted by historians in the censuses listed in the Bible. "Again the surplus of men among those who returned from the Exile (Babylonian) made itself felt. There seems to have been some 30,000 men and only 12,000 women among the new arrivals. Hence the divergence between the figures of 42,360 Jews, besides servants, in the 'whole congregation' of the returning exiles and the itemized list of 'the men of the people of Israel' totaling roughly 30,000 (Ezra, 2.2-65)."[42] There is never mention of a surplus of women.

Biblical figures cannot be taken as reliable evidence. But in more recent history, too, scattered comments on the excess of males among Jewish populations are found. A classic volume on demography, published at the end of the nineteenth century, notes that "Jewish families have a notably large excess of boy births."[43]

In a book on medical statistics from Odessa in 1842, Rafalovich[44] commented about the Jews: "The surplus of males born over females is so remarkable that one must surmise that the Rabbi's information from which these figures were taken is inexact; no doubt not all girls were registered, especially those who died soon after birth."[45] Here again, we encounter the assumption that if sex ratios look odd, one sex must be undercounted. Professor Rafalovich's perplexity is understandable. He noted that in 1842, in Odessa, 345 males and 154 females were born,[46] creating a sex ratio at birth of 224! Apparently he took for granted that Jewish sex ratios at birth were normally quite high, for in order to back up his presumption that there must be an undercount of females, he reported that the sex ratios for Jews were 162 in Vienna, 114 in Hamburg, and 108 in Prussia, as compared with 104 for the general mass of the population in Prussia.[47]

Charles Darwin once noted:

> It is a singular fact that with Jews the proportion of male births is decidedly larger than with Christians; thus in Prussia, the proportion is as 113, in Breslau as 114, and in Livonia as 120 to 100; the Christian births in these countries being the same as usual, for instance, in Livonia as 104 to 100.[48]

In 1917, some other Russian demographers looked back at the reported sex ratios at birth for Jews in the 1897 Russian census and remarked that they must correct for "the inexact registration of female births."[49] When sex ratios deviate very far from 100, demographers usually tend to assume that one sex is undercounted. Yet, as we shall see, it is possible to have high sex ratios at birth that are real and not the result of infanticide.

For more systematic evidence, we turn to sex ratios at birth for Orthodox Jews as reported in censuses. These may provide stronger clues to the origin of high ratios, if they are found, since unlike ratios for adults or total populations, they are not affected by postnatal mortality or by migrations.

Census data on sex ratios at birth for Orthodox Jewish populations are very difficult to unearth. During medieval times, the Jews did not keep parish records.[50] Because of taxes and persecutions of various types, communities of Jews were often loath to report the actual numbers in their populations.[51] Even recent demographic works, such as statistics on infant mortality among Jews of the Diaspora,[52] unfortunately do not report the figures by sex. Moreover, census data generally do not provide reports for subpopulations of Jews, so that Orthodox Jews cannot be differentiated from assimilated Jews. The closest approximation to data on Orthodox Jews are census data taken from an historic period and place where many Jews were known to be Orthodox.

Recently, Russian censuses conducted in 1867, 1868, 1870, 1872, 1873, 1879, 1881, 1882, and 1884 have come to light.[53] These nine years of census data report births by sex for different religious groups in every area of Imperial Russia, with the exception of Siberia. The sex ratios at birth of Jews,

TABLE 4.1 Summary of Sex Ratios Based on Data from Russian Censuses (1867-1884)

Religious Group	1867	1868	1870	1872	1873	1879	1881	1882	1884
Orthodox	104	105	105	104	104	105	105	105	105
Schismatics	104	104	102	106	105	103	104	102	102
Armenian-Gregorian	104	108	98	104	101	118	108	104	103
Roman Catholics	106	105	105	104	105	105	105	104	104
Protestants	105	105	105	104	106	105	105	105	105
Jews	131	127	132	133	132	146	144	146	146
Moslems	106	106	104	105	106	107	106	107	106
Pagans	107	104	107	105	106	103	102	110	103

SOURCE: *Dvizhenie Naseleniia v Europeiskoi Rossii (Population Movement in the Russian Empire)*, Statisticheskii vremennik Rossiiskoi Imperii; za 1867 god: Seriia II, vyp. 8 (St. Petersburg, 1872), pp. 10-11; za 1868 god. Seriia II, vyp. 12 (St. Petersburg, 1877), pp. 6-7; za 1870 god. Seriia II, vyp. 14 (St. Petersburg, 1879); za 1872 god. Seriia II, vyp. 18 (St. Petersburg, 1882), pp. 18-19; za 1873 god. Seriia II, vyp. 12 (St. Petersburg, 1882), pp. 18-19; za 1879 god. Seriia III, vyp. 3 (St. Petersburg, 1884), pp. 20-21; za 1881 god. Seriia III, vyp. 20 (St. Petersburg, 1887), pp. 20-21; za 1882 god. Seriia III, vyp. 21 (St. Petersburg, 1887), pp. 20-21; za 1884 god. Seriia III, vyp. 24 (St. Petersburg, 1889), pp. 14-15.

compared with every other group, are so remarkable, and so consistent over time, that all of them are reported in Table 4.1. The sex ratios for Jews average 137, while for all other religious groups they average 105. With populations so large, and with nine nearly consecutive censuses, these sex ratio differences at birth are highly reliable. The difference between Jewish sex ratios at birth and all other religious groups, in every census year, is so great that they could not have occurred by chance.

Are there systematic biases in census data that could explain away these astonishing sex ratios? If anything, it appears that an underreport of Orthodox Jewish male births is the most likely error, making the obtained ratios even more startling. There are at least two reasons for such possible undercounting: male births would sometimes not be reported to avoid special taxes demanded from Jews by the government, and particularly to avoid mandatory conscription of young boys into the Czar's army. This much-hated conscription began in the early nineteenth century. Not reporting Jewish male births resulted in the problem of the "Nelumin." A "nelom" is a concealed person, a man not registered as a citizen.[54]

> As is known, the terrible conscription of the Czar Nicholai's regime resulted in many male Jews who were not registered at all. They were Nelumin; officially they did not exist and were not counted in the population census. There was yet another reason that drove many to be Nelumin; it was the terrible poverty among Jews ... [to avoid] special taxes the government demanded from Jews.[55]

Mendele Moicher Sphorim wrote in his autobiography: "My birthday was not recorded. Jews used not to pay any attention to such things, especially in small towns."[56] Despite the natural, but probably incorrect assumption of the St. Petersburg demographers, it appears that Jewish male births may have been underreported.

One swallow does not make a summer, although these Russian censuses are quite a large swallow. Three other early-nineteenth century censuses of single towns also give the sex of children at birth for each religious group. These towns have much smaller populations—in each case no more than a few thousand, and these censuses were conducted earlier in the century. For these reasons, they are much less reliable. Births in Vilna Guberniia, in 1834, show a sex ratio for over 2,200 Jews of only 90, and for 46,000 Roman Catholics of only 76. About 400 Greek-Russian Orthodox have a ratio of 125, and 1,600 Uniates, 114. Except for the Roman Catholics, however, these populations are too small to be reliable. The sex ratio for about 3,300 Jews at birth reported in the Grodno Province in 1840 is an astounding 156, while the sex ratios for all the other populations of any size are close to the usual. But here too, the numbers are very small, and thus equally unreliable. In the Odessa census of 1866, the sex ratio for about 1,200 Jews is 111, and for all other groups it is below 100. Again, the numbers are small and the chance of unreliability correspondingly great. There is one census report for sex ratios among Jews at birth in the city of Odessa from 1892 to 1917, which is odd. It gives sex ratios at birth as 106 for nearly every year.[57] Upon investigation, the astounding regularity of the figure turns out to have been the work of Russian demographers who did not believe the much higher sex ratios at birth that had been determined from the census data. They decided to "correct" the figures downward to 106 in order to bring them in line with their own personal expectations!

One of the reasons that the large differences in sex ratios at birth have remained obscure has been the tendency of demographers not to believe what is reported and to correct the figures so that they conform with a hypothetical model of what they believe the sex ratios should be. The reasoning of one Russian demographer who changed the figures of Odessa's Jews is revealing:

> Before we proceed to the tables, we must remark on the following: as is well known, Jews do not rush to register girls. They have already learned to register boys, since they must be presented to the military, but when a girl is born, such does not apply. And therefore a strange situation arises. For example, in Vilna from 1893 to 1902 Jews gave birth to 196 boys to 100 girls. From 1911 to 1915 156 boys per 100 girls. One does not have to bring a lot of evidence to prove that this is impossible. But there are very good proofs that Vilna Jews were not so poor in females. In 1916, when the Germans occupied Vilna and bread was distributed by ration cards, so many girls appeared among Vilna Jews that the percentage was 114 girls for 100 boys. Dr. Shabad in the above-cited work deliberates on this precise point and comes to the conclusion that if we want to use the materials of the state rabbis about births among Jews, we must correct them in the following manner. We must accept that for 100 girls there are 106 boys born. In Odessa in regard to this fact, the situation was much better than in Vilna. For example, for 20 years from 1897 to 1916 the state rabbi's books showed that there were 112.2 boys per 100 girls. this was both in the first ten years from 1897-1906. . . This is already very close to the proportion between boys and girls that Dr. Shabad proposes to accept for the Jewish population.

> For Odessa we have made the following corrections for the reader. To see how much this correction changes the character of the tables, we will bring the

TABLE 4.2   Uncorrected Sex Ratios for Jews in Odessa

Year	Total No. Jewish Births	Sex Ratio
1892	3673	110
1893	3595	109
1894	3536	112
1901	4916	118
1902	5213	115
1903	5384	117

SOURCE: Y. Leshtsinski, "Geburtn, shtarb-faln, un khasenes ba idn in Odes fun 1892 biz 1919 (Births, Deaths and Marriages among Jews in Odessa from 1892 to 1919)," in Jacob Lestschinsky, *Bleter far yidishe demografie, statistik un ekonomik*. Berlin, 1923, Vol. 1, no. 2, table 1, p. 72. Our thanks to Patricia Herlihy both for finding the Odessa census from 1892-1917 and for discovering that the demographers had "corrected" it.

number of girls according to the state books of the rabbis and according to the corrected figures.

We see that there were years in which for every hundred girls Odessa Jews registered 118.1 boys (1901) or 117.2 boys (1903). Now there is absolutely no reason to believe that Odessa Jews in these years had such an abnormality, especially since such an abnormality is not repeated everywhere among the Jewish population, but only in those countries in which the registration of births was the responsibility of such people as the former state rabbis of Russia. It is therefore clear that according to the corrections we are a lot closer to the truth than if we were to remain with the figure that is taken from the books of the state rabbi. It is evident that in the years in which the number of registered girls was such that the proportion was 106 boys to 100 girls, we did not apply the correction. There were a total of five such years in the 26 years included in the table, 1908, 1910, 1912, 1914, 1916.[58]

Table 4.2 provides some *uncorrected* figures for the Odessa censuses, taken around the turn of the century. Clearly, the uncorrected sex ratios at birth are well above what is commonly found. But they are not as high as the Vilna figures of 196 for a similar period, nor are they as high as some of the all-Russia censuses reported in Table 4.1. This is not difficult to explain, however. The all-Russia census excluded Siberia, but included most of the rural countryside where the shtetls were located. Like Vilna, these were almost wholly Orthodox. Younger, more assimilated Jews were attracted to the cities, and there they became even more assimilated. Later, we will see that only Orthodox Jews have high sex ratios.

The period from the turn of the century through the first World War brought great social change for the Jews in eastern Europe. It was a time of great intellectual ferment, especially among young adults. The Enlightenment (The Haskala) was an important secular movement. Young adults became active socialists and revolutionaries, or ardent Zionists. Both these intellectual movements departed strongly from religious traditions; the change was violent and occurred within one generation.[59] It was particularly marked in cities like Odessa, which was a leader in the intellectual ferment of the era.[60] Thus, one would expect Odessa to contain many more assimilated Jews, who do not have sex ratios appreciably different from other peoples. The overall ratio at birth for Jews in Odessa should be based on a mixture of Orthodox and assimilated Jews, thus greatly attenuating the high ratio obtained for Orthodox Jews alone. Finally, the appreciable rise in the number of births and in the sex ratios for the later censuses could most plausibly be explained by the in-migration of more Orthodox, less assimilated Jews who gave birth after moving to Odessa.

Another way to obtain information on sex ratios among Orthodox Jews is to obtain family histories of individuals from strictly Orthodox backgrounds. Three recently collected oral histories from known Orthodox groups also provide personal data about high sex ratios. The genealogy of the Chochem family from the shtetl of Zvanetz circa 1905 yields a sex ratio of 140 in one generation.[61] In the past generation of the Blaus, an Orthodox family of Kabbalists from Safed, Israel, with a documented family genealogy, there were 16 males and 4 females.[62] An oral history of the shtetl Krechnev in 1927 reported sex ratios for adults of between 118 and 128.[63]

One might also compare sex ratios at different ages in a population that would have gone from largely Orthodox in the older generation to more assimilated in the younger generation. Naturally, there are many sources of possible error when one looks at sex ratios among adults—most notably, differential mortality and migration. For instance, in census data from eastern Europe immediately after World War II, there would most likely be many fewer adult males. Yet in the registered Jewish population of Slovakia in 1945, the sex ratio for those 50 and older was 113. Many men of this age group were doubtless killed by the Nazis, but they were also very likely to be born into families still practicing Orthodox Jewish sex rules. The sex ratio for the 40-49-year-old age group was an astounding 149, and even for the youngest group, under 15, where Orthodox sex practices are unlikely to have characterized the parent population, the sex ratio was 108.5[64] The registered Jewish population of Bohemia, Moravia, and Silesia, in October 1945, showed a sex ratio for the over-51-year-old group of 125. The younger age groups, especially those under age 15, showed a sex ratio of 100.[65]

These are suggestive figures, but one should be quite cautious in interpreting them, since sex ratios for adults are subject to may sources of error, especially for populations that experienced the Holocaust. The oldest males would probably have been born to Orthodox parents, but with the Holocaust, one would anticipate that few of them survived. The high sex ratios found for this age group, despite many probable casualties, suggest that original sex ratios in the oldest population must have been quite high. Using only partial data, it is of course possible that more older *women* perished instead.

Some additional data, reported by James[66] from modern Israel, appear to contradict the thesis of high sex ratios at birth associated with Orthodox Jewish practices. He reports sex ratios at birth for Jews in Israel between 1957 and 1971 to be 106, while for non-Jews in Israel during the same time period, they are 106.8[67] Modern Israel, however, is a highly secular society where Orthodox Jews make up only a small percentage of the population.[68]

As we shall see, high sex ratios should only be expected for Orthodox Jews who practice strictly *all* of the various codes governing behavior. James himself says: "It is not known what proportion of the Jewish births occurred to couples practicing Niddah (rules governing women), but is is probably not negligible."[69] On the contrary, unless the Orthodox Jews are separated from other Jewish groups, it seems unlikely that an effect will be found. In fact, in 1973 an Israeli investigator who separated those couples strictly practicing Orthodox Niddah from Israeli Jewish couples who were not, found that among the Orthodox Jews, the sex ratio at birth was 130, while for the other Israeli Jews it was 105.[70]

Also in contrast with James, a door-to-door family survey conducted in 1976 among the Libyan Jewish community in Israel,[71] which was one generation removed from strictly Orthodox practice, showed a sex ratio among the young of 121.

The most recent data on sex ratios at birth for Jews in the United States and Canada include largely assimilated Jewish populations. Nevertheless, these data show higher sex ratios at birth than are found in the non-Jewish populations. In Montreal, in 1950, the sex ratio at birth for Jews was 113, while for the French it was 105, and for the Anglo-Celtics, 99.[72] In Providence, Rhode Island, in 1964, the sex ratios for Jews under age 15 was 111, while for the non-Jewish population it was 103.[73] This study noted that for the well-established Jewish community on the East Side of Providence (where, one assumes, there were more Orthodox), the sex ratio was 115 for those under the age of 20. In 1956, in the greater Washington area, the sex ratio for Jews under age 5 was 115.[74]

Factors Contributing to High Sex Ratios

Why do Orthodox Jews have such high sex ratios at birth and in adulthood? And why do sex ratios fall when Jews become assimilated? Why are there no other peoples in the world with such high sex ratios? And why has this distinctive feature of Jewish populations lasted for centuries—possibly even for thousands of years? We can immediately rule out two possible factors: female infanticide and unknown genetic factors. High sex ratios among Jews cannot have their origin in their genetic constitution, for as soon as Jews are assimilated, the sex ratios at birth fall sharply. Furthermore, the commandment, "Thou shalt not kill," prohibited infanticide among Jews as far back as biblical times. Tacitus remarked that "the Jews take thought to increase their numbers; for they regard it as a crime to kill any late-born (*agnatis,* or not-desired) child."[75]

In view of what we have discovered about sex ratios among Jewish populations, any explanatory factor would have to meet the following criteria:

(1) It would have to remain relatively constant over many centuries.
(2) It would have to be characteristic of Jews and no other population.
(3) It would have to change for assimilated Jews.

Taken together, these criteria clearly point to practices associated with Judaism. They are most likely to be practices that are salient in Jewish codes and laws, and that have remained relatively constant until assimilation occurred in modern times. One conceivable (but unlikely) candidate is diet. While the Talmud and other sources contain some dietary prescriptions and prohibitions, it is likely that diet has changed in association with changes in food supplies at different periods of history. Moreover, since diet is so habituated, it seems unlikely that there would be marked changes in diet as a result of assimilation. Finally, it also seems improbable that the diet of Orthodox Jews would be so unique as to make them the only people who have very high sex ratios at birth.

While diet apparently can not account for the very high sex ratios at birth among Orthodox Jewish populations, it appears that it may in one sense contribute to a higher than usual *adult* sex ratio as part of a larger condition that it shares with certain other population subgroups, and which is known to produce somewhat higher sex ratios. This factor is parental commitment to offspring, which results in better care of infants and older offspring, including adequate feeding. Although males are less robust than females, both prenatally and during infancy, with especially adequate care these males survive, thus raising the sex ratio above what it otherwise would have been. Thus, parental care in the broad sense, including prenatal care, medical care, and adequate diet apparently accounts for the substantial differences in the sex ratios at birth, ranging in contemporary populations from about 110 for the highest socioeconomic class to about 100 for the lowest. This is discussed in more detail in Chapter 8; here we will confine ourselves to demonstrating that the parental investment in Jewish children is exceptional.

That Jews have historically had a greater parental investment in their children can be demonstrated in a variety of ways. Jewish codes prescribe care and attention to both the infant and the mother out of concern for their health and well-being. As a result, infant mortality rates are lower for Jewish populations than for most other populations in the world. Family stability and the importance of the mother among Orthodox Jews are vividly pictured in a study of nineteenth-century Odessa where Jews made up 34 percent of the population in 1897.[76] In this city,

> among Russian women, 33.33 percent were independently employed, as opposed to only 19 percent of the Jewish women. This seems to reflect the peculiar strength of the Jewish household in Odessa, which tended to retain its females, and did not send them forth in large numbers to household service or to outside employment.[77] Among the Jews, the ratio of dependents to employed is 1.52—more than a third greater than that found in the entire urban population.[78]

Although Odessa had a large number of immigrants from other religious groups who had come to the city alone, most Jewish men emigrated to Odessa with their wives.[79] "The Jewish population in particular seems to have lived in large households, with members well balanced between the sexes and with relatively numerous children."[80] "For every 100 babies born and surviving in Russian families, there were 127 Jewish babies."[81]

> In many respects the Jews seem to have been the most stable component of Odessa's population. The sex ratio among them is nearly normal (98 men per 100 women) and the Jewish household appears to have been large and cohesive.[82]

> The growth of Odessa's Jewish community was partially due to continuing immigration, but also to high fertility among Jewish women and comparatively low death rates among their children . . . Not all the Jews of Odessa were wealthy, and this high rate of survival was not entirely a reflection of affluence. Stable family life and the traditional care of Jewish family and child benefitted from both material and cultural resources.[83]

Even quite recently, there are many other scattered indications of strong family stability, among Jewish populations, such as a man's commitment to his wife. For example, among the refugees who came to the United States before and during World War II, the percentage of married persons among

Jews was much higher than for other refugees. This was also true for immigrants to Australia.[84]

Concern for the well-being of Jewish mothers extends back to the earliest sources of Jewish codes and laws. In Maimonides one finds the following: "A man should not marry a woman belonging to a family of lepers or epileptics, provided that there is a presumption based on three cases that the disease is hereditary."[85]

The Talmud, in specifying what should happen to a nursing child under unusual circumstances, reflects the favored treatment which mother and infant are to receive:

> As long as the wife is nursing her child, the amount of her work should be reduced, while her maintenance should be augmented with wine and other things that are beneficial for lactation.

> If having been granted the maintenance due her, she develops a desire for more food, or for other kinds of food, due to an abnormal craving in her belly, she may eat all that she desires at her own expense; and the husband may not hinder her by claiming that if she eats too much or eats injurious food, the child will die; for the suffering of her own body has priority.[86]

> If she vows not to nurse her child, the husband may compel her to nurse it until it is twenty-four months old, regardless of whether it is a boy or a girl.

> If she says, "I will nurse my child," while he does not wish his wife to nurse, because nursing may make her unattractive, her own wish must be honored, even if she has several maidservants, because it is painful for her to be separated from her child.[87]

> A divorcee may not be compelled to nurse her child, but if she is willing to do so, her ex-husband may pay her her fee and she may then nurse it. If she is not willing to nurse the child, she may hand it over to him and he himself must attend to its needs.

> When does this apply? When she had not nursed the child before it grew old enough to recognize her. If the child already recognizes her, even if it is blind, it may not be separated from its mother, on account of the possible danger to its life. Rather she should be compelled to nurse it for a fee, until it is twenty-four months old.[88]

> A divorcee is not entitled to maintenance, even if she nurses her child. A husband, however, must give her, in addition to her fee, such things as the child may need, in the way of clothing, food, beverage, ointment, and the like. A pregnant woman, however, has no claim to anything.[89]

A variety of sources provide information on infant and child mortality rates among Jews. Schmelz has compiled infant mortality statistics for many European countries, in addition to the United States and Canada, for various periods ranging from 1819 to 1967.[90] In 21 countries, the median infant mortality rate among Jews was 74, while for the general population it was 130. Schmelz has also collected reports from the same period from 26 cities in these countries. The median mortality rate for Jewish infants was 88, and for the general population, 148. These differences are dramatic, for in country after country and city after city, the infant mortality rates are virtually always lower for Jewish infants, most often about half as high as for others. Moreover, the infant mortality rate among Jews is not only extremely low, but the death rate for female infants appears to be greater than for male infants. This is the reverse of what is found for non-Jews.

Schmelz, a leading authority on Jewish infant mortality, offers the following explanation for the lower mortality rate:

> In general, there are accounts, inter alia by physicians, of the greater attention to their children's health and rearing that was also bestowed by Jewish rather than non-Jewish parents. This is mentioned also for Jewish groups who lived in very unfavorable circumstances.[91]

> Some religious observances and traditional patterns of behavior among Jews have been beneficial to health and may have assisted in reducing infant mortality more rapidly among Jews than non-Jews. For example: the custom of handwashing before meals, the rarity of alcoholism and venereal diseases and allegedly, a greater readiness to attend to their own health and that of members of their family.[92]

> In medical reports from the turn of the 19th and 20th centuries, the frequent practice of Jewish mothers to give their children breast-feeding—and to refrain for this reason from going out to work, even in the poor classes—is thought to have avoided many Jewish infant deaths from gastro-intestinal diseases.[93]

The Jews of Europe and America have been more urbanized and often more educated and socioeconomically better off than the general population, but this alone does not account for differences in mortality rates. Even when comparisons are made within the same social class, Jewish infant mortality rates are significantly lower than those of other groups. Infant mortality data are not usually given by social class, and especially not by religion, but where available, comparisons support this conclusion. Table 4.3 shows the infant mortality rates in Baltimore in 1915 for Jews and non-Jews by economic class.

TABLE 4.3 Infant Mortality Rates in Baltimore in 1915 by Economic Status among the Jews and the General Population

Population Group of Mother	Yearly Income of Father	
	Below $650	Above $650
Colored	162	133
American-born White	127	79
Polish Immigrants	160	153
Italian Immigrants	106	49
Jewish Immigrants	49	41
Other Immigrants	112	87

TABLE 4.4 Infant Mortality Rates in Budapest in 1926-30 by Social Class among the Jews and the General Population

Social Class	Jews	Non-Jews
Workers (1929)	85	152
Middle Class (1926-30)	49	71

SOURCE: From U. O. Schmelz, *Infant and Early Childhood Mortality among Jews of the Diaspora* (The Institute of Contemporary Jewry at the Hebrew University of Jerusalem, 1971), p. 47.

Infant mortality among the Jewish and non-Jewish working class and middle class in Budapest in 1926-30 shows similar low rates for Jews in each class (see Table 4.4). Even in nonindustrialized countries like Tunisia, the Jewish infant mortality rate is approximately 65 percent lower than the Moslem rate.

In Mexico's about 20,000 strong Ashkenazi Jewish community, there was no infant mortality case through several recent years.[94]

Reports by British and American physicians at the turn of the 19th and 20th centuries singled out for favourable mention the greater care bestowed by the Jews, particularly the Jewish mothers, on their infants in the poorer quarters of London, Manchester, Liverpool, and New York, and the consequently smaller infant mortality among the Jews as contrasted with the rest of the population there. In keeping with these statements, statistics from London at the time showed comparatively low infant mortality rates among the total population of poor quarters which had absorbed many Jewish immigrants."[95]

It is particularly interesting to note that "if the percent distribution of the infants deceased according to age at death is examined, it is found that the proportion dying within the first month of life was higher among the Jews than among the corresponding non-Jewish population . . . This agrees with the generally accepted view that biological factors play a greater role in neonatal mortality (i.e., during the first month of life) than in post-neonatal infant mortality, which is more prominently influenced by environmental factors."[96] This is a strong indication of considerable parental investment in the care of the Jewish infant. "Already at the beginning of this century it was noted by an author that Jewish children had especially low mortality in respect of those gastro-intestinal, infectious and respiratory diseases which were avoidable or amenable to treatment with the methods and therapies then known, so that the greater care of the Jews for preserving and restoring the health of their children could be largely credited with the observed mortality differentials."[97]

A further indication of the significance of the male parental investment in the Jewish family is the higher infant mortality rate among the few illegitimate Jewish births.

In Eastern and Central Europe, there was rather high infant mortality among the relatively fewer illegitimate births by Jewish women . . . The differential between the infant mortality rates of the legitimates and the illegitimate children was greater for the Jews than for the non-Jews. . . . This casts a strong sidelight on the importance of parental care in accounting for the usually more favorable level of Jewish child mortality, compared to the general population.[98]

The high sex ratios at birth, the significantly lower infant mortality rates, and the greater survival of males all add up to high sex ratios for Jewish populations. Thus we have a self-perpetuating cycle in which high sex ratios lead to male commitment to the family and parental investment in children, which in turn lead to higher sex ratios among the next generation.

Jewish sex practices. While it is demonstrably clear that the investment and care that Jewish parents bestow on their children account for the survival of many males who would otherwise die, the resulting increase in the sex ratio falls far short of the ratios that we reported earlier for Orthodox Jews. We can probably assume that parental investment alone would not raise ratios above 110, a sex ratio characteristic of the highest socioeconomic class level for whites in modern societies. Yet populations consisting mostly of Orthodox Jews apparently have ratios of about 130. Even more crucial is the tendency for sex ratios *at birth* to be this high. Obviously, parental care of the child cannot account for sex ratios at birth; only care of the mother during pregnancy and before would have an effect on sex ratios at birth. Some other condition must account for these high ratios at birth.

The only plausible explanation that we can find for the high sex ratios at birth among Jews is that they result from Jewish sex practices. These practices meet all the criteria outlined earlier and that are required to provide an adequate explanation. Sex practices among Orthodox Jews have a basis in Jewish codes and laws dating back to earliest times, and so far as we are aware, they are unique to Jews. We can also reasonably assume that when orthodoxy is abandoned, sex practices change along with other features, resulting in lower sex ratios. Finally, while research in reproductive biology has many methodological weaknesses, it does provide some positive support for the link between Jewish sex practices and high sex ratios at birth. The last section of this chapter will review Jewish sex practices in relation to reproductive biology and show how they could account for the high sex ratios.

Let us look first at the Talmudic codes pertaining to sex practices. First, it is clear that it is the duty of the husband to procreate. Moreover, much advice and admonition pertain to satisfying one's wife sexually and remaining faithful to her. These two elements, as we will see later, relate to several possible conditions that might affect the relative balance of male-female conceptions. These conditions are: female orgasm, frequency of intercourse experienced by the female, and male abstinence except when having intercourse with one's wife.

First, on the issue of abstinence, the Talmud says: "The more continent a man is, the more is he praiseworthy, provided he does not neglect his marital duty without his wife's consent."[99] On male masturbation, the Talmud, in accordance with the Mosaic code, states: "It is forbidden to expend semen to no purpose. Consequently, a man should not thresh within and ejaculate without, nor should a man marry a minor who cannot yet bear children. As for masturbators, not only do they commit a strictly forbidden act, but they also expose themselves to a ban. It is to them that Scripture refers in saying, 'Your hands are full of blood' (Isaiah 1.15), and a masturbator's act is regarded as equivalent to killing a human being."[100]

Sexual intercourse between husband and wife is a duty for the man and a privilege for his wife.[101] The Talmud is quite explicit about the husband's sexual responsibility, as well as those sexual activities that are absolutely prohibited, and it emphasizes the psychological as well as the sexual commitment of the man to his wife. The following are some of the Talmudic laws concerning a man's sexual responsibilities:

> If, for example, a man betroths a woman on condition that he is to be free from the obligation of providing her with food, raiment, and conjugal rights, he should be told, "Your stipulation concerning food and raiment, which are money matters, is valid, but as for your stipulation regarding conjugal rights, it is null and void, because this latter duty is imposed upon you by the Torah. This woman is therefore now betrothed, and you owe her her conjugal rights, and therefore you cannot free yourself from them by names of your stipulation."[102]

> A woman may not be betrothed except with her consent, and if one betroths her against her will, she is not betrothed. On the other hand, if a man is coerced into betrothing a woman against his will, she is betrothed.[103]

> The Sages have likewise ordained that he who marries a virgin should rejoice with her for seven days. He should neither ply his trade nor buy and sell in the market, but should rather eat, drink, and be merry, whether he had been a bachelor or a widower.

> If a woman is a nonvirgin, he should rejoice with her for not less than three days, because it is an enactment of the Sages concerning the daughters of Israel that a man should rejoice with a nonvirgin three days, whether he had been a bachelor or a widower.[104]

> A woman who after marriage gives her husband permission to withhold her conjugal rights from her, is permitted to do so, but only after having children: "When does this apply?" When he has children, for in that case he has already fulfilled the commandment to be fruitful and multiply. If, however, he has not yet fulfilled it, he is obligated to have sexual intercourse with her according to his schedule until he has children, because this is a positive commandment of the Torah, as it is said, "Be fruitful and multiply" (Gen. 1.28).[105]

As part of the husband's sexual responsibilities to his wife, and reflecting the personal power of choice that women had in the intimate conjugal relation, the husband is required to treat his wife's preferences and aesthetic sensibilities with deference. The following three passages from the Talmud emphasize sensitivity, mutual respect, and faithfulness:

> The Sages have likewise ordained that a man should honor his wife more than his own self, and love her as himself; that if he has money, he should increase his generosity to her according to his wealth; that he should not cast undue fear upon her; and that his discourse with her should be gentle—he should be prone neither to melancholy nor to anger.[106]

It is the duty of every man to warn his wife against infidelity, and the Sages have said, "A man should warn his wife only because the spirit of purity has entered into him." Nevertheless, he should not carry his jealousy of her beyond reason, nor should he compel her to have intercourse with him against her will. Rather, he should do it only with her consent, accompanied by pleasant discourse and enjoyment.[107]

Similarly, the Sages have forbidden a man to have intercourse with his wife while thinking in his heart of another woman. Nor should he have intercourse while intoxicated or in the midst of strife or hatred. Nor should he have intercourse with her against her will while she is in dread of him, nor when one of them is under a ban, nor after he has made up his mind to divorce her. If he does one of these things, the resulting children will be degenerate; some will be shameless, others will become renegades and sinners.[108]

In keeping with the respect the wife is accorded, a married woman cannot be forced to have sexual intercourse with a husband she has come to loathe. The Talmud says:

The wife who prevents her husband from having intercourse with her is called "a rebellious wife," and should be questioned as to the reason for her rebelliousness. If she says, "I have come to loathe him, and I cannot willingly submit to his intercourse," he must be compelled to divorce her immediately, for she is not like a captive woman who must submit to a man that is hateful to her. She must, however, leave with forfeiture of all her *ketubbah,* but may take her worn-out clothes that are still on hand, regardless of whether they are part of the property brought by her to her husband, for which he had become surety, or are melog property, for which he had not become surety.[109]

While the duty of procreation falls heavily on the men, the Talmud is less stringent about the woman's procreative restrictions. As one interpreter of the Talmud has put it:

The law does not account the unmarried woman guilty of sin. Basically this is due to the fact that the bachelor woman was unknown in Talmudic days. But the haskalah has another explanation—that the duty of procreation does not fall upon the woman. However, one would expect the celibate woman to be condemned by Jewish law on the basis of her being exposed to immoral temptations; yet the law does not even agree to that. Evidently it considers the many social restrictions set upon woman's conduct sufficient guarantee that she will not violate her chastity. Nevertheless, the law urges the woman too to be married lest she be suspected of immoral conduct.[110]

Woman is not included in the prohibition of waste of nature, since she is not included in the duty of procreation. Therefore, anything the woman can do after the act of cohabitation to destroy the seed is perfectly permissible, so long as the intercourse was natural and normal. But nothing may be done to make the intercourse useless to begin with.[111]

Finally, the Talmud suggests in four different places that the timing of female orgasm with respect to male orgasm can alter the probability of conceiving a male or female child. The following advice is given to a man who wants to have sons:

> At first it used to be said that "if the woman emits her semen first she will bear a male, and if the man emits his semen first she will bear a female." . . . Scripture thus ascribes the males to the females and the females to the males. [112]

> Now is it within the power of man to increase the number of "sons and sons' sons"? But the fact is that because they contained themselves during intercourse in order that their wives should emit their semen first so that their children shall be males, Scripture attributes to them the same merits as if they had themselves caused the increase of the number of their sons and sons' sons. This explains what R. Kattina said, "I could make all my children to be males." [113]

From the foregoing, it is clear that the Orthodox Jewish husband, in the course of procreation, is expected to be sensitive and attentive to his wife's sexual needs, to remain faithful to her, and to be abstinent except when having sex with her. These codes favor sexual compatibility and, because the husband does not divide his attentions between a wife, a mistress, or other women, Jewish wives should have more frequent intercourse than do those wives whose husbands consort with other women. As we will see shortly, some tantalizing research findings in reproductive biology suggest that these conditions contribute to more male births. But these findings are suggestive rather than conclusive, and we turn now to a sex practice prescribed by the Talmud that receives slightly more support—although still tentative—from reproductive biology.

The Talmud is very explicit about specifying one period during each month when the husband must abstain from intercourse with his wife and may have no other sexual outlet. This interval is ended when the wife takes a ritual bath. Marital intercourse is prohibited during the wife's menstrual flow and for seven days after it ceases:

> The menstruant is classed with all other forbidden unions. If a man initiates the act of intercourse with her, whether naturally or unnaturally, he is punishable by extinction, even if she is a minor three years and one day old, as in all other cases of forbidden union, seeing that a female is rendered unclean by menstruation from the very day of her birth onwards. [114]

> The daughters of Israel have imposed upon themselves a further restriction, and made it a custom that wherever Israeli may live, when any daughter of Israel has a flow, even if it is a drop no larger than a mustard seed, she should, upon the cessation of the flow, count for herself seven days of cleanness, even if she has the flow during the period of her menstruation. It is immaterial whether she has a flow of only one day, or for two, or throughout the seven, or even longer: when the flow ceases she must count seven days of cleanness . . . and must then immerse herself on the eighth night . . . Thereafter she is permitted to her husband. [115]

> R. Johanan stated: A woman conceives only immediately after her ritual immersion, for it is said, "And in cleansing did my Mother conceive me" [116]

During the time of his wife's menstrual flow and for seven days thereafter, the husband's sexual abstinence is to be complete—neither masturbation nor intercourse with a woman who is not his wife is permitted.[117] While polygyny would of course lift this requirement (when wives are not menstruating at the same time), polygyny was rare even among the ancient Jews. After the Babylonian exile in the sixth century B.C., only monogamous relationships are mentioned for nonroyal men.[118] Even royal polygyny was prohibited by the laws of the Essenes,[119] which date from the beginning of the Christian era. Therefore, throughout the thousands of years during which these codes have been observed by Orthodox Jews, abstinence was to be total, because nearly all were in monogamous relationships.[120]

Another condition prescribed by the Talmud is frequency of intercourse. This is done for different occupations, which is probably irrelevant for our purposes, but of special importance is the prescription that intercourse should take place after the micvah, or ritual bath, and what is even more remarkable, that if a man wants sons, he should have intercourse twice in succession at that time. The Talmud says:

The conjugal rights mentioned in the Torah are obligatory upon each man according to his physical powers and his occupations.

How so? For men who are healthy and live in comfortable and pleasurable circumstances, without having to perform work that would weaken their strength, and do nought but eat and drink and sit idly in their houses, the conjugal schedule is every night. For laborers, such as tailors, weavers, masons, and the like, their conjugal schedule is twice a week if their work is in the same city, and once a week if their work is in another city.

For ass-drivers, the schedule is once a week; for camel-drivers, once in thirty days; for sailors, once in six months; for disciples of the wise, once a week, because the study of Torah weakens their strength. It is the practice of the disciples of the wise to have conjugal relations each Friday night.[121]

A wife may restrict her husband in his business journeys to nearby places only, so that he would not otherwise deprive her of her conjugal rights. Hence he may not set out except with her permission.

Similarly, she may prevent him from changing an occupation involving a frequent conjugal schedule for one involving an infrequent schedule, as for example, if an ass-driver seeks to become a sailor.

Disciples of the wise, however, may absent themselves for the purpose of studying Torah, without their wives' permission for as long as two or three years. Similarly, if a man leading a comfortable and pleasurable life decides to become a disciple of the wise, his wife may not hinder him.[122]

If a man subjects his wife to a vow that he will have no intercourse with her, he is given a week's grace; beyond that, he must divorce her and pay her her *ketubbah*, or else effect a release from his vow.

This applies even to a sailor, whose schedule is once in six months, because once he makes the vow he has caused her suffering and despair.[123]

Thus, with the exception of men in unusual occupations, the husband is required to have intercourse with his wife at least twice a week, and sometimes more often.

How can one be reasonably sure that immediately following the period of abstinence for Orthodox Jews, intercourse would take place? From the Talmud: "R. Meir used to say, Why did the Torah ordain that the uncleanness of menstruation should continue for seven days? Because being in constant contact with his wife (a husband might) develop a loathing toward her. The Torah, therefore, ordained: Let her be unclean for seven days in order that she shall be beloved by her husband as at the time of her first entry into the bridal chamber.[124]

As we have seen, the Talmud says that a woman becomes fertile at just this time (physiologically, the period just before ovulation). The Talmud further says that if a man wants all of his children to be sons, he "should cohabit twice in succession.[125]

The combination of total sexual abstinence for about twelve days, plus the requirements that a husband have intercourse with his wife at a high frequency and the additional advice that if sons were wanted, that intercourse should occur twice in succession, all make it highly likely that intercourse would be timed shortly before ovulation, and that the coital rate (number of times intercourse occurred) would be frequent following a period of male abstinence. We turn now to examine the extent to which evidence from research on reproductive biology supports the view that following Talmudic codes may produce high sex ratios.

Reproductive biology and sex ratios. The literature on relationships between sex practices, the physiology of reproductive processes, and gender at conception is largely prescientific. Wild mysticism, superstitious practices, and physiological studies that vary greatly in the reliability of their techniques and in their bases for generalization are all freely intermixed. In popular writeups, the anecdotes of a mystery writer about one farmer's bulls[126] receive equal credence with controlled studies of manipulated physiological variables.[127] Anecdotes may be factually grounded, but they are hardly scientific evidence. One is reminded of the medical reports on bloodletting in previous centuries. The literature also contains many clinical tracts on how couples can conceive a baby of the desired sex. Scientific work is rare in which the effects of single variables have been carefully manipulated and controlled under conditions that would make sound scientific inferences possible.

Three serious flaws occur repeatedly, as follows: The first is that normal and abnormal populations are not differentiated. For example, many studies are based on couples who have had trouble conceiving, and who have therefore come to a fertility clinic for help.[128] Much evidence reveals that sex practices may have very different physiological effects for fertile as versus infertile couples.[129] For example, the effects of abstinence on the sperm count of men who have normal sperm counts compared with men who have abnormally low counts are quite different.[130] To understand some of the reported and conflicting results, it is therefore necessary to know the characteristics of the population studied. Normal populations provide the strongest basis for generalization.

A second serious flaw in a great many studies is that several different sexual practices are all instituted at the same time. For example, instructions may include the timing of intercourse following abstention, along with acid or alkaline douches.[131] This procedure results largely from the clinical orientation of much of the work, which is designed to maximize the chances that an infertile couple will conceive and have a baby of the desired sex. These couples are therefore told to do everything simultaneously, which is believed to enhance the chances of conceiving a child of a particular sex.[132] For this reason, it is often impossible to know whether any one of the multiple practices is irrelevant or even detrimental to the outcome.

Because the effects of each sex practice have not been carefully isolated, some sex practices that may have no scientific basis continue to be suggested to couples wishing to conceive. Like all superstitious practices, the coincidence of their use along with practices that do have a real effect on desired outcomes serves to perpetuate them. Until controlled studies are conducted of the effects of each practice alone, it is nearly impossible to generalize about their relative contribution to sex ratios at conception. To further complicate the matter, several of the sex practices have interactive effects, so that one of them in isolation does not produce what several of them together cause physiologically.[133]

A third deficiency is the tendency of some authors to assume that any condition that is associated with high or low sex ratios actually causes the high or low ratio. As is well known to researchers, two conditions can be strongly associated with neither being the cause of the other. Instead, they may both result from some other factor. For example, in England there are more babies born in areas where storks are found—not because storks bring babies, but rather because the high birth rate and the presence of storks are characteristic of rural areas. Erroneous assumptions of cause are most often made in studies that relate changes in sex ratios at birth for entire populations to a change in the society. For example, the rise in male births following wars is presumed to be correlated with servicemen's demobilization leaves.[134] A hypothetical model is proposed of the processes that intervene between these two social phenomena. It is assumed that there is a higher rate of intercourse with wives when servicemen are home on short leaves.[135] However, such an increase in coital rate is inferred rather than observed. A variety of other plausible alternative hypotheses could account for the increase in male births that cannot be ruled out, since the key intervening variables are not directly observed. Such analyses must always be considered only partial as long as there is no more direct evidence that can fill in the causal links between the two phenomena.

A fourth dubious practice is generalization from animal husbandry experiments to the relationship between human sex practices and the physiology of sex at conception. This approach is questionable, since the processes of sperm production in human males differ significantly from those of any other mammalian species.[136] Moreover, unlike other animal species, human females are continuously sexually receptive.[137]

Despite these considerable difficulties, let us proceed now to see what legitimate inferences, if any, can be drawn. We will consider first what is apparently the most important contributing factor—the timing of intercourse. Along with this, we will discuss the cyclic physiological and other changes that might relate to sex ratio balances. While adequately controlled experiments might be able to demonstrate that the timing of intercourse influences the sex ratio, confidence in this association would be increased if the physiological processes accounting for this association could be identified.

We have seen that following the practices outlined in traditional Jewish dicta would delay first intercourse after menstruation to a period shortly before ovulation (one to three days). The menstrual cycle averages about 28 days long, beginning with the first day of menstrual flow, and ovulation generally occurs on the 14th day of the cycle.[138] The length of time between ovulation and the start of the next menstrual flow is a relatively constant 14 days. The first part of the cycle—the period between the end of flow and ovulation—is more variable.[139] If the cycle is shorter or longer than 28 days, it is this first interval that varies in length. If a woman has a menstrual flow for five days, and then waits another seven days before ritual immersion and intercourse with her husband, she would be at about the 12th or 13th day of her cycle, within 24 to 48 hours of ovulation.

Much recent research has been devoted to studying the relationship between the precise timing of intercourse and male/female conceptions, but there are many methodological problems associated with this research. In some reports, generalizations have been drawn from too few cases. Other studies have confounded fertile and infertile populations that apparently yield sex ratios in opposite directions.[140] Other conditions that are likely to interact with the timing of intercourse, such as male abstinence[141] or coital rates,[142] are difficult to control. In considering the possible role of physiological processes in relation to timing, further difficulties arise. For example, in studying sperm mobility in relation to the female cycle, experimental studies might examine the sperm mobility *in vitro* (in a test tube), while clinical studies examine motility *in vivo* (in the body), probably producing noncomparable results. Sometimes artificial insemination is used. The physiological processes related to these different approaches are not well enough understood to enable us to draw firm conclusions. With respect to artificial insemination, for example, female sexual excitement is lacking, and its presence in natural insemination may be essential to produce more male births when intercourse occurs near ovulation.[143]

Despite the many difficulties with research in reproductive biology, some tentative support can be found for the idea that intercourse taking place near ovulation produces more males than females. One of the best controlled studies was conducted in 1975 by Seguy with a population of 100 couples with normal fertility. He used stringent controls to insure a normal sperm count, and accurately recorded thermal shift in the women to determine the time of ovulation. Furthermore, intercourse was permitted only during that time. These 100 couples produced 77 boys and 23 girls—a sex ratio of 335! Another study by the same investigator resulted in 61 males and 39 females.[144] Other investigators in less well-controlled investigations have also found extremely high sex ratios resulting from intercourse at the time of ovulation.

But many studies fail to achieve results like this, either because their controls are inadequate, or because other unknown factors might be operating. One investigation that gave results exactly the opposite of what would be expected in connection with Talmudic practices was conducted by Guerrero.[145] He found a greater number of males born when intercourse had been timed to occur 6-9 days *before* the thermal shift (a rise in body temperature which occurs approximately one day after ovulation).[146] That would be 5-8 days before ovulation, typically shortly after the end of menstruation. For natural insemination, sex ratios decreased from then until the day before the thermal shift, when they were lowest. But for artificial insemination, Guerrero found the reverse: More males resulted from insemination at the time of the thermal shift, while more females were conceived earlier in the cycle.[147]

Thus, in this study, results with *artificial* insemination were consistent with our sex ratio thesis, but were in the opposite direction for *natural* insemination. The other way around would be more consistent with our thesis, but a possible explanation is at hand: The couples used for the natural insemination experiments were atypical. One group consisted of fertile couples who used the rhythm method to avoid conception but who conceived in spite of this attempt, and the other consisted of infertile couples who had failed to conceive without medical intervention. Considerable evidence from other studies indicates that non-normal populations show different reproductive patterns from normal ones. Finally, only a small number of births occurred on several of the days reported, expecially those days early in the cycle, making the calculation of sex ratios somewhat questionable.

Rather less direct, but still positive support for the relationship between the timing of intercourse and sex at conception is provided by an analysis of the sex of dizygotic (based on fertilization of two separate ova) twins. If the timing of intercourse influences sex, and if two separate ova are most apt to be present nearest the time of ovulation, then dizygotic twins should be more likely to be of the same sex than chance would predict.[148] This has indeed been reported.[149]

We can get a better understanding of the probable effects of the timing of intercourse if we examine what is known about reproductive physiology. From knowledge of the processes that relate the timing of insemination to gender at conception, it is possible to trace a probable sequence of events. During all but the period around the time of ovulation, the cervical mucus is less favorable to sperm penetration.[150] The mucus before ovulation is usually scanty in amount, and slightly alkaline. It is thick and viscous, and the cells composing it are greater in number (more closely packed).[151] Just before and during ovulation, there is an increase in the amount of mucus, a decrease in its viscosity and cell content, and some increase in alkalinity. These changes make the ovulatory cervical mucus optimal for sperm migration through the female reproductive tract.[152]

Recent work on differential sperm motility, both *in vivo* and *in vitro,* shows that the Y sperm have an advantage in migration to the ovum.[153] They are lighter and move more quickly through the cervical mucus at this time than do the X-bearing sperm. Even under varying experimental conditions, the Y sperm continue to show this advantage. After intercourse at the time of ovulation, the percentage of Y sperm rises from 48.8 percent in the man's ejaculate to 57.2 percent in the cervical mucus, with 57.1 percent in the uterus. This suggests that if intercourse occurs prior to ovulation, the condition of the cervical mucus is apt to favor conception of a male.

Work with the new technique of fluorescent microscopy has revealed that the X sperm are slightly behind. During passage through the cervical mucus, the Y sperm advance ahead of the X sperm, forming a vanguard that progresses toward the ovum. Because of this, they may very likely reach the ovum first, though it is not known how conditions further on, in the oviducts, affect sperm migration.[154] Although it is probable that the X sperm eventually catch up to the Y sperm at the ovum, the delay may be significant in giving an advantage to the vanguard of Y sperm in fertilizing the ovum.[155] The effect, if present, would increase the probability of a male conception and would be consistent with our finding that Orthodox Jews have high sex ratios at birth. Several reservations here are: (1) the total number of sperm present at any stage of migration is usually not known; (2) it is difficult to say whether a vanguard of Y sperm would be large enough to initiate fertilization; and (3) not all the Y-bearing spermatozoa can be demonstrated by fluorescent microscopy.

For these reasons, and because of other limitations on the research, a firm and final conclusion concerning the relative migration of Y and X spermatozoa is not possible. What is needed is direct evidence that the relative advantage of the Y sperm is lessened if ovulation is more remote in time; a search of the literature failed to uncover this vital datum.

Some early theories favored ovulation as the optimal time for male conception on the basis of the differential survival rates of X and Y sperm. Since X sperm were thought to live longer, it was plausible that intercourse close to ovulation would insure that the Y sperm would be fresh and able to cause insemination. If intercourse occurred much earlier, it was believed that many of the Y sperm would die before ovulation, leaving mainly X sperm in the reproductive tract at the time of ovulation.[156] But recent physiological studies of X and Y sperm survival rates contradict the assumption of different rates. Both X and Y sperm appear to survive equally well in the reproductive tract.[157]

We can conclude that although it is highly probable that the timing of intercourse is related to the sex ratio at birth, the determination of exactly which time is most favorable for male conception needs further investigation if firm conclusions are to be reached. Moreover, various other conditions that might affect gender at the time of conception must be more precisely specified. For the present, combined findings suggest that high sex ratios are associated with intercourse timed before the day of ovulation, but not after ovulation or for the earlier period between ovulation and the end of menstruation. The Orthodox Jewish proscription against intercourse during menstrual flow and for an additional seven days would make first intercourse most likely to occur during this crucial period.

As mentioned earlier, the timing of intercourse very probably has different effects on sex ratios at conception, depending on a variety of other conditions that may or may not be present. One that appears prominently in Jewish codes is male abstinence during and after menstruation until intercourse near ovulation. Here too, physiological research is more suggestive than conclusive. Reliable evidence shows that with periods of abstinence of up to 8-10 days, the seminal volume increases, as does the sperm count per c.c. for fertile men.[158] This is not true for infertile men.[159] The rise in the sperm count levels off after about 10 days of abstinence.[160] No significant changes in sperm morphology take place as a result of abstinence,[161] but an increase in the days of abstinence appears to be associated with a decrease in the percentage of motile sperm.[162] Nevertheless, there is no evidence that such a decrease is differential between X and Y sperm,[163] or that the decrease has any significant effect on the advantage the Y sperm have in migration.[164]

Does the increased sperm count due to abstinence favor male conceptions? The Y sperm migrate ahead of the X sperm and form a vanguard that reaches the ovum first. Is it possible that with an increase in the overall sperm count, the vanguard of Y sperm contains more members with which to bombard the ovum? Although the ratios of Ys to Xs in the male ejaculate does not change with an increased sperm count, it is possible that the increase in the total number of Ys, combined with their vanguard position in migration, relatively improves their success in fertilization. Knowledge of total numbers of sperm and their effects, rather than percentages, is needed before a clear picture can be formed. One may speculate that the combination of an increased sperm count and seminal volume, plus the timing of intercourse just prior to ovulation may have an additive effect, making Y inseminations somewhat more likely, but hard evidence is lacking.

Another potentially important condition discussed previously was frequency of intercourse. We can conceive of this separately for each partner. In monogamous couples who have no sex outside of the marital union, the frequency is the same for the male and the female. But in other instances, we can think of these frequencies independently, for it might be the case, for example, that frequent intercourse for the female has different effects from frequency for the male. As we shall see, research suggests tentatively that increased frequency for the female (especially near ovulation) produces more male conceptions, while high frequency for the male, wih his wife only occasionally a partner, leads to more female conceptions. Thus, male promiscuity would produce low sex ratios (see Chapter 8). Unfortunately the evidence is only tantalizingly suggestive rather than conclusive.

One criterion that would fit in with and provide a test of these notions involves a comparison of polygynous with monogamous marriages. Here again, the Talmud has something to say. When there is more than one wife, the conjugal rights are to be divided among them.[165] Thus, frequency for any given wife would be comparatively low. We might expect, however, that even without the Jewish code, wives in polygynous marriages would experience less frequent intercourse. Bailey has worked out this line of reasoning:

> For example, a female in a monogamous marriage will most likely have a higher coital rate, on average, than a female in a polygynous marriage. Similarly, a polyandrous female will have, on average, a higher coital rate than a monandrous female. These expected differences in marriage patterns should be related to sex ratio at birth—monogamous couples and polyandrous females having children at a higher sex ratio than polygynous couples. (If a female's coital rate is some negative function of the number of her co-wives, then men with many wives will produce at a lower sex ratio than men with just two wives.)[166]

Anecdotal evidence suggests that women in harems produce fewer males.[167] But is there any hard evidence on the sex ratios at birth in monogamous and polygynous families? A recent anthropological survey looked at sex ratios at birth in monogamous and polygynous households among the Kikuyu (1963-73) and Gusii (1961-75), two peoples in Kenya. The percentage of male births in these groups under the different marital arrangements are highly significant and quite different. For monogamous families, they were 120 and 118, respectively, and for polygynous families, 66 and 87![168] Whiting has also taken a sample of 500 populations from the Human Area Relations File and found the following sex ratios at birth: for monogamous groups, 113; for limited polygynous, 104; and for full polygynous, 99.[169]

The Kikuyu and Gusii data are particularly interesting because they are from people of the same cultures, and thus many conditions were held constant. The only difference between the comparison groups was in the number of wives present, yet the sex ratio differences at birth are striking. Thus it seems that a higher coital rate for the female favors male conceptions, and a lower rate, female conceptions. It may be that in the monogamous situation, both coital rate with the same woman and some degree of abstinence—perhaps during her menstrual cycle—interact. Although this is strong inferential evidence, the frequency-of-intercourse hypothesis remains unsubstantiated until data on actual, rather than inferred, coital rates are gathered and linked to sex ratios at birth. Even within the same culture, there may be ways in which polygynous families differ, such as various housing arrangements that influence sex practices. Nevertheless, such cross-cultural data are the strongest evidence yet to correlate high female coital rate with high sex ratios at birth.

Several other investigators have suggested that high coital rates on the part of a couple increase the probability of male conceptions. James identifies peculiarities in the sex ratios at birth of special populations, hypothesizing that they result from increases or decreases in frequency of intercourse. A high coital rate is presumed to lead to more male births:

> These high wartime sex ratios are directly associated with short home leaves of servicemen and the concomitant unusually high coital rates. The high sex ratios just after wars would be due to the high coital rates when men are on demobilization leave. Bernstein (1958) noted that a higher proportion of

males are born to women who conceive after this interval. . . . I have unpublished data which powerfully suggests that coital rates in the first month of marriage are higher than any subsequent month. . . . Renkonen (1964, 1970) corroborated this with data from Finland and Australia. He observed that for nuptial conceptions the sex ratio is higher for first month conceptions than for conceptions in any subsequent month.[170]

The sex ratios among sibships of dizygotic twins have provided further evidence to support a relationship between coital rate and sex ratios at birth.[171]

An explanation based on male abstinence, or on a combination of abstinence and high coital rate, seems equally reasonable. "It has been suggested (James, 1972a) that when maternal age is controlled for, (high) coital rates are associated with the probability of dizygotic twinning. If this is correct (and if the present hypothesis were correct), then sibships containing twins should have high sex ratios. Such a feature has been reported (Schutzenberger, 1950)."[172]

Though provocative, these reports can hardly be considered more than speculative. They are not even correlational, since they are inferences based on only one source of data, and high coital rates are assumed rather than observed. Yet these ideas about the possible positive correlation between coital rates and sex ratios do lead to some testable hypotheses.

Some physiological effects of frequency of intercourse, particularly for the male, have been discovered. When the frequency of emission ranges from 2.0-4.4 times per week (as among many Orthodox Jews), sperm quality and quantity are not affected.[173] That range is an optimal one for high sperm count and quality.[174] If the same woman is the partner in each coition, then her reproductive tract might have a larger total number of the faster moving Y sperm.[175] In the cervical mucus, sperm remain alive for 28-48 hours.[176] Two coitions at ovulation, following male abstinence, would create optimum Y sperm penetration conditions that might favor the chances of male conception.

But when frequency of emission increases from 3.5 to 8.6 times per week, there is a

> marked and uniform decrease in sperm concentration (-55%), specimen volume (-33%) and motility (-15%). The increase in emission frequency has no effect on morphology and no significant effect on forward progression. . . . The total number of spermatozoa per week declined, at the higher frequency of emission, while the total volume of semen per week increased.[177]

At these high rates of emission, sperm quality decreases.[178] Extremely high rates of intercourse for a male, such as might occur with promiscuity with a harem, or with many concubines and/or wives, would temporarily lower sperm quality.[179] The Orthodox Jewish coital rate requirements are in the optimal range, but not so high as to lessen sperm quality. Again, this evidence only bears indirectly on the possibility of higher sex ratios.

We also saw that the Hebrew text was explicit about the woman having an orgasm first if a male child is to be conceived. This is one Talmudic instruction for which there is, at present, no supporting physiological evidence. One theory holds that female orgasm occurring first creates conditions favorable to male conception because secretions released during her orgasm raise the alkalinity of the vagina or cervix. These theories assume that the internal female reproductive environment is hostile to sperm survival because of its acidity, and in fact some researches have hypothesized that acidity is differentially harmful to Y-bearing sperm.[180] Recent studies show, however, that the cervical mucus is slightly alkaline during the entire menstrual cycle, with a slight rise in pH acid-alkaline balance at ovulation.[181] In some well-controlled recent studies, solutions differing in alkalinity did not affect either the differential survival rate or the migration rate of Y and X sperm.[182] No change was found in the vaginal pH after female orgasm,[183] although after prolonged excitation there is a slight decrease in acidity.[184] Further, there is an immediate and complete neutralization of vaginal acidity by the male ejaculate,[185] which effectively buffers a potentially harmful environment, and the cervical mucus is naturally more alkaline than the vagina.[186] No influence of the cervical pH on sperm has been found.[187]

There has also been speculation that female orgasm may in some way affect the transportation of sperm.[188] There are two different views on this. One is that an "insuck" is created in the cervical mucus at orgasm which acts to pull the sperm through the tract.[189] However, for this to work, male orgasm would have to be simultaneous, or preferably precede female orgasm.[190] The second type of speculation is that the contractions of the uterus associated with orgasm are expulsory and would therefore tend to hamper rather than aid sperm migration.[191] Neither of these views supports the notion that female orgasm preceding male orgasm has an influence on male conception, although if there were two coitions and the "insuck" theory were correct, the sperm already in the cervix would be affected by the movement during the second female orgasm. We can conclude that at this time there is no physiological substantiation for the role of female orgasm in male conception.

Yet the puzzle remains as to why the timing that results in male conception is so different for natural and artificial inseminations. Is the difference related to female sexual response, which is involved only in natural insemination? Parkes[192] has summarized data which he believes indicate that sexual excitement in women can accelerate ovulation. In some lower animals, like the rabbit and ferret, ovulation is dependent on mating. But these animals differ so much from humans that no reasonable analogy can be made. Parkes says: "On the other hand, the idea that a follicle due to ovulate in a few days might do so more rapidly as the result of intense sexual excitement is not inherently improbable, and cases of isolated coitus indicate that conceptions may occur well before the expected onset of the fertile periods."[193] An unusually high rate of pregnancies occurring after rapes, even at strange times in the menstrual cycle, "are of considerable interest in suggesting that the anger and fear evoked by rape may have the same effect as intense sexual excitement is said to have in accelerating ovulation."[194]

A recent review of the effects of intense coital stimulation on ovulation found that "it is quite possible that in women who get sufficiently intense coital stimulation during the post-menstrual period, when the follicles are ripening, coition may induce early ovulation."[195] A recent study of the high fertility rate following rape "associate(s) the high fertility rate following the rape of women with the fact that in rape thrusting is likely to be more intense than in most other instances of coitus. They speculate that 'this increased intensity could be an important factor in producing ovulation under these circumstances.'"[196] "Coition may be reproductive several days before the expected date for spontaneous ovulation. . . . one reason to think that vigorous coitus in women on an occasion that involves strong physical and emotional reactions can hasten the rupture of a ripening follicle."[197] But applying conclusions from rape cases to normal conceptions is stretching the line of inference to the breaking point, and such reasoning is of doubtful value. The role of female excitation and orgasm in influencing gender at conception is the least substantiated of any of the influences thus far discussed. Nothing has been proved, and much has yet to be learned.

Summary of sex practices and sex ratios. Several more recent studies illustrate the complexity of the issues involved in producing variation in sex ratios. The length of time that women can conceive during each month is not precisely known; estimates vary from as long as eight days[198] to 24-36 hours.[199] A few days seems more probable than the longer period, but more research is needed. What has recently become somewhat clearer is that during the short fertility period, the timing of intercourse has appreciable effects on the gender of the fetus conceived. It now appears that conceptions occurring early *and* late in the fertile period are more likely to be male, while those in the middle are more likely to be female.[200] Since sex ratios can thus be influenced depending on the timing of intercourse that varies by as little as 24 hours, more uncertainty is introduced concerning the notion that conceptions among Orthodox Jews are more often male because of their proximity to ovulation.

One possibility remains, however. Intercourse occurring early in the fertile period does produce more males. If the abstinence practiced by both male and female during the days following menstruation increases the likelihood that they will have intercourse just as soon as ritual permits, and if this first intercourse is followed relatively soon by another, we still have the possibility of more male conceptions among Orthodox Jews who follow the prescribed practices carefully. Yet it is also clear that this alone could hardly account for sex ratios of 135 at birth reported earlier for the shtetl Jews in eastern Europe. Except for one study by Seguy, reported earlier, other studies involving the timing of intercourse tell of effects on the gender of the zygote that are much smaller.[201] Thus we must conclude that the reported high sex ratios at birth for Orthodox Jews remain largely unexplained.

The results from various studies of reproductive biology suggest that a whole complex of factors are apt to have some influence on the sex of a zygote; moreover, at least some of these interact with each other.[202] It may well be that other conditions prevailing for nineteenth-century shtetl Jews combined with Talmudic practices to produce the high sex ratios at birth, but what these might be are presently unknown. The possibility also remains

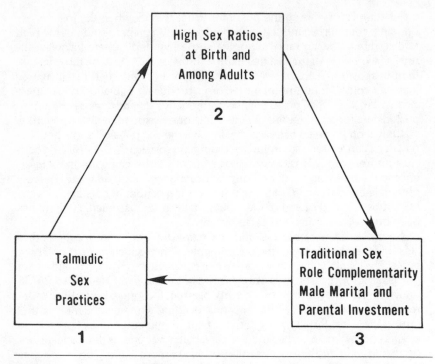

Figure 4.1   Feedback Cycle for the High Sex Ratio Society of Orthodox Jews

that the sex ratios of 135 were somewhat inflated by the failure to report female births as painstakingly as male births. Yet the evidence seems strong that Orthodox Jews in other places and times had sex ratios high enough to demand some sort of special explanation.

CONCLUSIONS

Our thesis has been that high sex ratio societies are traditional and have stable families in which males make a long parental investment in children. The stability of the family and the focus on the children, in turn, pass on the traditional values of the society to the next generation. If we assume that somehow this is accompanied by practices that favor higher sex ratios, a complete feedback cycle becomes apparent. Sexual customs create the physiological conditions at conception that favor more male births. High sex ratios perpetuate a relatively high sex ratio society in which men want to marry and invest in children. Thus the traditional Orthodox Jews passed on unchanged the traditional sex practices. The cycle was continuously repeated until some link in the feedback system was broken or weakened.

This feedback cycle for Orthodox Jews might be as shown in Figure 4.1. When for any reason there is a change in any part of the cycle, the pattern is apt to be disrupted, and other parts may change also. For example, if orthodox sex practices are not strictly followed, sex ratios at birth would not be unusually high, and this in turn would lead to a less strictly traditional society as women married assimilated Jews or even non-Jews. Male parental investment would drop to a more universal level, so that sex ratios at birth would be much the same as for other traditional populations. Whether or not a self-perpetuating cycle for low sex ratio societies could exist is even less clear, but we will return to that question in Chapter 8 in our discussion of sex and family among American blacks.

5

Frontier, Southern, and Victorian Women in Early America

Our strategy so far has been to examine periods and locations where the imbalance between the sexes was substantial and visible. In this way we can be confident of a disparity in numbers and can anticipate that appreciable social effects will follow from it. Several points in the history of the United States provide us with an opportunity to continue this strategy.[1] During the early Colonial period, sex ratios were almost universally high, with an acute shortage of women. Later, the changing frontiers in America were also characterized by high sex ratios. In the eighteenth and nineteenth centuries, America always had a frontier somewhere—one that was moving ever westward.

Two more settled regions can also be contrasted. Colonial New England's initially high sex ratios dropped off quickly, before long falling below 100 and remaining there throughout the eighteenth and nineteenth centuries right up to the present. Colonies in the South began with extravagantly high sex ratios which, after an initial downward plunge, dropped much more slowly, remaining slightly above 100 until the Civil War. These periods and regions also provided differing economic roles for men and women, enabling us to examine the effect of economic conditions on sex ratio imbalances.

The colonies and frontier areas also provide us with a very different kind of societal context from those in earlier chapters. By and large, in classical antiquity and the medieval period, tradition played a considerable part in determining the roles assigned to women and the constraints placed on them and their relationships with men and with the world outside of the home. Even in classical Greece, and certainly in the Roman Republic and Empire, many aspects of women's roles became codified into laws that were enforced by the judicial system. While these women were not always so unambiguously placed, certainly in contrast with women in frontier areas, they were under much greater societal constraints.

We saw earlier that whether or not high sex ratio societies give women an advantage because of their scarcity depends on certain other features of the society in which they live. Where men hold the balance of political and economic power, excluding women from direct participation, high sex ratios often make matters worse. Women are apt to be controlled by men and to have few rights of their own. This is especially apt to be the case where the society has long-established traditions and is highly stable over time.

Frontier societies contrast with these conditions. They are fluid; along with the lack of tradition, their boundaries and populations are constantly changing; new ways of doing things and new attitudes and values are repeatedly being introduced. Opportunities for changing one's place in life are ever present. The economy of the frontier is a developing one, with an acute scarcity of labor. Under such circumstances, women are not likely to be rigorously excluded from participation in productive activities outside the home.

Some frontiers, of course, are colonial, in the sense that the colonists represent some one mother country. While these colonists are apt to bring with them certain traditions, the conditions of life in the new territories may force abrupt changes in many traditional ways of doing things. Moreover, many colonists are self-selected for their willingness to depart from tradition in a new land. In the case of the American colonies, as well as in the early history of the United States and its territories, peoples from different countries with different traditions were involved. Hence there is little doubt that Colonial and early American society was one of extreme fluidity and social change. Under these circumstances, we would expect the high sex ratio condition, reflecting a severe shortage of women, to be favorable for them and to provide them with a certain degree of social power. It should be no surprise to find William Dixon, after a trip in 1875 to the new frontier, California, writing that one "pretty young woman of San Francisco had remarked: "Guess my husband's got to look after me and make himself agreeable to me if he can; if he don't, there's plenty that will."[2] But that is getting ahead of our account. Let us turn to the data on sex ratios in Colonial and early America.

THE COLONIES

The colonies varied markedly from one to another, as did the same colony in different periods. This is to be expected, for two of the factors that affect population demography, migration and mortality, are especially active in colonization. Not only did many of the larger migrations drastically alter the composition of the existing colonies, but famine, Indian wars, and disease occasionally decimated a colony population, sometimes selectively with respect to sex. Moreover, migrations to the different colonies consisted of populations with different features; some received many black slaves, white indentured servants, or convicts, while others did not, and these categories of people were not always systematically accounted for in the censuses.[3] Nevertheless, as is noted in an excellent study of the populations of the British colonies, some features of the various censuses can be regarded as sufficiently accurate to use for demographic studies.[4] While reports of population size have to be carefully evaluated, sex ratios, especially of adult populations, are probably less subject to error.[5] At the same time, it should be kept in mind that census-taking in the Colonial period was very sporadic—often only a few censuses were taken in a colony during a whole century.[6]

Sex Ratios in the Colonies

In the initial period of colonization, in the early seventeenth century, both the New England colonies and Virginia had a considerable excess of males. In New England, this amounted to about three adult males for every two women, a sex ratio of 150; and in Virginia, up to about 1640, there were seven males over 20 years of age for each woman, a sex ratio of 700! By the time of the Massachusetts Census of 1764, however, the sex ratio for Massachusetts was below 100 in most counties, and the urban counties that included Boston and its surrounds averaged only 87 for adults over 16 years of age.[7] The ratio remained slightly above 100 in the more rural counties.

In Virginia, while the proportion of adult males had fallen drastically by 1700, as estimated from the number of men listed in the militia rolls, the sex ratio remained well above 100. The sex ratio in Virginia was kept high by the mass importation of white indentured servants. The population was probably like Maryland's, which had a sex ratio of about 150. One estimate is that the sex ratio in Virginia did not approach an approximately even balance until late in the eighteenth century.[8]

Other early colonies had a similar history in being critically short of women.[9] Except for New England, indentured white servants had a large part in populating the colonies, although they were not counted in the censuses.[10] Few women were among the first shipment of colonists to Maryland, and little is known of the early women in North Carolina. The colonists from New England who helped found Carolina did include women, mainly wives and women servants, but like the other colonies, there were not enough of them.[11] South Carolina in 1672 had 268 men able to bear arms, and only 69 women.[12] The Georgia colony concentrated at first on attracting poor men with families rather than single women, who might have taken as husbands soldiers from the garrison, thus weakening the defense of the colony against the Spaniards to the South.[13]

On the whole, one of the major contrasts in sex ratios for these British colonies was the considerably greater ratio for Virginia and, later, for some of the middle and southern colonies, as compared with New England. While the latter had an initially high sex ratio, it was nowhere near that of the early ratios in the other colonies, and it was relatively short-lived. We will see later, when we discuss the nineteenth and twentieth centuries, that this low sex ratio situation continued to prevail in Massachusetts and generally in New England, and that it even exists today. In contrast, the southern colonies continued to have high sex ratios throughout the Colonial period, and they remained above 100 until the Civil War.

Social Consequences of High Sex Ratios in the Colonies

It is clear that a central demographic fact characterizing the colonies in the seventeenth century, as well as a good part of the eighteenth century, was an acute shortage of marriageable women. This was recognized from the outset, and many pleas were made for the situation to be corrected. Although the Virginia colonists started out as a communal body, it was soon realized that they would be more motivated to work if they had property of their own, and when Sir Thomas Dale arrived as governor in 1611, he provided every *family* man with a house, a year's provisions, 12 fenced-in acres, tools, and some farm animals.[14] A few years later, the London Company expressed concern about the large number of bachelors who, it was feared, would only be interested in making a fortune and returning to England.

In November 1618, the Virginia Company expressed interest in stabilizing the settlement and requested "that a fitt hundreth might be sent of women, Maidens young and uncorrupt to make wives to the Inhabitants and by that meanes to make the men more settled and lesse moveable."[15] The company also promised to provide servants first to those planters who married women who were recruited and, as a further incentive, gave an additional allotment of shares to men who married.[16] The small number of women who were transported to the colonies was eagerly courted by crowds of settlers waiting for them at the harbor.[17]

Lord Baltimore encouraged women to come to Maryland, offering an equal share of 100 acres for a wife, 50 for each child, 100 for each manservant, and 60 for a female servant. Women who were heads of families received the same number of acres as a male head.[18] One observer in Maryland noted in 1658 that: "As for women, they no sooner arrive than they are besieged with offers of matrimony, husbands being ready soon for those whom nature had apparently marked out, and predestined for lives of single blessedness."[19]

In Georgia, too, it was not very long before the importance of women in creating greater stability was realized. Bachelor soldiers and farmers began to demand wives. Moreover, landowners demanded that they be allowed to bequeath land to their daughters. Married soldiers and farmers were recognized as more industrious than bachelors, and the Georgians continued to ask for more single, eligible women throughout the seventeenth century and well into the eighteenth.[20]

Pressure on women to marry was strong in many places in the colonies. This is reflected in a bill passed by the Maryland assembly, but vetoed by the proprietor:

> That it may be prevented that noe woman here vow chastity in the world, unless she marry within seven years after land shall fall to hir, she must either dispose away of hir land, or else she shall forfeite it to the next of kinne, and if she have but one Mannor, whereas she canne not alienate it, it is gonne unless she git a husband.[21]

The greater value of women was also reflected in the scarcity of dowries.[22] In Europe, a poor girl without a dowry had hardly any chance of marrying, unless the dowry was provided by a charitable institution. In Colonial America, lack of a dowry was no handicap. Even female servants had excellent marital opportunities. Some of those who came to Maryland between 1634 and 1670 "married well and gained wealth and distinction."[23] This was true even though some were innocent country girls who had been kidnapped and shipped to America as servants. Sometimes these were courted as soon as they landed. Bullock, a plantation owner, says: "Maid servants of good honest stock may choose their husbands out of the better sort of people."[24] He complained that he could never keep one at his plantation for longer than three months.

In spite of the fact that it was not necessary for the bride to have a dowry, marriage portions were often paid where the father of the bride was a man of means. But also common were instances where the father of the groom promised a large settlement for his son upon marriage to a particular woman, a promise communicated directly to the family of the bride.[25] This is reminiscent of the bride-price encountered in some primitive societies, at certain times in Classical Greece and Rome, and in southern France and Spain in the later medieval period.

Another answer to the sex ratio question is that, where women are in short supply, they will have more choice of a suitor, and under some circumstances are treated in the romantic tradition. The position of women with respect to choosing men was so advantageous that apparently Wyatt, an early governor of Virginia, issued a proclamation to prevent them from committing themselves to more than one man:

> Women are yet scarce and in much request, and this offence has become very common, whereby great disquiet arose between parties, and no small trouble to the government . . . (Such conduct must cease and) every minister should give notice in his church that what man or woman soever should use any word or speech tending to a contract of marriage to several persons at one time . . . as might entangle or breed scruples in their consciences, should, for such their offence, either undergo corporal correction, or be punished by fine or otherwise, according to . . . quality of the person so offending.[26]

While parents in New England exerted considerable control over marriage arrangements, young women nevertheless had considerable independence of choice.[27] If a daughter firmly asserted that she could not love and respect a potential mate suggested by her parents, the suitor usually lost out. One observer cites a number of these cases where daughters were given veto power over suitors, as well as instances where young colonial women eloped with their lovers, who were then accepted by their fathers, and draws the following conclusions:

> It seems clear that the virgin, as well as the widow, was given considerable liberty in making up her own mind as to the choice of a life mate, and any general conclusions that colonial women were practically forced into uncongenial marriages by the command of parents has no documentary evidence whatever.[28]

Sometimes, however, practical considerations of Colonial life loomed large, and marriages were economic bargains with little pretense to romance. A study of Puritan families indicates that often men (of some standing) made a decision to marry *before* they had picked out the potential bride.[29] Only then did they look about for a suitable bride.

In low sex ratio societies, widows are often especially disadvantaged. Not only are they somewhat older than the usual age for marriage, but they may be burdened with children and be in financial straits. But in the high sex ratio colonies, widows were intensively wooed, and they quickly remarried. Adam Smith stated that:

> a young widow with four or five young children, who, among the middling or inferior ranks of people in Europe, would have so little chance for a second husband, is there (in America) frequently courted as a sort of fortune.[30]

Numerous cases were known of women who married three, four, and even five times. Widows were often social belles: George Washington, Patrick Henry's father, Thomas Jefferson, and James Madison all chose widows as wives.[31] Even in Colonial New England, where sex ratios were not very high, marriage was the normal state of affairs, and bereaved spouses married within a year or two.[32]

That the opportunities of widows were related to high sex ratios is suggested in an exceptional instance where ratios were considerably below 100. In 1765, in Plymouth, the sex ratio for adults over 21 years of age was only 86. Of all adults who did not die before the age of 50 years, approximately 42 percent of the widowers had remarried at least once, but only 28 percent of the widows had done so.[33] Further evidence on factors that depress the chances of widows comes from detailed evidence on marriages that took place at the beginning of the eighteenth century in the small town of Woburn, Massachusetts.[34] These marriages lasted more than 20 years on the average, and in those instances where the husband died, most widows were 50 years of age or more. Moreover, the adult sex ratio for Woburn in 1765 was 87.9. Most of these widows did not remarry; apparently their age and the shortage of males made marital opportunities scarce.

More dramatic findings on widowhood were reported in a study of the 1773 census in New Hampshire and the 1774 census in Connecticut. A striking inverse relationship was found between local sex ratios in New Hampshire and the number of widowed females. Remember that as unattached men move westward, sex ratios in the settled areas left behind drop, and that toward the frontier, they rise. The further the county from the Atlantic coast, the higher was the sex ratio and the smaller the proportion of widows among the population.[35] Portsmouth, on the coast, had a median sex ratio for whites of 86, and about 10 percent of all the women living in Portsmouth were widows who had not remarried. On the New Hampshire frontier, Chesire and Grafton counties had sex ratios of 112 and 126, respectively, and there the proportions widowed were only 2 and 1 percent, respectively. Consistent with this finding is that as the proportion of unmarried men increased, so did the proportion of women who were married.

The 1774 census taken in Connecticut illustrates further the importance of marital opportunity. More men than women were married in the three northeastern counties, where adult sex ratios were 92, 94, and 95, respectively, while in the remaining three counties, where adult sex ratios were 100, 103, and 111, more women than men were married.[36] The conclusion from this study was:

> Thus men appear to have married at a fairly constant rate throughout the colony, but the chances of a woman marrying depended on the number of eligible males present. When men were relatively common more women married, but when men were scarce there were more spinsters and widows.[37]

Finally, the same investigator called attention to another practice. He noted that men over 70 years of age had wives about as often as younger adult males, but that only about 42 percent of the women in this age bracket were married, compared with about three-quarters of the women below age 70. By estimating how many of the elderly women would be married if men over age 70 had wives about their own age, he deduced that the unmarried state of these elderly women was due primarily to the fact that widowers remarried more often than widows, and at the same time took younger wives.[38]

Another expected consequence of high sex ratios is early marriage for women and late marriage for men. Many Colonial historians have claimed that most brides were extremely young. For example, one well-known historian asserted that early marriage was a reality in seventeenth-century Virginia. He stated that marriage at 15 years was common, and even at 13 was not unusual.[39] It should be recognized, however, that statistics on age at marriage were almost nonexistent, and early historians of the Colonial period often cited only a few cases to make a point—admittedly, sometimes the only cases that were available to them. More modern historical demography indicates that early marriage for women was not universally true.

Intensive studies of single communities where vital records were available yield much higher ages at marriage. One study reports an average age of 23.8 years for brides at first marriage in seventeenth-century Andover, Massachusetts;[40] a study of Plymouth Colony reports a figure ranging from 20.6 years early in the seventeenth century to 22.3 years in the late seventeenth century;[41] in Woburn, around 1700, it was 23.6 years.[42] A study of three groups of Quakers in the middle colonies yielded an average age at first marriage of 22.8 for women and 26.5 for men. The investigator noted that ages at first marriage were generally concentrated within a limited span of years, not only among the Quakers, but in other parts of the colonies. Three-quarters of the brides married for the first time between the ages of 16 and 25, and four-fifths of the men between 20 and 29. He suggested, with good reason, that such practices probably reflect marriage customs prevailing in the seventeenth and eighteenth centuries.

These relatively late marriage ages for brides in the early seventeenth century may not be typical of all the colonies; the sex ratio for Andover colonists over 21 years of age was 117, though well below 100 in Plymouth and in Woburn. We have seen that the sex ratios in Virginia and many other parts of Colonial America were far higher; hence, the ages of women at first marriage may have been considerably lower in those regions. The relation to the sex ratio of age at first marriage is reflected in the above report, indicating that in Plymouth Colony toward the end of the seventeenth century, women married at a later age. Moreover, at century end, men married at age 24½, compared with age 27 early in the century. This is consistent with the decline in the sex ratio throughout the century, reflecting a considerable surplus of women in Plymouth toward the end of the century, and thus making it easier for men to obtain a suitable partner. The more settled areas of a colony lose males to the frontier parts, leaving behind a surplus of women. This surplus apparently results in (1) a smaller proportion of women married, (2) women marrying at a later age, and (3) lower fertility rates.[43]

It is important to keep in mind the nature of the Colonial economy and its consequences for the age at which men first married. Agriculture loomed large, both to ensure subsistence and to provide a means of exchange. Family households were the main sources of production, often augmented by servants, slaves, or more rarely, hired men who also lived on the land. For unattached individuals, there was almost no gainful place of employment or anywhere to live. While this varied somewhat from colony to colony, and was less true in urban areas, notably seaports, the family farm or plantation was the major economic unit and dwelling place.

This economic fact had important consequences for family structure and for relations between the sexes. For example, an intensive study of the seventeenth-century community of Andover, Massachusetts, underscores the difficulties encountered by the second generation.[44] While daughters married at an average age of 23, sons did not marry until 27, on the average. This was related to their dependency on their fathers. Until their father was willing to give them part of his land to settle on and develop, they had no means of supporting themselves and a wife. Of course, eldest sons were favored, as illustrated by the fact that they married at an earlier age, about 25½ years on the average. Typically, they were set up before the younger sons. But even having one's own share of the farm with a separate residence did not constitute complete independence. Usually the father retained title to the land, making it impossible for the son to sell his shares and leave the community. Since Andover men commonly lived into their seventies, this meant that family structure was patriarchal, in the form of a modified extended family. It is important to point out, however, that there was enormous variation in family patterns and households, and the Andover situation is not necessarily typical. In Plymouth Colony, for example, there were no married sons or daughters at all living in the same household.[45] Frequently, however, young married couples did live on adjoining property provided by parents.

When sex ratios are so high that there is an acute shortage of potential wives, we may expect wives to be tempted to change husbands, and occasionally to yield to such temptations. Apparently, the number of colonial women who broke off relations with their husbands was in considerable contrast to European women.[46] Often the woman was known to have eloped with another man. Presumably, this difference between colony and motherland was a function of the widely different sex ratios rather than differences in marital satisfaction between colonial America and Europe.

At the same time, the sex ratio question suggests that when women are in short supply, constraints will be placed on their interaction with other men, especially on the sexual behavior of married women. While it is true that the Puritan ideology would also require this, we can at least examine whether such constraints existed. It is abundantly clear that they did. In early Massachusetts, the penalty for adultery was whipping, branding, banishment, or even death. Especially noteworthy and consistent with our thesis is that much more mention is made of the punishment of *women* for adultery; apparently, the male partner was less often punished or more lightly sentenced. A few Massachusetts women were actually put to death; others had the letter "A" branded on their forehead or, as every reader knows, were required to wear a scarlet letter on their sleeve or bosom. Sometimes the letter was burned into the breast instead. Another form of punishment consisted of a symbolic hanging, carried out by putting the individual in the gallows with a rope about the neck for a fixed period of time, followed by a public whipping.

The existence of these punishments, horrendous compared with modern attitudes toward adultery, easily leads to misinterpretation of Puritan views of human nature. In fact, the Puritans viewed sexual behavior as a natural expression of human nature; they did *not* believe in an ascetic life. This was as true of the New England clergy as of their congregations. But they did stress that sexual intercourse should be confined to marital partners. At the same time, they viewed humans as weak in spirit, and expected transgressions to occur: "Sexual intercourse was a human necessity and marriage the only proper supply for it."[47]

In fact, the Puritans stressed that sexual intercourse was a necessary, right, and important part of marital relations. Many instances were recorded of actions by the Church or even the courts against individuals who denied conjugal rights to their spouses by absenting themselves or otherwise failing to participate in sexual intercourse. The one limitation placed on marital sex by the Puritans was that it must not interfere with religion; on days of fast, for example, sex was denied.[48]

Sexual breaches outside of marriage had to be punished; they were acts against the community and against God. They were not met with surprise or secret gossip, but were expected, given man's frailty since the fall of Adam. Apparently, illicit sexual intercourse was fairly common; many records of offenses survive. This is what would be expected from the high sex ratio, representing a considerable surplus of unattached males. But even intercourse prior to marriage between couples who later married received community censure if it was detected. One sure way of detection was the birth of a child in less than seven months subsequent to the wedding. In these instances, the errant couple had to confess and provide full details concerning the circumstances and nature of their premarital intercourse before the entire congregation. They were then forgiven and the child was protected in the eyes of God.

Servants contributed a separate source of illicit sexual behavior.[49] They lived in the homes of their masters, under contract for a specified number of years. Generally, they could not marry unless the master approved and the spouse could live in the same home. Even servants not bound in this way were usually single. Male servants who worked for wages often quit and set up their own household as soon as they accumulated enough money.

With such a large number of unattached adults, it is only to be expected that they would engage in sexual intercourse. Ordinarily, this could only happen surreptitiously, because of the master's total control over his servants' lives. But many records exist reporting nocturnal escapades of both male and female servants. A further source of illicit sex was between the master and his female servants; many such cases are documented. Apparently there were enough children born to unattached women to arouse community concern about the care of bastard children.[50] In 1668, the General Court of Massachusetts ordered that any man who was legally convicted to be the father of a bastard child would be required to assume the care and maintenance of the child, along with assistance from the mother. The court went on to add, remarkably, that in instances where the court did not satisfactorily establish the identity of the father, the man charged by the woman to be the father should nevertheless be responsible for the child's maintenance, unless he could prove his innocence in court.[51]

Another facet of the sex ratio thesis pertains to the social class, age, racial, and other constraints that are ordinarily reflected in marital practices. When ratios are imbalanced, these may be expected to weaken. Thus we might expect that in the case of the colonies, where men were in considerable oversupply and unable to find a wife, they would ignore the usual social class, age, and racial constraints on long-term relationships with women, including marital relationships. Indeed, we find Captain John Bargrave, a planter in Virginia and investor in the Virginia Company, suggesting in 1623 that social class considerations be ignored in creating marital unions:

> But to the end that love may bee mayntayned, and that theise degrees may not estrange the upper orders from the lower, wee wish that the heires and eldest sonnes of the upper orders may marrie with the daughters of the lower orders, soe to rayse their wives fortunes. And that the daughters of the upper orders being heires may marrye with the sonnes of the lower orders, makeing choice of the most vertuous, soe as vertue may advance both men and woemen to marriages, and that all degrees may bee thereby bound togeather in the bonde of love that none may be scorned but the scorner.[52]

Bargrave also points out the dangers to the company of allowing private estates to be combined through marriage, and suggests that where both parties have estates, one should be required to give up his or her estate and take the surname of the spouse. What is interesting about this, in light of the great scarcity of women, is his suggestion that sometimes the sacrifice may be made by the groom: "Except shee marryeing of a husband soe enamored with her that he shall sell or give away his owne patriotshippe and soe shall take the sirname of his wifes auncester."[53]

Colonial men also responded to the scarcity of women by accepting as marriage partners women of advanced age.[54] No solid information is available on this, although one publicist for the Province of Carolina made the following claim mentioning age:

> If any Maid or single Woman have a desire to go over, they will think themselves in the golden Age, when men paid a Dowry for their Wives; for if they be but civil, and under 50 years of age, some honest man or other, will purchase them for their Wives.[55]

With respect to the racial barrier, during the latter half of the seventeenth century the early French colonists, who had an exceedingly high sex ratio, had no prejudice against alliances with Indian women. This seldom took the form of a formal marriage, but living together occurred frequently. Throughout the eighteenth century, concubinage with young Indian women was the rule in West Canada and Louisiana, as well as in other frontier areas where white women were scarce. Many children emerged from these mixed unions. In some frontier areas with extreme imbalances, many white men married Indian women. These included the Dutch in New Netherlands, and during the early years of the Virginia colony, black women were also involved.

Crossing racial lines was greatest among lower-class whites, especially indentured servants and convicts. Both of these groups had a much higher sex ratio than the rest of the population, and thus were more likely to break through the racial constraints on intermarriage.[56] In the island colonies during the seventeenth century, the surplus of white males apparently encouraged more sexual contact between the races. But in the eighteenth century, when white women were in the majority in the Caribbean region, interracial contact apparently did not occur.[57] This is clearly related to social class constraints; women typically marry up, not down. The only area where white women occasionally married black men was early seventeenth-century New England, when sex ratios were still very high. In general, freedom to cross racial lines was for the most part confined to frontier areas and perhaps a few other restricted areas where sex ratios were extremely high. In the more settled parts of the colonies, fairly strong antagonism toward miscegenation had become established by the end of the seventeenth century.

By the time of the Revolution and afterward, sex ratios in some parts of the colonies had reached a more even balance; women were no longer so scarce. Incoming immigrant populations were no longer predominantly male, and men from the more settled regions continued to migrate westward to the frontiers. This immediately raises the question of whether the lowered sex ratio gave rise to more independence for women in the form of opening up for them roles other than domestic ones. One demographer cites evidence suggesting that the earlier strong emphasis on marriage and family, as well as the suspicious attitudes expressed toward single men, weakened somewhat. After the Revolution, men were more likely to accept women as equals in some respects, such as owning property. Women also demanded more of marriage, showing an increased concern with love and happiness.[58] These changes are consistent with our earlier discussions of low sex ratio societies.

In general, our discussion indicates that the high sex ratios in the colonies greatly enhanced marital opportunities for women. Circumstances that have often worked against marriage, such as plainness, being older than the norm, being a widow, lacking a dowry, or belonging to an ethnic or social class category that was an object of prejudice were apparently of little consequence in the colonies. Desirable women who were single, moreover, received much attention from men and occasionally attracted a settlement of monies or properties to share with the man whom they agreed to marry. In those occasional locales where sex ratios were not high, a smaller proportion of women were married, and fewer widows remarried—in contrast to widowers, who remarried frequently, often choosing younger women.

In the comparatively open society of the colonies, the strong constraints on women that we found in earlier societies, such as an emphasis on virginity, on seclusion, protection, and sheltering, and on prohibiting adultery for married women were less in evidence. Adultery was strongly condemned in New England, but this could be attributed to the Puritans; moreover, New England typically had low sex ratios after it became well established. It seems clear that high sex ratios in open societies provide women with more advantages and fewer constraints on their freedom than do high sex ratios in societies with strong traditions. We turn now to examine sex ratios and their consequences in the frontier regions that emerged during the development of the United States.

THE FRONTIER

What needs to be clear from the outset is that America had many frontiers at many different times. In Colonial times, western New England and western Virginia were frontiers, entered only by the fur trader and the adventurer. After the Revolutionary War, the first great frontier area was bounded by the Allegheny Mountains on the east and by the 98th meridian on the west. The western boundary bisected what are now the Dakotas, Nebraska, and Texas, and included most of the area now covered by Kansas and Oklahoma. The area was similar to the Atlantic coastal plain in climate and topography, heavily timbered except for the prairies of Iowa and Illinois. The earliest trade links into this area were the Ohio and Mississippi Rivers, making New Orleans an important trading center in the late eighteenth and early nineteenth centuries. In 1825, the Erie Canal provided an important link for the Great Lakes area, but it was not until after the mid-nineteenth century that the last railroad links to the east were completed, providing strong competition for water transport.[59]

Just before the middle of the nineteenth century, the remainder of the country began to open up to settlers. This included the Rocky Mountains and the wooded areas of the Pacific coast. The Great Plains area was much less hospitable than the wetter, more fertile plains of the middle west, but the Rocky Mountain area and most of the Pacific coastal areas had ample water. In particular, the absence of wood for fuel was a problem in the Great Plains. While the menace from the Indians had come to an end by 1890, the public lands of the Far West continued to be thrown open to prospective settlers until 1914. Hence there was always a frontier somewhere in the U.S. territory from Colonial times to just before World War I, and it is important to keep in mind which frontier one is referring to in connection with sex ratios and their consequences.

Sex Ratios in the Midwestern
and Western Frontiers

The most general characteristic of sex ratios in early America is that they were highest at the edge of the frontier and lowest in the most settled regions. This occurred in large part because of the greater proportion of males who migrated westward to new lands. We have already seen this phenomenon in the Colonial period; sex ratios were higher in western and northern New England than they were in the eastern parts. And in the South, ratios were higher in the west than in the east. This phenomenon occurred again in the development of the midwestern region of the United States, and in even more exaggerated form in the development of the mountain states to the west, where the principal attractions were gold and silver, and other activities ancillary to mining these ores that held out the prospect of large returns.

Although they have many limitations for our purposes, the U.S. censuses, which began in 1790 and were repeated every ten years, provide us with more systematic information on sex ratios than were available for the colonies. Here we are able to report sex ratios for total populations in particular regions or states. Figure 5.1 provides sex ratios from 1790 to 1900 for four states in the northern part of the midwestern frontier. From east to west, these states are: Ohio, Illinois, Iowa, and Kansas. Their population density in 1900 is given in Figure 5.1 after the name of each state. We can see that the least populated state, Kansas, had the highest sex ratios during the nineteenth century, and that the most populated state, Ohio, had the lowest. Choosing any particular census year, say 1860, we can see the effect of the degree of settlement on sex ratios: Kansas had a ratio of 123, but Ohio only 104. Population density also reflects development: the lower the density (18 persons per square mile in Kansas versus 102 in Ohio), the more frontierlike the state.

Also clear from Figure 5.1 is that within any large region like the midwestern frontier, considerable variations in the sex ratio occur. This limits our discussion to dealing with fairly broad generalizations, since social effects or consequences of sex ratios are difficult to pinpoint by state. Yet this is consistent with our strategy for earlier times. The problem is mitigated by dealing with sufficiently contrasting ratios and large or even dramatic effects. A case in point is the difference in the ratios for the far western region, consisting of the Mountain and Pacific states, and those for the midwestern frontier. The attraction of the latter was fertile farmland, and judging from the sex ratios taken from even the earliest censuses, it appears that the majority of immigrants to the midwest consisted of families who came to settle on the land. The median of all the ratios in Figure 5.1 is only about 110, so we can consider the frontier effect to be relatively short-lived in this region.

The Mountain and Pacific states had as a major attraction the lure of gold and silver mining, and later, other ores. Along with the miners came mer-

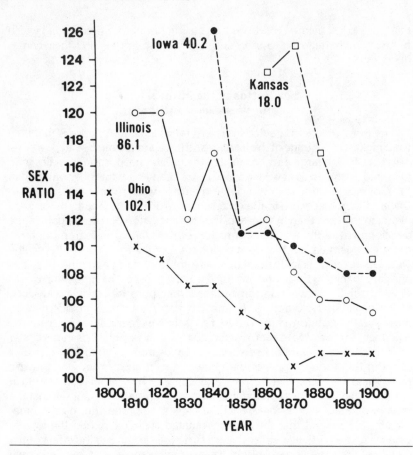

Figure 5.1   **Sex Ratios in the Nineteenth Century for Selected States in the Midwestern Frontier Region**

SOURCE: U.S. Bureau of the Census, *Historical Statistics of the United States, Colonial Times to 1970,* Bicentennial ed., part I. Washington, DC: Government Printing Office.

chants, saloonkeepers, entertainers, wagon freighters, steamshipmen, stage-coachmen, and food producers, all hopeful of capitalizing on the free flow of precious metals and money.[60] Much of the land in this region did not lend itself to growing crops, so it was not especially attractive to farmers. Aside from mining, it was more suited to grazing cattle on the open range. Presumably because of these circumstances, immigrants to the western frontier contained a much greater proportion of men. Figure 5.2 provides sex ratios for the half-dozen western states whose development was greatly accentuated by the discovery of gold and silver.

From Figure 5.2, it is immediately clear that sex ratios in the Far West were astronomically higher than those for the midwestern region. All of these states started out with ratios of 300 or more. California in 1850 had a ratio of 1228, and Colorado in 1860 had one of 1659! Moreover, sex ratios re-

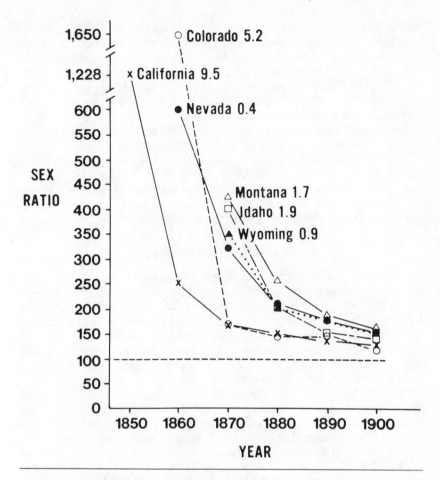

Figure 5.2 Sex Ratios in the Nineteenth Century for Selected States in the Western Frontier Region

SOURCE: U.S. Bureau of the Census, *Historical Statistics of the United States, Colonial Times to 1970,* Bicentennial ed., part I. Washington, DC: Government Printing Office.

mained far above 100 for at least several decades. By 1900, these states still had ratios as high as or considerably higher than the highest ratios previously reported for the midwestern frontier. We can anticipate that sex ratios on the western frontier will have had far stronger effects than those in the Midwest.

Some historians have opined that the high sex ratios and other demographic attributes found on the frontiers did not last long, perhaps less than a decade. This impression was probably created by a well-known demographic study of frontier America from the period 1800 to 1840.[61] But the findings leading to this conclusion were based on a study of five counties located in the South and five in what we have called the midwestern frontier. Neither of these test areas are relevant to the later frontiers in the Far West, where the results were very different. From Figure 5.2, it is clear that for the six states in the Far West, sex ratios remained high for several decades within the period from 1850 to 1900. In 1900, moreover, these states still had ratios ranging from 125 to 162, and that covers a 50-year period for California. Even in the midwestern frontier area, as can be seen from Figure 5.1, the initial sex ratios, ranging from 114 to 126 for the various states, also stayed well above 100 for several decades.

Even more decisive is a comprehensive demographic study of 88 frontier counties located in states and territories ranging from Lake Michigan to the Pacific Ocean for the period from 1840 to 1860. The average sex ratio was 125 for the general population, and for ages 20-39, the ratios ranged from 148 to 165. Moreover, these ratios actually increased over the 20-year period! It seems clear that sex ratio imbalances in the two frontier regions discussed here were lasting enough to have appreciable effects.[62]

The Midwestern Frontier

The rich, fertile land of this region, with its agricultural potential, its undeveloped, primitive nature, and the balanced sex ratios, with only about a 10 percent excess of men, combined to create a distinctive set of circumstances for women. Most of the original sources for the life of women in pioneer days come from diaries, commentaries, notes and observations of a few of the pioneers themselves, or from travelers. Many of these have been assembled in a social history of women in the West.[63] Several types of migrants to this frontier were noted: backwoodsmen or squatters, hunters using some agriculture, and finally, farmers.[64] Hardships were greatest for women accompanying the first types. Backwoodsmen's cabins were described by one observer writing in 1819 as "miserable holes having one room only, and in that one room, all cook, eat, sleep, breed, and die, male and female all together."[65]

The scarcity of goods and labor on the frontier greatly affected the lives of women. Many men desired wives because of the domestic goods and services they could provide and the farm chores they could perform. Observers described women as spinning and weaving clothes for the whole family, and cooking for them at great risk in open fireplaces. Stoves did not become common until the 1840s.[66] When there were dairy cattle, women did all the milking, until about 1820.[67] Given the absence of any commercial accommodations, it was an accepted but burdensome custom to accommodate travelers.[68]

Perhaps the most arduous task of all was the continual bearing and raising of children under primitive conditions. Effective birth control was nonexistent; in fact, children were welcome because of the scanty population and inadequate labor supply. Many pioneer women were pregnant throughout most or all of their childbearing years. This situation was aggravated by the long-term absences of husbands. They were frequently gone in search of new land or minerals, or on hunting or trading trips. At these times, the entire burden of maintaining herself and her children fell to the wife.

It might be thought that wives of professional men, such as physicians and lawyers, would be comparatively well off on the frontier. Yet the frontier made demands on the husband that often affected the wife's circumstances unfavorably. The sparsely populated area meant that professional men had to serve very large areas, so that they, too, were often away from home for days or weeks at a time.

The description of the hardworking, industrious pioneer woman contrasts with that of midwestern frontiersmen. While not providing statistical evidence, one writer believed that the traditional image of the hardworking pioneer (perhaps generated by the New England image of the Puritans) was not confirmed by the behavior of many flesh-and-blood frontiersmen. He describes men spending days at a time in idleness in small towns, sometimes drinking and gambling. He thought it not uncommon for men to go off on leisurely hunting trips, leaving their wives home to care for the children and cope with the problems of staying well or even alive in rugged areas.[69] It is impossible to tell the extent of idleness versus industry on the part of the midwestern pioneers without statistical data. But no doubt some women suffered by virtue of having such husbands.

Women were not accorded the deference and respect that they later received in the Far West. Fathers and sons might eat first, waited on by the mother and daughter(s) who only got to eat their own meal after their service.[70] Women lacked social diversions and frequently felt lonely in the absence of civilized company.[71] But because unattached women were not easy to find, they were in great demand and had high status. Many comments are already familiar to us from the Colonial times: Even the least attractive woman could get a husband, and it was almost impossible to keep a servant girl—she tended to be snatched up as a bride. But while it was easy to find a husband, the circumstances of married life were not necessarily pleasant. Often the practicalities of frontier life meant a hard and arduous life for a wife and mother. A man could not farm without the help of a couple of sturdy sons and a wife who could feed the hogs, grow vegetables, milk the cows, make clothes, cook meals, and keep house, in addition to helping at times with the crops. That life on the midwestern frontier was seen as difficult and arduous by Easterners is illustrated by a song popular in 1840, entitled "To the Prairie I'll Fly Not." The song describes the rough life and terrors of the prairie from the point of view of an Eastern woman emphatically rejecting a suitor.[72]

Unattached women on the midwestern frontier, however, benefited from the scarcity of labor, especially women's labor. Women who worked for pay at tasks not normally performed by men received high wages. Female servants were in tremendous demand, and those doing laundry or dressmaking were able to extract high prices. The labor scarcity also made it possible for women to do men's work for high pay.

Another familiar feature typifying societies where women are greatly desired is the derogation of the bachelor. The *Western Citizen,* a Paris, Kentucky, newspaper said of him in 1824: "A bachelor is a sort of whimsical being which nature never intended to create. He was formed out of the odds and ends of what materials were left over after the great work was over."[73]

While Kentucky had a sex ratio of only 105 in 1820, Paris was in the western part of the state, and was very probably a frontier town with a much higher ratio. Moves were also made to tax bachelors, and some desperate souls resorted to advertising for wives. One unnamed observer describes the plight of single men in frontier Tennessee:

> In 1824 there was no society worthy of the name. There were no ladies to visit. Indian women and black girls were in abundance; but not a respectable white woman was to be seen once a month. Two or three respectable men married Indian women, with the excuse that there were no white women about. In the Chattanooga region, some Scotch settlers courted and married Indian girls.[74]

One feature characterizing the midwestern frontier is not ordinarily typical of high sex ratio societies: Young women received almost as much education as young men in most of the state, unlike the more settled East.[75] Ordinarily in high sex ratio societies, women are less apt to be educated. This has been borne out in virtually all of the societies we have discussed. And yet a good reason for this exception is not hard to find: The great labor scarcity of the frontier meant that young men could not be spared to carry their education very far; in fact, as boys they were almost inevitably apprenticed to follow an occupational pursuit similar to that of their father—typically farming or hunting. That young women were more restricted to domestic roles meant that on successful farms, they could be spared for the time it took to get an education. So it is not surprising that frontier daughters equaled or outdistanced frontier sons in the amount of education they received. Many of these educated women became school teachers, especially after normal schools for training teachers began to flourish in the midnineteenth century.

In sum, what stands out in the midwestern region during the last half of the nineteenth century is the development of its rich and fertile farmland, which required hard work and much privation.

Sex ratios of 110 or so were not sufficient to create favorable conditions for married women, who were in great demand for their domestic services and productivity, as well as for farm chores. Certainly single women and widows had no difficulty finding a husband, but along with a spouse went the assumption of a considerable domestic burden under unfavorable conditions. The slight shortage of women made them desirable as wives and mothers, but did not seem to create any special status for them. This is consistent with our thesis that sex ratios have to be considerably above 100 before they have dramatic social consequences. We turn now to look at the western frontier.

The Western Frontier

We have already noted that the western frontier in the nineteenth century had very high sex ratios. Roughly speaking, it was often the case that there was only one woman for every two men (see Figure 5.2). The high sex ratio societies that we discussed in earlier chapters, however, differed in a crucial way from the western frontier: they were typically tightly controlled, traditional societies. We noted that high ratios in such societies often work to the disadvantage of women. We saw in Chapter 2, for example, that in Greece, when sex ratios were high, women were in some respects treated as chattel.

They were virtually the property of men, who had strong control over them; they had few rights of their own.

The western frontier provides an opportunity to examine a high sex ratio society in the absence of tradition. With the continual influx of migrants, the sense of growth and change, and of transience, there were few supports for traditional ways of doing things. The society was a wide-open one, with few restraints. Under these circumstances, we might expect to find that women would be treated well, and that few constraints would be placed on their actions.

Before looking at the larger western society, we have an opportunity to look at the situation of women in a traditional, closed society in the West, created by some unusual circumstances: the Chinese-Americans.[76] It will serve as a sharp contrast with the larger, open society, although it appeared toward the end of the frontier period, in the latter half of the nineteenth century and extended well into the twentieth century. From 1850 to 1882, Chinese laborers were brought to this country largely for the purpose of building the transcontinental railroad. Nearly all were male, and although most of these were married, Chinese custom required that married men traveling abroad leave their wives at home with the husband's parents. From 1850 up to the Chinese Exclusion Act of 1882, only about 9,000 Chinese women came to this country, compared with over 100,000 Chinese men. Many of these women returned to China or died during the next few decades. As a result, in the last few decades of the nineteenth century, the average sex ratio for Chinese-Americans was roughly 2,000.[77]

The Chinese-American society differed sharply from the open society characterizing the frontier and later America. Three sources of community organization in mainland China operated in a similar fashion in America. These were: *hui kuan,* based on village affiliation; the clan, based on kinship; and the secret society, or *tong.* Cohesiveness among the Chinese in America was further intensified through the isolation resulting from the language barrier and racial prejudice.

Some of the scarce Chinese women in America were prostitutes in mining or railroad camps, and those in cities were mainly in brothels. Prostitution was often highly organized and controlled by the tongs, which brought Chinese women to this country on the pretense of a proxy marriage or through outright kidnapping. Only an occasional woman was married to a Chinese-American of means; such women were sheltered and protected to a degree that almost amounted to imprisonment.[78] Thus we see here another instance where a strong traditional social structure meant that scarce women were mere chattel, severely constrained and guarded, and very tightly controlled so as to serve the needs of men.

The example of the Chinese-Americans highlights through contrast a significant feature of the frontier: its openness and looseness of structure. This was probably accentuated by the large number of frontier men who were more interested in making a fortune than in settling down. Miners participating in the various gold rushes were prime examples, as was the large number of unattached men who had migrated to the frontier areas simply because of the job opportunities in these labor-scarce regions. Often these men had only temporary, though well-paid employment that ended when a project was completed (for instance, mining or building a railroad). Usually they were living under very rough conditions (in tents). Instead of building a community, they more often thought of making a lot of money and getting back to civilization. The presence of so many men with this orientation meant relatively few community controls over the behavior of men and women. The western frontier was a high sex ratio society lacking in tradition, and we might expect more interest in women for casual sex or for entertainment than as wives and mothers.

In some mining camps and towns, women were so scarce that the mere sight of one was a joyous occasion. One anecdote makes the point:

> The first woman to arrive at the "Coyotte Diggins" of California apparently reached the camp with her husband one night unnoticed by the miners, for the next morning these men were much surprised to find the covered wagon and a washing hung out to dry. Since among the suspended garments were several that only a female would wear, they immediately concluded that a woman was in the party, and soon a large crowd of miners had gathered. Upon drawing back the wagon curtain, the husband was at first greatly alarmed, but the leaders of the assembled group assured him that they intended no harm, and only desired to obtain a good glimpse of the lady. She was extremely hesitant about stepping from the wagon, and hence, as an inducement, the miners raised a fund which actually amounted to between two and three thousand dollars. She was told that it would be hers if she would walk out so that all could see her, and receive it. Finally, after stepping out several times only to run back, the woman summoned sufficient courage to reach the spot where the leader of the men was holding the coins.[79]

Given life under such harsh, primitive conditions, and the unsettled nature of many of the temporary communities, diversions were naturally overvalued. Drinking, gambling, and all forms of entertainment were popular on the western frontier, and the scarcity of women played a part in making the most of exploiting for monetary gain, in a variety of ways. For example, once the railroad connection between the East and Denver was completed, dance halls were established with young women imported from the East who cooperated with their employers in extracting money from nearby mining and railroad camps. In fact, stores, saloons, gambling houses, and dance halls were put on railroad cars and moved as rail construction ended in one area and began in another, leading to the origin of the phrase, "hell on wheels."[80]

In all of the areas where a large population of miners collected, saloons, gambling houses, and entertainment halls quickly appeared. Many of these made use of women to attract large numbers of customers. Here was the situation in Denver:

> These glorified saloons and gambling halls had fifteen to twenty numbers a night of dancing, singing, magic, and farce. Another attraction was the bevy of pretty, flashily dressed girls who allowed male patrons to buy them beer at a dollar a bottle and wine or champagne at from two to five dollars. For each sale

the girl received a check from the waiter and immediately thrust it into her stockings; these slips showed the management whether she was to be retained at her job. Some of these women sold men keys to their hotel rooms for three or five dollars and few of the dupes later had the courage to complain that there was no such room number.[81]

Diversion was so highly valued that entertainment did not have to be skilled, and was often outrageously amateurish. But at the same time, serious entertainment was also highly valued. Shakespearian and other plays, ballet, and opera were successfully presented, even in rough mining camps.[82] Touring companies with versatile repertories traveled from town to town and camp to camp, with great success.[83] As soon as it could be built, every prosperous mining community had its entertainment hall, and the larger ones went still further. For example, Virginia City, Nevada, the site of the famous Comstock Lode, built a Grand Opera House that still stands today as a tourist attraction, and the riches of the community attracted the best opera stars of the day for performances.

Not all men desired women for frivolous purposes. The opening of public lands during the nineteenth century, especially the Homestead Act of 1862, which offered immigrants 260 acres of land for only incidental fees, meant that many young men came west to settle on the land, and many of these desired a wife. In many of the Oregon settlements, the only women present were married. Various attempts were made to attract young single women to far western frontiers, but efforts at group recruiting generally failed, as they had during Colonial times.[84] Individual men advertised for Eastern women who might want to marry, and made extensive inquiries of friends and relatives in the attempt to find a woman, but of course little is known of the success of such efforts. As in Colonial times, women were thought to have an important civilizing influence, and newspapers and other sources emphasized their value in this respect.

Our review of the western frontier indicates that very high sex ratios greatly intensified the desire of many men for a woman's company and companionship, and often led them to extend themselves greatly in a variety of ways, whether merely to obtain a brief glimpse of a woman, to watch a professional performer, to drink with a bar girl, or to find a wife. While this need born of scarcity was often exploited for money, both by women and by their employers, it also may be seen as contributing to the deference and respect shown toward women by western frontiersmen, which persisted long enough to become a tradition and which can be seen in somewhat exaggerated form in fictional films having settings in the Wild West.

SOUTHERN BELLES AND NEW ENGLAND SPINSTERS

Two regions from early America that differed appreciably in sex ratios, thus lending themselves to useful comparison, are New England and the South. New England, especially in its more populated regions, had characteristically low sex ratios even while still a colony.[85] These persisted after the

Revolutionary War and through the nineteenth and twentieth centuries, and still prevail at the present time. During much of our history, these low sex ratios were brought about and maintained by the continual drain of young men seeking their fortunes on successive frontiers to the west, and also by the selective migration of women into New England to work in the textile mills during the nineteenth century.

Both regions were alike in that they represented more settled areas, compared with the raw territories, though they differed in other important respects besides the sex ratio. The fathers of New England were of stern Puritan stock, whereas the early immigrants to the South were varied in religious outlook. The South was a plantation economy, producing primarily cotton and tobacco, while New England became a manufacturing area, principally textiles. The South was rural, having few large concentrations of population, while New England's population was more urban, having many people living in or near small towns, with a few large cities. In 1850, Massachusetts and Rhode Island were over 50 percent urban, while the most populous state in the South, Virginia, was only 8 percent urban. The only southern state with an appreciable urban population was Maryland, with 32 percent.[86]

Of special interest for the sex ratio question is the image of Southern women that emerged in the plantation society of the South. In spite of the greatly varied character of the different southern states, a coherent view of home and family and woman's place in it became central to the subculture of that region.[87] Of course, this image was held up primarily for women of the upper classes or those with aspirations in that direction; the poor farm woman, servant, or slave was not expected to conform to the image. As we will see, the image of the Southern woman had most of the features of the traditional role of women that we have already discussed in connection with other societies, although this role also had some distinctive features.

The New England woman presented a less uniform image. While the Victorian role ascribed to many New England wives had much in common with that of the Southern lady, certain differences stand out. Even more important is the less complete agreement in New England on the proper role for women. If nontraditional roles were frowned on, the traditional role had less strict limits and more facets, which made it possible for women to suit their role somewhat more to their individual tastes.

We turn first to discuss the demography of the sex ratios of these two regions, and follow with an examination of their possible correspondence to the roles of Southern and New England women.

Sex Ratios in the South and New England

For the southern colonies, census data are fragmentary. As we noted earlier, during the initial colonization sex ratios there were very high. While these fell to more moderate levels and reached a rough balance by 1750, they persisted beyond this point for a much longer period in the South than in New England,[88] staying above 100 for another century, almost until the Civil War. This is shown by U.S. Census data which were regularly collected each decade, starting in 1790.

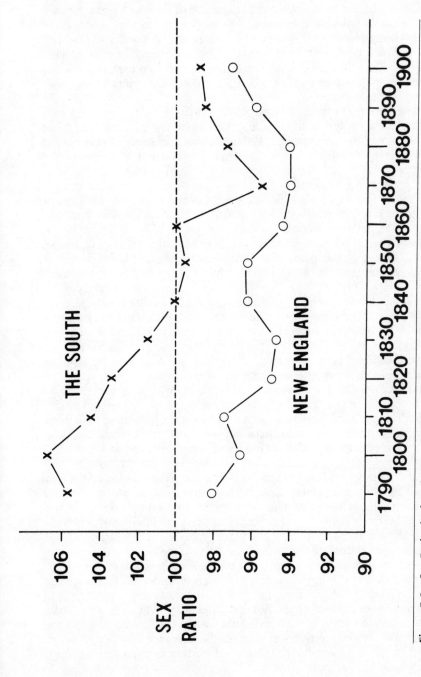

Figure 5.3   Sex Ratios in the Nineteenth Century for the South and New England

SOURCE: U.S. Bureau of the Census, *Historical Statistics of the United States, Colonial Times to 1970,*
Bicentennial ed., part I. Washington, DC: Government Printing Office.

Figure 5.3 provides sex ratios from 1790 to 1900, calculated from the U.S. Census figures for the more settled, populous areas of the two regions, which of course have lower sex ratios than the frontier portions. These areas are represented for New England by Massachusetts, Rhode Island, Connecticut, and New Hampshire, and for the South by Virginia, North Carolina, South Carolina, Maryland, and Georgia. The more settled parts of these two regions are emphasized because it was there that the social patterns under discussion were represented.

These ratios for the total white population indicate that the South entered the nineteenth century with ratios appreciably above 100, and that these dropped very slowly, not reaching 100 until about midcentury. New England entered the nineteenth century with ratios below 100 that fell several points further and reached a low point after the Civil War. The difference between New England and the South is not great—less than 10 points. Yet the sex ratios in the South typically reflected a slight excess of men, while those in New England reflected a shortage of men. After the Civil War, New England continued to have sex ratios below 100, but now the South, too, fell below 100, with a particular shortage of men at the ages most suitable for marriage.

In Chapter 1 we called attention to the fact that age and social class constraints on marriage appreciably worsen marital opportunities for women. We will discuss this further in Chapter 7, dealing with the modern period, where more detailed census breakdowns are available. Worth noting here is that, because of these marital constraints, sex ratios do not need to be much below 100 to have social effects. Thus, the difference of 5-10 points between New England and the South from the time of the American Revolution into the mid-nineteenth century seems worth examining, especially since it shifts the balance from one gender to another by crossing 100.

One final point is that we would dearly like to know what the sex ratios were among the upper classes, although, of course, these data are not available. Their importance is that the Southern traditions pertaining to women and family, as well as to relationships between unmarried young men and women, were largely a product of the aristocratic plantation society. In particular, we suspect, but cannot demonstrate, that the situation resembled that of southern France and Spain in the medieval period referred to earlier (see Chapter 3), where many men desired to move up in social class by marrying a noble lady. If this were also the case in the South, then the population sex ratio of 105 or so would not be indicative of the special demand for plantation daughters as marriage partners. Considering the continued growth of the United States through migration, in addition to the lack of historical family records in such a new country, it is reasonable to expect that the ranks of men interested in winning plantation daughters as brides would be considerably swelled by adventurers and pretenders whose true identity either could not be ascertained or did not really matter, providing that they had achieved a niche in the New World. This, then, would create both demographic and societal parallels between southern France and Spain, as described earlier, and the romantic culture of the aristocratic plantation society in the South.

The Antebellum South

As is usual for historical times, we know most about women in the upper social classes and very little about the average or poor woman. But we can at least determine the extent to which the knowledge we have fits our expected patterns. We will find that the South, up to the Civil War, had all of the characteristics of a high sex ratio society—in spite of the fact that in the nineteenth century, ratios were not much above 100. But what is probably of greater importance is that the plantation society of the South had its origins in Colonial times, where, for example, in Virginia, the proportion of men to women was initially as great as 6 to 1. Thus, this society had its beginning long before the first U.S. Census of 1790, during a period where sex ratios were probably no lower than 150, and often considerably higher.

We have already indicated that sex ratios by themselves do not bring about societal effects, but rather that they combine with a variety of other social, economic, and political conditions to produce the consequent effects on the roles of men and women and the relationship between them. One possible perspective here is that the plantation society of the South was shaped by the aristocratic origins of the plantation owners, along with their desires to establish themselves in the New World and to achieve recognition from representatives of the mother country. This would help to account for the emphasis on honor, courtesy, good manners, and gracious living. It also underscores the point that our expected patterns apply to upper-class men and women of the South and to those who aspired to enter such classes. The whole cultural complex is accentuated further by the presence of two underclasses: indentured servants and slaves. Neither were present in appreciable numbers in New England.

The rural nature of the South and its economy is also important here, for it would contribute to a homogeneous culture centering around the plantations, in contrast to the greater heterogeneity and diversity found in the cosmopolitan cultures of urban centers. Moreover, once established, such a society would be more resistant to change because of the isolation provided by the rural setting, even when sex ratios were no longer so high. It was not until after the Civil War that the plantation society of the South disintegrated, and even then, views of Southern womanhood persisted in some quarters into the twentieth century.

Southern belles and ladies were key figures in plantation society. In literary journals, novels, sermons, and other writings and speeches, the antebellum Southern lady was described by men as the "most perfect example of womankind yet on earth." One historian has neatly captured the image:

This marvelous creation was described as a submissive wife whose reason for being was to love, honor, obey, and occasionally amuse her husband, to bring up his children and manage her household. Physically weak, and "formed for the less laborious occupations," she depended upon male protection. To secure this protection she was endowed with the capacity to "create a magic spell" over any man in her vicinity. She was timid and modest, beautiful and graceful, "the most fascinating being in creation . . . . the delight and charm of every circle she moves in.[89] Part of her charm lay in her *innocence*. The less a woman knew of life, Ellen Glasgow once remarked bitterly, the better she was supposed to be able to deal with it. Her mind was not logical, but in the absence of reasoning capacity her sensibility and intuition were highly developed. It was, indeed, to her advantage that the "play of instincts and of the feelings is not cramped by the controlling influence of logic and reason." She was capable of acute perceptions about human relationships, and was a creature of tact, discernment, sympathy, and compassion. It was her nature to be self-denying, and she was given to suffering in silence, a characteristic said to endear her to men. Less endearing, perhaps, but no less natural, was her piety and her tendency to "restrain man's natural vice and immorality." She was thought to be "most deeply interested in the success of every scheme which curbs the passions and enforces a true morality." She was a natural teacher, and wise counselor to her husband and children.[90]

Home and the family were honored and upheld on all sides: in the pulpit, in literature, in speeches of politicians, they were the very core of a man's honor. Moreover, maintenance of home and family were viewed in large part as the only legitimate creative task that could be undertaken by a woman. It was the Southern lady who brought up her sons to be gentlemen and her daughters to be ladies. As in so many other traditional societies, her sphere of influence was supposed to be limited strictly to the home and to domestic affairs. Deference to the authority of males, particularly her husband, was to be absolute. From earliest childhood, Southern girls were trained to the ideals of perfection and submission. A magazine for children published in Charleston had stories filled with pious, obedient little girls, and the popular boarding schools for young girls emphasized devotion, obedience, and modesty.

A typical example of male thinking on the proper role of women in relation to men is taken from the letter of a college president to his newly married daughter. Deference to authority is the central theme:

The wife's conduct alone, he asserted, determined the happiness or misery of a marriage. She must resolve at the outset never to oppose her husband, never to show displeasure, no matter what he might do. A man had a right to expect his wife to place perfect confidence in his judgment and to believe that he always knew best. "A difference with your husband ought to be considered the greatest calamity," wrote her father, adding that a woman who permitted differences to occur could expect to lose her husband's love and all hope of happiness. He concluded with the usual injunction that she should be amiable, sweet, prudent, and devoted, that she should regulate her servants with a kind but firm hand, cultivate her mind by reading history and not corrupt it with novels, and manage her domestic concerns with neatness, order, economy, and judgment.[91]

A clearer example of the strong socialization pressures on young women to conform to the image desired by men could not be found. Of course, the example is not an isolated one; such prescriptions for young women abound in virtually every extant source for the antebellum period. Especially noteworthy here is the strong emphasis on the authority of men, particularly fathers and husbands: Women are expected to be respectful, deferent, sub-missive, and obedient. A clash of wills between a husband and wife is consid-ered disastrous.

This is consistent with our sex ratio patterns; we are apt to find strong conformity pressures on women whenever the sex ratio is high, with women in short supply. These pressures usually take the form of constraints on women's freedom. Purity, chastity, and submissiveness, with great depen-dence on men, becomes the norm for women. They are to be protected and guarded, their fate decided by men.

We saw in Chapter 2 that high sex ratios in classical Athens were also associated with strong male authority. Women there were in some respects chattels; daughters were the property of their fathers, and later, their hus-bands. Women had few rights before Athenian law; they had to be repre-sented by a husband, father, or guardian in order to receive any consider-ation. This was not so with the low sex ratios in Sparta. Women there had more independence. Thus, if we assume that this dependence of the antebel-lum Southern woman on male authority, along with her other supposed attributes, was established during the early high sex ratio period and per-sisted even when sex ratios dropped to more modest levels, we have a pat-tern consistent with the other high sex ratio societies discussed.

Relationships between men and women, gentlemen and ladies in the South were characterized by another feature we have encountered when sex ratios were high—the romantic view of women as paragons of virtue and beauty, requiring chivalrous, tender attention and protection. The medi-eval period saw a similar emergence of the complex of romantic love, with the appearance of the troubadours, love poetry, and the chivalrous service of knights to their ladies (see Chapter 3). The image of Southern belles and ladies had as salient features charm, beauty , and graciousness. In Chapter 4 we found that another high sex ratio society, that of Orthodox Jews, while similar in assigning the traditional domestic role to women, specifically downgraded charm and beauty. Perhaps the difference here is one of social class. The Southern image is derived from the upper classes, but Jewish people have been the object of persecution throughout much of history and have mostly been poor. The image of the domestic, hardworking Jewish wife in whom charm and beauty are unimportant is best illustrated by the late nineteenth- and early twentieth-century eastern European shtetl cul-ture, where Jewish families were poor, and where both husbands and wives had to work hard to maintain themselves and their children (see Chapter 4). This suggests that the romantic tradition embellished by formalities and rit-uals is more apt to appear among the upper classes. The Southern romantic tradition is best represented by the plantation aristocracy and contrasts sharply with the blunt and pragmatic manners of the New England Yankee of the same time period.

We have identified the image of the Southern woman with the projected desires of men; the description fits what they see as an ideal. We might expect that while women may try to shape themselves in the direction of this ideal, and even be partially successful, they would in actuality fail to live up to it and, moreover, would resent the constant pressure to be such paragons. One historian has cogently argued that this is indeed the case.[92] The actual lives of Southern women were fraught with difficulties. The change from courted belle with many suitors to plantation lady with a lord-and-master husband was something of a shock. Suddenly a girl not yet out of her teens had to take charge of a large household and its servants, be responsible for the feeding, care, and health of all the plantation slaves, as well as give attention to the constant demands for gracious hospitality toward the many guests who stopped overnight.

> No matter how large or wealthy the establishment, the mistress was expected to understand not only the skills of spinning, weaving, and sewing, but also gardening, care of poultry, care of the sick, and all aspects of food preparation from the sowing of seed to the appearance of the final product on the table. Fine ladies thought nothing of supervising hog butchering on the first cold days in fall, or of drying fruits and vegetables for the winter. They made their own yeast, lard, and soap, set their own hens, and were expected to be able to make with equal skill a rough dress for a slave or a ball gown for themselves. It was customary for the mistress to rise at five or six, and to be in the kitchen when the cook arrived to "overlook" all the arrangements for the day. A Virginia gentleman's bland assertion that "a considerable portion of her life must be spent in the nursery and the sickroom" was a simple description of reality.[93]

Wealth and a large plantation did not relieve the Southern mistress; it simply meant a larger retinue to look after. Wives whose husbands had smaller plantations had to do more of the actual work themselves, so their task and role was different only in kind, not in quantity. Similarly, the town-dwelling wife, with only a few slaves, was busy making clothes, cleaning, tending the vegetable garden, and supervising food-getting, meal preparation, and care of the many children. The reality is summed up succinctly:

> The real life of the Southern lady was more varied and more demanding than the fantasies of Southern men would suggest. She became, as the myth assured her she must, a wife and mother as soon as the opportunity offered. Thereafter, she was likely to work hard for the rest of her life, having a baby every year or so, developing in the process of her experience a steely self-control, and the knowledge that the work she did was essential and gave meaning to her life.[94]

For some Southern women, the romantic myth *was* partly realized in marriage, judging from personal documents that have survived.[95] But for most, while we would not expect open rebellion, we would anticipate private doubts, resentment, and anger. Evidence of discontent is widespread among letters and diaries that are available from the antebellum period. Some women likened themselves to slaves, and there was a saying that the mistress of a plantation was the most complete slave on it.[96] A particular source of resentment was the husband's liaisons with his slave women. Mary Chestnut wrote:

A magnate who runs a hideous black harem with its consequences under the same roof with his lovely white wife, and his beautiful accomplished daughters . . . poses as the model of all human virtues to these poor women who God and the laws have given him. From the height of his awful majesty, he scolds and thunders at them, as if he never did wrong in his life.[97]

Ladies could tell you who was the father of mulatto children in any household but their own. Of particular concern was venereal disease, contracted by the husband from his slave women and passed on to his wife, who did not have recourse to modern medical treatment or knowledge. In addition, there was the resentment of the double standard, requiring women to suppress or, more strongly, to *deny* their sexuality. A review of available personal documents concludes that women were not the asexual creatures that the idealized image made them out to be, and that they often resented having to deny their own sexuality.[98]

Like many other high sex ratio societies, emphasis on the traditional domestic role included the beliefs that women were intellectually inferior and that they would benefit little from education. Boarding school and seminaries were for the purpose of teaching women social graces and domestic skills, not for stretching their intellect, which was thought to be rather weak. And marriage in the teens further cut off possibilities for higher education. This too was a source of discontent, often voiced privately by women. As the nineteenth century progressed, however, many college presidents challenged the prevailing view and suggested that both men and women would be better off if women received more education.

It is clear from our discussion that after it was well-established as a colony and up until the Civil War, the South had the characteristics ordinarily associated with a high sex ratio society. Consistent with the sex ratio thesis, the image held up for womanhood was the traditional domestic one. Special emphasis was placed on submissiveness to the authority of the male— father, husband, guardians, and male authorities in general. Deference, respect, and obedience toward males were required. An integral part of the image was that women were incompetent in affairs of the world outside of the home, and in fact that they lacked the intellectual capacity to participate in or make valid judgments concerning worldly affairs.

These aspects of the image have much in common with those in other high sex ratio societies, such as some primitive societies, classical Greece, and some parts of early medieval Europe. A further facet of the image is the emphasis on beauty, grace, and charm, and its association with courting the Southern belle. These attributes were important for the Southern lady, too, who was expected to maintain a gracious, hospitable home in which guests were entertained and charmed. This is comparable to the medieval image of women in southern France and Spain, with its emphasis on chivalry and romance. This particular feature is absent from the traditional image of the Orthodox Jewish wife as represented in the eastern European shtetl culture, which specifically denigrates beauty and charm (see Chapter 4). The romantic love complex, when it appears, seems to be associated mainly with the upper social classes. In the next section, however, we will discover that it was not a prominent feature of the low sex ratio society of New England, even in the upper classes.

We have limited ourselves to the antebellum South in our discussion of the Southern lady. The Civil War shattered the economy of the South, as well as many of its cherished traditions and beliefs. Roles change when those who enact them are placed in new settings or circumstances that require them to behave in ways contrary to normal expectations. The war itself thrust women into emergency situations of all imaginable kinds, including many that they had formerly left only to men, and which certainly were incompatible with the image of the Southern lady. In the devastated South after the war, many women were forced to earn a living. With the passage of time, many turned to enterprises that had been unthinkable earlier. They went to college or obtained professional training, they found employment in the expanding towns or cities, they formed women's clubs having serious purposes, and they fought for the vote and for other causes that were liberating for women.[99] But we will not discuss the postwar South in any detail because, while the sex ratio dropped precipitously as a result of the war, and was undoubtedly especially imbalanced at the ages when men and women are most eligible for marriage, there were many other factors besides imbalanced sex ratios that surely played a part in changing women's roles. These included the shift from a rural society to a more urban one, a rebuilding of the economy in new directions, and a shattered subculture. We turn instead to look at New England, which had low sex ratios throughout all but its earliest history as a colony.

New England Wives and Spinsters

We have repeatedly noted the importance of the workplace in relation to the effects of high or low sex ratios. Its importance has intensified over the last two centuries of American history, so it becomes necessary to identify those economic changes that affected women.[100] During the Colonial period and for the rest of the eighteenth century, production was largely centered in the home. This meant that often the whole family—husband, wife, children, relatives, and servants—was engaged in productive work at home. This included activities that might center around a farm, or it might involve a craft of some sort, such as making leather products or repairing wagons. In addition, almost every home, whether rural or urban, was involved in spinning yarn, weaving, sewing, and tailoring, and these were typically female tasks. Food production and preparation were, of course, centered in the home. All these tasks, added to the continual bearing and care of children, meant that scarcely any married women were to have any responsibility outside of the home and, moreover, that unmarried sons and daughters were needed at home. The saying "A woman's work is never done," would certainly have been appropriate for Colonial America and for the several decades succeeding the American Revolutionary War. In spite of this daily life of industry and hard work, the tasks of women were considered secondary to those of men.

Men were considered to be the providers. Men bought and worked the land, or led craft production.[101]

A few years after the American Revolution and the establishment of independence, certain features of the economy in New England began to change in a way that affected the central role of women, so that by 1835, the economy had a mercantile and commercial base. Merchant capitalism began to produce standardized goods on a larger scale and at lower cost. This widened markets and reduced the importance of home production of goods. The New England shipping trade flourished and worked hand in hand with merchants, leading to additional business enterprises such as shipbuilding, warehousing, and banking. This mercantile activity served as a transition and preparatory period for the further development of manufacturing, especially of the factory system. During this transition period, some entrepreneurs contracted with families to produce certain goods or perform certain tasks in goods production. Ultimately, they marketed the finished product or served as intermediary wholesalers.[102]

The impact on the home of this new commercial activity was important. Spinning at home was no longer done simply to meet the needs of one's own family; those who needed outside income could now spin yarn at home for a meagre income. Because so many unmarried females engaged in this activity, both in England and the United States, the meaning of the term *spinster* shifted from "female spinner" to "unmarried woman." Of course, more than spinning was often involved: carding, combing, weaving, bleaching or dyeing the fabric, as well as cutting, sewing, or tailoring.[103]

In the late eighteenth century, industrial spinning machinery was introduced, and "manufactories" that had earlier collected spun yarn and woven material from various homes gradually began to take over these operations themselves, hiring many women and children. As the market-oriented production of textiles advanced, one of the chief tasks of women at home diminished, and by the beginning of the nineteenth century, young single women took up school teaching in increasing numbers. In 1814, the power loom appeared, and by 1830, industrial manufacture of textiles was in full swing, largely removing this function from the home.[104]

These developments brought about a drastic change in the lives of young unmarried women:

> Textile mill operatives, who were almost all between the ages of fifteen and thirty, were young women who followed their traditional occupation to a new location, the factory. New England textile factories from the start employed a vastly greater proportion of women than men.[105]

This introduced variety and mobility, as well as uncertainty, into the lives of young women. While their earnings often went back to the family, this new element brought young women into association with their peers, put some distance between them and home, and provided some disposable income. In some instances, it led to careers in literature, education, or religion.[106] Yet it is important to keep in mind that the fraction of women so employed remained very small, and that these changes could be regarded only as a foretaste of what would not become a virtual revolution in the workplace until more than a century had passed. While the production of domestic goods left the home forever, women did not. The improvement in living conditions brought about by industrialization gradually allowed women to leave gainful employment and return to the home; by mid-nineteenth century, the great majority of working-class mothers had returned.[107]

The actual proportion of women working in the early nineteenth century was quite small; the significance of these changes lies elsewhere. What is important is the diminished importance of the home as a unit of production. Fathers moved out into the world to a greater extent, and the home became more of a woman's sphere, with purely domestic duties at its center. Along with this came another change: The sexuality of women became muted. Victorian sexual ideology in America, in its earlier form, extends roughly from the end of the eighteenth century to about halfway through the nineteenth. It has as its central core the view that women do not have a strong desire for sex, nor do they greatly enjoy it. Those of us who became adults before the middle of the twentieth century will recognize a variant of this ideology that persisted for another 100 years, until mid-twentieth century. This is the idea that women should remain virgins until marriage, but that men need not. Moreover, virginity in an adult man raised questions about his manliness and occasionally suggested pathology.

The interpretation of nineteenth-century Victorian ideology is a subject of considerable controversy among social historians and other writers. Medical authorities of the day considered Victorian views of womanhood to define women's natural state. One current view is that such an ideology was imposed on women by men for their own advantage. Still another is that it was more an ideology than reality, and did not represent actual behavior. Moreover, some argue that it had some definite advantages for women.[108]

At least one authority has rejected the notion that women's supposed lack of passion can be attributed solely to men, tracing its origins in New England to other sources.[109] This is important for our sex ratio question. We have noted repeatedly that a common condition of high sex ratio societies is that women's sexuality is highly controlled; a variety of constraints designed to protect their virginity and prevent adultery are found. Along with these constraints often goes a muted view of women's sexuality; they are considered much less passionate than men. We have suggested that when sex ratios are high, men help to generate this image. But there is no reason for constraints on the sexual behavior of women invariably to be associated with a belief that they lack passion. Quite often, such a belief might well grow out of repeated observations of their behavior toward men, which in such societies must be nonprovocative, reserved, passive, and proper. But a kind of paradox emerges: If women are passionless, why are special constraints required? One answer is that men are sexually aggressive and will seduce any woman they can. Barring that way out, however, such constraints require explanation.

An equally cogent logic could be offered to the effect that social constraints on women's sexual behavior are required because they are highly passionate and lack good control over their impulses. In fact, we do find high sex ratio societies where this belief prevails. Chapter 4 has discussed in detail sex roles among Orthodox Jews in the late nineteenth and early twentieth centuries in the shtetls of eastern Europe, where sex ratios were very high. We emphasized that in shtetl societies, all women were considered dangerous and given to excesses, and that a man must remain alert to the possibility that a woman might arouse desire that is stronger than his will and good judgment.[110] Sexual temptations might involve any woman in the shtetl, and the burden of control was placed on the men. While sexual intercourse was regarded as natural and good, it had a time and place. It was especially sinful to entertain sexual thoughts while studying the Talmud or while in the temple. Men were expected to avoid women in their daily activities; their attraction was so potent that men must avert their eyes in order to protect them both.[111]

Our findings for Orthodox shtetl Jews are consistent with a thesis concerning the Victorian ideology of women as passionless. One view is that throughout most of history, with few exceptions, women have been regarded as at least as sexually passionate as men. In fact, in many societies the image has been that they are more emotional and impulsive than men, less rational and less controlled, and thus dangerous.[112] Such an image, after all, begins with the Bible story of Eve leading Adam into temptation. But this historically representative view of women was turned around during the seventeenth and eighteenth centuries, resulting in the Victorian ideology during the first half of the nineteenth century.

Our logic so far does not account for the Victorian ideology that women are passionless in New England's *low* sex ratio society. We have suggested that in low sex ratio societies, women's sexuality is more apt to be openly accepted. Men no longer need to exercise stern control over women's sexual encounters because of the surplus of available women. A further consideration derives from the institutionalized attitudes of society toward sexual behavior. History has demonstrated that during the Victorian period in New England, women participated extensively in the church and its doctrines.[113] Religious leaders emphasized the spiritual qualities of women as taking precedence over their more physical aspects, and no doubt the earlier origins of the New England church in the ideas of its Puritan fathers contributed to a view of promiscuity and permissiveness as sinful. One study also identified attitudes in women's magazines dating from 1820 to 1860 toward "true womanhood" as emphasizing purity and spirituality.[114] With this kind of cultural tradition, the persistence and low sex ratios with an oversupply of women is apt to lead not to open or liberated sexual behavior for both sexes, but to a more moderated form.

Our suggestion here is that under these circumstances, while men would have no desire to control unattached women, they would still, as a rule, not want a woman with whom they have a close relationship to be promiscuous. Thus the change in sexuality takes a moderated form; instead of adopting a single image for women, two quite different ones are assumed: passionless women and sexy women.

These two forms of imagery are well known. Fiedler, in his analysis of American novels, has identified them as the Fair Maiden and the Dark

Lady.[115] Praz has called attention to other related types in French literature, such as the "fatal woman," who may be readily associated with the Dark Lady.[116] Both types can be found in the literature of almost any period, as well as in other writings about women. The Fair Maiden is blonde, pure, good, and sexually passive. The Dark Lady is passionate, sexually and otherwise, and is very dangerous, sometimes evil.

Such imagery would seem appropriate to the Victorian period in New England, where sex ratios were below 100. We are suggesting that men helped to build a morality and imagery of women that facilitated their control over them. They picked a Fair Maiden for a fiancee or wife if they could, but there was no need for them to have such imagery concerning other women to whom they were not attached, and who might be available for sexual satisfaction. The only difficulty was that some of these available women were Dark Ladies, whose depth of passion was dangerous and possibly ruinous to a man who was a solid citizen.

Although it does not explicitly deal with the dual imagery, one analysis of the Victorian period in New England from 1790 to 1850 fits this interpretation well.[117] It shows how women of that period accepted and even helped to create the image of the Fair Maiden, in whom passion was displaced by spiritual attributes. At the same time, female sexuality was recognized as double-edged; inherent female licentiousness was attributed to those women who strayed from the spiritual path through lack of character or because of the temptations created by unscrupulous seducers.[118]

The same analysis calls attention to the part played by evangelical religion during the period in question, in generating the image of women as more spiritual than passionate. Women of that day flocked to church, and the church in turn praised female character as the essence of morality. We are reminded here of the late Middle Ages, when the Beguines enabled women to commune directly with God, without the intervention of a male priest. A central part of that morality was its lack of passion, or control thereof:

> By replacing sexual with moral motives and determinants, the ideology of passionlessness favored women's power and self-respect. It reversed the tradition of Christian mistrust based on women's sexual treacherousness. It elevated women above the weakness of animal nature, stressing instead that they were "formed for exalted purity, felicity, and glory" . . . It postulated that women's influence was not ensnaring but disinterested. It routed women out of the cul-de-sac of education for attractiveness, thus allowing for more intellectual breadth.[119]

Sex ratios in New England had fallen below 100 before the end of the eighteenth century and stayed there throughout the nineteenth century. We have seen that women married later, men earlier, and that fewer widows were able to remarry. The surplus of women made them more vulnerable to exploitation.[120] By and large, most women had no means of economic support, except that provided by a man—their father, their husband, or a relative; only a few jobs had so far emerged for women in the workplace. The Victorian ideology helped with this problem. By deemphasizing their sexuality, women could escape exploitation by men and lay the ground for bringing other attributes to the fore—not just spiritual qualities, but intelligence and aptitude for education, which in turn would make it possible for them to enter places outside the home that were formerly for men only. This move has been seen as an early form of feminism, which is disadvantageous only if it goes so far as to put women out of touch with their own sexual functioning.[121]

It is not difficult to support the dual image view of women in the nineteenth century. An intensive analysis of the medical literature concerning views on women countered the popular impression among historians that medical authorities of the day viewed women as passionless.[122] While many medical writers took this view, many others took an opposite view, to the effect that sexual feelings were natural for women and that failure to express them could be harmful. Moreover, one observer has shown clearly that the views of Dr. William Acton, a leading advocate of the "passionless" belief, were more prescriptive than descriptive; it represented a kind of desirable goal, in Acton's mind.[123] That women were often seen as Dark Ladies rather than Fair Maidens is also apparent from the voluminous letters, diaries, and personal papers written by women of the period who complained about the double standard and who were angry and bitter because their husbands and men in general consorted with the "other woman" or with many other women.[124]

What seems to be the case, then, is that in low sex ratio New England, the muted sexuality of women developed partly under the leadership of evangelical religionists who augmented their flock by emphasizing the spiritual qualities of women, and partly because women were able to turn this imagery to their advantage by reducing the extent to which men could exploit them, by emphasizing qualities other than their sexuality.

Nineteenth-Century Feminism

Another characteristic feature of low sex ratio societies is that some form of feminism emerges. Once again, because of the low sex ratios in nineteenth-century New England, and in the South after the Civil War, we would expect such movements to appear. Feminist movements, as we have stated, take a form that is shaped partly by the social context of the society in which they emerge, so that movements from different historical periods are by no means the same. Still, all of them have in common some sort of special plea made by women on behalf of women.

Contemporary scholars have identified and described a variety of feminist movements in the nineteenth-century America, most of them emerging in the later part of the century, and many having their origins in New England. By the last quarter of the nineteenth century, several divergent groups of feminists nevertheless agreed on their stand toward motherhood: It should be voluntary.[125] Motherhood should not be an automatic and regular accompaniment of marriage; women should have the right to decide whether or not to have a baby. These feminist groups included suffragists, who had two different national organizations and many local ones; women from various moral reform causes, such as the temperance movement; and women who belonged to the free love movement.[126]

What is of interest for our purposes is that all of these groups argued for greater independence for women. We have asserted that when low sex ratios prevail over any substantial period of time, the level of exploitation of women rises, and an appreciable number of women in traditional societies have unsatisfactory experiences with men, or have difficulty in finding a husband. If they are married, their relationship to their husband may be a source of stress. One reaction that results from these three factors taken together is that women strive for greater independence and self-determination. Each of the various feminist groups in the late nineteenth century conforms to this thesis in that they severely criticized and tried to change the marriage relationship and the various constraints on women's independence.

The free love groups, which were quite small, often led by men, and never very popular, argued against the constraints induced by the institution of marriage, believing that it stifled "real love." Both the suffragists and the moral reformers were more concerned with popular acceptance, and couched their arguments for change in language that would avoid outraging common sensibilities.[127] All three movements believed that the legal and moral constraints on birth control were unfair to women, and that women had a right to limit and restrict sexual intercourse, even with their husbands, in the interest of controlling pregnancies, as well as, for some feminists, for moral or spiritual reasons. Because today we think of birth control as synonymous with contraceptive techniques, it is worth noting that "birth control" in the nineteenth century meant abortion and even infanticide, but especially voluntary restraint from sexual intercourse, as well as such techniques as coitus interruptus. Some who favored birth control condemned contraceptive techniques—for example, moral reformers advocating sexual restraint saw them as encouraging lustful sex.[128]

One observer has argued that the muted sexuality of Victorian women could be seen as a form of "domestic feminism."[129] This is consistent with our earlier discussion emphasizing that under the guise of being passionless, women could emphasize other desirable qualities to a greater extent, including intelligence and the aptitude for rational self-direction, as well as spiritual and moral values. But we need not discard the idea that men also contributed to this imagery; at least one advantage to them was that it helped to perpetuate the double standard of sexual morality.

Another feature expected in low sex ratio societies emerged along with feminism in late nineteenth-century New England, a feature that suggested that by then, the Victorian image of women was more fantasy than reality. A sharp rise occurred in premarital pregnancies, from below 10 percent of first births at mid-century, to 20-25 percent of first births toward the end of the century.[130] While this cannot be wholly attributed to a change in sex ratios, it is at least consistent with the prevailing low sex ratios at that time.

CONCLUSIONS

Taking a backward look at the whole history of Colonial and early America, what can we conclude concerning the sex ratio question? First, we have encountered a high sex ratio society rather different from any that we have discussed in connection with the medieval period or earlier times. A few of the colonies, but especially the western frontier, were characterized by very high sex ratios in an underpopulated setting with little tradition, constant change and growth, and requiring much flexibility and adaptability in order to meet the exigencies of maintaining oneself in a new land under harsh circumstances. In this high sex ratio setting, women were greatly admired and desired. Men deprived of their company for long periods of time found great pleasure in the mere sight of a woman. Their reaction was not unlike that of military personnel stationed in isolated settings in World War II when they were visited by USO entertainers. Their appreciation of the female entertainers was extravagant beyond all normal bounds.

Single men on the frontier who wanted to marry searched desperately for an unattached woman. Often constraints that ordinarily operate in marital selection were cast aside. Few women on the frontier remained unmarried, regardless of their attributes. Social class was no barrier; servant girls were soon taken in marriage. Widows, even those with many children, were eagerly courted and soon remarried. On the frontier, even racial bounds were sometimes crossed in marriage. Although evidence is very scanty, it appears that married women in these very high sex ratio societies were also well treated.

What is important about these high sex ratio settings is their contrast with high sex ratios in traditional societies. There we saw that men used their political and economic power to build a set of social constraints, customs, legal restrictions, and even moral proscriptions that limit women's freedom and make them second-class citizens, even to the point of making them the property of men. This did not happen with the high sex ratios on the far western frontier because of the openness of these societies. In the one exception on the frontier, that of the Chinese-Americans, who had several strong sources of cohesive social organization, it did happen, and women were once again subjugated to men under extremely high sex ratio conditions.

The midwestern frontier was different. Migration to that region most often included pioneers who wanted to turn rich land into farms, and who brought a family. So the ratios were not so high (very roughly, about 110 or so), with great variations at different times and places. The domestic role of the wife in that setting, with its tremendous labor scarcity, was arduous and demanding. Wives were especially desired because they could perform all of the domestic duties, such as cooking, making clothes, and butchering animals; many of the farm chores, like feeding the chickens and hogs, milking the cows, and tending a vegetable garden; as well as bearing and raising children, who would labor on the farm at a very early age. While single women were much in demand and intensively courted, their role changed drastically after marriage.

In many ways, we can contrast the midwestern frontier with the South. Although the South started with very high sex ratios, and apparently maintained them for a much longer period than was the case for the midwestern frontier, by the end of the eighteenth century, ratios in the South were slightly lower than they were in the midwestern regions, although they remained above 100. Thus the two regions were roughly comparable with respect to sex ratios, except for their early histories. But we have seen that the role of women was very different in the South from that on the midwestern frontier. While this may have been due in part to its earlier period, with the very high sex ratios, it undoubtedly was also due to the difference in the economies of the two regions. Because the South had slaves and indentured servants, it was not labor-scarce, making it possible to operate large plantations. This created important class distinctions between large landowners and those with smaller farms, as well as the large underclass of tenant farmers, indentured servants, and slaves. In spite of the fact that the sex ratio was not very high, the upper classes developed a society in which the virtues of Southern ladies were honored and extolled, as we have seen. The familiar romantic tradition was prominent in this society and almost totally absent from the midwestern region. The South, once it became settled, was like a high sex ratio society, and the romantic tradition that developed was similar in some respects to that of the Middle Ages in southern France and Spain. Possibly the demography was also similar, in that there may have been a considerable excess of male aspirants for the hands of plantation daughters, although direct evidence of this is not available.

Finally, except for the earliest period of its history, New England had sex ratios persistently below 100. Although the Victorian image of women that developed there toward the end of the eighteenth century and into the nineteenth had some features in common with that of the Southern lady, society there lacked the elaborate manners, customs, and romantic features of the South. Ordinarily, it would be more in accord with sex ratio patterns to anticipate Victorian attitudes toward women in a high sex ratio society, because our view is that men react to a scarcity of women by building a protective morality around the women whom they possess. Certainly this happened in the South, but why did it happen in New England, with its low sex ratios? What is revealed here is the possibility that such circumstances can readily lead to a double sexual standard involving dual images for women. Women are divided into respectable and loose categories—Fair Maidens and Dark Ladies—and men are free to maintain relationships with both. Men married respectable women, had a family, and maintained a home. But many also had an underlife with one or more women who, because they were sexy, were not considered respectable. In this regard there was little difference between New England and the South.

But women were emancipated much earlier in low sex ratio New England. We have seen that there was much less agreement on the Victorian image of women in New England than there was on the Southern lady. New England provided more opportunities for women to adopt different roles, and spinsters and widows were much in evidence. Young girls before the mid-nineteenth century spent some time out of their homes in textile factories, taking them out of the sheltered and controlled environment of their homes and exposing them to a very different world. Feminist thrusts developed and were more vigorous in New England than in the South, and in the latter half of the nineteenth century received much attention. Women in the South were slower to become emancipated; it took the Civil War to begin this process. It seems likely that the low sex ratios of New England were in part responsible for these differences.

II

OBSERVATIONS FROM
RECENT TIMES

By the nature of the task, our historical review in Part I was forced to deal with periods of a century (or even several centuries) with huge, poorly defined populations that were suspected of having either very low or very high sex ratios. While this historical analysis has been remarkably supportive of the sex ratio thesis, even stronger support would be provided if we could show effects for sharply defined populations differing from each other in some precise but not very large disparity in sex ratios. Part II will attempt to do that.

The last few decades provide us with an opportunity to examine sex ratios and their effects in more depth, since more adequate data on populations and social conditions are available. It may be surprising to find that there were severe limits on the data available in the first half of the twentieth century, yet this was certainly the case. For example, it was not until 1966 that a U.S. Standard Certificate of Marriage and a similar certificate for divorce were adopted and recommended for use by all of the states.[1] Of course, this helps to put our historical studies of sex ratios in their proper perspective—if census and vital statistics have been inadequate even in the twentieth century, one can imagine the grossness of the data from earlier centuries.

Carter and Glick have ably reviewed the history of efforts to collect national statistics on marriage and divorce, and there is no need to repeat their review here.[2] Nevertheless, it is important to point out that published data of the sort that would permit a rigorous test of hypotheses are often not available, even today. Major limitations on published data for our purposes include the impossibility of getting a sufficient variety of information on the same individuals, grouping people into age or other intervals too large to allow examination of certain hypotheses, the unavailability of detailed breakdowns of the population during the years in between the censuses, and the noncomparability of reports from one period to another. None of these comments is intended as a criticism of the relevant government agencies; after all, our purposes are rather different from the mandate given them by Congress.

Two major sources of data are the Division of Vital Statistics of the National Center for Health Statistics, and the Bureau of the Census. A third valuable source consists of analyses published by demographers; these often include unpublished data available to them, as well as published data. Since, at this writing, the last census was conducted in 1970, our consideration of the current scene will lean heavily on these analyses, as well as government sources such as *Current Population Reports* and periodicals such as the *Population Bulletin.*

Our other concern in Part II will be to sharpen our ideas to achieve approximate theoretical formulations. Part I, for example, said little about how demographic conditions are linked to psychological states and social effects. In order for the sex ratio thesis to be convincing, we must spell out in detail just how an oversupply or undersupply of one sex is connected with the various social effects that we have claimed. Part II will begin with a chapter that attempts to do this.

Finally, after having reported the state of affairs in contemporary times, we will give some attention to the broader and deeper implications of the sex ratio thesis and, along with that, indicate what the future is likely to hold for men and women and their relationships. This is not as presumptuous as it might seem, for the basis of such prognostications is the age-sex structure of that portion of the population that has not yet reached adulthood. Of course, this alone is inadequate, for we shall also have to consider how the future will be affected by changes that have already occurred, such as the new standard of permissiveness in sexual attitudes and behaviors, more effective birth control methods, the trend toward women entering full-time careers, and the growth of feminism.

6

From Sex Ratios
to Sex Roles

In Chapter 1 we described women's roles in two imaginary societies, EROS and LIBERTINIA. In both, their behavior and that of the men with whom they interacted seemed strange and absurd. In EROS, men were romantic love objects and enjoyed staying home and taking care of the children. The double standard of morality was more strict for men, who had weaker sex drives. Women dominated the business world and government as well, and many preferred their husbands to stay at home, while they provided for them. In LIBERTINIA, women and men had roles similar to those in EROS, but families were much less stable. Divorce, illegitimacy, and abortion rates were all high. Standards of sexual morality were low for both sexes, and men, in particular, were often exploited as sex objects by women.

These imaginary societies seem impossible to us, and the reason for this is that they dramatically reverse certain core features of the role-identities of women and men. These features, in their normal form, have been so unvarying throughout history that they are taken for granted, and most of us have come to think of the behaviors they represent as stemming from the biological natures of men and women. The key elements depicting men and women have been reiterated countless times in history, literature, drama, and in our daily lives. No other human roles have been so constant.

EROS and LIBERTINIA were constructed with a purpose, namely, to show what would logically follow if an underlying condition that has pervaded all of human history were to be changed. This condition is the key to understanding the sex roles and identity of men and women. In EROS and LIBERTINIA, the usual prevailing condition has been reversed—there, women, not men, hold what we have termed *structural power*. This power derives from their superior economic, political, and legal position in society, as well as from the sheer weight of the social values and practices that implement these powers. This alone could account for all of the strangeness of these two societies when compared with more familiar ones. There, men are like women, and women are like men. But men in EROS are different from men in LIBERTINIA, and the same is true of women. This occurs because EROS has a low sex ratio, with men in short supply, and LIBERTINIA a high ratio, with a surplus of men. As we explained earlier, these ratios alter the *dyadic power* of women and men, combining with the existing balance of structural power to produce different overall effects.

The central question of this chapter concerns the means by which sex roles are generated and maintained. We have a particular interest in explaining the means by which an imbalance in sex ratios combines with the prevailing imbalance in structural power to produce changes in the attitudes and behaviors of men and women in relation to each other and, with sufficient time, to produce changes in the associated sex roles and institutional structures, such as the family. Our thesis would be more complete if we could detail the various links between the demographic conditions and the psychological and social effects. At this point in our knowledge, however, no final explanation can be provided. All that can be done is to sketch some plausible mechanisms and look for evidence that might support or reject them. Such an approach should increase our understanding and sharpen further research so that definitive answers might ultimately be provided.

Explanations such as we are seeking are bound up with questions about human nature itself, and with the value positions taken on human nature by social scientists and others. Issues arise, such as the biological differences between men and women and their consequences for sexual and other behaviors; the nature of love between men and women; parental behavior and attitudes, especially commitment to children; and the relative contributions of economic, cultural, and societal factors to relations between the sexes. For these reasons, many diverse, impassioned views about man-woman relationships have strong effects on the manner in which such relationships are conceptualized and explained. Consequently, it should be no surprise that many different and contrasting mechanisms could be proposed to explain the social effects of imbalances in sex ratios. Our reaction will be to thread our way through this maze of contradictions by sticking to the main lines of argument and evidence and avoiding lines of explanation that seem implausible or illogical, or that are contrary to the facts as we see them.

In what follows, we will outline our argument in sharp profile. To clear the ground, several assumptions must first be made explicit.

SOME BASIC ASSUMPTIONS

To deal more sharply with the arguments and evidence, we will put aside until the last chapter the issue of the biological natures of men and women. In spite of the advances that have been made in understanding the biology of gender, no definitive conclusions can yet be drawn about the effects of biological properties or conditions on *behavior.* This is true not only for differences between male and female behavior, but also for variations in the behavior of different individuals of the same sex. We do not have any firm evidence that some biological condition or constitutional property makes one individual more sexually active, more aggressive, more emotional, or more perceptive than another, nor do we know of any such biological conditions that account for the other behavior differences that are usually imputed to males and females. For the present, we assume that males and females are not biologically different in ways that produce important behavioral differences, in order to better zero in on the societal and social differences that might account for the different behaviors of male and females. Once the societal factors are worked out, we can return to the question of the biology of male and female natures.

Another basic assumption that we make here is that men and women need each other. Obviously, this is partly biological and specifically sexual, although the variety of forms that sexual behavior takes under various social conditions makes it clear that sexual biology is not simply and directly expressed in a narrow band of sexual behavior, nor even exclusively toward the opposite sex. Moreover, the needs of men and women for each other are obviously not solely sexual; companionship, nurture, play, maintaining a home and family, and a great variety of other forms of expression characterize male-female transactions. Once again, to focus on the societal and social determinants of relationships, we assume no difference between men and women in the strength of their needs, sexual or otherwise. In the absence of strong evidence, making the assumption that men have stronger sex needs than women—or the reverse assumption—would simply beg the question we are trying to answer.

A key condition that must be stressed is the unequal division of structural power that has prevailed from the earliest recorded history and that is deeply embedded in the background of current societal structure and sex-role identities. The balance of this power has been overwhelmingly in the hands of males, and this has had a profound effect on the roles and identities of men and women, the forms that relationships between them have taken, and the social institutions, such as the family, that have evolved to maintain such relationships in keeping with the accepted value systems of society.

It is men who have been lawmakers, business executives, entrepreneurs, heads of families, judges, police officers, presidents, governors, dictators, and generals. This imbalance of power has been so pervasive and ever-present that it has often been taken for granted and simply ignored when the natures of men and women have been considered. Quite possibly, many of the differences between men and women that are taken to be natural or biological are in fact consequences of the unequal distribution of structural power between the sexes. Since an unequal distribution has been virtually always present, it could well be that what we see as "natural" differences between men and women are simply due to this ever-present difference. The broad sweep of history that we have made may provide some insights into this issue, and we will examine this possibility.

THE ORIGIN AND MAINTENANCE OF SEX ROLES

Social scientists take for granted that social roles are shaped through socialization. Age-sex roles, for example, are shaped by parents and others from infancy onward, in the kinds of behaviors they encourage and approve of in a child, depending on its gender. Socialization is more than conscious shaping; adults and others often serve as role models that children may copy on their own. This socialization process continues throughout adult life, whenever individuals assume new role positions (such as becoming a husband or wife, a soldier, a minister, or a newly retired person).

But role socialization in this sense is of little help in explaining how particular roles emerge in a society in the first place, or how these roles change over time. It only shows how the new generation gets recruited into old ways of doing things, and how an individual in society progresses from one role to another. Much less attention has been given to how particular roles change (for instance, why mothers today behave differently from their grandmother or even from mothers of 20 years ago), and to the twin problem of why roles stay the same over time. Only in more recent years have social scientists come to think of social roles as dynamic, in the sense that they must be constantly renewed by the individuals enacting them if they are to survive, and further, that a full explanation requires identification of the originating and sustaining forces, as well as of the pressures toward change. This chapter details some of these forces in connection with sex roles, with special attention to the effects of imbalanced sex ratios.

Adult sex roles are shaped, maintained, or changed through what can be thought of as two relatively independent sources: the social exchanges of the role partners, and the task demands that bear on those roles. These two sources are not, of course, completely independent; task demands may influence social exchanges, and vice versa. But the interactions between two role partners, such as husband and wife, and the task demands that bear on each role, can only be understood in the larger context of the society in which they occur. That men hold the balance of economic and political power in society has profound effects on the nature of the exchanges between any two role partners, as well as on the task demands that each partner bears. The society itself specifies what kinds of exchanges and task demands are appropriate for each role actor, at least within limits, and these have been accepted for the most part by the two parties.

Task demands originate partly in the physical and social setting of the role position, sources that are often beyond the power of the role actors to alter. We saw in the chapter on early America, for example, that frontier women in the midwestern region were thrust into the role of farm wife, which automatically imposed upon them all of the domestic and farm chores necessary for maintaining the farm, and further, that because they were female, they would bear many children as a matter of course.

The task demands of a social role are relatively fixed by physical or societal conditions, whereas social exchanges are more subject to negotiation between the role partners. Task demands are partly social, in the sense that they derive in part from the structure of society. For example, if we think more broadly of an adult woman's role (as contrasted with that of wife/ mother) in the midwestern frontier, we can see that frontier society provided little in the way of alternative roles for an adult unmarried woman. With few exceptions, women had no means of supporting themselves and were apt to be dependent on relatives for shelter and means of subsistence. Thus, in a sense we can think of this midwestern frontier society as providing a rather narrow, single set of task demands for its adult women—always recognizing a few exceptions, of course. The importance of this concept of task demands as imposed by the physical and social setting of a role cannot be overestimated, and we will return to discuss it in more detail in our final chapter, in connection with the future role identities of women.

SOCIAL EXCHANGES AND DYADIC POWER

Sex ratio imbalances produce their effects by disturbing the balance of social power between the two sexes. How this comes about can be conceptualized in terms of a theory of social exchange that has been generated by adapting the economic model of exchange to the social realm. We will provide a brief, informal sketch of the theory and then discuss it in more detail, particularly in association with imbalanced sex ratios.[1]

Dyadic power in a relationship between two persons derives from the psychological resources that one partner has for satisfying the needs of the other partner. The more such resources a person has and the stronger the needs of the partner for those resources, the greater the dyadic power. This effect is tempered by the extent to which the weaker person is dependent specifically on one partner for satisfaction. For example, when the weaker party in a relationship can gain satisfaction outside of the relationship, the power of the stronger party is weakened. We have referred to this social power deriving from dependencies in a two-person relationship as *dyadic power.*

In relationships between members of the opposite sex that are open to change or dissolution, demography is linked with dyadic power in the following way: When one gender is in short supply, it becomes more difficult for the opposite sex to find a partner. Moreover, relationships are apt to be less satisfying for the gender in oversupply. This follows because the scarce gender has more sources of satisfaction alternative to the partner, while the partner has fewer. These conditions generate more dyadic power for the party with more alternative sources of satisfaction because of the way they affect the exchange of resources. This party is less dependent on the partner and can turn elsewhere for satisfaction. The partner, on the other hand, has fewer options and thus must provide a level of satisfaction sufficiently above the first party's alternative sources in order to keep the relationship alive.

This is the substance of the argument, but it needs fleshing out to be fully understood. In an economic exchange, each party experiences costs and benefits in a transaction with another party. Further, competition and supply and demand all bear on the exchange. In like manner, the focus of *social* exchange theory is on the social transactions in a relationship between two persons as they take place in the context of the larger set of options that each party has in other relationships. The relationship may be initial or temporary, or it may be of long duration.

As in economic exchange, interactions between a man and a woman can be viewed as exchanges where each party experiences certain benefits and costs. The benefits and costs are largely psychological, including not only sexual pleasures, but enjoyment of intimacy, companionship, feelings of self-worth, or whatever. Costs are also psychological, such as "spending" one's time, embarrassment or rejection, guilt or deception, and so on. These benefits and costs, taken together over a period of time, yield each party's outcomes.

The degree of satisfaction yielded in an exchange depends both on the resources of one's partner to benefit one, and the intensity of one's need for such benefits. For example, the ability to carry on a good conversation is a resource if one has a partner who likes to participate in such conversation. A person may be beautiful or handsome, sexy, fun to be with, emotionally supportive, able to take charge of a situation, a good listener—these are common resources that most people enjoy in a partner—but clearly, whether they are valuable resources depends on what one wants from a partner. For example, some would rather take charge of a situation themselves, or do the listening instead of the talking. The beauty of a woman may be a resource desired by the man she is with, but if she is with a woman, it may be a liability.

The extent to which resources and needs determine the level of satisfaction in the outcome of social exchanges depends on yet another important condition that varies with prior experiences in and out of the relationship. Outcomes by themselves neither tell us about satisfaction with a series of exchanges nor whether further exchanges will take place. The model of economic exchange makes this clear. Whether or not a woman who has just purchased something thinks that she has just made a good buy depends on what she thinks the going price is. Similarly, satisfaction with the outcome in a social relationship depends on the level that is expected.

In economic exchange, the going price is the expected level. Just as this is based on other transactions of the same kind from the past, on tentative pricings from other sellers, and even on prices that one *thinks* might be obtained, the level of expectation for a social transaction is based on similar transactions in the past and on the alternative transactions that a party perceives as available. A desirable man may be accustomed to highly satisfying interactions with women; he expects more and would be less satisfied with or even disappointed by some actions than would a less desirable man. The concept of *alternatives* is crucial: Human satisfactions are always relative; their evaluation depends on what might have been experienced instead. These potential experiences may be estimated from past experiences or from optional alternatives, real or imagined.

From these concepts of outcomes, expectations, and alternative options follow implications about the relative satisfactions of each party, the relative dependencies of each on the other, the relative power each has over the other, and the desire to continue or discontinue the relationship.

Worth noting in passing is the point that the most common objection to this application of exchange theory is that it makes friendship and love appear calculating and self-serving. In answer to this objection, it should be clear that social exchange theory does not require a conscious weighing of costs and benefits in a relationship—that would indeed belie the very meaning of friendship and love. Exchange theory does not even make any assumption of "equitable" exchanges between partners, because each partner's satisfaction depends on his or her own expectations and outcomes. The viewpoint taken in social exchange theory is quite different—namely, that the *feelings* of satisfaction, warmth, love, rejection, or bitterness are often all that is consciously experienced, but that these feelings result nevertheless from an unconscious assessment of the balance between outcomes, expectations, and alternatives.

While a calculus may enable prediction or explanation of the kinds of emotional reactions that will occur, it need not imply a deliberate, self-conscious calculation of benefits and costs by people in a relationship. An analogous situation may help here. Consider the case of a child who has received too little attention. He is apt to engage in exhibitionism, attention-getting tactics, and even unpleasant or inappropriate behavior. This does not mean that he has consciously calculated the amount of attention he has received and compared it with some expected level, yet he reacts as if he had such knowledge and responds to the lack of attention. Innumerable human behaviors are based on quantitative assessments that occur below the level of awareness. This is obviously true of skilled movements, such as those in piano playing or touch typing. We may safely assume that complex quantitative assessments also underlie some social behaviors.

A further complication that must be understood is the interplay between resources and needs and the shaping of these by societal structures and processes. A simple example is beauty. Patterns of physical attributes that are seen as beautiful, and thus as a resource of their possessor, are socially determined. This is clear from the wide cultural variations in what is considered beautiful. In the same way, more complex attributes such as status and power constitute resources only by virtue of societal processes. What conveys status depends on central social values. Constraints on freedom to negotiate are socially conditioned in a similar way. Some features of a relationship are not negotiable because society rigidly defines them, and deviation from the rules results in disaster for the perpetrator. In some societies, for example, if a young woman loses her virginity, her identity is permanently spoiled and she cannot achieve a good marriage. Finally, we noted earlier that the task demands stemming from the physical and social setting of the sex role in question are in many respects independent of the social exchange process within a given relationship.

Social exchanges are seen in clearest outline where both participants in a relationship have maximum freedom to behave in a variety of ways, including leaving the relationship. There are two sources controlling this freedom. One is the extent to which the social roles of the participants have been prescribed and limited by society, and the other is the stage of the relationship. Thus, the exchange process is most dramatically demonstrated in relationships that are tentative or new, or in an early stage, and where the roles are not narrowly prescribed. Even though they are strangers to each other, the exchanges that might take place between a bank teller and a customer are strictly limited by the narrow prescriptions of their respective roles. On the other hand, two strangers meeting at a cocktail party might have a wide range of exchanges that they could engage in. This is directly analogous to free market conditions under sufficient demand, where both buyer and seller have the freedom to reject or accept an exchange, and have available alternative sources of exchange.

The subtleties involved in constraints on social exchanges may be illustrated by another example. Consider the "sex game," as played through encounters at singles bars. It might appear at first that such encounters are open to a wide variety of exchanges. In fact, though, only the usual constraints on sexual intercourse between strangers are lifted; most other social exchanges unrelated to this outcome are not available in such encounters. Indeed, perhaps this is the reason why many single people find encounters at singles bars distasteful. The unwritten but clearly understood rules constrain the participants to a rather narrowly prescribed set of acts that end in sexual intercourse. Freedom to interact in alternative, nonsexual but satisfying ways is mostly ruled out by the mutually shared expectations that singles-bar frequenters hold. Thus, while the usual constraints on sex between strangers are lifted by such games, behaviors that fall outside of the game theme are ruled out.

In contrast to brief encounters, when a relationship between two persons is long-standing and has many personal and institutional commitments, certain types of exchanges are no longer available. Examples are provided by the perennial concerns about losing their freedom experienced by single men or women when contemplating marriage. But it should also be recognized that long-term relationships, like friendships and marriages, also open up and facilitate kinds of social exchanges that are not available in the early stages of such relationships.

Finally, a society that is stable and that has long-standing traditions places more constraints on the forms that relationships may take, thus limiting the exchanges that are open to negotiation. We have already seen in earlier chapters, for example, that when women are strictly limited to the traditional domestic role of wife/mother, they have fewer choices in the way they relate to a man and in the life "career" that they may adopt. This interlocking of exchange processes with societal structures and contexts is a theme that will recur throughout this chapter, and it is crucial to understanding how sex ratio demography affects relationships between men and women.

Attraction, Dependency, and Dyadic Power

From the viewpoint of social exchange theory, two elements are of foremost importance in any relationship between a man and a woman: attraction of each to the other, and the dependency of each on the other. Attraction has to do with the level of outcomes that each experiences in transactions with the other, relative to what each party expects, and dependency, with the alternative options that each party has. Let us consider attraction first, and dependency second.

A simple principle is that the level of attraction to the other party in a relationship is a function of the level of outcomes experienced in relation to the level that is *expected*. The expected level is relatively stable and has become established as a result of the outcomes experienced in past exchanges with the same party, in similar exchanges in other relations, and in optional exchanges in alternative relations. The more the actual outcomes exceed the expected level, the more attraction will be experienced. Put simply, a strong liking or attraction for another person results from rewarding exchanges with the person that appreciably exceed those ordinarily experienced.

The other component of social exchange theory, dependency on the relationship, is at the heart of our thesis concerning imbalances in sex ratios. Staying in or leaving a relationship depends on the extent to which outcomes in the relationship exceed those that are available in alternative relationships. It is this fact that brings in competition and supply and demand in social relationships, and it is this fact that alters the balance of power within the relationship when sex ratios are out of balance. If the outcomes in alternative relationships are perceived by an individual to be highly satisfying (whether they actually are or not), this perception will raise the level of what is expected within the existing relationship. This makes it less attractive because the outcomes are then closer to the expected level. At the same time, this party is less dependent on it for satisfaction. Remember that we are discussing tentative or early-stage relationships, for alternatives loom larger in this phase and often become more psychologically remote when a mutual commitment has taken place.

Sex Ratios, Dependency, and Alternatives

If the number of single men only slightly exceeds the number of single women, the number of alternative options in finding a partner will be approximately equal for both partners. We noted earlier that the age and social class constraints on pairings of men and women require this slight excess of eligible males. But let us consider the situation where there are appreciably more single women than men. Under these circumstances, men have, on the average, more alternative relationships than women. This provides more freedom of choice for men, as well as a sense of control over the way they relate to a woman. Of crucial importance is their level of expectation for optional relationships, particularly that alternative relationship that carries the highest expected outcomes. In a relationship without commitment, the outcomes must exceed those in the best alternative relationship if the man is to stay in the existing relationship. In fact, only if a woman can maintain her partner's outcomes at a level above those of alternative relationships will he remain. The more alternatives he has, the less dependent he is on the relationship.

Consider now the position of the woman in this precommitment relationship, in a context where women outnumber men. She may have no visible alternatives at all, except the one of being alone; therefore, unlike her male partner, she is highly dependent on him. She is in the position of having to provide high outcomes for him, but whether she receives them in exchange or not, she has to continue the relationship or risk being alone. In fact, if she particularly dislikes the alternative of being alone, she may stay in the relationship even though it provides outcomes that are well *below* what she would ordinarily expect. Outcomes below the level of expectation produce dissatisfaction and feelings of rejection, yet she remains in the relationship. This effect of alternatives helps to explain the common but puzzling observation that couples often remain together even when they both seem very unhappy with each other. In that instance, the alternatives to staying in the relationship appear worse to both parties.

Vis-à-vis her partner, the woman in a low alternative situation feels powerless, while her partner has a feeling of power over the relationship. She may have to put up with various behaviors on his part that she finds distressing or obnoxious. She may have to provide outcomes for him that are psychologically costly for her, while he can easily balk at providing outcomes for her if they are costly to him. From a theoretical viewpoint, he will not engage in exchanges that are costly for him and which thus produce net outcomes for him that are below his level of available options. Thus, he has the power to control her behavior so as to maximize his own outcomes without at the same time having to make sacrifices that would keep her outcomes at a high level.

If, in spite of her efforts, he abandons her for another woman, her feelings of rejection and her resentment are apt to be multiplied by the uneven exchange in which she has given more than he has. She will have a strong sense of having been unfairly treated, which may intensify her feelings of being impotent and powerless. She put forth extra effort and yet was rejected.

What is important to understand here is that it is not necessary for men or women to be directly aware of the imbalance in the relative numbers of men and women who are available. It is not a matter of directly perceiving the sex ratio. Rather, as a result of continuing experiences in encounters with the opposite sex, the average individual whose gender is in the minority occasionally has more alternatives in terms of actual or potential partners, whereas the opposite sex has fewer such alternatives. From time to time, this produces a one-up, one-down situation that leads the party whose gender is in the minority to have higher expectations for outcomes in an existing relationship and less willingness to commit oneself, while the individual of the opposite sex feels a greater dependency on the existing relationship and is willing to give more. When the sex ratio is considerably out of balance, the widespread effects increase the visibility of desirable alternatives for the scarce gender, and the injustices and exploitations undergone by the gender in oversupply become more salient.

COMMITMENT AND INSTITUTIONALIZED RELATIONSHIPS

An important concept in relationships is *commitment*. Perhaps the most formal commitment in our society between a man and a woman is marriage, but we can also conceive of commitments that are progressively weaker until they reach the point of no commitment. Most relationships have some degree of commitment. Even voluntarily spending one's time with another person on only one occasion may set up at least a weak anticipation that one might see him or her again. Commitments need not be formal. They amount to an expectation on the part of both parties that they will continue to see one another and behave toward each other as they have in the past; in other words, a commitment has to be shared or mutually understood.

At some point the commitment may be made explicit, perhaps when the couple decides to share the same residence, or to get married. But a commitment could become quite strong through mutual understanding without even being explicitly discussed. With this understood, let us now leave the precommitment stage of a relationship and assume that it has continued to the point where making an exclusive commitment to each other is being considered. Again, our discussion continues to focus on the exchange process as it would occur in modern Western societies, where both parties would have some freedom of choice. Whether a commitment involves marriage or not, living together or separately, such a commitment usually carries with it an agreement not to engage in intimacies outside of the relationship, and sometimes additional constraints are placed on relating to third parties. It involves commitment of a considerable block of one's time; at the very least, much of one's recreational or spare time is shared with the other party. Along with it comes an implication of emotional support and caring on the part of the other party, who becomes someone to depend on in time of need or trouble. But at the same time it implies an agreement to take the bad with the good; one puts up with the other's tantrums, quirks, or obnoxious habits. Both parties receive some benefits from the commitment. They feel more secure; they no longer need to try to impress, or to always be on their best behavior; they can relax and be more comfortable. Note particularly that a joint exclusive commitment implies a kind of sharing, a give-and-take attitude on the part of both parties. These various positive and negative features combine to yield an outcome for each party that results from the commitment. Each party must feel that he or she will be better off with the arrangement—again, not necessarily a conscious calculation, since the only tangible manifestation of it may be a desire for the commitment—than without it. Where such a desire exists, both parties value each other highly, and this in turn raises the outcomes of both.

Imbalanced Sex Ratios

Now consider the decision to make an exclusive commitment where the prevailing sex ratio involves a considerable excess of unattached women. Remember the core principle: dependency on a relationship is a function of the extent to which outcomes in that relationship are above the level of expectation for alternative relationships. Generally, it is the level of expectation in the best alternative relationship that counts as the basis for comparing outcomes in a current relationship.

When there are many unattached women to whom a man can relate, his level of expectation in the best alternative relationship is apt to be considerably higher than it would be when the sex ratio were equally balanced and his choices limited. This means that he will be less dependent on the current relationship. Moreover, it means that he is less likely to make a commitment, because its outcomes do not appreciably exceed what he could attain in multiple relationships. The existence of any alternative relationships with high outcomes means that a commitment would carry the cost of giving them up. In a word, when unattached women are available, men are reluctant to make a long-term commitment to one woman.

What about exclusive commitment from the point of view of the woman in the current relationship? Her alternatives are low when sex ratios are low since, few unattached men are available. This means that she is highly dependent on the relationship. Because of this dependency, a lack of commitment on the part of her male partner will be experienced as psychologically costly; it may even mean that she has to bear feelings of jealousy, the pain at times of being slighted, or being alone, or occasionally being rejected by her male partner. All this means that she will be especially eager for and desirous of a mutual commitment. Her outcomes in the relationship, even with their costs, are still above what she could expect in alternative relationships that are either nonexistent or not very attractive. But above all, an exclusive commitment would greatly reduce or even eliminate her heaviest costs, thus markedly raising her outcomes.

Under different circumstances, where the alternatives available to two lovers are limited, both could easily experience highs as the result of a mutually exclusive commitment, which is self-enhancing—a special recognition of self-worth. In the case described here, however, the male partner is unlikely to anticipate a euphoric state resulting from an exclusive commitment, and thus may either decide against it or immediately regret having made it. The regret follows from the costs experienced in having to give up alternative relationships.

Finally, staying with the circumstances where male alternatives are plentiful, let us look at those relationships where a mutual commitment has taken place, either in the form of marriage, living together, or simply exclusive intimacy. Once firm commitments are made, there is a considerable cost in breaking them. Leaving a mate involves inflicting pain, facing accusations, and raising questions of fairness, breach of trust, and guilt. All of these are costs that reduce the outcomes of an alternative relationship. Some costs, perhaps, may be of temporary duration; others may endure for years. Where alternative relationships are more potential than actual, both parties are apt to stay in the current relationship. But under the circumstances where male alternatives are abundant, the constant possibility of alternative relationships remains a threat to the woman and an opportunity for the man.

It may well be that for many men who are committed to a relationship with a woman, the alternatives are not psychologically real or salient. But for those men for whom the alternative seems real enough and attractive enough, the commitment may be threatened or actually broken. At the very least, a man who perceives potential alternative relationships may feel less dependency on the existing relationship and have a feeling of greater power in it. Obviously, this is much less likely to happen where sex ratios are more balanced; moreover, where sex ratios are high, involving many alternatives for women and few for men, commitments are also apt to last longer.

Effects of Structural Power on Exchanges

So far in this chapter we have focused on the generation of dyadic power through social exchanges, ignoring the impact of larger societal processes on two-person relationships. Obviously, the roles of men and women in the larger society and the relative power they have there also have profound effects on the form that exchanges in relationships take. We have referred to economic, political, and other powers that derive from societal structures as structural power. The relative structural power of men and women also has profound effects on the form that exchanges in relationships take. It should be clear that such power can restructure psychological resources and each party's dependence on them. This is accomplished by putting limits and constraints on what is negotiable, by defining resources in ways that are favorable to men and unfavorable to women, and by generating moral values that work to the advantage of men. The unequal division of these powers between the two sexes is responsible for the characteristic forms that sex role identities have taken throughout history.

We can put the matter this way: When structural power is in the hands of the gender that is on the low side of the sex ratio, that power is augmented by dyadic power. Under these circumstances, exchanges are most favorable to the stronger party. When the sex ratio is the other way around, the dyadic power at the disposal of the party whose gender is scarce may serve as a counter to structural power.

More specifically, since men always have the structural power, when they are also fewer in number than women (low sex ratio), their structural power is augmented by dyadic power and thus constitutes a potent source of change in sexual and other relationships between men and women. Even when women are scarce (high sex ratio), the structural power of men may, under some circumstances, provide some advantages in relation to women. Whether or not this occurs depends on the *degree* of imbalance in structural power and in the sex ratio; we have seen that extreme shortages of women have sometimes failed to create better conditions for them and, on occasion, even made matters worse.

Two factors create asymmetries in power imbalances, and quite different situations prevail, depending on whether men or women hold particular kinds of power. In the first place, men have virtually always held the balance of structural power. Thus, this asymmetry is a constant. In Chapter 1, our descriptions of EROS and LIBERTINIA have shown how different sex role identities could be if women held this form of power. The second factor creating asymmetry is also important. The psychological resources that each sex provides for the other are very different. Of course, these are socially determined, and we could envision a very different distribution, yet certain features have been common to men and women in most societies. When women are scarce, the ability of individual men to provide high outcomes for women becomes more important. This usually means that men who possess status, income, and power will be more apt to have female partners than men without these attributes.

When men are scarce, it is often beauty, youth, and more intangible womanly attributes that give a woman an advantage in attracting a man. In this latter situation, contradictory pressures shaping women's roles are apt to be prominent. On the one hand are pressures toward adopting a role much despised by feminists, one that emphasizes a woman's sexual attraction for and complementariness to a man, as reflected in extreme form today in such magazines as *Cosmopolitan,* or in books like *Total Woman.*[2] This role may also emphasize motherhood and homemaking. The direction taken includes doing things specifically to please a man, such as dressing according to his tastes, participating in activities that he enjoys, and catering to his needs. Family activities centering around the children may also have a central place.

This move is one kind of response to the background competition for men in a situation where they are scarce. But an entirely different set of pressures also follows from our analysis and may coexist with the former. The difficulties that women face under these competitive circumstances and the low outcomes that many women have in interaction with men, including successive rejections or abandonments, create pressures toward lessening their dependence on men, and toward attempts to increase women's structural power—either social, economic, or political, as reflected in the current feminist movement. The direction taken here emphasizes being oneself, instead of being what some man wants one to be, giving some attention to one's own needs, and developing an independent identity as a person.

These two directions are essentially incompatible, and presumably the same woman would not attempt to move in both of them at the same time. In fact, to the extent that these reactions to overdependency and the lack of dyadic power are organized into group actions, the groups would be expected to be in opposition to one another. Roughly speaking, the feminists and anti-feminists among women fit these directional movements. In connection with group organization, it is worth noting that the more imbalanced the sex ratio, the larger the number of individuals who get the short end of social exchanges, and the greater the possibility that these individuals will interact to form organizational efforts at correcting the situation. This is one of the reasons why low sex ratios give impetus to feminist movements. Concerted action by men when sex ratios are too high is not without precedent, either. Recall attempts by legislative bodies to limit the bride-price when it had been driven very high by the scarcity of women in the medieval period, or the fact that the Chinese-American tongs put many of their women into brothels when sex ratios were astronomically high.

Those women who already have a satisfactory relationship with a man involving mutual commitment may possibly remain unaware of or unconcerned with the lack of marital opportunities for women. On the other hand, direct threats to their own relationship may stimulate active efforts on their part to improve it. Unfortunately, these may take the form of emphasizing a subordinate feminine role instead of making an effort to achieve a more meaningful relationship. If they are in a relationship that is more transient, where commitment is uncertain, women may even be more active. Most women cannot fail to observe what happens to their close female friends and acquaintances in their relationships with men. They may be called on to provide emotional support for those female friends who experience difficulties or rejection in their relationships with men, and sometimes this may lead them to give more attention to their own relationship with a man.

Some women move, instead, in the direction of more independence and a separate identity. A series of rejections and failed relationships may lead to consciousness-raising, to a redefinition of self and of one's relationship to men. Social, economic, and sexual independence apart from men may become goals. But this does not mean that all feminists, or even a majority of them, have had or currently have inadequate relationships with men. Marked inequities and inequalities experienced by women in most spheres of life may be sufficient motivation for changing the existing state of affairs. Moreover, a woman may have a successful and satisfying relationship with a man but still be exercised by inequality in her career situation or by the unfortunate experiences of her women friends in relation to men.

It is important to keep in mind that the primary condition to which women are reacting is the unequal balance of dyadic power in relationships with men which results from the shortage of men as marital partners, and as aggravated by the fact that men also possess superior structural power. A shortage means that an appreciable number of women will have emotionally disturbing experiences with men; moreover, the surplus of women will lead men to value women less, to be less committed to any one woman, and to deemphasize traditional relationships between men and women and the traditional roles that accompany them. But when the situation is the other way around, when sex ratios are high and there is a shortage of women, men value women more and treat women very differently, though on their own terms. They emphasize and reinforce traditional relationships in which women have a subordinate role. This is possible despite the shortage of women, because men possess superior structural power.

We have considered social exchange processes mostly in the context of low sex ratios, where men are in short supply, and here we add some additional comments within the other context, where sex ratios are sufficiently high (say, above 125), so that for most men, unattached women are not at all easy to find. We need not discuss in detail all of the features of exchanges and alternatives. Obviously, they resemble those outlined for low sex ratios, except that here they are reversed for the two sexes. In addition, some features are different and require discussion.

Let us assume that in love relationships, most of the initiative remains with the male. While this has been weakening in modern times, it is doubtful whether initiative is equally divided yet between male and female. At any rate, when male alternatives are plentiful, male initiative is an advantage to men; it makes it less costly for them to sample optional alternative relationships because the probability of rejection is lower. Male initiative, combined with low female alternatives, makes it doubly costly for women to try out alternative relationships.

We are now discussing a different situation from the earlier one—a situation where female alternatives are plentiful and male choices few. Under these circumstances, male initiative is more costly because the probability of rejection is high. Beyond this, the male is now in the position of having to offer more; if he is to maintain a relationship with a woman, he either has to create high outcomes for her or find a way to limit her alternatives. This latter path more readily leads him to make a mutually exclusive commitment. But much more is involved. Typically, men have more structural power than women; they are in a better position to shape social practices. Hence, the ways in which men raise the outcomes of women differ sharply from the ways in which women raise the outcomes of men when the reverse circumstances prevail. Moreover, men can and do use their power to limit women's alternatives.

One example is the creation of the romantic tradition in which women are highly valued as sweethearts, wives, and mothers. This tradition also emphasizes mutually exclusive, monogamous commitments in the strongest form. Thus, at one stroke, women's outcomes are raised, while at the same time their alternatives are limited. Strong family values are favored; virginity becomes prized. If society considers women who have lost their virginity to have spoiled identities, men have succeeded in controlling female alternatives, at least with respect to sexual intercourse. Women who bear children are often exalted as mothers; the family and the home are cherished. Men give enough to women under these circumstances and make strong commitments so that women often accept the morality that is imposed upon them and support it themselves. Like men, they too believe in virginity, monogamy, motherhood, and family.

In those societies where men have sufficient power, many other customs may arise to control the alternatives that women have in relation to men and to make them the exclusive "property" of one man. Woman's activities and roles are limited; in some societies they may be extremely cloistered. Keeping women from the world of work, preventing them from gaining economic independence, from owning property, from having rights of various sorts, and from gaining an education that might prepare them for a career makes them more dependent on men because it maintains the advantage that men hold in structural power.

In modern industrial societies, a new factor arises to alter the balance of power: Women gain economic power through working. This lessens the structural power of men over them, and men are less able to dictate the forms that relationships between men and women will take. As a larger and larger proportion of women work for a living, the structural power of men vis-à-vis women weakens. Women become able to live apart from men and to relate to them on their own terms. Their greater independence permits them to turn to pursuits other than in the home, such as politics or professional careers. Since women seem to be moving increasingly in this direction, we should anticipate that the marked changes in the relative structural power of the two sexes will bring about profound changes in their roles and identities. We will return to this issue in the last chapter of the book.

Finally, we have been arguing that men have used their favorable balance of power to shape women's roles to their own advantage. One objection that might be raised is that many women not only accept these roles, but even defend and support them, and are happy with them. This is true even when sex ratios are low. In effect, those women who defend traditional roles do not see their relationship to men as having unfavorable outcomes. Why don't they? If a social exchange perspective is to provide maximum understanding, this circumstance requires explanation.

This condition might be reconciled with social exchange theory in several ways. In the first place, the value to be placed on rewards and costs in an exchange is partly an individual matter. How much a particular outcome is worth depends on the individual's psychology. Some features of the traditional role are valued more highly by some women than by others. For example, they may especially enjoy children, or the leisure that comes from being supported by a husband, or even doing things just to please their male partner. So they may perceive the outcomes in their relationship with a man as meeting their expectations, even if the relationship is a traditional one.

Still another aspect of social exchange theory may be invoked to explain how women might be satisfied with traditional roles. Females acquire their values by growing up in a society controlled largely by men. Central values and the social practices that reflect them are acquired through socialization, and these values and practices in turn play a part in defining the outcomes experienced in social exchanges. Consider, for example, the Muslim woman in Morocco who, from our (American) perspective, has a social role far inferior to that of a man.

More than two dozen elements demonstrating this inferiority have been identified.[3] They include the following: adult men can marry on their own decision, while women must obtain the consent of a male authority; polygyny is permitted to a man, but not to a woman; husbands may divorce as they wish, but wives are required to have substantial grounds; virginity is required for a woman's first marriage, but not for a man's; a husband can withhold conjugal sex, but a wife cannot; extramarital sex if prohibited by law for both sexes, but men are not punished, while women are; in case of divorce, children legally belong to the husband; for management of property belonging to children, a *male* representative is nearly always required; women must observe a curfew from sunrise to sunset, while adult men are not restricted; women must be secluded, but men have no restrictions; husbands select the household of residence, since women have no say; mosques are completely open to men, but women must use women's prayer rooms; women may not make eye contact with strangers, but men may; women must dress so as to cover all but the eyes and fingertips, while men may expose their faces and lower arms; brides have restrictions on visiting their family and friends, but men do not; women cannot work without the consent of their husband or father, unless they are widows or divorcees; in inheritance, a female generally gets one-quarter, while a male gets three-quarters; most property in a marriage belongs to the husband, since the wife owns only her personal possessions; women are generally excluded from the courtroom, while men are not; women are restricted from holding such offices as judge, prayer leader, and sultan; adult women can vote, but typically do not because of modesty.[4]

While Muslim women in Morocco often protest some of these restrictions, it is clear that many of them not only accept most of them, but also consider them appropriate and right.[5] Obviously, their outcomes are defined by them in a manner very different from how an American woman might see them. This situation presents no problem for social exchange theory. Remember that satisfaction with a relationship is a function of the degree to which outcomes exceed the level that is expected. Moroccan women come to expect to enact certain roles in relation to men, and these expectations are more or less in line with what is accepted by their society. Thus, there is no reason to expect them to be more dissatisfied with their role than American women are with theirs.

Another point here is that social exchange theory does not require the assumption that exchanges be "equitable." No set of concepts common to both parties permits the calculation of equity. Each role actor expects to be treated in certain ways by the partner. These are the "role rights" that are the partner's "role obligations," and exchanges in role settings go on most smoothly when both parties share each other's definitions of rights and obligations. Still, these are separate for each social role; they are not measured in a common frame of outcomes by the partners themselves or by some concept of "equity."

Instead, in exchange theory, each individual's satisfaction or dissatisfaction with a relationship depends on his or her outcomes in relation to their level of expectation—always remembering that the latter is influenced not only by one's previous experiences in and outside of the relationship, but also by potential alternative relationships. Dissatisfaction with a relationship is brought about either by changes in the level of what is expected, or by changes in outcomes. Thus, if consciousness-raising leads women to expect more from men, they can readily become dissatisfied with relationships that were formerly satisfying. Or, when potential alternative relationships appear more attractive, dissatisfaction may arise. Of course, potential alternative relationships may change one's level of expectation in an existing relationship. For example, a woman might perceive that her friends relate to their husbands in a way that permits them to have a satisfying career in the workplace, and she might imagine a potentially satisfying relationship with a man that would permit her to do so as well.

To sum up this last argument, from the perspective of a participant in social exchanges with a partner, outcomes may be seen as satisfactory or unsatisfactory, depending on whether they are above or below the participant's level of expectation. But since each party's own expectations and outcomes are qualitatively different from the other's, the two sets of outcomes are not usually seen within a single framework as matching each other or as equitable. It is only from the perspective of observers outside of the relationship that this type of comparison can be made, and it is only from this viewpoint that we can make the assertion that women's roles have been shaped to the advantage of males.

This is why many women in the U.S. today do not understand the feminist position. They see their own role as qualitatively different from that of a man, and they have no desire to compete with him in the workplace, so long as they can find a man who will partially or wholly support them in exchange for their performance of the homemaking/mother role. Given their perspective, it is impossible for them to perceive such arrangements as inequitable, since inequity can only be seen from a perspective that is outside of the relationship.

A final comment. The emphasis on outcomes, power, and dependency in social exchanges between men and women as a function of alternative relationships available to one or the other party is apt to appear cynical. It may well give the impression that the track to happiness is best traveled by the jockey who is most skilled at maneuvering to achieve a dominant position. But this would be a gross misreading of our position. Under this misinterpretation, men (or women) would be happiest when women (or men) are widely available and when one refrains from anything but half-hearted commitments. Such a view would overlook the core value of human relationships: the social bond of commitment. A mutual commitment between two persons is a bond of trust, faithfulness, and sometimes love; each party cherishes the interests of the other as his or her own. The outcomes of exchanges in such a relationship are usually immeasurably higher than in relationships where commitment to each other is low.

Why, then, doesn't everyone make such commitments and thereby greatly increase outcomes? The answer is that almost everyone tries to do so, and many couples succeed. Nearly all divorced persons remarry, most of them relatively soon. According to projections made in 1977, slightly more than one out of every three marriages will end in divorce.[6] But it is easy to forget the other side of this statistic: Almost two out of every three marriages will survive until disrupted by death.[7]

None of these data is inconsistent with social exchange theory. We would assume that not all couples are capable of establishing an adequate social bond with firm commitments to each other. The reasons are many: partners may be unsuited to each other in any of a variety of ways; some individuals may be too immature for a long-term, sustained relationship like marriage; still others may not be equipped for the role of father, mother, or even wife or husband. We also suspect that some of these precarious relationships would remain intact under some sex ratio conditions, but not others. When existing relationships are marginal, expectations in alternative relationships are apt to appear attractive, but when a man and woman are bound in a loving commitment, anticipated satisfactions in alternative relationships tend to approach zero, and the existing bond endures.

We move on now to consider the demography of the contemporary period and whether or not the social consequences are those that would be anticipated by the sex ratio thesis.

7

Sex Roles and Family
Among White Americans

A collection of writings on the Women's Liberation Movement[1] entitled *Sisterhood is Powerful* contains titles such as the following:

The Oppressed Majority
Know Your Enemy
The Secretarial Proletariat
It Hurts to be Alive and Obsolete: The Aging Woman
The Politics of Orgasm
Must I Marry?
Song of the Fucked Duck

Two themes concerning men are expressed in different motifs over and over throughout these essays by American women. One theme revolves around a war between the sexes, focusing on the struggle to gain economic and political power, and on various forms of independence and equality. The other involves feelings of oppression, outrage, abandonment, manipulation, exploitation, and rejection. Many woman feel that in men's eyes, they are mere objects for the satisfaction of men's lustful desires, having no other value. Both themes are familiar from the feminist movement.

Several of the titles listed above illustrate this latter theme. The essay about aging is by an anonymous woman of 43 who feels cast aside and isolated. She describes herself as gregarious, interested in others, thoughtful, and intelligent. Divorced, she doubts that she could love and marry again and live that close to another individual. She wants to get to know others and to have them know her, yet she dare not show a man that she finds him attractive, since she thinks that the revelation would be met with withdrawal and repugnance. She feels herself an object of disgust, a mere cipher.

Why should women in these contemporary times be fighting so hard for power, independence, and equality? Why should they feel that they have been used, manipulated, exploited, and cast aside? Although they are far from having status and power equal to that of men, women have been vastly more oppressed in other times and places than they are in America today. Is it only that today they are more aware of the inequalities, and in a better position to fight for a more equal standing? Or is there something more that contributes to the surge of feminism in these contemporary times? We have argued that low sex ratios provide a strong impetus to such movements and contribute to a host of changes in relationships between men and women and in related social institutions. This chapter will look at these phenomena in contemporary America.

Suppose that we could find a period when the sex ratio dropped appreciably, say 10 points below 100, and persisted over a decade or more. What sorts of social changes would we expect to find, and why? Some changes would follow quite directly from the shortage of men or oversupply of women; others would require a mediating psychological process to link low sex ratios with other demographic indices; and still others would involve a complex process resulting in widespread societal changes. Let us first list these expected changes, and later try to explain those that have been found.

With low sex ratios, changes should occur for both men and women in age at first marriage, the proportion who remain single, length of marriage, rate of divorce, the proportion of individuals divorced, and the proportion who remarry. Changes should also take place in the age, social class, and ethnic or racial constraints that ordinarily affect marital selection. We would also anticipate social and moral changes. With low sex ratios, these would include weaker commitments on the part of men toward women, a lower parental investment, more illegitimate births, and an increase in sexual promiscuity. Since the conditions created by low sex ratios impact on women in a number of unfavorable ways, we would expect them to become more aware of their weak economic and social position and, as a result, to engage in organized protest. This would provide impetus for feminist movements. The present chapter discusses all of these issues for the white population in the United States, and in the next chapter, for the black population.

The following section examines sex ratios for population data provided in the last few censuses. After that we discuss the changes that have occurred along with the decline in the sex ratio.

CURRENT SEX RATIOS AND THE MARRIAGE SQUEEZE

Chapter 1 called attention to the "marriage squeeze" prevailing in recent years.[2] The total number of live births in the United States reached a low point in 1945, during World War II. Thereafter, it continued to rise, not reaching a peak until 1957. This meant that ever-larger cohorts of male and female infants were born each year. When these individuals reached adulthood, the customary practice of women marrying men who were older than they meant that women had to seek partners from the smaller number of

TABLE 7.1   Sex Ratios for Unmarried Women Aged 20-24 Years

Cohorts	Year of Census	
	1960	*1970*
Unmarried men 22-26 years		
Unmarried women 20-24 years	111	84
Unmarried men 23-27 years		
Unmarried women 20-24 years	93	67

NOTE: The unmarried include white, single, separated, widowed, and divorced persons. The ratios are calculated from tables of single years of age.
SOURCE: Census of the Population, U.S. Summary, Vol. 1, Tables 156 and 176. Washington, DC: Government Printing Office, 1960, 1970.

men born a few years earlier. The effects of this marriage squeeze are revealed dramatically if sex ratios are computed so that the average age difference between men and women at marriage reflects prevailing practices.

One approximate way of doing this is shown in Table 7.1, which provides marital opportunity ratios for selected age cohorts for the census years 1960 and 1970 among unmarried white men and women (single, divorced, or widowed). These sex ratios were previously reported in Chapter 1 but are repeated here for convenience. The lower the marital opportunity index, the poorer the chances of a woman in finding a male partner of the right age.

From Table 7.1, we can see that opportunities in 1960 for finding men two years older were appreciably above parity (111 men for every 100 women). There were even 93 men available who were three years older. But by 1970, because of the marriage squeeze, marital opportunities had fallen drastically. Each 100 women aged 20-24 years seeking a man two years older had only 84 men to choose from. Even worse, every three women wanting a man three years older than themselves had only two men to choose from. This reflected a critical social situation for the unmarried men and women involved.

It should be understood that the method of computing sex ratios presented in Table 7.1 is an arbitrary one that does not take into account everything about the actual marital situation of these men and women. For example, while the *average* difference between men and women in age at first marriage is 2.5 years, many women marry men considerably more than 2.5 years older than themselves, some who are the same age as they, and a few even younger than themselves. A statistical model representing these actual practices would give a more accurate picture of marital opportunities, but limitations of census data prevent us from developing a wholly adequate model without making some very arbitrary assumptions. One other limitation, even with an adequate statistical model, is that given the imbalance in sex ratios, individuals may very well react to this situation by breaking the age or social class constraints by taking a mate outside the usual bounds.

Another way of getting a broader and more representative view of the sex ratio imbalances in 1960 and 1970 is to obtain marital opportunity indices for a whole set of age cohorts. Since the two-year age interval appears to be

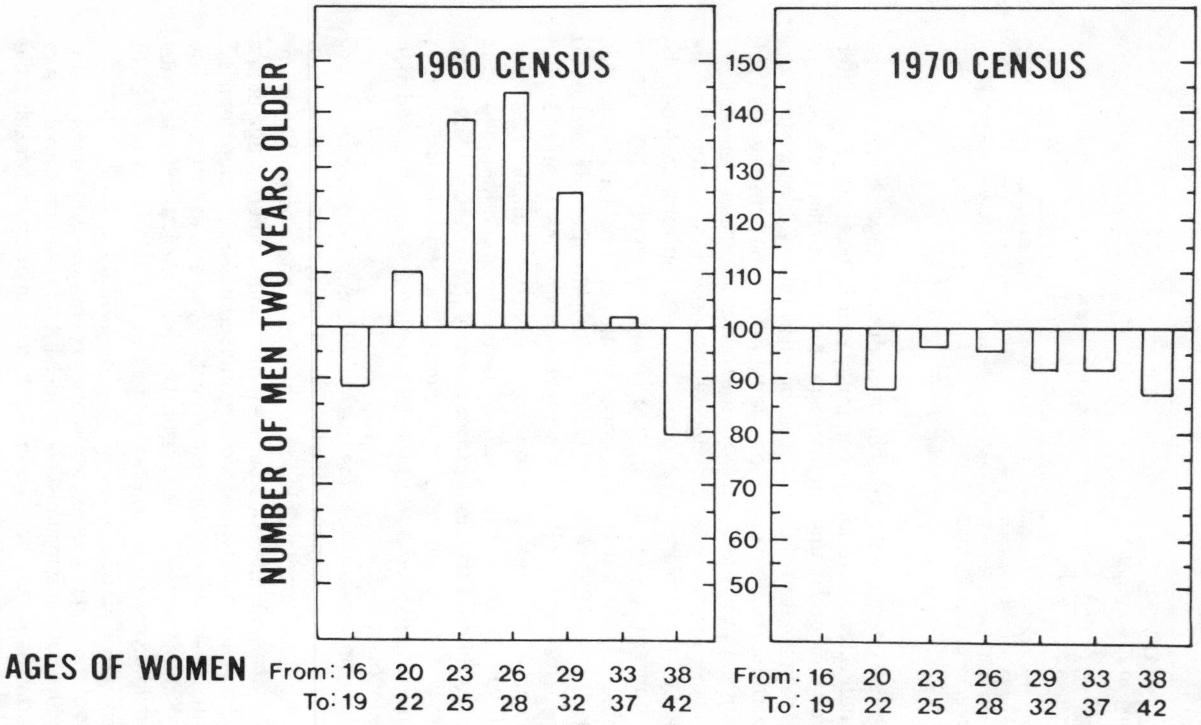

AGES OF WOMEN

Figure 7.1   Marital Opportunities Indices for White Women in 1960 and 1970, by Age

SOURCES: U.S. Bureau of the Census, *Census of the Population: 1970, Subject Reports, Marital Status,* Final Report PC(2)-4C, Table 1; *Census of the Population: 1960, Subject Reports, Marital Status.* Washington, DC: Government Printing Office.

the most common in marriages, we have chosen it for our indices. The number of single men available per 100 women reaching various ages in 1960 and in 1970 is shown in Figure 7.1.

Figure 7.1 reveals at a glance the very different age-sex population structures in 1960 and 1970. We see immediately that, in 1960, women between 20 and 37 years of age had a surplus of potential partners two years older than themselves. For each 100 women, partners ranged from 101 men for women between 33 and 37 years of age to 144 men for women between 26 and 28 years. Women 19 years or younger, along with women 38 years of age or older, were short of potential male partners. Overall, though, the outstanding feature in 1960 is the ample supply of surplus males of suitable ages for women between 20 and 32 years of age.

Now contrast 1960 with 1970. In 1970, *all* women between 17 and 52 years of age had restricted marital opportunities. For women 19 years or younger and 38 or over, there is little difference in marital opportunities between 1960 and 1970; they were too young or too old to be caught in the marriage squeeze. It is the women aged 20-32 years, born during the rising birth rate (1945 to 1957), who are dramatically affected by the marriage squeeze. Ten years earlier, women of their age enjoyed a considerable surplus of males, but now marital opportunities are appreciably below parity.

This analysis also demonstrates that overall sex ratios based on wide age ranges may well conceal imbalances in marital opportunities at certain ages. While such overall sex ratios have been useful for determining gross historical trends or for making very rough comparisons, more precise information about marital opportunities for specific age brackets should be obtained whenever it is available. Once again, we caution that even these age-adjusted ratios have their limits, for they do not assess marital opportunities for the broader range of ages within which women actually obtain a marital partner. We are assuming that these ratios provide only a rough approximation to some precise, but as yet undevised mathematical estimate of marital opportunities.

Throughout this chapter we shall be concerned primarily with comparisons between 1960 and 1970, and also with the 1970s. Although less complete information is available for the 1970s, population surveys provide considerable additional social statistics that follow up trends observed in the 1970s census data. However, marital status is not available by single ages for these years, so we could not obtain a strictly comparable marital opportunity index for the years after 1970. Nevertheless, it is important to examine marital opportunities during the decade of the 1970s and in future years. In order to provide a rough answer to whether the shortage of men will continue well into the 1980s, marital opportunities for selected years up to 1990 have been estimated by a method to be explained shortly.

At the time of writing, single-year age data with marital status were not yet available from the 1980 Census. The last complete data from which the marital opportunity indices could be computed were from 1970. In 1977, however, the Census Bureau published projections of the population size from 1976 to the year 2050, providing figures for each single-age year. This was done by projecting the younger age cohorts of the existing population into the future while making appropriate adjustments for mortality and immigration. The future marital status of these cohorts, of course, is unknown. But in order to compute sex ratios based on the unmarried, we have used the percentages married for each single-year cohort as given in the 1970 Census, subtracting this from the total for each age year. From these estimates of single persons in each future year, we computed marital opportunity ratios, following the same procedures as for known population figures. The result of this analysis is provided in Figure 7.2.

Before examining this figure, we would like to caution that these are crude estimates of the shortage of marital partners, for several reasons. One is that projecting the percentage married for each year of age from the 1970 census begs the question, in a sense, for we expect these proportions to change according to changes in marital opportunities. Thus, the answer to the very question that we are asking is being biased by using the 1970 baseline. Unfortunately, this is the only one available for single-year age cohorts. Moreover, removing the married from the totals, even if poorly estimated, probably gives us better predictions of marital opportunities than would be obtained by using the total figures for married and unmarried. The projections given include armed forces overseas, a factor that would produce an overestimation of marital opportunities for women, especially those seeking marital partners among men aged 20-29 years of age.[3] Of course, this may be somewhat counterbalanced by the fact that using the 1970 baseline for marital percentages is likely to produce an underestimate of marital opportunities for women.

Figure 7.2 shows the number of single men two years older for the years from 1960 to 1990, for various female cohorts. From the figure, the unmarried reader can easily estimate what his or her chances of being married were in 1980, or what they will be in 1985 or 1990, by calculating which age cohort he or she will belong to at that time. For example, unmarried women who will be between 26 and 28 years old in the 1980s will enjoy a surplus of men ranging from about 7 to 16 extra men per 100 women. Those between 29 and 32 years, however, will experience a shortage of single men in the 1980s. This shortage gets much worse for women who will be 33 years or older in the 1980s.

To determine their situation, male readers need to subtract two years from their own age to find the female cohort that contains their potential partners. Thus, men who will be 31 years of age or older in the 1980s will have a surplus of unmarried women 29 years of age, and the older the men, the greater the surplus of unmarried women two years younger. On the other hand, men who will be 16-19 or 23-28 years of age in the 1980s will experience a shortage of potential partners two years younger.

Again, it is worth looking at the four age categories from 20 years to 32 years, for the entire span from 1960 to 1990. In 1960, these four age groups enjoyed a considerable surplus of potential male partners two years older. By 1970, the new cohorts of women reaching these same age categories had the opposite experience—a considerable shortage of men. Through the 1980s, or even by 1990, those cohorts reaching ages 20-22 and 29-32 will not have a surplus of single men two years older.

Those women in the middle groups, from 23 to 28 years of age, do experience a small surplus of men by 1976 and on through the 1980s, increasing by 1990 to about 116-118 men for every 100 women from 23 to 28 years of age. Of course, all of these differences between cohorts are reflections of the marriage squeeze. The year in which a male or female is born can have a profound effect on the marital opportunities experienced at adulthood.

Figure 7.2 also indicates that the younger age cohorts between 16 and 19 years of age were not subjected to the marriage squeeze. Their opportunities were somewhat worse in 1960 than later on, and the variation in the opportunities of these successive cohorts is much less than that for the middle groups. Those women reaching age 33 or older in the years shown will continue to experience severely constrained marital opportunities through the 1980s and into the 1990s. Contrary to what one might think, very little of the plight of older women is due to the fact that men are more mortal than women. By age 40, only about 1 percent more women than men have survived.[4] The shortage of men for women of these ages is more probably due to the fact that divorced men whose ages would be appropriate often marry women more than two years younger than they are, passing over these older women.

DEMOGRAPHIC AND SOCIAL CHANGES

Now that we have demonstrated the striking decline in marital opportunities during the 1960s and continuing into the 1990s, we can examine whether the social changes anticipated by the sex ratio question have in fact occurred.

Supply and Demand

It is possible to make straightforward projections based on the oversupply or undersupply of one sex, although these may well be modified by other conditions. Following a simple supply-and-demand thesis, if there is a shortage of men, we can expect that women will have more difficulty in finding a marital partner from among the available pool. Without making any assumptions about how women might be affected psychologically by this condition, or how men might be affected, we might expect that more women will remain single, marry at a later age, remain divorced longer, and be less likely to remarry if divorced or widowed simply because of difficulties in finding a partner.

We will look at such direct consequences of supply and demand in a moment, but first let us note that psychological factors can very readily be introduced to modify the effects of the male shortage. For example, a woman frustrated in the attempt to find a suitable mate might turn to categories of men that she would not otherwise consider: someone of a different race, or considerably older than she is. She might entertain the possibility of remaining single for an extended period of time and decide to get additional educational training to prepare for a career. Such psychological effects would alter the consequences of the scarcity of men. After discussing the

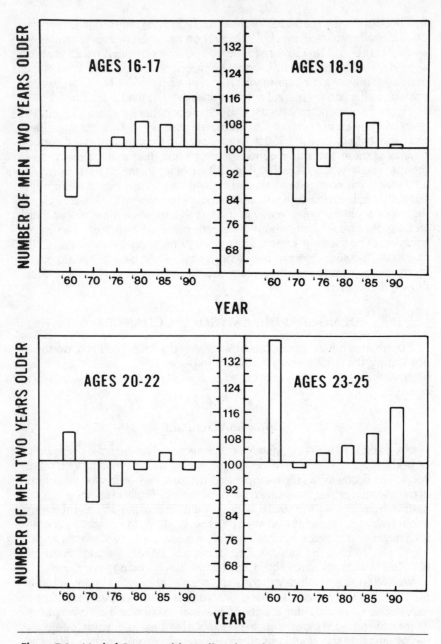

Figure 7.2   Marital Opportunities Indices for White Women from 1960 to 1990,
          by Age

SOURCES: U.S. Bureau of the Census, *Current Population Reports, Projections of the Population of
    the United States: 1977 to 2050,* Series P-25, No. 704, Table 6; *Census of the Population: 1970,
    Subject Reports, Marital Status,* Final Report PC(2)-4C, Table 1. Washington, DC: Government
    Printing Office.

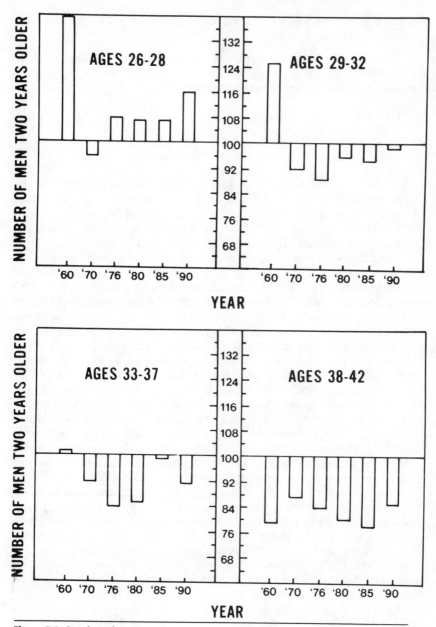

Figure 7.2 Continued

direct consequences of supply and demand, we will take up these more complicated considerations.

Direct effects on women of the scarcity of men. First we will look at those demographic indices that might be directly affected by the shortage of males. Those most relevant to our interests are:

(1) first marriage at a *later* age;
(2) an *increase* in the proportion of women who remain single;
(3) a *larger* pool of divorced women at any one time; and
(4) *more* divorced and widowed women who would *not* remarry.

All of these predictions from the lesser availability of men are confirmed by demographic data. The median age for all women at first marriage increased by only a half-year during the decade between the censuses, from 20.3 years in 1960 to 20.8 years in 1970. During the nine years following, however, it increased by well over a full year to 22.1 in 1979.[5]

The proportion of single (never-married) women has also increased, as shown in Figure 7.3. The height of the black bars represents the percentage of single women aged 20-24 years, and the white bars, those from 14 to 34 years. The substantial increase in the height of the black bars from 1960 to 1979 reveals dramatic changes during the ages when women most often marry—20-24 years. Compared with 1960, in 1979 about two-thirds more women aged 20-24 years had never married, and the largest part of this change took place in the low sex ratio years from 1970 to 1979. Not shown in the figure, but also significant, is the fact that among women aged 25-29 years, little change took place between 1960 and 1970, but by 1979, over one-sixth more of these women were still single.[6]

Unlike many women in their 20's, women who were 35 years or older in 1970 or 1979 (not shown in Figure 7.3) were slightly *more* likely to be married than women who were of the same age in 1960.[7] This too is consistent with sex ratios, for these older cohorts, born earlier, had a larger pool of men to draw from than did those who were under 35 in 1970 or 1979.

Much more dramatic than the increase in single persons was the acceleration in divorce. A common measure of divorce used by demographers is the number of divorced persons per 1000 persons married and living with their spouse. This is a good measure for revealing the proportion of divorced persons in the population at any one time. Figure 7.4 shows the great increase in the proportion of white women of all ages who were divorced—from 38 per 1000 in 1960 to 102 per 1000 in 1979—an increase of 168 percent.[8] The greatest acceleration in divorce took place in the low sex ratio 1970s—121 percent over the 1960 base. By 1979, then, for every 10 married women in the United States, there was one who was currently divorced.

Specific age categories were available only for whites and nonwhites combined. The increase was greatest among women under 30 years of age. For them, the ratio was 246 percent higher in 1979 than in 1960. Almost as high an increase took place among women between 30 and 44 years of age—232 percent.[9]

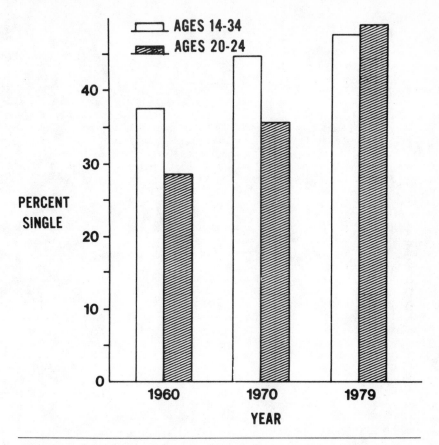

Figure 7.3   Percentage of Never-Married White Women, by Year

SOURCE: U.S. Bureau of the Census, *Current Population Reports*, Series P-20, No. 349. Washington, DC: Government Printing Office, March 1979.

Finally, the remarriage rate for women 35-44 years peaked in 1968 and declined thereafter. Carter and Glick suggest that this might mean that many men were passing over these divorced women and remarrying women who had not been previously married.[10]

In conclusion, all of the demographic conditions involving women that we have deduced directly from a supply-and-demand principle have been found to be associated with the low sex ratios of the 1970s. We have deferred for the moment the many changes that require consideration of more than supply and demand. Now let us ask the question for men: Do they too react in terms of a supply-and-demand principle?

Direct effects on men of the oversupply of women. If we use the same reasoning for men that we have applied to women, based solely on supply

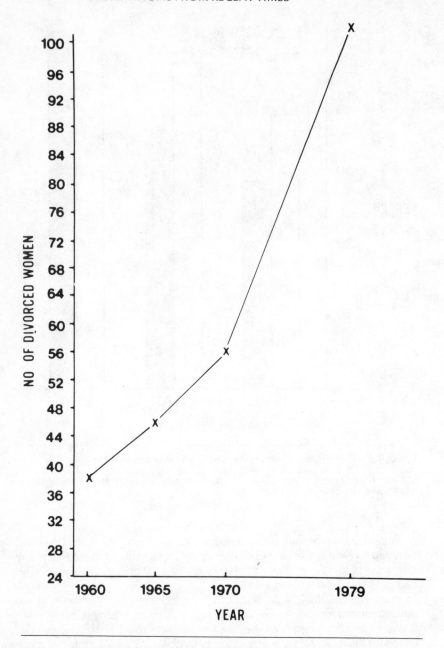

Figure 7.4   Number of Divorced White Women per 1000 Married Persons with Spouse Present, by Year

SOURCE: U.S. Bureau of the Census, *Current Population Reports,* Series P-20, No. 349. Washington, DC: Government Printing Office, March 1979.

and demand, because of the oversupply of women we would anticipate effects opposite to those for women. The following would then be expected:

(1) first marriage at an *earlier* age;
(2) a *decrease* in the proportion of men who remain single;
(3) a *smaller* pool of divorced men at any one time; and
(4) *fewer* divorced and widowed men remaining unmarried.

But what we find is that none of these are true! This fact is of profound importance. It means that we cannot work from simple rules of supply and demand. Psychological, economic, or other conditions are moderating their effects. This means that we need to take a closer look at demographic trends in terms of the social exchange theory developed in the previous chapter to see if we can explain these trends for men. It also means that although the demographic trends for women were consistent with an interpretation in terms of supply and demand, this explanation is probably wrong because it doesn't work for men. Would a social exchange interpretation work for both sexes?

Low Sex Ratios and Social Exchange

We can use the theory developed in the previous chapter to state hypotheses concerning the demographic changes that should be associated with low sex ratios. From the ideas stated there, it follows that since men are in short supply, they have more dyadic power in relation to women, because they have more possible alternative relationships with women. Women, on the other hand, are more dependent on the man with whom they have a relationship, because they have fewer alternatives among the limited number of unattached men. We shall call this a favorable balance of exchange, in this case, for men. Let us now look at the situation for men from this point of view.

Effects on men of the favorable balance of exchange. We will state predictions from social exchange theory first, and then discuss the rationale and the data for each. There should be:

(1) first marriage at a *later* age for men;
(2) an *increase* in the proportion of men who remain single;
(3) a *larger* pool of divorced men at any one time;
(4) *more* divorced and widowed men who do not remarry.

These four hypotheses are exactly the opposite of what we could predict from supply and demand. Supply and demand theory works only for women and makes predictions directly counter to the facts for men. On the basis of supply alone, since women are abundant, we would expect men to marry earlier and to remarry sooner, rather than to remain single. Why don't they? Let us see whether a sex ratio thesis built on social exchange theory will adequately explain the demographic findings for both men and women.

When women are in oversupply, men can more readily have simultaneous or successive multiple relationships with them. Because of the tradition of monogamy, marriage would strip away these alternatives. Presumably, men marry in order to have a woman as a companion and sexual partner, and perhaps to have children. It is not at all clear that the majority of marriages take place because the parties desire children; it may well be the case that this desire in most cases only arises sometime after marriage. With an oversupply of women, it becomes less necessary to marry in order to have a woman as a companion and sexual partner. In fact, if an unmarried man has a relationship with more than one woman, either simultaneously or successively, a monogamous marriage would reduce these to one relationship. From this line of reasoning, the four previously stated hypotheses follow, given the oversupply of women.

The demographic findings are all consistent with these predictions. Age at first marriage went up appreciably in the 1970s. For white and black men combined who are over 14 years old, age at first marriage went up less than one-half a year for the decade of the 1960s, from 22.8 years in 1960 to 23.2 years in 1970. Just as it had for women, this trend accelerated during the 1970s, increasing by almost a year and one-half to 24.6 in 1980.[11]

Many more men chose not to marry in the 1970s. We have calculated the percentage of white men remaining single (never married) in 1960, 1970, and 1979. Once again, for the decade of the 1960s, little change occurred, while rapid change took place in the decade of the 1970s. In 1960, 53 percent of the men aged 20-24 years were still single; in 1970, about 55 percent; but by 1979, 66 percent of the men in this age category were still single! Among white men aged 25-29 years, a similar change occurred. Figures were 20 percent for 1960, 19 percent for 1970, and 29 percent for 1979.[12]

But the marriage rate did not fall off by 1970, and at first sight this might seem confusing. It rose substantially in the 1960s, peaked in 1972 at 11 per 1000 population, and declined thereafter.[13] As it turns out, this is not inconsistent with our explanation. Marriage rates are based on marriages per 1000 population (for all ages) and thus vary with the age composition of the population. A proportionately larger number of young adults in the population should be associated with the higher marriage rates. Thus, the increase in the marriage rate is largely a function of the high birth rates after World War II and the resulting larger proportion of young adults reaching the most eligible ages for marriage during the last decade or so.[14]

The sex ratio question should be answered differently with respect to marrying, since the *proportion* of young adults choosing to marry should decline when sex ratios decline. This expectation is borne out. During the 1960s, the population 18-24 years old increased by 57 percent, while the marriage rate increased by only 25 percent.[15] In effect, the proportion of individuals in these marriage-prone categories who actually married declined during the 1960s, which is, of course, perfectly consistent with the fact that more young men and women remained single.

For white men, the divorce ratio also rose dramatically in the 1970s, although in contrast to women, it underwent only a slight rise in the 1960s.[16] This can be seen in Figure 7.5. The increase during the 1970s is about a 100 percent boost. As among women, the increase was greatest among the men under 30 years old (for whites and nonwhites); it was over four times as high

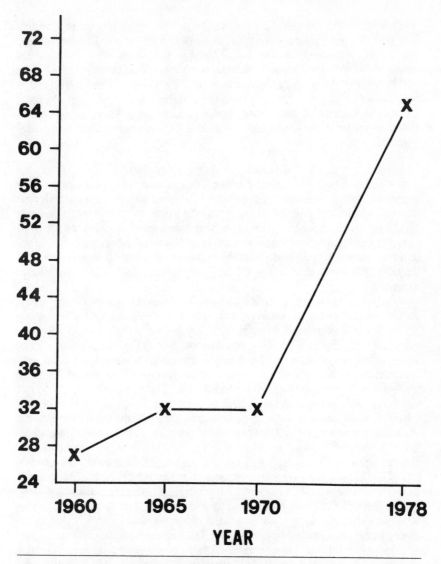

Figure 7.5 Number of Divorced White Men per 1000 Married Persons With Spouse Present, by Year

SOURCE: U.S. Bureau of the Census, *Current Population Reports,* Series P-20, No. 338. Washington, DC: Government Printing Office, 1979.

in 1979 than in 1970. Divorce was also high among men aged 30-44 years—having more than doubled during the 18-year period.

We do not wish to claim that these demographic trends result solely from the social effects of sex ratios. As some demographers have observed, we might expect that young men stay single or divorced men fail to remarry because of economic recession, because of the larger age lump of young men in the population during the 1970s who had to compete for jobs, because of deferring marriage to get more education, or because more men had to serve in the military forces overseas.[17] Yet what we have found is that men under 25 years of age, to whom these notions would most apply, have more often remarried than those over 25 years of age. This suggests a lifestyle change for those men between 25 and 44 years, rather than a financial inability to remarry.

Marital selection and social class. Let us turn now to the social constraints that affect selection of a marital partner. The practice of women marrying up in social class is widespread across many different societies, and in different historical periods.[18] That this is an established practice in our own society is clear, especially in recent times. The best measure of social class for both sexes in published population reports is educational attainment. While income is an often used and valuable indicator of social class, it has severe limitations in the case of women, limitations that are not true of educational attainment.

A question of great interest is whether social class constraints have aggravated the low sex ratio situation prevailing by the later 1960s and early 1970s. We will examine demographic analyses and population data for evidence of such effects. First, let us consider women at the highest educational level. If they are constrained by social practices from marrying a man with less education than they have, their marital opportunities will be far more limited than those women with less education. This condition is created not just because fewer men attain a high educational level, but also by the fact that men at this level, along with college graduates, are the most married and the least divorced. In 1970, 80 percent of the men in this educational category who were 35-44 years old were still married to their first wife, and only 3.4 percent were divorced.[19] In 1975, 82 percent of the men 35-54 years of age at the highest educational level were still in an intact first marriage, compared with an average of 72 percent for men at all educational levels.[20]

Our expectations are, then, that more women at the highest educational level would never have married and, if divorced, would be less apt to remarry because of limited opportunities. The most striking finding in support of these expectations is the number of these women who have never married. In 1970, almost 19 percent of women with a graduate education who were 35 to 44 years of age were still single. This is compared with a figure of between 5 and 6 percent for all women.[21]

That situation was even more extreme ten years earlier. In 1960, even more of these women—24 percent—had never married.[22] One suggested explanation is that it is becoming more acceptable for women both to be married and to have a career.[23] Another report provides a figure of only 11.9 percent single for 1975 among women with five or more years of college, but aged 35-54 years (rather than 44 years).[24] Since, like the 35-44-year group, 19 percent of these women were single in 1970, it appears that the proportion remaining single is continuing to drop. But it should be kept in mind that these women were born in 1940 or earlier, and thus escaped the marriage squeeze.

Turning to divorce, and considering men and women at an age where they have had an opportunity to obtain a divorce (35-44 years old in 1970), we find that for males and females who have completed college but have not continued beyond, the proportion divorced is about the same, a little over 9 percent.[25] But women with one or more years of graduate school were much more likely than men to have been divorced (of those who had married, 16.2 percent versus 9.2 percent).[26] For women aged 35-54 years with five or more years of college in 1970, the figures are 17.0 percent divorced, and in 1975, 18.3, representing a further increase. Figures for the comparable male group are 10.4 percent in 1970 and 10.8 percent in 1975.[27]

Here we must consider the possibility of economic factors in combination with low marital opportunities. Demographers have noted that women at the highest level of education—the graduate level—are more likely to have adequate incomes and therefore to have a choice of lifestyles, which includes remaining single or not remarrying after divorce.[28] In 1970, about three-quarters of the women between 35 and 44 years of age at this educational level were in the workforce, as compared with two-thirds in 1960. Only about half of the women *below* this educational level were in the workforce in 1970.[29] This suggests that these women place a higher priority on satisfaction through work outside the home than do other women.[30] While this may well be true, it is still quite possible that the reduced marital opportunities associated with low sex ratios in the 1970s may not give single, divorced, or widowed women in this high education category much choice about being in the workplace. Of course, this constraint does not apply to married women in this category, most of whom presumably have the option of working or not.

We might expect results similar to those for graduate education if we look at men and women in the highest income brackets, and we do indeed find them. Men and women 35-44 years of age in the highest bracket reveal sharply different divorce patterns. Only about 10 percent of the men who married at least once got a divorce; this was much lower than for men with smaller incomes. Meanwhile, the comparable figure for women was 30 percent! Demographers have suggested that much of this difference may occur because women in this bracket can support themselves and can thus get a divorce without suffering too much of a drop in their standard of living.[31]

It would be of great interest to know whether, under the pressures of restricted marital opportunities, women at the highest educational level violate the common social class constraints by frequently marrying men with less education than they have. Unfortunately, this marital information is not available in a form that allows us to answer the question, but we will see in the next chapter that women in this educational category violate another constraint on marital selection, that of race. We will find that marriages of white women with four or more years of college to black men occurred more frequently as marital opportunities shrank because of declining sex ratios. This was not due to a reduction in race prejudice, for during the same period, marriages of black women to white men dropped off sharply.

SOCIAL AND MORAL CHANGES

Perhaps the most important but also the most difficult to study are the social and moral changes that take place in times of low sex ratios. Many observers have referred to current society as overly narcissistic, with each individual interested only in his or her own gratification and advancement, with little concern for others.[32] It has been dubbed the "me-generation," a term not intended to be limited to the young, but to the general population. Much of this bears on sexual behavior and expressions which, in the new ethos, should be free and uninhibited. Elaborate rationalizations for this freedom have been developed in the name of mental health.

This ethos runs counter to the social bond of commitment. Relationships between men and women, as discussed in the previous chapter, go through various stages of increasing commitment. Commitment is the emergence of a mutual understanding that the interests of both parties will be given top priority, and that each party will behave in accordance with these priorities. In relationships between men and women, one part of this commitment typically means that their sexual relationship will be limited to each other and will exclude other persons as potential sex partners. Marriage is an end-stage in the progressively binding commitments that develop among couples. It is formal and backed by legal authority. While of course there are variations among individual couples (for example, open marriage), by and large marriage, especially, implies sexual exclusivity.

One part of the sex ratio thesis is the idea that under conditions of low sex ratios, which mean that unattached men are scarce and that unattached women are plentiful, the social bond of commitment in male-female relationships becomes weakened. This is true both of premarital and marital relationships. Why this comes about has already been explained in terms of social exchange (see Chapter 6). In a nutshell, the argument is as follows:

(1) In relationships between men and women, men are apt to be less committed, because they typically have more economic power and status, thus making women dependent on them.

(2) Male commitment is strongest when sex ratios are high and unattached women scarce. Under these circumstances, women gain some dyadic power to offset the superior structural power of men. Thus they can negotiate exchanges that are somewhat less unfavorable to them.

(3) Male commitment is weakest when sex ratios are low and men are scarce. The structural power that men have is then augmented by their dyadic power, and they can negotiate exchanges that are most favorable to them. When sex ratios are low:

(a) Men are more reluctant to make a commitment to any one woman, and if they make it, it is a weaker one, and is more apt to be broken.

(b) Women are apt to feel exploited, because even when they meet a male partner's demands, he may break off the relationship.

(c) This feeling of being exploited generates attempts by women to redefine male and female roles in a relationship, to reject a male partner, and/or to reduce their dependency by becoming more independent.

Many of the demographic findings already discussed in this chapter reflect a weakened commitment between the sexes. This is represented quite directly, for example, in the delay in first marriages, in the larger proportion remaining single, in the rising divorce rate, and in the greater proportion of individuals who are divorced at any one time. These findings represent weakened commitment simply in an objective sense; we have not proven that they are brought about by weakened commitments, nor do the data by themselves suggest a subjective sense of weakened commitment.

The question arises as to whether weakened commitment characterizes both sexes or just males. From social exchange theory, it might seem that only men are reluctant to make a commitment—often because of the high level of satisfaction in alternative relationships. Actually, it follows that women too may, under low sex ratio conditions, rapidly become less willing to make a commitment to a relationship with a man. The reasons are several: Under low sex ratio conditions, the outcomes in relationships with men are relatively poor; women are more likely than men to have experienced abandonment, desertion, or betrayal; and they are more likely to develop a feeling of having been exploited. Thus it should not be surprising that they too should become more wary of commitments. Of course, it is the weakened commitment on the part of the male that is critical, for even if women were willing to make full commitments, the supply of men is insufficient to allow them to do so. Considering the oversupply of women, it is this unwillingness to make a commitment on the part of men that could account for their delay of marriage to a later age, and for their greater tendencies to remain single or in the divorced state rather than to remarry.

Several demographic indices not yet discussed can be viewed as indicators of weakened commitment. These include the number of illegitimate births, the number of couples living together without marrying, and the number of single-parent families headed by women. Illegitimate births are clearly related to weakened commitments; either the father or mother or both are unwilling to commit themselves to an enduring relationship with each other through marriage. Two common indices are available: the illegitimacy rate and the illegitimacy ratio. The rate is in terms of the number of births per 1000 unmarried women of childbearing age in a given year. A similar rate for legitimate births is ascertained per 1000 married women of childbearing age. The illegitimacy ratio is slightly more complicated, and changes in it over time may occur in several ways. The ratio is usually reported as the number of illegitimate births in a given year, per 1000 live births, both legitimate and illegitimate. What this amounts to is a proportion: If there were 100 illegitimate births out of every 1000 live births, this would be 100/1000 or 1/10 of all births.

As shown in Figure 7.6, for white women, the illegitimacy rate rose slightly but steadily for two decades to over 14 per 1000 unmarried women in 1970, and then dropped to below 12 in 1975. The illegitimacy ratio, on the other hand, showed a sharp increase, especially from the mid-1960s to the 1970s, reaching a peak in 1975 (the last year figures were available) of about 72 illegitimate births per every 1000. This came about partly because of the

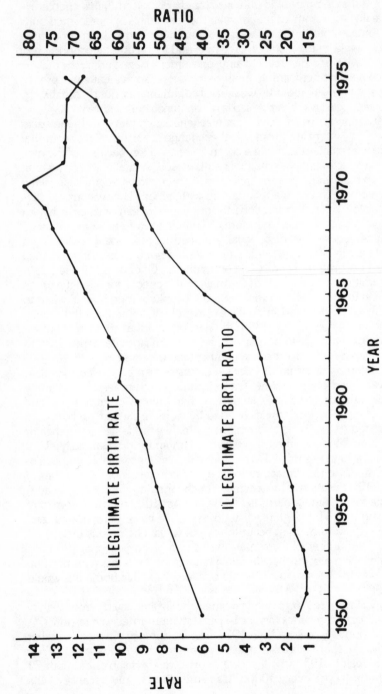

Figure 7.6 Number of Illegitimate Births per 1000 Unmarried White Women of Childbearing Age and per 1000 Live Births, by Year

SOURCE: National Center for Health Statistics, *Vital Statistics of the United States, 1975*, Vol.1— *Natality*. DHEW Publication No. (PHS) 78-113. Washington, DC: Government Printing Office, 1978.

large number of unmarried women in the population, and because of the large number of illegitimate births. This is more than three times the ratio in 1960, which was only about 23 out of every 1000. Clearly, unmarried people who have a child are less willing to marry and form a family.

Another reflection of weakened commitment would be living together with a member of the opposite sex without marriage. While the proportion of couples living under these circumstances remains relatively small (about 3 percent in 1979), the increase in the fraction was dramatic during the 1970s and coincides with the falling sex ratio. In 1970 there were about 523,000 unmarried couples, up from 439,000 in 1960. By 1979, this figure had almost tripled, to 1,346,000 couples. Even the one-year interval increases are impressive: 19 percent from 1977 to 1978, and 18 percent from 1978 to 1979.[33] About three-quarters of these couples had no children, and almost half of them were under 34 years of age. About one-half had never been married, and less than a third had been divorced.

There is no way of estimating precisely how many of these couples were sexual partners. Some no doubt had a landlady-tenant relationship, but since the great majority were in the same age group or in an adjacent one, and had no children present, it appears that most of them were roommates, companions, or friends.[34] Demographers report that age comparisons indicate that many more couples in 1960 than in the 1970s were apparently an older landlady with a young male roomer. For similar reasons, it is difficult to estimate the proportion of all couples, married and unmarried, who are living together in the unmarried state. At least 1 percent of all people and all households in the United States includes unmarried couples living together, but the true percentage could be as high as 4 percent.[35] As many as 8.3 percent of divorced men under 35 were living with an unrelated woman.[36]

Still another measure directly reflecting lack of male commitment is the number of single-parent families headed by women—the great majority of these arising through divorce or desertion. The proportion of such families has risen steadily since 1960, from about 4,500,000 in 1960 to 8,458,000 in 1979, an increase of about 88 percent.[37] Two-thirds of these women have their own children under 18 years of age living with them. About one in every seven families is headed by women with no husband present. While well over 11,000,000 children are living with their mother as family head, only about 1,000,000 live with their father. Many of these families are black, and we will discuss this further in the next chapter. Nevertheless, the number of white families headed by women has increased by about two-thirds, so that at least 11.5 percent of all white families are currently headed by women.

The increasing ratio of illegitimate births and the increase in the number of couples living together without marriage represent not only weakened commitment, but also weakened constraints on sexual behavior. Various other evidence points clearly to more permissive attitudes toward sexual intercourse outside of marriage. Most colleges and universities, for example, now have coeducational dormitories with only weak constraints on temporary or enduring sexual liaisons between those living in them. Gone are the days before mid-century when colleges and universities served as parent-surrogates, when house mothers monitored contacts between men and women in the living room of the house and saw to it that women were in their rooms by 10:00 p.m.

Numerous surveys of college students and of younger adolescents indicate that, compared with earlier decades, premarital intercourse increased markedly in frequency by the late 1960s and into the 1970s.[38] Especially notable, because of its relevance to the sex ratio question, is the point that the increase has been largely among females, so that they are approaching the same frequency as males. This is consistent with the idea that lower frequencies for females when women are in the minority result from special constraints placed by society on their sexual behavior. We have interpreted the older double standard of sexual morality as a system of constraints that are most likely to be imposed when there is a surplus of men. The constraints are imposed upon women by their parents so as to preserve exclusive sexual rights, although eventually these constraints become a commonly shared morality. When women are no longer scarce, the constraints disappear.

While the increase in premarital intercourse on the part of females is consistent with the sex ratio thesis, it cannot be demonstrated that the increasing surplus of women caused it, primarily because of other changes that took place concurrently. For example, improvements in and a greater availability of birth control devices both occurred during the same period, thus potentially reducing the fear of pregnancy that might otherwise deter females from engaging in coitus. At the same time, it should be kept in mind that a very large proportion—at least half—of premarital encounters among the young occur *without* the use of any birth control devices or methods, or else with only older, less effective techniques, such as withdrawal or douching.

Other demographic data also point to more liberal attitudes toward sexual intercourse. In addition to extramarital intercourse, represented by the illegitimate birth ratios already discussed, many legitimate children are conceived prior to marriage, which takes place after pregnancy occurs, but before they are born. Of those women who in 1975 had ever been married, 9 percent reported that their first child had been born before they were married! In addition, another 24 percent of first births in the 1970s occurred less than nine months after the date of marriage. As Glick and Norton note, this means that about one-third of all first births in the 1970s were premaritally conceived![39]

Increases in sexual behavior are not limited to premarital intercourse. Apparently, erotic activity in general has increased. Shorter has compared data collected by Kinsey in the 1940s with that gathered by Hunt in the early 1970s and concluded that sexual activities and styles have undergone a dramatic change.[40] Erotic activity within marriage has greatly increased in frequency and variety. Coital frequency and length of intercourse have both increased substantially, as has length of foreplay. These data also show dramatic increases in oral/genital sex. Greater variety is suggested by the fact that three-fourths of the 1970s couples reported experimentation with the female on top, as compared with only one-third of Kinsey's couples. While rear-entry vaginal intercourse was reported by only 10 percent of Kinsey's sample, it characterized 40 percent of the 1970s groups.

While it is true that both Kinsey's and Hunt's studies can be criticized on the grounds of sampling representativeness and other shortcomings, the differences between the two are so great that it seems likely that a real increase in and diversification of erotic activity has occurred. This is consistent with the thesis that in societies where sex ratios are low, protective norms toward women weaken and constraints on sexuality fade. We have seen that promiscuity increases in such societies, but what is clear from the increased eroticism within marriage is that the trend is a general one, and that low sex ratio societies have more liberal attitudes toward all sorts of sexual expression.

The various demographic indices that we have discussed, along with the evidence of increasing sexual permissiveness, clearly suggest less willingness to commit oneself to marriage and family living. This interpretation would be further strengthened if we had some evidence that attitudes valuing the family had weakened by the 1970s. Especially desirable would be a comparison of the attitudes that men held toward women in 1960 with those in 1970, especially with respect to exclusive commitment and marriage. Fortunately, at least one study can be cited for each of these kinds of evidence.

One way to look at commitment to the family is to analyze the content of women's magazines over time. To the extent that such magazines reflect the changing values of the reader audience, they can constitute a quantitative measure of change. One such study of the *Ladies Home Journal* is illustrative.[41] Articles and stories portraying the family as stable, warm, and fulfilling for the woman characterized the late forties and early fifties. References to moral education, a moral life, and a moral code were frequent. But in the late sixties, issues that had earlier been viewed in moral terms now were characterized in terms of personal fulfillment or other personal perspectives. While the family and a secure marriage were still considered important, their support as a *moral* imperative was much less in evidence, and personal fulfillment for the woman came to the fore, including the responsibility of greater sexual freedom.

Men's attitudes toward women, sex, love, and marriage were indirectly assessed for the period from 1957 to 1960, and from 1970 to 1974, in an Ed.D. dissertation stimulated by the sex ratio question and carried out under the supervision of the second author of this book.[42] The method used was the following: It was assumed that, by and large, the attitudes toward women attributed to the main male characters in best-selling American novels published in these two periods would reflect to some extent the attitudes that men in the society at large held at those times. While there would be many exceptions to this generalization, the hypothesis seemed worth testing. The first period was one where sex ratios were relatively balanced, and attitudes associated with the high sex ratios of earlier times should still have been prevalent. Later, the substantial drop in sex ratios evident by the early 1970s should have brought about associated changes in attitudes.

Ten best-selling American novels published between 1957 and 1960, and another ten from 1970 to 1974, were selected. All had to have leading male characters who made statements about women, sex, love, and marriage. The investigator first identified a large set of attitudes or actions that should be associated with a high sex ratio society and another set for a low sex ratio society. Examples associated with a high sex ratio are:

Adultery is morally unacceptable.
Marriage is an attractive prospect.
Sexual intimacy is an expression of love.
Marriage is a permanent relationship.
Family life is important.
Breaking up a relationship is painful.
A loved woman should be prized and protected.

Examples associated with a low sex ratio are:

Adultery is morally acceptable.
Marriage is not an attractive prospect.
Single life is attractive.
Love or sexual attraction are bases for a temporary relationship.
Casual sex is attractive.
Self-sufficient women are desirable.
An existing relationship does not inhibit new contacts.
Family and children are not considered desirable.
Disappointment but not pain is felt at breaking up a relationship.

Every statement or incident in these books that could be classified as belonging to either set was identified. Scores were then obtained by counting all of the attitude statements in each of the 20 books and determining the proportion that were low sex ratio attitudes. Our expectation was that, given the considerable difference in sex ratios between the two periods, the circa 1960 books would have a few low sex ratio attitudes, and the circa 1970 books, many low sex ratio attitudes. We were not disappointed; the findings were overwhelmingly supportive. For the ten books for the period 1957-1960, the proportion of low sex ratio attitudes ranged from 0 percent to 48 percent, with the median book about 22 percent. In contrast, for the ten books for the period 1970-1974, proportions of low sex ratio attitudes ranged from 43 percent to 94 percent, with the median book about 65 percent. Nine of the ten books from 1970 to 1974 had larger percentages of low sex ratio attitudes than any of the ten books from 1957 to 1960. This is striking confirmation of our sex ratio thesis.

CONCLUSIONS

In closing this chapter, let us return to the issues raised in the beginning of the chapter and go beyond the cold demographic facts that we have described. The 1970s have seen an intensification of several trends. Among these were an increase in sexual freedoms, including more premarital and extramarital sex; a weakening of the family, in terms of delays in marrying and more divorce; and a stronger push by women for sexual, economic, and political independence. Many social observers have suggested that individuals in our contemporary society are more concerned with their own pleasure and satisfaction than with concerns that are more social and that involve the welfare of other persons. This is suggested by, for example, the repeated success during the 1970s of books that emphasize how to satisfy

one's own needs and how to express oneself; by the emergence of encounter groups and various other weekend group activities intended to help one
get more personal satisfaction out of life; and by the appearance of swinger's
clubs and other sexual freedoms.

Is any of this brought about by the low sex ratio conditions of the 1970s
associated with an abundance of unattached women? We have suggested
that low sex ratios *are* contributory to social conditions such as these. But
since we suspect that they alone are not responsible, it seems important to
review the background context, which, when combined with a low sex ratio,
brings about the effects. First and foremost is the fact that, compared with
women, men have overwhelming structural power. Males hold almost all of
the positions of power in government, in business and industry, in the military, in science, in education, and in the professions. While women are gaining ground in this respect, they are still far behind. Although these areas are
all sources of formal power, it seems reasonable to assume that those who
hold formal power are also more influential in shaping informal social norms
that people in society live by. What we are suggesting in answer to the sex
ratio question is that, given the abundance of unattached women, men will
shape to their advantage the form that relationships between men and
women take. With a surplus of women, sexual freedoms are more advantageous to men than to women. Decreased willingness to commit oneself to an
exclusive relationship with one woman is consistent with that fact.

All of this encourages one to serve one's own satisfaction, whether or not
at the expense of others. It follows further that the persistence of such circumstances would leave many women hurt and angry. Other women, not themselves without a man, would nevertheless often be aware of the unfortunate
experiences of their women friends in relations with men. These circumstances should impel women to seek more power and, incidentally, turn
them more toward meeting their own needs. Most forms of feminism are
directed to just such ends.

This interpretation in terms of power or control is considerably strengthened if we look at what happens in high sex ratio societies where unattached
women are relatively scarce. Once again, the baseline condition is that men
hold the structural, or societal, power. But the important difference is that
women, can, under certain circumstances, mitigate the effects of this male
dominance by virtue of the fact that because of their scarcity, they have
dyadic power. This means that they are less dependent on a particular
man—there are a lot more of them out there—and they can negotiate a
better bargain in their relationship with a particular man because they have
alternatives and he does not. Thus, individual men are put in the position of
having to woo unattached women and to make various concessions.

Since even under conditions that are optimal for women, men have
much more societal power than women, the form taken by social norms
governing the relationships between men and women still favors men, although under high sex ratio conditions, women can use their dyadic power
to modify that form somewhat. It is easy to see that under high sex ratio
conditions, sexual freedom for women would be disadvantageous to men.
The surplus of men and shortage of women would mean that women would

have more control over most relationships. They would be able to select their partners and would be more in control. But this tends not to be the case; women usually do not have sexual freedom under high sex ratio conditions. Typically, strong constraints are present. Women are sheltered and protected—not only wives, but also daughters. Virginity at marriage is often insisted upon, and dire penalties for violation are imposed, making premarital sex dangerous. Constraints on the freedom of women provide men with more control over their relationship to women—particularly daughters and wives. It seems reasonable to assume that it is their possession of structural power that brings this situation about. But under low sex ratio conditions, with an abundance of unattached women, such constraints are no longer necessary in order to afford men access to women. Aptly enough, these constraints appear to have faded in our own contemporary United States.

What of the fact that in some societies, women themselves accept sexual constraints, even to the point where they consider them a moral good? Is this consistent with our line of argument? We have asserted that male societal power is the key to understanding these constraints in a high sex ratio society. That they become a moral issue is not inconsistent with our argument, although it requires additional explanation. From the male point of view, of course, identifying the constraints as moral would only strengthen them, and serve their purpose that much better. The probability is that sexual constraints placed on women become a moral imperative only after the constraints have been the standard practice; in that case, they could not be used to substitute for our argument in terms of societal power. The constraints become a moral value for women as well as men in the same way that other standards become moral, but there is no need here to enter into this complex issue.

Perhaps the usefulness of the imaginary societies introduced in Chapter 1, EROS and LIBERTINIA, will now become more apparent. In both of those societies, women had the societal power. In EROS, with low sex ratios and thus a shortage of men, we found women shaping a protective morality for *men*. But men had dyadic power, and women wooed them. Only in LIBERTINIA could women take full advantage of their superior societal power, for with the high sex ratios there, they could take advantage of the abundant supply of unattached men. They created a sexually permissive society very much like our contemporary United States, except that the sex roles were reversed.

In the final chapter, we will ask about future trends in relationships between men and women and in the family. We have some idea now of what sex ratios will be like, at least for the next decade, but what is also important is the future distribution of societal power. We think that we have demonstrated that both societal and dyadic power are crucial to relationships between men and women, and we shall see that both of these are apt to change in the future. Before going to that chapter, we turn now to the next chapter to look at the situation of black men and women in recent times in the United States.

8

Sex Roles and Family
Among Black Americans

Just as the eastern European Jews living in shtetls provided a rare opportunity to examine a high sex ratio society, American blacks offer unusual insights into a low sex ratio subculture. Aside from postwar shortages of men in various countries, American blacks present us with the most persistent and severest shortage of men in a coherent subcultural group that we have been able to discover during the era of modern censuses. Such acute shortages are apt to make clearer other demographic conditions that accompany low sex ratios. They also make it easier for us to identify crucial conditions or circumstances that bring about the low sex ratios themselves. This chapter will examine the case of American blacks in order to enlarge our knowledge of the causes of low sex ratios and to examine further their social consequences.

Our focus here is on demographic characteristics and their social consequences, such as high rates of divorce and illegitimate births. Nothing reported here is intended to suggest that the racial or biological characteristics of blacks produce the social consequences described. So far as we have been able to ascertain, the social conditions that we report all follow from demographic features of the black population, rather than from any biological characteristics of the black race. We assume that a white population having the same demographic features as the black population would demonstrate the same social consequences. Moreover, these social conditions do not seem to be directly produced by the historical circumstances that American blacks have experienced. For example, some social scientists have suggested that the high incidence of single-parent families headed by black women has occurred because "matriarchal families" are a part of "black culture."[1] Explanations of that kind are unwarranted, given the simple fact that there is an acute shortage of black men. Finally, being black *has* contributed indirectly to the social conditions we describe, in that some of the demographic characteristics of the black population are accentuated or even wholly produced by the fact that blacks have been an object of prejudice, and thus have lower incomes and less education than whites. We will see that some of the social conditions are thereby aggravated, and that sex ratios are lower because of these effects.

By this time it should be clear what characteristics are to be anticipated in a subculture with very low sex ratios. We should find considerable family disruption, displayed in very high incidences of divorce, single-parent families headed by women, illegitimate births, remaining single, and failing to remarry. Men should be reluctant to make a commitment to remain with a woman and to share in raising children. They should have misogynous attitudes toward women. Women should experience considerable stress, despair, and anger, some of it directed at exploitation by men. Such psychological pressures should in turn produce a variety of symptomatic effects among young women who face the most trying circumstances. Married men should be more satisfied with their marriages than women, because they hold a favorable balance in social exchanges, and thus are apt to have more control over their marital circumstances. Conversely, married women are less apt to be content. None of this is intended to characterize *all* relationships between men and women under low sex ratio conditions, but under such conditions, a larger proportion of such relationships are expected to be unsatisfactory than would be the case if sex ratios were balanced or above 100.

SEX RATIOS AMONG BLACKS

Here we will not only present statistics on sex ratios, but because they are unusually low, we will also attempt to identify some of the conditions that depress sex ratios. Our discussion will weave back and forth from descriptive presentation to explanation of the reasons for the findings. In considering these data, it should be kept in mind that prior to 1970, blacks were included in the census category, "nonwhite." While most of the nonwhite population was black, it also included other races. Thus, figures prior to 1970 should be regarded only as estimates.

Sex ratios are available for the total population of nonwhites of all ages, both married and unmarried, all the way back to the Civil War. While these are of very limited use for our purposes, they do show the historical trend. Nationally, the overall ratios for the nonwhite population rose during the decades from 1880 to 1920, to 99.2.[2] After that they fell continuously but gradually until 1970, which yielded a ratio of only 90.8. Thus, nonwhites have experienced sex ratios below 100 for a considerably longer period than whites. They are similar, however, in that for both populations, 1970 represents the lowest point.

Of much greater value for our purposes are marital opportunity indices of the sort that we presented in the previous chapter for the white population. These are presented in Table 8.1 for the years 1950, 1960, and 1970. Since the men are between 18 and 44 years of age, while the women range from 16 to 42 years, the men are, on the average, two years older than the women. We

TABLE 8.1 Marital Opportunity Indices for Unmarried Black Men and Women

Census Year:	1950	1960	1970
Sex Ratio:	105	87	73

NOTE: These ratios have been computed for unmarried black males aged 18-44 years, and for unmarried black females aged 16-42 years. Unmarried means single, widowed, or divorced.
SOURCE: U.S. Bureau of the Census, *Census of the Population: 1970 Subject Reports, Marital Status.* Final Report PC (2)-4C, Table 1. *Census of the Population: 1960 Subject Reports, Marital Status.* Final Report PC (2)-4C, Table 1. *Census of the Population: 1950, Marital Status,* Vol. IV, Part 2, Chapter D, Table 5.

can see immediately that the nonwhite population had a balanced opportunity index in 1950, but that by 1960, this ratio had fallen sharply to only 87. Further, it underwent another sharp drop during the decade of the 1960s, reaching a low of 73 in 1970. With opportunity indices this low, we would expect to find dramatic social effects—and we will not be disappointed.

Because of the wide age range, these indices are very crude and may be quite inaccurate for some cohorts within the range. We can get a more precise estimate of marital opportunities by only including cohorts within a narrow range of ages. In the early twenties, when most first marriages commonly take place, even lower indices are obtained, using a three-year difference between men and women. Figure 8.1 depicts these indices for both whites and non-whites for 1960 and 1970. Both the dramatic change from 1960 to 1970 and the especially depressed ratios for nonwhites are apparent.

From these figures, it appears that in 1970, for the age cohorts most eligible for marriage, there were almost two black women for every man. This is for the United States as a whole. Regional variations create even worse situations in some locations, and better ones in others. As will be spelled out later, the migration of black men and women since World War II in differing proportions from rural to urban areas, or from one region of the United States to another, has accentuated the shortage of black men in some places, especially the larger cities of the Northeast and South.

We can get a better picture of marital opportunities for blacks by examining indices for the whole range of ages, computed in the same manner as previously for whites (see Chapter 7). These give us a clear picture of the severely restricted marital opportunities experienced by black females. Figure 8.2 reports these indices for 1960 and 1970. Recall that the indices for the overall nonwhite black population for these years, mentioned earlier, were 87 and 73, respectively. As a result, we would expect 1970 to be much worse than 1960. This is confirmed by Figure 8.2. The year 1970 shows severe shortages of black men in every age category—30 or more out of every 100 black women do not have a potential partner in the marriage pool, except for ages 16-19, where 21 women lack a partner.

The effects of the marriage squeeze on black women are similar to those for white women, except that the squeeze is even more painful for blacks. As in the case of white women, black women who reached an age between 23 and 32 in 1960 were close to parity in the number of suitable black men who were available. But because they were born during the rising birth rate, black women reaching these ages in 1970 experienced a severe shortage of single

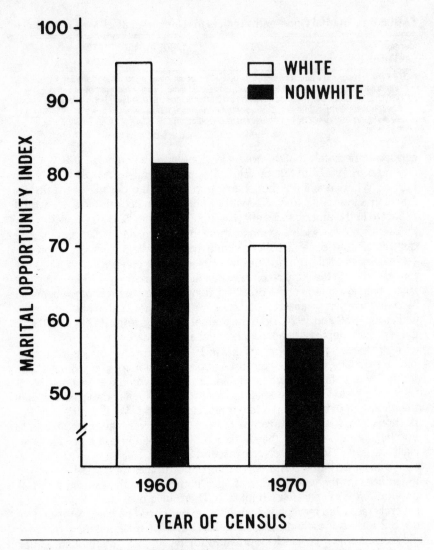

Figure 8.1 Marital Opportunity Indices in 1960 and 1970 by Race for Unmarried Females 20-24 Years Old

SOURCE: U.S. Bureau of the Census, *Census of the Population, 1960, U.S. Summary,* Vol. 1, Tables 156 and 176; *Census of the Population, 1970, U.S. Summary,* Vol. 1, Tables 156 and 176. Washington, DC: Government Printing Office.

black men. One difference from the white pattern is that even the other age categories are no better off, except for those who are 19 or under. This reflects other conditions that characterize the black population, which will be discussed shortly.

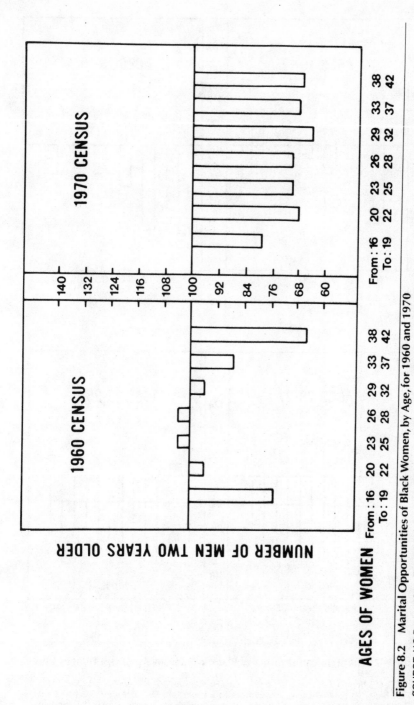

Figure 8.2 Marital Opportunities of Black Women, by Age, for 1960 and 1970

SOURCE: U.S. Bureau of the Census, Census of the Population: 1960, Subject Reports, Marital Status, Final Report PC(2)-4C, Table 1; Current Population Reports, Projections of the Population of the United States: 1977 to 2050, Series P-25, No. 704; Census of the Population: 1970, Subject Reports, Marital Status, Final Report PC(2)-4C, Table 1. Washington, DC: Government Printing Office.

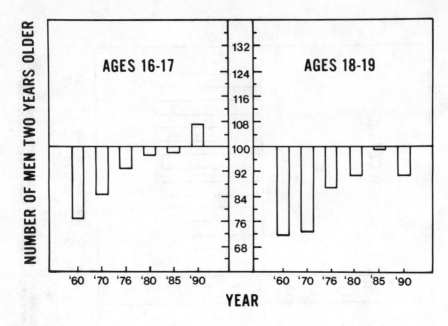

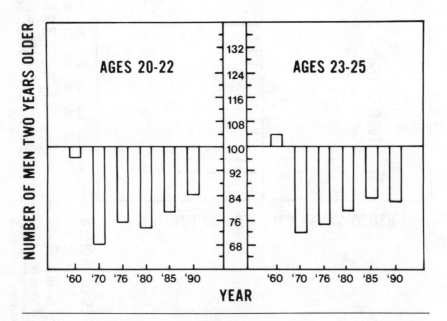

Figure 8.3   Marital Opportunities of Black Women, by Age, from 1960 to 1990

SOURCE: U.S. Bureau of the Census, *Census of the Population: 1960, Subject Reports, Marital Status,*
    Final Report PC(2)-4C, Table 1; *Census of the Population: 1970, Subject Reports, Marital Status,*
    Final Report PC(2)-4C, Table 1; *Current Population Reports, Projections of the Population of the*
    United States: 1977 to 2050, Series P-25, No. 704. Washington, DC: Government Printing Office.

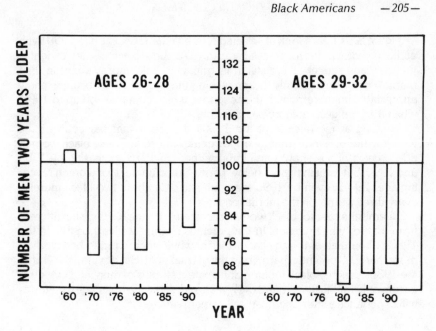

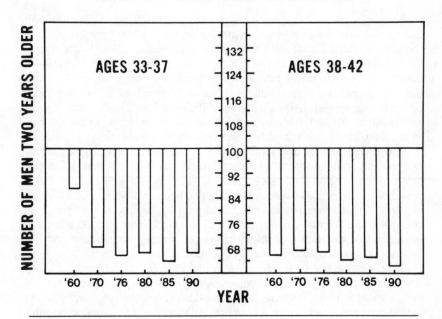

Figure 8.3 Continued

Figure 8.3 offers a look at selected future years, ranging up to 1990, with earlier years included for comparison. In 1976, those black women caught in the marriage squeeze were still in its grip, with little improvement in their marital opportunities. Only those reaching the ages of 16-19 begin to show appreciable improvement in their chances, which continues on up to 1990, when the youngest category passes parity.

Looking at the decade of the 1980s, it is clear that the younger the woman, the sooner her marital opportunities improve. Those black women 20-25 years of age show some improvement in 1976, increasing by 1985 and 1990, but remaining well below parity. Unfortunately, for women reaching ages 29-42, even by 1990 there are still only about two black men for every three women in the marital pool.

Overall, the case for black women revealed in Figure 8.3 is vastly different from that for white women. In the previous chapter we learned that in the 1980s, about half of the age categories of white single women had close to more than 100 potential partners in the marital pool. But not until the end of the 1980s can *any* black women anticipate a surplus of men, and even this occurs only for black women 16-17 years old. All of the other age categories will experience a shortage, nearly all of them severe.

Effects of Underenumeration in the Census

Although census-taking is residence-based, attempts are made to include individuals who are away from home during the counting period, such as those in hospitals, hotels, prisons, or other institutions. Those in the armed forces who are stationed in the United States are included in the resident count, but those in the armed forces overseas are tallied separately from military records and are not included in the resident tables. Clearly, this focus on residence for census-taking creates difficulties for including people who are transient. Among the very poor, some drift from abode to abode, and many sleep in parks, automobiles, and various other nonresident locations.[3]

Because of the presumption that many black men do not have a permanent abode, some authorities believe that census methods overlook a disproportionate number of black males. Our ratios and indices have been based on actual census counts, without any corrections being made. Generally speaking, the assumption that some people are missed in any census count, especially if they are transient, is a reasonable one, and some corrections are in order. But a problem arises concerning the amount and the manner in which corrections should be made.

Census corrections are involved in a highly technical controversy. Years after a census has been published, articles by demographers and other experts appear from time to time suggesting sets of corrections to be applied to the earlier census figures. Unfortunately, little agreement exists among the experts concerning the proper corrections. The suggested corrections range from quite small percentages, having little significance, to rather substantial ones. One extensive study published in 1974, for example, recommends very large upward adjustments for black males, but not for black females, a result that would raise sex ratios based on actual counts in an amount ranging from 6 to 13.7.[4] For example, blacks 25-34 years of age who were found and reported in the 1970 census yield a ratio of 84.2, but the 1974 recommendation would raise it to 96.4. Similarly, the 1960 count yielded a sex ratio of 82.8, whereas the corrected figure would be 96.5.

Many different methods of correcting underenumeration have been suggested, but these methods do not agree in the figures they yield. A discussion of the logic and data on which the underenumeration hypothesis rests is provided by the U.S. Census Bureau.[5] Essentially, the final figure for sex ratios depends on the relative credence given to the assumptions on which the statistical corrections are made, as well as to the figures reporting the people actually found by the census.

Clearly, the matter of the "true" sex ratio for blacks cannot be resolved here. But several important points need making. One is the probability that those men who are overlooked in the census count and again in a recount are less likely to be good candidates for the marital pool from which women might choose. They are more likely not to have a stable residence, and may not even be employed. Another point is that, as we have seen, when black sex ratios are based on male and female cohorts two or three years apart in age, the severely restricted marital opportunities for black women become especially clear. Substantial shortages of males would still appear in marital opportunity indices even if the largest of the recommended corrections were made. Finally, a much larger proportion of black than white men are in penal and other institutions and are thus removed from the marital pool even though they are counted in the census. Hence, we can safely conclude that marital opportunities for black women are severely constrained. Before discussing the social consequences of these reduced marital opportunities, we shall inquire further into the reasons that black men are in such short supply.

Causes of Low Sex Ratios Among Blacks

Besides the census underenumeration, a variety of other factors combine to lower marital opportunity indices and sex ratios in the black population. These include the disproportionate number of black men in the armed forces and in prisons and other institutions, lower sex ratios at birth, high mortality among black male infants, children, and adolescents, and large gender differences in the migration of young blacks, especially in the post-World War II period. Each of these factors needs some discussion.

Exclusion of the Armed Forces and Other Categories

One reason that sex ratios or marital opportunity indices based on resident census tables are so low for blacks is that, relative to the white population, a disproportionate number of them serve in the armed forces overseas and are thus excluded from our figures. The effect of this on young men would be especially strong in 1970, for well over one-half of the males in the armed forces at that time were between 20 and 24 years of age. Yet the exclusion seems reasonable in view of the fact that the great majority of single men overseas are not available as potential marriage partners for the women back home. It could even be argued that men in the armed forces at home should be excluded, since their residence on military bases is essentially transient, and their contacts with the civilian population are somewhat limited.

Marital opportunity indices that include men overseas are not available, but we can get some idea of the effect of this exclusion by looking at sex ratios for men and women of the *same* ages. In 1970, the overall sex ratio for white *and* nonwhite persons aged 20-24 years was 101; with the armed forces overseas excluded, it dropped to 94. The effect of this adjustment was less for 1960 ratios because fewer military personnel were in these age ranges.

The effect on sex ratios of excluding the armed forces overseas and at home is more critical for blacks than for whites. For all ages, the civilian sex ratio for whites in 1970 was 94, but for blacks, it was only 89. Moreover, for ages 20-24, it was only 83, while for whites, it was 95. Even at older ages, sex ratios for civilian blacks remained far below ratios for whites. At age 37, for example, the black sex ratio was 78, while for whites, it was 94. Remember that these are not marital opportunity indices, which would be still lower, but sex ratios based on male and female cohorts of the *same* ages.[6]

The inclusion of certain other categories of black men in our indices over-estimates marital opportunities. Compared with white men, a dispropor-tionate number of black men counted in the resident census are in prisons and other institutions, and thus are not available for marriage. Excluding these men would lower opportunity ratios still further.

Mortality Among Black Men

Sex ratios among blacks at birth are significantly lower than those for whites, for several reasons. The lower socioeconomic status of blacks has been associated with poor nutrition and lack of medical care, which results in more fetal deaths *in utero.* Because male fetuses are less robust, more females than males survive to parturition. A much higher illegitimacy ratio among blacks accentuates this problem; pregnancies among single black women probably receive less medical care. Families at the lowest socioeconomic level have approximately an 8 or 9 percent lower chance of giving birth to a male than do middle- and upper-class families. This is apparently independent of a small racial difference between whites and blacks, with males 3 percent less likely to be born to blacks than to whites. Finally, a small contribution to low sex ratios comes from the fact that later-born children in families at the lowest socioeco-nomic level are slightly more likely to be female.[7]

These conditions explain why sex ratios at birth are significantly lower for blacks than for whites, as shown in Table 8.2.[8] In 1940, for example, the average white sex ratio at birth was 106.0, while for blacks it was 102.6. This significant difference in sex ratios at birth between whites and blacks occurs in every cohort. In 1960, the white sex ratio at birth was 105.5, while the black sex ratio was 101.6. By 1970, it had narrowed somewhat, to 105.9 versus 103.1, but the difference was still appreciable.

Lower sex ratios for blacks apparently extend to even before birth. The loss rates for nonwhite fetuses exceed those of whites by a wide margin, and the difference between black male and female fetal death rates has been

TABLE 8.2   Sex Ratios at Birth, by Race, United States, 1940-1970

	White	Black
1970	105.9	103.1
1965	105.6	102.6
1960	105.5	101.6
1955	105.6	102.0
1950	105.8	102.4
1945	106.1	102.0
1940	106.0	102.6

SOURCE: Vital Statistics of the United States, 1970, Vol. 1: Nationality. U.S. Department of Health Education and Welfare, Public Health Service, National Center for Health Statistics, Rockville, MD, 1975, Table 1-18.

substantial throughout this century.[9] In the early 1960s, the average fetal death rate (all fetal deaths of 20 weeks or more gestation per 1000 live births) for whites was 14.7 for males and 13.4 for females, a difference of only 1.3. For blacks, the figures were 30.4 fetal deaths for males and 26.1 for females, a difference of 4.3.[10] The highest fetal death rates occur among nonwhite illegitimate children. We can conclude that the lower sex ratios at birth among blacks amount roughly to about 3 fewer males per 100 females. While this is a significant contributing factor to lower sex ratios for blacks, clearly it is only a partial contribution.

Another decrement comes from infant mortality rates. Considerably more black than white infants die, and more of these are males. One study indicated that from 1959 to 1961, the infant mortality rate for nonwhite children was 86 percent above the rate for white children. In addition, the chances of dying during infancy were 29 percent greater among males than females.[11] This difference between white and nonwhite infant deaths is far from new; it has existed for decades. Though the rates for both black and whites are declining, the decline is faster among whites. Moreover, the decline has been greater among females than among males, and the gap has remained at about 30 percent. Together, these two factors mean that the sex ratio for blacks by the age of one year falls further behind that for whites.

As children grow older, their death rates generally decrease, although boys continue to have a higher mortality rate than girls throughout life. This accounts for a further decline with age in the sex ratio among blacks, since blacks have higher overall mortality rates than do whites. Mortality rates remain especially high for young black boys. Rates at ages 10-14 are almost as great as those at ages 5-9, a pattern not true for white boys. In some years (the 1940s and 1950s), the mortality rate for nonwhites between 10 and 14 has actually exceeded the rate at younger ages.[12] These particular figures are not broken down by sex, but it is reasonable to assume that the major contribution to these rates comes from the deaths of black boys.

The various forms of mortality that we have discussed so far apparently relate to sex ratios primarily through two causal factors: the lesser robustness of males, as reflected in infant mortality rates and in longevity; and differences in parental and medical care, including nutrition and care of the mother during pregnancy. In Chapter 4 we discussed the remarkably low infant mortality rates among Jewish people all over the world, and attributed them primarily to parental investment in and care of the infant. These conditions are basic, but they relate in an important way to another factor—the proportion of births that are illegitimate. It is reasonable to assume that women pregnant with an illegitimate child, whether white or black, are less apt to have good medical care, and further, that more illegitimate children than legitimate ones are not wanted. Since the proportion of illegitimate births among blacks is very high, their relation to sex ratios deserves special attention.

Of special import is the long-known fact that sex ratios at birth and later are lower for illegitimate children than for legitimate ones. The phenomenon is not a local one nor limited to a particular race. The sparse data that exist indicate that regardless of race, more illegitimate female than male children survive.

The U.S. Bureau of Vital Statistics does not regularly report the sex of infants born illegitimately, but in 1930 reported a sex ratio for legitimate black children of 103.5, and for illegitimate, 101.1; in 1931, these figures were 103.5 and 100.7, respectively.[13] As we have stated, one reason for the lower sex ratios at birth for illegitimate children is probably the loss of more males *in utero* because of poor care of the mother during pregnancy.

After birth, too, illegitimate infants have a higher death rate than legitimate infants.[14] This is true not only for blacks, but also for whites. In New York City, in 1961-1963, for example, the neonatal infant mortality rate among white and black illegitimate children was practically the same: 40.7 for whites, and 41.4 for blacks.[15] Probably, though, the inadequate care given to young illegitimate children beyond infancy has a much larger effect on sex ratios. Often they are not wanted, and even when they are, they typically have only one parent, who is most often a teenager with only marginal means to care for them.

We can conclude that the greater proportion of illegitimate births among blacks occurring in the 1960s and 1970s makes a small contribution to the lower sex ratios for the black population taken as a whole. Of course, it should be clear that since our marital opportunity indices exclude anyone below 16 years of age, they do not reflect these differences in male/female proportions among the young. They are relevant, however, to sex ratios projected for the black population in future years as reported in Figure 8.3.

One other possible reason lower sex ratios among black illegitimate infants, and possibly illegitimate ones as well, has not yet been discussed. While the evidence is tentative and suggestive, it is especially intriguing, for if it were valid, it would produce systemic effects that persist from generation to generation. This is the possibility that more females are conceived when mothers experience a low coital rate because their mates are promiscuous. We discussed the relation between male promiscuity and sex ratios at birth in Chapter 4. Our tentative conclusion was that sex ratios at birth are somewhat lower when the mother had relatively infrequent intercourse. Presumably, this would be the case if her mate was promiscuous rather than monogamous. We noted a considerable difference in sex ratios for monogamous and polygamous tribes; in the former, they were well above 100, and in the latter, well below 100. This is consistent evidence, for we can assume that wives in polygynous marriages, with only one husband, have less frequent intercourse than those in monogamous marriages. A variety of other, less direct evidence was also discussed in Chapter 4. Sperm quality was found to decrease with very high emission frequencies on the part of the male, approaching 5-8 times per week. This might produce fewer male conceptions. Further, in monogamous marriages, male abstinence during the menstrual period of the wife may also contribute to higher male/ female ratios. Abstinence would not be necessary for men with several wives having different menstrual periods. And, of course, abstinence would not be present among men who are promiscuous.

We did conclude, however, that evidence demonstrating that low frequencies of intercourse for the female produce a lower sex ratio at birth is more tentative and suggestive than firm. Nevertheless, the possibility should not be dismissed entirely. A relation between promiscuity and sex ratios would contribute to a stable cycle whereby low sex ratio societies would be perpetuated from generation to generation because of the presence of male promiscuity.

Finally, adult black males are susceptible to deaths from a variety of sources that affect black females to a lesser extent. Young black men are overrepresented in the overseas armed forces. Some of the steep drop in sex ratios for young adult blacks between 1960 and 1970 occurred because of the war in Vietnam, in which a disproportionately large number of young black men served.[16] Finally, "black males generally die earlier than black females from heart and lung diseases, chronic alcoholism, automobile and industrial accidents, homicide and suicide... Deaths from drug overdoses are presently more common among black males than black females."[17]

In sum, these various sources of mortality for black males contribute to lower sex ratios for black populations. But they are far from sufficient to account for the observed shortage of males. Another factor that is of especial importance for certain regions, especially central cities, is in-migration, discussed in the next section.

Black In-Migration

In-migration—that is, migration from one state or city to another by the indigenous U.S. population—has caused large-scale population shifts within the United States. For blacks as for whites, the motive for migration has been jobs and economic betterment. Sex differences in migration are pronounced, especially for blacks. The U.S. Census reports in-migration, out-migration, and net migration, by race and sex, for every state, and also for each region in the United States. These figures provide some idea of the pronounced sex differences in black migration.

In 1930, four-fifths of all black families lived in the South, and most were rural. But by 1960, fewer than three-fifths of black families were Southern, and three-quarters of all blacks were urban. Between 1940 and 1970, more than 20,000,000 Americans, of whom over 4,000,000 were nonwhite, moved to the city.[18] With the expansion of industry during World War II, many blacks moved to industrial cities like Chicago and Detroit. After World

War II, blacks in the rural South migrated first to Southern cities, and then to the North and West.

Net migration figures from region to region are provided in Table 8.3 for nonwhites for 1960 and for blacks for 1970. In these two five-year periods, the South lost over 500,000 nonwhites/blacks, of whom 57 percent were female and 43 percent male. Moreover, equal numbers of males and females went west; the Northwest and the North Central regions received the entire surplus of nonwhite/black females. The Northeast gained almost two nonwhite/black females for every male, while the North Central region gained about three nonwhite/black females for every two males.

Migration from the South to the various states within a region was highly selective. Some states received larger numbers and more imbalanced proportions of the sexes and, of course, cities in particular often changed mark-

TABLE 8.3   Net Migration of Nonwhite/Black Population

	Emigration from: South	Net Migration from 1955 to 1960 Migration to: Northeast	North Central	West
Male:	−120,000	36,000	27,000	57,000
Female:	−158,000	58,000	44,000	56,000
		Net Migration from 1965 to 1970		
Male:	−108,000	16,000	46,000	46,000
Female:	−142,000	34,000	62,000	46,000

NOTE: These net figures represent nonwhites/blacks who, by the time of the census, had moved to a new residence from their place of residence five years prior to the census. Net figures are obtained by subtracting the number who moved out of a region from the number who moved into the region.
SOURCE: *U.S. Census of the Population: 1970,* Summary Reports: *Mobility for States and the Nation PC(2)-2B.* Washington, DC: U.S. Bureau of the Census, Table 58; *U.S. Census of the Population: 1960,* Summary Reports: *PC(2)-2B.* Washington, DC: U.S. Bureau of the Census, Table 27.

TABLE 8.4   Local Shifts in Net Migration of Nonwhite/Black Females

State	1955-1960	1965-1970
New York	14,217	8,949
Pennsylvania	4,669	2,922
Illinois	6,839	5,230
Ohio	3,893	4,739
Michigan	6,337	5,675
District of Columbia	2,968	5,964*
California	862	5,958

NOTE: Figures given represent the excess of nonwhite/black females migrating into a state, obtained by subtracting the net number of males migrating in from the net number of females migrating in.
*The District of Columbia lost both male and female nonwhites/blacks from 1965 to 1970. The figure given represents the excess of males lost.
SOURCE: *U.S. Census of the Population: 1970,* Summary Reports: *Mobility for States and the Nation PC(2)-2B.* Washington, DC: U.S. Bureau of the Census, Table 58; *U.S. Census of the Population: 1960,* Summary Reports *PC(2)-2B.* Washington, DC: U.S. Bureau of the Census, Table 27.

edly through these migrations. Table 8.4 provides the figures for the excess of nonwhite/black females moving to states where the excess was at least 4000 females. The states listed were the heaviest recipients of an excess of nonwhite/ black females. We can also see changes in the migration patterns from 1960 to 1970. Most notable is that by 1970, California was also receiving an excess of nonwhite/black females.

These dominant migration patterns for blacks had changed considerably by the end of the mid-1970s. During the period from 1975 to 1978, the number of blacks moving out of the South and the North Central region was about the same as the number moving in. No doubt this shift was due in part to the economic growth of the cities in the Sunbelt region. The West, however, continued to have a net increase of black migrants in 1978.

The most striking migration data are found not in these regional or state figures, but in the gains in the nonwhite populations of cities. In 1978, about three-fourths of the black population resided in metropolitan areas, and more than one-half of all blacks (55 percent) lived in central cities within these areas. Because of the long-term shift from rural to urban areas, we can anticipate that most of the migration gains among nonwhite populations were experienced by central cities. Figures for metropolitan areas, in contrast to those for central cities, are less revealing, for they include gains in suburbs reflecting out-migration by whites from central cities, as well as from

TABLE 8.5   Gains in the Nonwhite Population of Central Cities

| City | Percentage | |
	White	Nonwhite
Boston	17	22
Charleston	7	−28
Dallas	1	36
Denver	−9	35
Detroit	−33	20
Fort Wayne	−8	22
Grand Rapids	−5	28
Hartford	−26	48
Honolulu	22	−20
Houston	9	26
Los Angeles (and Long Beach)	−2	29
Milwaukee	−14	35
Minneapolis	−20	46
Newark	−40	23
New York City	−14	38
Phoenix	17	22
Portland	−2	22
Rochester	−23	69
San Francisco (and Oakland)	−15	28
Seattle-Everett	−14	21
Wilmington	−37	20

SOURCE: *U.S. Census of the Population and Housing: 1970, PHC (2): General Demographic Trends for Metropolitan Areas, 1960 to 1970.* Washington, DC: U.S. Bureau of the Census, Table 3.

other locations. Table 8.5 lists all the central cities showing changes of at least 20 percent in the nonwhite population in 1970. Even a cursory examination reveals a sharp increase. Breakdowns by sex are not available, but since the preponderance of nonwhite migration to the regions in which these cities are located was female, it is clear that sex ratios would be appreciably lowered as a result of the migrations.

One other feature of these migrations important for our thesis is that such migrations consist overwhelmingly of young adults. This is important because of their effect on marriage pools, family stability, and other consequences. Young black women have moved in much larger numbers than black men to most of the major cities of the United States. In 1950, young black women were in excess primarily in urban areas in the South. For example, in Southern urban areas, in 1950, for ages 20-24, there were 181,000 black males to 237,000 young black women. That is a sex ratio of 76! In 1960, there were 115,000 more black women than black men in Northern cities. By 1970, this excess had expanded by more than half, to 176,000, creating the lowest sex ratios for blacks that have *ever* existed in Northern cities. We turn now to look at these urban ratios.

Sex Ratios for Black Urban Dwellers

In 1970, and even before, most urban areas had serious shortages of young black men. Sex ratios for black/nonwhite young adults 20-24 years of age are shown by census year for selected cities in Table 8.6. These ratios are very low, mostly ranging from the mid-60s to the low 80s. But since these ratios include married as well as unmarried adults, and are not based on age differences between men and women at marriage, they still overestimate marital opportunities for black females. With such adjustments, they would undoubtedly be even lower than the opportunity indices we discussed earlier, for those included blacks in rural areas, which have higher ratios.

Table 8.6 reveals several conditions that affect sex ratios. The changes in these ratios between 1930 and 1970 may appear at first glance to be chaotic, but two clear trends are noticeable. All cities but Atlanta—which was

TABLE 8.6   Sex Ratios for Nonwhites Aged 20-24 in Selected Cities, 1930-1970

City	Census Year				
	1930	1940	1950	1960	1970
Atlanta	65	65	74	79	76
Baltimore	87	82	82	79	76
Chicago	79	71	78	73	72
Detroit	87	77	81	69	79
Philadelphia	77	71	74	74	75
New York	76	59	68	73	72
Average Ratio:	79	71	76	75	75

SOURCE: Calculated from U.S. Bureau of the Census, *Census of the Population*, 1930, 1940, 1950, 1960, 1970. Washington, DC: Government Printing Office.

already very low—dropped sharply by 1940. This was probably due to the selective out-migration of young black males during the Depression years. A sharp upward turn occurs by 1950, after World War II, for all cities but Baltimore. This reflects the selective in-migration of young black males during the postwar industrial expansion of these cities.

That the situation is grave is clear from Table 8.6. First, it is clear that for all of these cities, black/nonwhite sex ratios for these young adults have been below 87 since 1930. The shortage of young black/nonwhite males has apparently been a chronic problem for at least a half-century, at least in these cities, and probably in some others. Second, the gross overall trend has been for the situation to worsen, for by 1970, all of these cities had ratios below 80. Clearly, urban black women have very poor marital opportunities because of the limited number of black males available. In the next section, we discuss the consequences of these scarce marital opportunities.

CONSEQUENCES OF FEW MARITAL OPPORTUNITIES FOR BLACK WOMEN

The lack of marital opportunities for young black women has had far-reaching effects. Predictions for the cluster of social, sexual, and cultural consequences of low sex ratio demography include the following: black men would be reluctant to make a long-term marital commitment to one woman throughout her childbearing years; black men would be reluctant to marry and to invest in parenthood; black men would have a number of women sequentially or simultaneously; sexual libertarianism would be the ethos, and illegitimate births would be common; brief sexual liaisons with black men would be frequent; black male attitudes would be misogynistic; women would not be highly valued or respected; sex roles would be less differentiated; and black women would seek and possibly achieve economic, sexual and social independence for themselves, rather than acquiring economic or social status through marriage. Indices of family instability such as divorce, single-parent families headed by women, and the ratio of illegitimate to legitimate births would be high. Black women in these circumstances would be aware of the low value placed on them by black men. Their unhappiness would be reflected in higher rates of depression, especially among the many who had been abandoned and who had young children to raise by themselves. These consequences deserve further discussion.

To avoid any misunderstanding, let us first emphasize that none of these social consequences has anything to do with being black. We do *not* derive these consequences from characteristics of the black race, from qualities of the character of black men, from "black culture," "matriarchal culture," or any other characteristics peculiar to blacks. We argue instead that these social consequences follow from acutely low sex ratios, along with other aggravating influences such as depressed income and less schooling. Moreover, our position is that the same social consequences would follow for a *white* population having similarly low sex ratios and similar accentuating conditions. The only relevance of being black is that some of the facilitating conditions, such as depressed income and fewer years of education, result in part from prejudice against the black race, and that these conditions intensify the effects of low sex ratios.

Sex Ratios and Illegitimacy

In Chapter 7, we described two indices of illegitimacy. The illegitimacy *rate* is the number of illegitimate births occurring in a given year per 1,000 unmarried women 15-44 years of age. If, on the average, each 1,000 women so classified had 50 illegitimate children in a given year, the illegitimacy rate could be 50.

The illegitimacy *ratio* is the obtained by the following formula:

$$\text{Illegitimacy ratio} = \frac{\text{No. of illegitimate births}}{\text{Total live births}} \times 1000$$

Essentially, this ratio is the proportion of all live births that are illegitimate, multiplied by 1000. An illegitimacy ratio of 200 would mean that one-fifth of all live births in a given year were illegitimate $(200/1000=1/5)$. The reason that a clear understanding of the illegitimacy ratio is important is that changes in it can be produced by several different demographic changes.

One possible contributor is simply a rise in the number of illegitimate births. On the other hand, the ratio can also go up even when the number of illegitimate births goes down! This is because of the other demographic contributors: the proportion of unmarried women in a population, and a change in the number of legitimate births. Thus, the number of illegitimate births could remain constant, but if the number of legitimate births fell off, the illegitimacy ratio would go up. With these cautions in mind, let us look at what has happened.

Figure 8.4 provides information for whites and nonwhites on both legitimate and illegitimate birth rates since 1950. The trends are similar for both races, although both rates are higher for blacks. The legitimate birth rate for both races peaked around 1956 and fell off, more sharply for nonwhites than for whites. Meanwhile, the illegitimate birth rates for nonwhites rose to a high point, and in about the middle of the 1960s began to fall off, with another small peak in 1970. For whites, illegitimate birth rates have risen slightly and quite steadily, but they are considerably lower on the whole than those for blacks.

If we turn now to report illegitimacy ratios, it should be clear that for both nonwhites and whites, a considerable rise in ratios would be due primarily to a drop in legitimate birth rates. Since the drop in legitimate birth rates is much steeper for nonwhites, the rise in the illegitimacy ratios would be much greater for them than for whites. All of this makes sense in terms of the sex ratio thesis, for we would expect that with very low sex ratios, the number of black women who remained single or divorced would be much greater in proportion to married black women. These demographic facts contribute to fewer legitimate births and to relatively more illegitimate births.

The findings confirm this interpretation, as shown in Figure 8.5. Since the mid-1950s, for blacks, and the late 1960s for whites, a sharp rise in the ratio of illegitimate to legitimate births has occurred among both blacks and

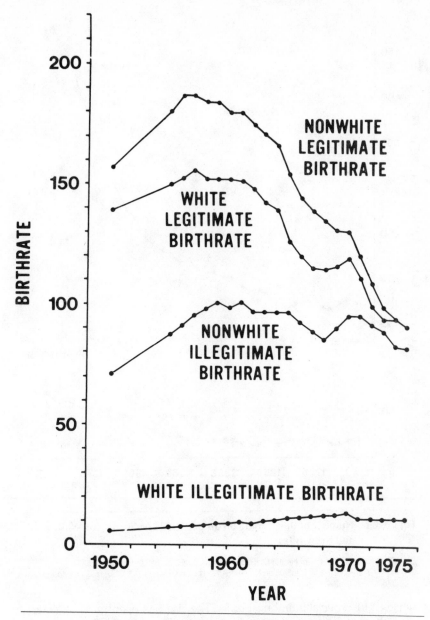

Figure 8.4   Legitimate and Illegitimate Birth Rates for Whites and Nonwhites

SOURCE: National Center for Health Statistics, *Vital Statistics of the United States, 1975,*
    Vol. 1—*Natality.* DHEW Publication No. (PHS) 78-1113, 1978. Washington, DC: Government Printing
    Office, 1978.

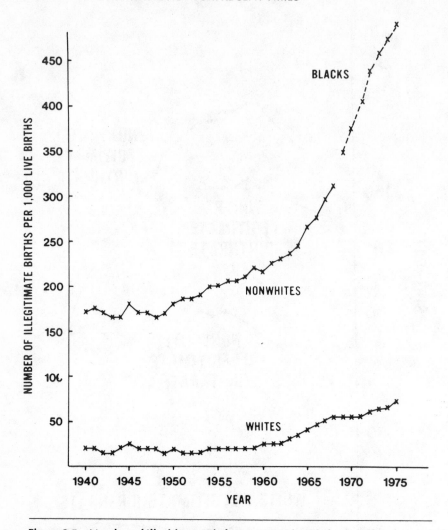

Figure 8.5   Number of Illegitimate Births per 1000 Live Births, for Whites and Nonwhites

SOURCE: National Center for Health Statistics, *Vital Statistics of the United States, 1975,*
Vol. 1—*Natality.* DHEW Publication No. (PHS) 78-113. Washington, DC: Government Printing Office,
1978.

whites, but especially among blacks. The rise has been particularly steep since the mid-1960s. As discussed earlier, sex differences in black migrations, especially for young adults, were particularly marked during the same years.

Our thesis predicts that illegitimate births would be negatively associated with sex ratios: the lower the ratio, the greater the proportion of illegitimate births. To test this, state-by-state correlations were computed between sex ratios for nonwhites and the proportion of nonwhite live births that were illegitimate. In 1960, the correlation was -0.76, and in 1970, -0.75. For blacks (instead of nonwhites) in 1970, it was -0.87! These correlations may somewhat overestimate the relationship, because both the sex ratio and the ratio of illegitimate to all live births are affected by the proportion of women who are married. But illegitimacy rates, which would not be subject to this bias, are not available by race and state. Moreover, the sex ratio thesis incorporates the view that the percent married is a function of sex ratios, so that this relationship is not a statistical artifact. There seems no doubt that sex ratios and illegitimacy are, in any case, very strongly related.

These correlations mean that a larger proportion of black babies are illegitimate in states where black women considerably outnumber black men. In states where the sex ratio among blacks is high, that is, where men outnumber women, the proportion of births that are illegitimate is much smaller. Further, these high correlations mean that if the sex ratios by state are known for blacks, the illegitimacy ratios can be accurately predicted.

Relationships this strong are quite rare in the social sciences. Consequently, it seems prudent to pause here and look into possible contributions to this astonishing relationship. First, the correlation is based on data from the 40 states that provide information on illegitimate births. Most of the correlation is due to the states that have a small black population (fewer than 10,000). These are more rural than most, and have higher sex ratios than most, as well as low illegitimacy ratios. If these eight states are eliminated, the correlation drops almost to zero. Yet there is no theoretical reason for eliminating these states, and the relationship seems a valid one. Further statistical investigation does not weaken this conclusion. For example, the rural/urban difference cannot be shown to explain the high association, and while socioeconomic factors were found to be associated with sex ratios, they did not explain away the contribution of sex ratios to illegitimacy ratios.[19]

What is very clear is that the illegitimacy ratio is explained by demographic and economic factors, rather than by race. This is shown by the finding that the correlation between the proportion of illegitimate *white* births and state-by-state sex ratios in 1960 was -.24, and in 1970, -.27. This indicates a similar, but much weaker relationship for whites. But that it is weaker is not due to race, for two major reasons. Whites did not migrate selectively by sex in large numbers the way blacks did, particularly from 1960 through the 1970s, and thus the state-by-state sex ratio differences for whites are much less pronounced than they are for blacks. This lesser variation results in much lower correlations for whites because of a well-known property of correlations: Their magnitude varies with the range of differences reflected in the measures that are correlated. The second reason is an economic one. Amount of income is related to marital status. Men who are poor, *whether white or black,* are less likely to marry, even when they father children. The proportion of men who remain single diminishes sharply as income increases; virtually everyone in the highest bracket marries. What this means is that because there is an income differential between whites and blacks, the low sex ratios among whites are more likely to be reflected in divorce and remarriage rates of single-parent families headed by separated and divorced women, but less so in illegitimacy figures. These differences between blacks and whites are not racial or cultural, but economic.

The matter can be put this way. When sex ratios are low, both white and black men move successively from woman to woman and father children along the way, but white men (who can more often afford it) marry and divorce these women, while black men marry them less often because they cannot afford to. The relationship between low sex ratios and sequential pairing is found in both races, but the correlation of low sex ratios with the proportion of illegitimate births is only high for blacks for economic reasons.

Separation, Divorce, and Single-Parent Families

Since black sex ratios are considerably lower than those for whites, and because of the poorer economic status of blacks, we would expect a larger proportion of blacks than whites to be divorced at any one time (since blacks can less afford to remarry). In fact, this is the case. In 1975, 27 percent of the black population between the ages of 25 and 54 was either divorced or separated. A comparable figure for whites of the same ages was only 8 percent. These rates had increased over 1970, when they were 20 percent and 6 percent, respectively.[20]

Further support for this reasoning comes from the percentages of the separated and divorced. Many more blacks than whites are separated. In about half of the states, the percentage of black women separated is higher than the percentage of blacks divorced, a condition that does not occur for whites in any of the 50 states.[21] Why? Because divorce, compared with separation, is expensive, and blacks are poorer than whites. In 1970, in a number of populous northeastern states, having low sex ratios for blacks like New York, New Jersey, and Pennsylvania, more than 10 percent of the black women residents reported that they were separated, whereas separation figures for whites were around 2 percent.[22]

Another way to test our ideas is to examine the correlation between sex ratios and divorce/separation, which should be strongly associated. Again, this is indeed the case. The correlation between percent divorced or separated and the state-by-state sex ratio for blacks is -.67. The correlation between percent separated (omitting divorced) among blacks and the sex ratio for blacks, state-by-state, is -.77. The largest contribution to the correlation comes from the states with extremely high sex ratios for blacks: North Dakota, South Dakota, Montana, Idaho, Maine, New Hampshire, Vermont, Wyoming, Alaska, Hawaii, and Utah.[23] Very few black women in these states report that they are separated. Each of these latter states has a small black population, and they are characteristically rural; what urban centers they have are relatively small. Probably for this reason, black females are not attracted to these states.

The most dramatic finding supportive of our reasoning concerns the proportion of black households headed by females. The proportion of families headed by women had accelerated alarmingly in the last decade, from about 1 in every 10 families in 1970 to 1 in every 5 in 1981. Again the situation is far worse among blacks. While 1 in every 6 white families is headed by only one parent, one-half of all black families have only one parent. The vast majority of these single-parent families, whether black or white, are headed by the mother.[24]

This dramatic state of affairs for black families has led social scientists to invent a variety of racially or ethnically based explanations Most notorious was the idea that this has occurred among blacks because they, unlike whites, have a distinctive matriarchal culture. But data reported by a black female sociologist demonstrate that single-parent families headed by women stem from the demography of sex ratios.[25] The correlation state-by-state, between black sex ratios and the percentage of female-headed, black families is -.83. The lower the sex ratio in a state, the fewer the men relative to women, and the greater the number of female-headed families. In states with a sufficient black male population, few black families are headed by women. For example, in North Dakota, where the black sex ratio was 160, only 2.9 percent of black families were headed by a woman. In contrast, in New York the sex ratio was 86, and 33 percent of black families were headed by a woman.

From these findings on illegitimacy, divorce, separation, and single-parent families, it is clear that the stability of black families has nothing to do with matriarchy or with any other social/cultural properties distinctive to blacks. Instead, it is a function of the sex ratio and of economic factors. In high sex ratio states where black men are abundant and black women relatively scarce, family stability is marked. Under these circumstances, black men make a long-term parental investment in their children, and illegitimate births, divorce and separation, and single-parent families headed by women are all relatively low.

Black Families in the Past

If there were any lingering doubts to the effect that being black was some-how connected with these conditions of family instability, they can be put to rest by considering certain historical circumstances of the black family.

In Colonial America during the eighteenth century, sex ratios for blacks were very high. In Carolina, in 1708, the sex ratio for black adults was 164; in Maryland, in 1755, it was 135; in New Jersey, in 1772, it was 133; in New York, in 1771, it was 120.[26] But data were sporadic; New York was the only colony with sufficient information to trace the evolution of the sex ratio among black adults. There, the sex ratio of adult blacks rose to its highest level in the early eighteenth century, a time when the largest number of blacks was brought into the colony.[27]

In the late eighteenth century, American slave imports had the high sex ratios characteristic of other slave imports, though less extreme.[28] The fact that the United States did not exhibit the gross imbalances in sex ratios characteristic of other countries was due to the very large proportion of American-born slaves.[29] Until 1830, the sex ratio for blacks was 100 or more, but after that it was always below 100, indicating a surplus of women. The ratio fell steadily until 1870, when it was at its lowest point for the nineteenth century, perhaps reflecting deaths in the Civil War.[30] Black sex ratios rose gradually from this low, reaching their highest point of the twentieth century in 1920 (close to 100), and then began a descent which, as we have seen, was most marked after 1950.[31]

In some urban areas in the nineteenth century, sex ratios were low, and there was a considerable shortage of black men. Presumably this created a problem for the black family.[32] But our interest is in the question of whether, with high sex ratios, black families were stable. Sex ratios in rural areas were typically above 100. One study reports slave sex ratios in North Carolina in 1860.[33] Although on some plantations the sex ratio was in the high 90s, in many it was above 100, and in many more, above 110. Further, since overall slave sex ratios from 1820 to 1860 were above 100, and since urban ratios were often lower, it follows that rural ratios would be higher.[34]

An analysis of plantations provides a special opportunity to examine the thesis that with high sex ratios, black families were stable. Early historical opinion was that the plantation slave families were disorganized, but two extensive studies suggest that such assumptions were unfounded. It now appears that stable nuclear families were the rule, rather than the exception.[35] A great many plantation slave couples had long-lasting marriages.

A recent analysis of sex ratios on 540 plantations is persuasive.[36] The analysis reveals that sex ratios differed systematically by plantation size. As shown in Table 8.7, plantations with less than 25 slaves had the lowest sex ratios. The average sex ratio for small plantations was 85, while for the larger ones it was 110 (25-74 slaves) or 117 (more than 75 slaves). The key theme in these data is the relationship between adult sex ratios and sex ratios at birth. The relationship is rough and imperfect because of the relatively small number of children from which the ratios were computed, but it is nevertheless striking.

Higher sex ratios for children under 1 year of age are associated with higher sex ratios in the adult population. This may be seen in Table 8.7 by comparing the low adult sex ratio of 85 for the small plantations with the

TABLE 8.7   Sex Ratios of Slaves by Age and Plantation Size

| | | | Plantation Size | | | |
| | Small | | | | Large | |
	No. Slaves 1-24	Sex Ratio	No. Slaves 25-74	Sex Ratio	No. Slaves Over 75	Sex Ratio
All Ages						
Males	1638		2237		1838	
Females	1921	85	2035	110	1571	117
Under 1 Year						
Male	106		99		94	
Female	93	114	70	141	59	125
Under 5 Years						
Male	460		412		333	
Female	489	94	453	91	302	110

SOURCE: Based on R. Stekel, personal communication, 1977.

higher ratios of 110 and 117 for the larger plantations, and noting that this corresponds to the lower infant sex ratio of 114 for the small plantations and the higher infant ratios of 141 and 125 for the larger plantations.

This intergenerational relation between sex ratios fits our thesis that, given Western marriage patterns, high sex ratios among adults create male fidelity and family commitment. As we found among the Jews in the shteltls of eastern Europe, this greater male commitment results in better conditions for the family and in turn produces higher sex ratios at birth and in infancy. Thus, one would predict that among slaves, the most stable nuclear families would be found in the rural areas, especially on the larger plantations, where sex ratios were high. This pattern would be less pronounced on the small plantations and in the cities, with their lower sex ratios. Moreover, observers have noted that stable families and a lack of promiscuous sexual behavior was the norm among plantation slaves. It has been reported that the average age of slave mothers at the birth of their first child was quite high. This was not due to infertility, for after marriage, the birth rate was high. What these facts suggest is that slave daughters were protected from free sexual contact, and the the "prevailing sexual mores of slaves were not promiscuous but prudish." As we have seen in other contexts, in a high sex ratio situation, one expects to find a protective attitude toward unmarried daughters.

Intermarriage and Sex Ratios

Intermarriage across social class, ethnic, or racial lines provides an interesting test of the idea that sex ratios can be understood in terms of the supply and demand for marital partners. These categories ordinarily serve as constraints on the selection of marital partners, and we would expect these constraints to weaken when sex ratios become imbalanced. For example, when sex ratios are low among the white population, the oversupply of women means that some of them will accept or seek partners who they ordinarily would not consider. If we assume that in our society, white women have a higher status than black women, then the fact that the sex ratio is also low among blacks does not matter. Even though there is an ample supply of black women, some black men will choose white women as marital partners.

We would expect that when sex ratios are low among whites, the proportion of interracial marriages consisting of a black husband and a white wife would increase, while the proportion of marriages consisting of a black wife and a white husband would decrease. This is exactly what happened during the period when black sex ratios were declining, as may be seen from Figure 8.6. Among interracial marriages identified in census and population survey data from 1970 to 1977, marriages between a black husband and a white wife rose from 63 percent to 76 percent, while those between a black wife and white husband dropped from 37 percent to 24 percent.

While this increase is substantial and consistent with our thesis, we should keep in mind that only 1 percent of all marriages were interracial. It would have been desirable to compare 1960 as well; however, in the 1960 census, people were identified only as white or nonwhite. Moreover, there were only half as many interracial marriages in 1960 as in 1970.

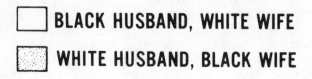

☐ **BLACK HUSBAND, WHITE WIFE**

▨ **WHITE HUSBAND, BLACK WIFE**

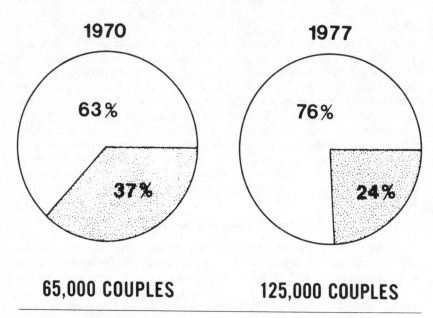

1970

63%

37%

65,000 COUPLES

1977

76%

24%

125,000 COUPLES

Figure 8.6   Racial Intermarriages Between 1970 and 1977

SOURCE: U.S. Bureau of the Census, *Current Population Reports, Special Studies*, Series P-23, No. 77. Washington, DC: Government Printing Office, 1978.

Table 8.8 provides regional differences in interracial marriages for 1960 and 1970. Black men most often married white women in urban areas and in the Northeast, North Central, and the West, but much less commonly in the South. This is consistent with the especially low sex ratios of the North, but subcultural attitudes in the other regions were apparently at work to modify the effects of sex ratios. This type of marriage increased in the South by only 5 percent during the decade, probably reflecting attitudes inhibiting the marriage of black men to white women. It might also stem from the smaller number of black men in the South with high educational and occupational status, for it is these men who most often marry white women. In the West, where the shortage of white men was actually less severe, this type of marriage had the highest proportion of any region. This suggests more permissive attitudes, resulting in either more marriages of this type in the region or in migration of that type of interracial couple to the West.

An analysis of the the 1970 census points out that about 2 percent of

TABLE 8.8   Interracial Marriages by Region

| Region | Percentage of Married Couples | | | |
| | Black Husband White Wife | | White Husband Black Wife | |
	1960	1970	1960	1970
Total United States	55	63	45	37
Northeast	54	61	46	39
North Central	54	70	46	30
South	42	47	58	53
West	57	75	43	25
Central Cities	53	69	47	31
Urban Fringe	47	65	53	35

NOTE: As usual, the categories for the identification of race in the two censuses were obtained
somewhat differently. The 1960 identification is actually nonwhite, and only the 1970 identification is
black. But the trends shown are roughly accurate, as most of the nonwhites in 1960 were black. In
each instance, the figures reflect the couples married during the decade prior to the census. The
regional data for 1960 and 1970 are based on samples; the U.S. totals are from the total census.
SOURCES: 1970 Census: *Subject Reports PC(2)-4C: Marital Status*, December 1972, Table 12. Race
and Spanish origin of wife by race and Spanish origin of husband and decade in which husband
and wife first married when married once.

1960 Census: *Subject Reports PC(2)-4E: Marital Status*, January 1966, Table 10. Race of husband
and wife—married couples, for the United States and regions, by type of residence, with year
husband first married, for the United States.

black men marry white women, and further, that about two to four times as
large a proportion of black men in the upper socioeconomic level, as compared with the lower, marry white women.[37] By and large, the women they
marry also tend to be at the upper levels in education and income—more
than twice as large a proportion of upper-level wives as lower-level are involved in interracial marriages. This too is consistent with the sex ratio thesis.
Because of the practice whereby women marry at the same level or upward
in social class, we would expect low sex ratios especially to reduce adversely
the marital opportunities of white women at the upper educational level
because of the limited number of men at these levels. One way of enlarging
their marital opportunities would be to consider taking a black man as a
husband. Another factor may be the lesser prejudice toward blacks on the
part of more educated women.

The prime condition underlying this discussion of racial intermarriage has
been low sex ratios among whites, which make white women available for
interracial marriage. What happens when the white population has high sex
ratios? We have already seen the answer in our discussion of Colonial and
early America. When women are in very scarce supply in a population, men
seek marital partners outside of their group, often from populations they
would not ordinarily consider. We found that under these circumstances white
men often chose black or Indian women as sexual partners, and sometimes as
wives. There is little doubt that during this period in history, marriages of white
men to black or Indian women were more common than were marriages of
white women to Indians or black men. Of course, interracial marriages were
restricted by the fact that blacks were slaves, which led to exploitation of black
women by white men and precluded marriage in most cases.

Occupational and Educational Status of Spouses

That some black men with high occupational and educational status marry white women instead of black women further aggravates a condition that creates marital strains for better-educated black women: More black women than men graduate from high school and from college. Moreover, more black women than men achieve occupational status levels that carry prestige. This is not true for white men and women. As a result, the common marital practice of women marrying a man with the same social status or higher is impossible for many black women. There are simply not enough of the right kind of black men to go around. Although black men have higher incomes than black women, differences in occupational and educational status are still apt to create incompatibilities for some married couples.

Roughly equal *percentages* of black men and women reach the various marker levels of schooling, such as high school or college graduation, but since there are more black women than men, many black women are left without a partner in the marital pool who has an education comparable to theirs. Among blacks 20-24 years of age, 1 in every 5 women completing high school does not have a potential spouse in the marital pool with a comparable education. One in every 9 women in the same age bracket completing one or more years of college similarly lacks a potential partner. Among blacks 25-34 years of age, 1 in 8 who have completed 4 or more years of college lacks a similarly educated potential partner.[38]

Of course, these results are largely due to the very low sex ratios reflecting the general shortage of black men, but it is worth noting that the failure of black men to obtain higher levels of education than black women aggravates the shortage of suitable marital partners for educated black women in a way that does not occur for the white population, especially at the college level. For example, in spite of the low sex ratios for the white population, in 1978, for every three white women between the ages of 25 and 34 with four or more years of college, there were four white males with a similar education.[39]

The occupational status of black women relative to black men improved markedly from 1960 to 1970, as may be seen in Table 8.9. One in every three black women had a white collar job, compared with only one in six black men. More than half of the men had blue collar jobs compared to only

TABLE 8.9 Occupational Statuses of Black Men and Women

	1960		1970	
Occupational Status	Men	Women	Men	Women
White Collar	11	17	17	32
Blue Collar	54	14	53	17
Household Service	1	36	—	15
Other Service	14	21	14	23
Farm	11	3	4	1

NOTE: Figures given are percentages of black men (or black women) at a given status level.
SOURCE: U.S. Bureau of the Census, "The social and economic status of the black population in the United States, 1790-1978." *Current Population Reports: Special Studies,* Series P-23, No. 80. Washington, DC: Government Printing Office, 1979, Table 53.

one in six women. Only in one category did black women have lower status. About one in seven had a job in household service, while virtually no men did, but overall black women had jobs higher in prestige.

Because of the shortage of black men with similar status, many black women are apt to marry men having different status from their own, and these status differences are apt to create value conflicts within the marriage. Since many studies have shown that different occupational and educational levels are strongly associated with different values and lifestyles, it seems reasonable to conclude that a woman married to a man having lower educational and occupational status than her own would, under some circumstances, experience considerable marital dissatisfaction and stress. This is a complex issue, however, for this outcome depends on accepting the stereotype that males should be dominant and females submissive. Much depends on how society structures the relationship between the family and the occupation, and also on the nature of the social exchanges between husband and wife.[40] We will return to this complex issue in the final chapter.

Attitudes and Feelings of Black Men and Women

While it is ordinarily difficult to document the effects of sex ratios on attitudes and feelings about the opposite sex, the sex ratios for black populations have been so low that many black observers have not only noted the shortage of black men, but have also described the effects of this shortage on relationships between black men and women, as well as the feelings that they have generated. In addition, a number of objective indices reveal the ways in which these relationships are affected by low sex ratios.

The effects on black women of the lack of family support and of desertion are expressed in at least three arenas where objective indices are available: having children, the economic role of the mother, and rates of depression. The sex difference in attitude toward having children is shown partly in the percentage of black men and women who come in for sterilization, as compared with whites. Approximately equal numbers of white men and women choose sterilization, but among blacks, 95 percent are women and only 5 percent are men.[41] Black women apparently feel the entire responsibility for the prevention of conception resting on their shoulders, while black men feel almost none.

The importance of their economic role is underlined by black women's awareness that they will have to be economically self-sufficient and that their social status will rest on their own achievements. Young black girls feel much pressure to achieve as adults.[42] Moreover, in an unusual study that asked children to designate which parent made decisions about their activities, children perceived black mothers as more powerful than white mothers, regardless of social class.[43]

Finally, women who head families with young children have higher rates of depression than men or women in other categories, and black women have considerably higher rates than white women.[44] That this occurs because of the greater sex ratio imbalance is of course not clear, because black women are also poorer and more likely to have other stresses because of their circumstances. It is tempting also to tie in the marked rise in suicide rates since 1960 for black women; however, the fact is that in spite of the increase, the rate of suicide has been low, with less than 500 suicides among black women in 1970.[45]

We turn next to more subjective observations made by many black observers from a variety of sources. Brief liaisons are common for black men, since they can and do have their choice of sexual partners. Black men are reluctant to marry and are less interested in parental investment. One study found that far more black teenage girls than boys hoped to be married some day.[46] As one black psychologist put it, in 1976: "An appropriate analog is witnessed every day in the American market place. As the availability of a commodity decreases and the need for that commodity increases the price will invariably climb. Black men in one sense may be viewed as a commodity in short supply and high demand. Black women unfortunately and invariably pay the price."[47] One black sociologist put it another way: "Where women are plentiful, they are likely to tolerate certain abuses because of a lack of alternatives.[48]

Another black psychologist has made the following observations:

(1) Black women are competitive and aggressive; they realize that they must go after men rather than waiting for men to come to them.
(2) Black men are insensitive and unaccommodating, expecting sexual favors while giving little in return.
(3) Black men expect monogamy from their women, but black women expect and tolerate unfaithfulness from their men.
(4) Black women are expected to compromise and give in, while black men are unwilling to change.
(5) Black men can easily be highly selective in choosing women; black women will often settle for much less than what they would like in a man.[49]

The black magazine, Ebony, ran a series of articles on relationships between black men and women that included the observations of a variety of black psychologists, psychiatrists, and sociologists. Material from these articles includes the following sorts of observations: "Black men show a lack of respect for black women; expect a woman to keep herself looking, smelling, feeling good while he doesn't make any efforts with his personal grooming."[50] "Black women are used to being mistreated and abused, and they have adopted a defensive attitude because of it."[51] Many observers note that black women feel exploited and abused.[52]

The sexual libertarianism to be expected in low sex ratio situations is also found. A black sociologist notes that black men have rarely insisted on sexual chastity for their women. Moreover, the pressure to yield on the male's terms is great because of the availability of other women.[53] One black psychologist has observed that sexual play and intercourse are experienced very early, that girls are viewed by black males as a challenge to a sexual conquest, and that black men often have one regular girlfriend but other women available as well.[54]

The libertarian ethos on the part of men, along with their disinterest in a permanent and stable relationship with one woman, becomes a part of the culture and is reflected in what each gender says about the other. In a 1976 Detroit *Free Press* story entitled "The Burdens on Black Couples," black men and women registered the following complaints about each other. Black men felt black women were too:

(1) Middle-class oriented and materialistic;
(2) Threatening and castrating;
(3) Independent and impatient with their men's lack of ambition;
(4) Sexually inhibited and unimaginative;
(5) Nonsupportive and unwilling to submerge their interests for their men; and
(6) Lacking in the subtle art of getting and keeping a man.

Black women, on the other hand, felt black men were too:

(1) Noncommunicative;
(2) Insensitive;
(3) Unstable and incompetent;
(4) Insecure, with very fragile egos;
(5) Spoiled and courted by black (and white) women; and
(6) Selfish, thoughtless, jealous, and resentful of black women's successes.[55]

In low sex ratio cultures, males are misogynists and women are not highly valued or esteemed by them. Black women know this—it is a part of their daily experience. The anger and despair that they experience is vividly expressed in songs, especially the blues, and in the poetry and stories written and told by modern black women. Black music is replete with songs of women who lost their man, who would do anything to be with him, who are sad because he has other women.[56] Themes of depression, worthlessness, bitterness, male cruelty, exploitation, and physical violence are prominent in the Broadway musical, *For Colored Girls Who Have Considered Suicide When the Rainbow is Enuf.*[57] Literature written by black women echoes similar themes; well-educated, middle-class black women complain that black men who would be a suitable match find them threatening and marry a younger woman with less education, or else a white woman.[58]

CONCLUSIONS

In concluding this chapter, it seems important to point out that, based on past and current data, the majority of black marriages will endure until the death of one of the spouses. It is easy to lose sight of this when looking at indices of family disruption. Despite this state of affairs, the low sex ratios for the black population prevailing for several decades and becoming worse in the 1970s appear to have had profound effects on the relationships between men and women. The form that these have taken is, of course, partially shaped by a number of other social/economic factors that characterize the black population. Given the depressed incomes of black people, the lower educational levels achieved, and the restricted occupational opportunities, the shortages of black men reflected in the low sex ratios have made an appreciable number of them reluctant to commit themselves to relationships with black women, especially marital ones, just as they are reluctant to support children. The large oversupply of black women makes such commitments unnecessary.

More subjective types of reports suggest that black men expect to have the upper hand in their relationships with women, and that they expect women to compromise their own needs in order to meet male demands. At the extreme, this leads to frequent exploitation of black women by black men. The facts that the black family frequently ends in divorce or separation, and that a very high proportion of black families are headed by women alone, both follow from these conditions. All of these various findings can be explained in terms of the favorable balance of social exchange possessed by black men as a result of the long-lasting oversupply of black women, although it is also facilitated by the fact that the incomes of black men are substantially larger than those of black women. There appears to be no need to attribute any of these conclusions to the fact that this low sex ratio population is black, given the very low sex ratios and the prevailing social/economic conditions that characterize this population. In other words, the social consequences for the family and for relationships between men and women follow from the low sex ratios and the accompanying societal circumstances that characterize this population. The only important sense in which being black contributes to this social complex is that black people have been objects of racial prejudice in our society, which in turn has created many of the unfavorable social/economic conditions under which they live. These have aggravated the social consequences of the long-time low sex ratios in the black population.

9

Future Trends in
Sex Roles and Family

Our discussion of high and low sex ratio societies at different times and places has identified for each a set of characteristic roles allocated to men and women, as well as the effects that these two forms of gender imbalance have on their relationships, their attitudes and beliefs about each other, and on marriage and the family. The characteristics common to each of these sex ratio conditions have appeared at widely different times and places, although their specific forms have reflected prevailing cultural beliefs, values, and practices. Yet if we were asked whether these sex ratio imbalances will continue to have similar effects in the future, our answer would be that they will not. Instead, they will appear in new forms, at least in the United States and in other countries with similar cultures. This chapter will discuss the reasons for these changes.

We noted earlier that the social roles allocated to females in both high and low sex ratio societies are not the only possible ones. In one sense, they are curiously asymmetrical. Although women have dyadic power in high sex ratio societies, and men when ratios are low, this power is used in vastly different ways by men and women. In both kinds of societies, women's roles are shaped more to the advantage of men, which we have attributed to the undisputed possession of structural power by men. In a nutshell, when women are scarce and men are readily available, a protective morality develops that favors monogamy for women, limits their interactions with men, and shapes female roles in traditional domestic directions. But when men are scarce and women are readily available, no such protective morality arises to favor monogamy for men. Instead, the traditional protective customs and practices pertaining to women and the pressures on them to fulfill domestic roles weaken or disappear. Men have multiple relationships with women and become less willing to commit themselves in marriage to one woman. These effects, as well as related ones described earlier, appear to us to stem directly from the structural powers that men hold.

BIOLOGICAL BASES FOR SEX DIFFERENCES

One other possibility, deferred until now, needs consideration. Quite possibly some, or even most, aspects of the roles of men and women, including those related to the possession of structural power, might ultimately be based on biological differences between the two genders. If this were the case, the prospects for gender roles that are radically different from presently known ones might be much dimmer. We turn first to consider the possibility of biologically based differences in the behavior of men and women.

Reviewing the arguments and research literature purporting to demonstrate biological contributions to differences in the behaviors of men and women would be impossible here; it would require at least a book-length monograph. Instead, a different tack will be taken. Our argument will start with a few major, undisputed biological differences between men and women and will assert that these differences have been of profound significance in human history in defining gender roles, primarily by placing structural power in the hands of men rather than women. The argument will conclude by showing how, under appropriate circumstances, cultural evolution can reduce these biological differences to minor importance, thus preparing the way for movement toward more equality between men and women.

A line of argument developed in some detail by Tiger and Fox[1] represents the position stressing the biological determination of behavioral differences between men and women. They believe that during the 65 million years that primates have been on earth, male and female primates, including humans, have evolved so as to be adapted for different roles, roles that favor survival of the genes associated with these adaptations. They believe further that this process continued as humans evolved, so that human males and females are best equipped to perform rather different activities. Briefly, they assert that during the millions of years that humans have been on earth, males became best suited for hunting and war, while women became adapted for domestic activities and for gathering fruit, berries, roots, and herbs.

Tiger and Fox review what is known about various primate species and argue that characteristic male and female behaviors are found across so many primate species that one can only conclude that these distinctive behaviors are biologically based. Further, the argument goes, humans are descended from primates and thus share much of their biology, including differences between males and females. Finally, they assert that commonly found behavioral differences between human males and females have direct parallels with those found among primates.

It has only been 10,000 years since our ancestors roamed the savannah in bands—too short a time for any further evolution to have taken place. Thus, contemporary male humans still have a biology best suited to hunting and war, and females a biology adapted to domestic activities. Hunting and war involve men in groups, forming cohesive bands or teams. Whatever biology underlies such behavior is currently at the base of the behavior of men in the arenas of sports, politics, government, and business, according to this perspective. While this ancient biological formula may not be suited to modern times, it cannot yet have evolved further; moreover, male biology is said to be better suited to such arenas than is female biology. Women, it is believed, are less interested and less capable in these spheres, and much more suited to home and family activities.

Unfortunately for this thesis, other scholars have also studied primates and have come to conclusions that fail to support Tiger and Fox's position. One primatologist, for example, has found just the opposite: Female monkeys and apes are fiercely competitive, sexually aggressive, and promiscuous.[2] In our own view, the only kind of evidence that would be conclusive is a detailed exposition of the *biological mechanisms* that are linked to such male or female behaviors. But there is no such evidence.[3] It will not do to point to the ways in which males and females have behaved differently from each other throughout history and then to attribute these to biological sex differences. It is always possible that such differences have social origins.

But even if Tiger and Fox were right and the structural power of men did indeed grow out of biological differences between men and women, this power imbalance cannot be assumed to continue into the future. The differences postulated would have evolved through natural selection among the primates and later among humanoids, but *only* because societies were structured so that physical strength was needed for hunting and warfare, and to some extent, for agriculture. As is well known, cultural evolution—as opposed to biological evolution—proceeds much more rapidly and produces changes that can easily subvert or render irrelevant any unchanging biological attributes. Since this is so, it may matter very little whether differences in the biology of men and women produce some behavioral differences. This possibility deserves further discussion.

CULTURAL EVOLUTION

Remember that the background conditions under which imbalanced sex ratios have had their effect have been relatively constant from the time of classical Greece until the advent of the twentieth century. Earlier we called attention to the importance of the fact that structural power—economic, political, and legal—has invariably been in male hands. This condition has prevailed in every high and low sex ratio society that we have examined in detail. What this means is that sex ratio imbalances might well have radically different effects in a society where women had appreciable structural power. We have, in fact, suggested that such societies would have some of the characteristics of the two imaginary societies described in Chapter 1, EROS and LIBERTINIA. The ways in which contemporary societies are changing must be considered, with a focus on possible shifts in the allocation of political, economic, and legal powers between men and women. Through their effects on the social exchanges between men and women, such changes in structural power would radically alter the manner in which they use the dyadic power acquired from imbalanced sex ratios. In order to illustrate how cultural evolution might bring about such changes, let us consider two obvious and indisputable biological differences between men and women:

(1) Men are larger and physically stronger than women. This makes them better equipped for warfare and hunting; moreover, they can settle disputes with weaker individuals, including women, by force.

(2) Women bear children. This means that during the childbearing years, they often have periods lasting many months where their pregnancies make some kinds of physical activities more difficult to perform. Often they suckle their young, which further restricts their activities.[4]

A glance backward into history is all that is needed to make clear that under primitive conditions, these differences between the sexes played a vital role in shaping the division of labor. Primitive hunting methods required physical prowess if one's prey were to be successfully caught and killed.[5] In warfare, with primitive weapons such as clubs, axes, knives, and spears, physical strength often meant survival. In contrast, women in warfare who were pregnant or nursing a child would put two members of the tribe in jeopardy.

It follows that the physical superiority of males and the childbearing task of females meant that males, not females, would do battle with the enemy. And to the victors in battle went the spoils. It seems highly plausible that the strongest and most effective warriors became the leaders, not only in warfare, but in most of the activities of the tribe. What is known about tribal chieftans is reasonably consistent with this idea. The only other attributes that are sometimes required for certain leadership roles are age and lineage, but hereditary chiefs are apt to favor and support their best loyal warriors, elevating them to high positions.

The best warriors or hunters, then, achieved high status in the tribe and control over its resources. This meant that women were not among these leaders. It seems probable, moreover, that conflicts of interest and power struggles were often settled by force, although various social mechanisms often emerged to reduce the destructiveness that would be wrought by internal violence. Under these circumstances, it was inevitable that women would be assigned to a low status in the power structures of the tribe. Directly or indirectly, men used their superior physical strength to subjugate women. Throughout history, women have often been the booty of war, to be sold as mistresses or slaves. Of course these are usually the enemy's women; the women of one's own society have typically been treated more favorably, but only because they have been wives, concubines, and the mothers of one's children. In early history, these women have often been regarded as the property of men—of their fathers, husbands, brothers, or a male guardian. A large body of law and custom emerged that was shaped to the advantage of men and to the disadvantage of women. We can conclude, then, that in the earliest human societies, the physical powers of males was a crucial factor in achieving leadership and in relegating women to a second-class status.

But culture has evolved, creating an enormous gap between early societies and contemporary ones. Without examining the progress of cultural evolution, let us simply jump to modern society and consider the current contribution of physical prowess to individual achievements within it. We will limit our analysis to the United States in order to make it manageable, but with the recognition that it will probably apply to many other technologically advanced societies, if not all, and that countries other than these may well be in different stages and have rather different futures in store for some time to come.

Men differ markedly from each other in physical strength, but we need only ask to what extent this strength provides them with dominant status. The answer is clear: outside of certain sporting contests, very little. Scarcely any jobs remain that require it—not even warfare, thanks to modern weaponry. Modern technology has reduced the importance of physical strength almost to zero. Today, people who achieve the highest posts in politics, the business world, the military, and the professions are not physically stronger than those of lesser status; the attributes for their success lie instead in ambition, hard work, and intelligence, probably in that order. Not a shred of evidence supports any assumption that these attributes are associated with the biological differences between men and women. That women are often more passive and less ambitious can be attributed to the way they have been socialized and to the conditions in society that tend to maintain those attitudes. At the same time, there are no grounds for believing that this state of affairs will persist indefinitely.

Conditions that contrived in past times to keep women in the home have also changed. Without effective means of contraception, many wives were pregnant most of the time, bearing one child after another. Before the advent of bottle-feeding, mothers also had to suckle their young, except for those who could hire wet nurses. In addition, in preindustrial times, the home was the center of domestic production. Women were engaged in making clothes and other items needed for daily living, and food preparation started with the raw product, often involving many steps before reaching the table. They were so fully occupied that there could be little thought of young daughters leaving home to get an advanced education or to earn an income by working outside on a full-time basis, much less of allowing the wife and mother to do so.

This situation has since changed markedly. Modern contraceptive techniques have made it possible for women to limit the number of children they have, as well as to plan births so as to cause minimum disruption to careers. With modern medical care, moreover, women have fewer complications during pregnancy or birth; for many, their childbearing function is now only a minor and temporary handicap. Child rearing, too, has changed. Domestic burdens are comparatively light in modern society, and various kinds of child care facilities have become common.

The effect of these various technological changes, then, has been to create a society with a technology that makes *task demands* on men and women that are vastly different from those of the past. These task demands in turn modify the social roles that society expects males and females to fulfill. Men no longer gain appreciable advantages from superior physical strength, and women are not confined solely to bearing and rearing children and performing domestic tasks. Women who are economically independent do not have an economic need to marry; therefore they feel less pressure to marry. They may still marry for other reasons, but marriage is not their only option. And those who choose not to be mothers, though married, may relate to men in markedly different ways from women who do.

CHANGES IN SOCIAL STRUCTURES AND PRACTICES

Technological changes are not the only ones that impact on imbalanced sex ratio conditions, bringing about changes in the way that men and women relate to each other. Various social changes are also important.

The Practice of Marrying Up

We have strongly emphasized that the widespread practice of women marrying men two to three years older than themselves has, under certain circumstances, limited their marital opportunities. We suspect that this practice follows from the traditional social meaning of male-female relationships as ascendant-dependent, a meaning accepted and desired by both parties. This would be consistent with females marrying up in status and age. Logically, this practice would be consistent with the fact that males have an overwhelming edge in economic and other forms of structural power. Were this power to be undermined and brought toward equality between the two genders, the practice of women "marrying up" might be much weakened.

Of course, many other reasons for such a practice could be suggested. Men might choose younger women because they find them more physically attractive. On the other hand, we are referring to a practice characterizing first marriages, which most commonly take place in the early twenties. Because the difference in age is only two to three years, it seems unlikely that it would be associated with differences in physical attractiveness. Many men may need to feel superior to the woman they marry. They may well feel threatened by a woman who is equal or superior in intelligence, education, income, or other qualities. One important consideration when marriage takes place in the teens or early twenties is that women of the *same* age are more socially mature, and that these young men may thus feel inadequate. By choosing a woman who is younger, they can lessen such threatening feelings. Similarly, women might well find an older man with more social and economic status more attractive. These subjective feelings, when experienced by men or women, however, are merely a reflection of the traditionally accepted interpretation of male-female relationships in which the male is supposed to be dominant and the female dependent.

Another factor that contributes to social status is education; women often marry a man with more education than they have. However, a long-term trend toward narrowing the gap in educational achievement between men and women promises to make marrying up in this sense more difficult. Throughout history, and until very recently, women have been far behind men in educational attainment. But at the end of the 1970s, the number of women enrolled in U. S. colleges and universities exceeded that of men for the first time. About 5 million men and 5 million women below the age of 35 were enrolled, but among older students, there were 900,000 women and only 500,000 men.[6] This continuing trend means that the practice of marrying men with more education than oneself will become more and more difficult to sustain, because there will be fewer such men available.

If male-female relationships in which neither party is dominant become common, the practice of men marrying women younger than themselves would be weakened. Both economic and educational trends are moving in this direction. This would dramatically wipe out the marriage squeeze for women who were born at a time when the birth rate was rising, as well as the reverse marriage squeeze for men born at a time when the birth rate was falling. At the present writing, however, no trend toward narrowing the age gap between bride and groom seems apparent from census and other statistics on marriage, so perhaps other unknown factors still support this practice.

Shifts in Economic Power

Current trends point to an eventual complete breakdown of traditional sex role divisions in business, industry, government, and even in the armed forces. The number of women who are gainfully employed, including married women, has been steadily increasing in modern times, and has especially accelerated during the past few decades. Modern technological societies apparently cannot afford the luxury of having one-half their population (its females) as nonparticipants who stay home and take care of the children. Most families apparently require more than one wage earner if their standard of living is to be adequate.

One recent forecast is that the number of working women will increase from 40 million in 1978 to 52 million by 1990, with the largest increases among married women with children. Only one in four mothers will spend all of her time at home with her children.[7] We can thus envision an ultimate state of affairs where virtually all men and women will work, and where women will eventually have incomes equal to men.

The increasing economic power of women will bring about further changes in the domestic roles of men and women. Although their economic status remains far below that of men, they have made appreciable relative gains, considering the low base from which they started. In a traditional marriage, the primary responsibility of the husband is his work. Not only that, but his work usually determines the status of the family, and the family's needs must be accommodated to the demands of his career. Often a high-level occupation will require moving on short notice to a new location; sometimes it will require work after hours or on weekends. When this occurs, the needs of the wife or children must take second place. When a wife is in the traditional role of homemaker, she can often alleviate the pressures of her husband's work by being accommodating, supportive, and nurturant.

Some of the ways in which the roles of married men and women might change may be gleaned from what is known about dual-career families.[8] While it is true that most studies have been limited to higher-level occupations, these in fact meet an important requisite for anticipating the future—

that the employment of both partners in a marriage be of equal importance and status. In a dual-career family, a wide range of role demands may come from *either* spouse, sometimes simultaneously. Each spouse may come home from work expecting strokes from the other. Or perhaps the children need special attention. Who gives it? The same goes for the chores of daily living—someone has to do them. And in the area of psychological support, high-status, hard-working people often need encouragement, respect, and deference from those close to them. When both spouses need this, who obliges?

Research so far suggests that solutions to these problems worked out by different couples may take widely varying forms.[9] In some, the woman's career may be temporarily deferred in favor of having children or staying home and taking care of young children, or else by reducing it to part-time work; this is an obvious accommodation in the direction of the conventional pattern. In others, both spouses may share virtually all facets of family roles, quite in contrast to the conventional form. Instances where the husband's career is down-graded in favor of the wife's and where he thereby takes over a larger share of the parenting and homemaking are still extremely rare, but may become more common in the future.

Worth noting is the point that dual-career couples are currently trying to function in a social world which, while it has loosened up slightly, is by and large structured to accommodate only the traditional family. Unconventional families, in addition to having greater role strains than conventional families, must cope with the lack of fit between their social/business world and their unusual private roles. There is the female professor at a reception for faculty and their spouses who frequently gets asked, "And whose wife are you?" Or the lawyer who tells of his difficulties in explaining that he can't schedule a meeting with an important client on Thursday afternoon because he has to take his son for piano lessons.[10] Some of these dual-career couples do very little entertaining because they are both committed to getting ahead in their professions, work long hours, and cannot spare the time to make the necessary preparations.

There is still another factor concerning the future problems of dual-career families. If working couples are to become the norm, then societies will gradually become more and more accommodated to such families, and role strains will ease. Having dual careers is a sharp departure from the conventional family pattern, and in time we can expect marked change in the workplace to accommodate it. Flexible working hours and shared careers, where both spouses spend half of their time at the same job, are different examples of adjustments that have already occurred in some places.[11]

Legal Rights of Women

Women have made some small gains in political status, in that many more women are running for political office and getting elected. Moreover, in the 1980 presidential election, for the first time in U.S. history, more women than men voted. The last few decades have seen the formation of active, strong organizations organized and led by women with the aim of achieving various political goals, especially more equality for women. So far, though, the assumption of these political roles by a small number of women probably has had little effect on our attitudes and beliefs about women in general.

Perhaps the most remarkable advances have been made in the realm of legal rights, especially when they are contrasted with past centuries. Consider, for example, legal changes in one arena, that of women's rights in marriage, divorce, and child custody. In most high sex ratio societies of the past, where women held dyadic power because of their scarcity, this power was effectively neutralized by many legal constraints. Given contemporary Western customs, when young women are scarce, they are able to use their dyadic power to their advantage as long as they remain single. But in most early societies of the past, young single women were firmly under the control of their fathers, who severely limited their interaction with the opposite sex and who chose their daughters' husbands for them. Once married, the husband in effect became their legal guardian. This was reflected in the fact that property usually came under his control. He could readily divorce his wife, while she would have great difficulty in obtaining a divorce. If the marriage dissolved in divorce, property most often went to the husband rather than being divided, and he got custody of the children. Thus, even when women were in short supply, neither the single nor the married state permitted them to exercise their potential dyadic power in such societies.

In contemporary society, all this has changed. Young single women are not confined to the home and have much experience with the opposite sex. They make their own decisions about male friends or the choice of a husband. Either party to a marriage can now get a divorce if they want one. These changes that free young single people to choose their own mates and loosen the marriage bond favor the gender that is in short supply. In a word, structural constraints that have in the past neutralized dyadic power, particularly that of women, have disappeared.

Changes in the legal rights of women have also extended beyond the home to the workplace. A woman being interviewed for a position can no longer be questioned about her marital status or her condition and/or intentions concerning motherhood by an employer who desires to acquire a basis for estimating her permanence and steady availability as a potential employee. The civil courts are considering numerous cases where claims have been made by women that they have been discriminated against in terms of pay or advancement, or that they have been sexually harassed by a supervisor. Such claims are only possible because constitutional or other laws now recognize the right of women to equal treatment before the law, both in and out of the home. One has to read history to grasp the full impact of this change. Except for the past century or so, women had virtually no place whatsoever outside the home.

ROLE IDENTITIES OF MEN AND WOMEN

Changes in technology, in social practices, and in social structures are apt to change our most fundamental beliefs about human nature. For many of us, the most interesting aspect of these changes is the impact that they have on our beliefs about the very nature of men and women. This occurs because, in part at least, the character that we attribute to categories of people is shaped by the kinds of task demands and roles that they fulfill. The roles that society allocates to them more or less define their identity as people, and this extends to beliefs and feelings about their identity. We can discuss sex ratios, marital opportunities, and social structures from the viewpoint of their impact on the role identities of men and women.

The identity attributed to men or women is, of course, partly influenced by the age category to which they belong. Keep in mind that our focus has been on the child-bearing ages—the twenties and thirties—and we stay within those boundaries here. Consider first the identity that is ordinarily attributed to women. While it is easy to get into a quarrel over any one feature, several central characteristics have traditionally been ascribed to them. Young women today have already changed to some extent; the list here is probably better attributed to earlier generations. Women have generally been considered to be unassertive, submissive, passive, soft, and dependent; affectionate, nurturant, and domestic; devious, manipulative, emotional, and irrational. Interesting contradictions arise over sexuality. Sometimes they are believed to have more control over their sexual impulses—to have a muted sexuality—but often they have been believed to be dangerously passionate and undisciplined.[12] In contrast with women, men are believed to have a strong sex drive, to be aggressive, assertive, competitive, strong, independent, rational, and tough. Of course, the qualities of men and women vary somewhat in different societies and in different periods, but the basic core stays much the same.

If it is true that societal conditions are bringing about marked changes in the role and task demands placed upon women, we could well be on the verge of observing marked changes in their collective identity. If appreciable numbers of women choose not to be mothers, their role-identity will have been shorn of one of its most central components. Since the childbearing function of women has been salient for thousands of years in virtually all societies, widespread choice of this new option would bring about drastic changes. One direction that this change might take would be a split in the role-identity of women into two sharply differentiated types: mothers and nonmothers. The latter category as yet lacks an appropriate modern name; certainly the old term "spinster" would no longer fit, and "career woman" would fit women with children as well.

Many of the attributes we have listed as typically ascribed to women follow quite directly from the traditional role of mother: nurturant, domestic, soft, and affectionate. All of the remaining ones follow from the weak power position of women vis-à-vis men: unassertive, submissive, passive, dependent, devious, manipulative, irrational, and emotional. This set stems from the greater power, authority, and status that men have traditionally had compared to women, whether as husbands, bosses, or societal leaders. Many wives are dependent on their husbands, and women in the work force are usually in subordinate positions. Their relationship to their husband in the traditional family is unassertive, submissive, and passive, and that to their boss has similar attributes.

That women are often believed to be devious and manipulative also stems from their "one-down" position. Women may conceal those values on which there is disagreement, may be ingratiating, may yield to pressures to conform to men's desires, and may actually shape themselves according to the image desired by men. What is seen as emotionality or irrationality also stems in part from disadvantages in trying to be direct when in a low-power position. But all of these are characteristics attributed to *every* low-status, low-power group, whether male or female. Such beliefs are commonly held about racial and ethnic groups, the lower socioeconomic classes, and servants, among others. They are a function of a disparity in status and power, and they change if that disparity changes.

Individuals in weak positions cannot directly assert their power against those in stronger positions, except at the risk of being crushed or squelched. Hence, they must be more indirect, more devious, more manipulative. Weaker parties try to negotiate exchanges where the advantages to them are not obvious or are concealed; the process is manipulated so that it appears to the stronger parties that they are getting the better of the deal, or at least equality. Our belief is that these behavioral characteristics are not inherent, but that they emerge from the social context.

At the present time, it is still easy to see a woman who succeeds in a profession or as a business executive as "different"—not like other women. But women are going into law, medicine, and business in rapidly increasing numbers, and will soon be too numerous to ignore. Certainly, enacting such roles contradicts the traditional image of women as dependent, passive, and domestically oriented. That many millions of working women support themselves contradicts the notion that women have to be taken care of. The declining birth rate reflects numerous decisions by women not to have children or to have fewer children. As the role of mother becomes less central in defining a woman's identity, we can expect those attributes associated with motherhood to become less salient in the common view of what a woman is.

These marked changes in women's role identities will have a powerful impact on the role identities of men. Many men who get ego support from the dependency of women on them are apt to suffer a loss of self-esteem upon realizing that these women no longer need them to lean on. Men married to career women will need to learn that family decisions must consider not only the husband's career, but also that of his wife. They will be under considerable pressure to share domestic duties and the care of the children. In the long run, their role identities will have to undergo marked changes if they are to relate in a compatible way to the modern woman.

One theme that runs through traditional relationships between men and women is that of male ascendance/female dependence. This has already been apparent in the allocation of the breadwinner role to men and the domestic one to women, but the theme is far more pervasive. Literature and other media have repeatedly cast men in the role of hero, problem-solver, and rescuer, while women appear as comparatively helpless creatures living in a dangerous world. Even in the sexual act itself, the male is commonly seen as the aggressor, with the female passive. But unless there are real biological differences supporting this interpretation of the sexual act, we can anticipate a continuation of the changes that have taken place in the last two decades toward more equal contributions to the sexual act from both partners.

The issues here are complicated. Some observers have suggested, for example, that the nature of the sex act itself and the capabilities that it requires are not suited to absolute equality between man and woman. One suggestion is that the male's ability to maintain tumescence may well be easily threatened by too aggressive or too passionate a woman, resulting in the embarrassment of impotence. Her demand for orgasmic experiences may be too much for him. Or, more generally, the common presumption is that when a woman is dependent on a man, he can more readily feel ascendant in carrying out the sex act and that it nourishes the male ego. Does this mean that when a man and a woman have equality in every respect that she needs to conceal or submerge her sexual desires and the true extent of her passion? It seems likely that, while men who are unable to accept women as peers may have difficulty, those who accept them as equals may well obtain more satisfaction from a woman who is aggressively passionate. In fact, the considerable increase in recent years in the intensity and variety of erotic behavior among married couples reported in Chapter 7 suggests that the female's contribution can become more intense and more varied, with both parties experiencing greater satisfaction.

More generally, equality in structural and dyadic power should make sexual behavior more mutually supportive. Each partner should be more caring toward the other, and more considerate, for no longer would sex be a resource bartered by women in exchange for financial support, status, or whatever. The image of women giving and not receiving comes from her dependency on men; she has had little choice in her traditional role. Most of what is immoral or unfair about sexual exchanges comes from the unequal division of structural power between males and females and the consequent distortions of the social exchanges that take place between them. Power corrupts sexual activity, just as it does every other form of human action. Thus, if we ever do reach a point where men and women have equal economic and political power, we will also see a new standard of morality in sexual behavior.

As equality between men and women is approached, we can anticipate that the role identities of both will shift gradually to incorporate more of the characteristics that have traditionally been attributed to the opposite sex. Social scientists have come to label such shifts as "androgynous." Along with this will come a greater variety of types within each gender. Each will be less stereotyped; people will be more ready to attribute widely different characteristics to individuals of the same gender. An appreciable number of men will be seen as nurturant, tender, and loving, along with whatever other characteristics they might have, and many women will be seen as aggressive, tough, competitive, and rational. At the same time, we can still expect that the old conventional roles and their identity attributes will still be prevalent, for they will continue to work well in some settings and with the right partner.

The ultimate effect of these structural changes is to make men and women more equal in their freedom to use dyadic power when the sex ratio imbalance is in their favor. This should eventually undermine the double standard of sexual morality in which men are free to have multiple relationships with women, while women are restricted to a single, monogamous relationship. Other changes reinforce this conclusion. Clearly, the last few decades have seen a sexual revolution take place; both premarital sex and sex within and outside of marriage occur more often. While this has been brought about partly by low sex ratios and the surplus of women, such changes eventually become a part of the forms of life of the society in which they take place, and thus are not so easily turned around. Moreover, this change is no doubt due in part to the perfection and greater availability of effective contraceptive devices that remove the fear of unwanted pregnancies from sexual encounters, as well as to the more ready availability of abortions should pregnancy occur. Should sex ratios once again create a scarcity of women, we would still not expect a return to the old double standard. At most, there might be a sorting out of the conditions under which sexual freedoms prevail, but American males no longer have sufficient structural power to bring back chastity for their daughters. Under high sex ratio conditions, they may not be able to enforce monogamy for their wives, either, unless they, too, accept it through mutual agreement.

Nothing we have said is meant to imply that radical changes in role identities for the majority of men and women are just around the corner. We anticipate a transition period of many decades, possibly even a century, before the structural powers of women really approach those of men. In the interim, the favorable balance of power that men currently hold will often be used to stave off change, or even to return to earlier conditions. In the end, though, eventual change seems inevitable by powerful technological and societal trends that show no signs of being arrested.

In conclusion, as these changes in social structures and role identities emerge, the high and low sex ratio societies that we have found in many times and places are not apt to recur in the United States and similar Western countries, at least not in the same form as in the past. Movement toward a more equitable distribution of structural power between men and women will mean that the kinds of role identities and relationships characterizing high and low sex ratio societies of the past will be replaced by male and female identities quite different from anything that history has seen before. The currently dominant image of woman as homemaker and mother will fade and be replaced by a radically different, more composite portrait. Men will fulfill much more diverse roles than ever before, and men and women will relate to each other in a new and different way.

Notes

Chapter One

1. U.S. Bureau of the Census, *Census of population: 1970 subject reports, marital status*, Final Report PC(2)-4C, Table 1.

2. P. C. Glick, D. M. Heer, and J. C. Beresford, "Family formation and family composition: Trends and prospects." In M. B. Sussman (Ed.), *Sourcebook in marriage and the family*, 2nd ed. Boston: Houghton Mifflin, 1963, pp. 30-40.

3. Social exchange theory has its origins in economics, social psychology, and sociology. Included among the extensive literature are the following major works: J. W. Thibaut and H. H. Kelley, *The social psychology of groups*. New York: John Wiley, 1959; P. M. Blau, *Exchange and power in social life*. New York: John Wiley, 1964; G. C. Homans, *Social behavior: Its elementary forms*, revised ed. New York: Harcourt Brace Jovanovich, 1974; G. S. Becker, *The economic approach to human behavior*. Chicago: University of Chicago Press, 1976; H. H. Kelley and J. W. Thibaut, *Interpersonal relations: A theory of independence*. New York: John Wiley, 1978.

4. P. C. Glick and A. J. Norton, "Marrying, divorcing, and living together in the U.S. today." *Population Bulletin*, 1977, 32.

5. E. Ardener, S. Ardener, and W. A. Warmington, *Plantation and village in the Cameroons: Some economic and social studies*. London: Oxford University Press, 1960.

6. S. Lyman, *The Asian in the West*. Reno, NV: Social Science and Humanities Publication No. 4, Western Studies Center, Desert Research Institute, University of Nevada System, 1970; S. Lyman, *Chinese Americans*. New York: Random House, 1974.

7. S. Rawlings, "Perspectives on husbands and wives." *Current Population Reports:* Special Studies, Series P-23, No. 77. Washington, DC: Government Printing Office, 1978.

8. Ibid.

9. L. Tiger and R. Fox, *The imperial animal*. New York: Holt, Rinehart & Winston, 1971.

Chapter Two

1. We are especially indebted to anthropologist Tom Beidelman for pointing out that *reliable* demographic data on preliterate societies are extremely difficult to obtain, and that they are not available in sufficient quantity to enable us to draw conclusions about the effects of sex ratios on relations between men and women.

2. M. Finley, "The Greek cities." In W. W. Tarn (Ed.) and G. T. Griffith (Rev.), *Hellenistic civilization*. London, 1952.

3. Ibid.

4. Sarah B. Pomeroy, *Goddesses, whores, wives, slaves: Women in classical antiquity.* New York: Schocken Books, 1975.

5. Finley, op. cit.

6. Ibid.

7. The stimulation for this study grew out of conversations between Ernst Badian and Marcia Guttentag, and was carried out by V. J. Harward. These conversations concerning the classical era were invaluable in organizing and writing this section, and our debt to Professor Badian is profound. Of course, any inadequacies or errors are entirely our own responsibility.

8. Robert Payne, *Ancient Greece: the triumph of a culture.* New York: W. W. Norton, 1964.

9. *The Iliad of Homer,* Richmond Lattimore, trans. Chicago: University of Chicago Press, 1970, 3.88-91.

10. Ibid., pp. 727-732.

11. *The Odyssey of Homer,* Richmond Lattimore, trans. New York: Harper & Row, 1967, 6.108-111.

12. *Iliad,* op. cit.

13. *Herodotus: The Persian wars,* G. Rawlinson, trans. New York: Modern Library, 1942, 1.146.

14. Ibid.

15. *Iliad,* op. cit.

16. *Odyssey,* op. cit.

17. Pomeroy, op. cit.

18. Ibid.

19. Ibid.

20. *Herodotus,* op. cit.

21. Pomeroy, op. cit.

22. *Odyssey,* op. cit.

23. J. Harward "Report on an investigation of the ratio between men to women in the Athenian population of the fourth century, B.C.," October 1976.

24. Ibid.

25. Ibid.

26. Ibid.

27. Pomeroy, op. cit., p. 66

28. Ibid.

29. Finley, op. cit.

30. Ibid.

31. Ibid.

32. Ibid.

33. Ibid.

34. Plutarch, *Lycurgus,* op. cit., p. 140.

35. Pomeroy, op, cit.

36. See Pomeroy, op. cit., pp. 58-60 for a summary of this controversy and also Pomeroy, "Selected bibliography on women in antiquity," for references to scholars contributing to the dispute.

37. Finley, op. cit.

38. W. K. Lacey, *The family in classical Greece.* London: Thames and Hudson, 1968, p. 215.

39. *Aristotle's Politics,* J. E. C. Welldon, trans. London: Macmillan, 1907, 1.13.

40. Pomeroy, op. cit.

41. Lacey, op. cit., p. 159.

42. Pomeroy, op. cit., p. 74.

43. Ibid.

44. Pomeroy, op. cit., pp. 63-64.

45. Pomeroy, op. cit., p. 63.

46. Pomeroy, op. cit., p. 62.

47. Pomeroy, op. cit., p. 64.

48. Ibid.

49. Ibid., pp. 64-65.

50. Pomeroy, op. cit., p. 74.

51. Pomeroy, op. cit., pp. 71-73.
52. Pomeroy, op. cit., pp. 81-83.
53. Lacey, op. cit., p. 113.
54. Ibid.
55. Phocylides: Diehl fragment 2, as cited in Pomeroy, op. cit., p. 49.
56. Lacey, op. cit., p. 115.
57. Pomeroy, op. cit., p. 78.
58. Finley, op. cit., p. 83.
59. Ibid.
60. Pomeroy, op. cit., p. 36.
61. Lacey, op. cit., p. 215.
62. R. F. Willets, *The Law Code of Gortyn*. Berlin: Walter de Gruyter, 1967, cols. 6.11-13.
63. Pomeroy, op. cit., p. 130.
64. Willets, op. cit., col. 2, 309.
65. Pomeroy, op. cit., p. 81.
66. Pomeroy, op. cit., p. 37.
67. Alcman, fragment 3. Judith Peller Hallett, trans. As quoted in Pomeroy, op. cit., pp. 52-53.
68. Pomeroy, op. cit., p. 56.
69. Pomeroy, op. cit., pp. 53-54.
70. Interested readers should refer to K. J. Dover, *Greek homosexuality* (London: Gerald Duckworth, 1978), for an extensive presentation of the evidence for homosexuality among the Greeks of classical times.
71. E. Badian, op. cit., p. 30.
72. Aristophanes, *Lysistrata: the Grecian temptress*. Norman Lindsay, trans. New York: Three Sirens Press, p. 101.
73. M. K. Martin and B. Voorhies, *Female of the species*. New York: Columbia University Press, 1975.
74. Papers by Mildred Dickeman, both published and unpublished, made available to the authors were of great value to us in writing this section of female infanticide and hypergamy, and we are deeply indebted to her. M. Dickeman. Demographic consequences of infanticide in man. *Annual Review of Ecology and Systematics*, 1975, 6, pp. 107-137; M. Dickeman, "Female infanticide and hypergamy: a neglected relationship," Unpublished paper, 1976.
75. Ibid.
76. M. Weissman and G. L. Klerman, "Sex differences and the epidemiology of depression." *Archives of General Psychiatry*, 1977, 24.
77. Dickeman, op. cit.
78. G. M. Carstairs, *The twice-born: A study of a community of high-caste Hindus*. Bloomington: Indiana University Press, 1958; W. Crooke, *The north western provinces of India: Their history, enthnology and administration*. London: Methuen, 1897.
79. Dickeman, op. cit.
80. Ibid.
81. Ping-ti Ho, *Studies on the population of China, 1368-1953*. Cambridge: Harvard University Press, 1959. Cited in Dickeman, op. cit.
82. I. Tinker et al., "Culture and population change." *American Association for the Advancement of Science Reports*, 1974. Revised and edited in 1976 by Tinker et al.
83. W. L. Langer, "Checks on population growth, 1750-1850." *Scientific American*, 1972, 226, 92-99; "Infanticide: a historical survey." *History of Childhood Quarterly*, 1974, 1, 353-365.
84. Tinker et al., op. cit.
85. J. C. Russell, "Late ancient and medieval populations." *Transactions*, American Philosophical Society, 1958.

Chapter Three

1. Much of this section uses David Herlihy's important work on the historical demography of the Middle Ages and is stimulated by his theories, particularly the following: "Land, family

and women in Continental Europe, 701-1200." In Susan Mosher Stuard (Ed.), *Women in medieval society.* Philadelphia: University of Pennsylvania Press, 1976; "Alienation in medieval culture and society." In *Alienation: Concept, term and meanings.* New York: Seminar Press, 1973; "The medieval marriage market." In Dale B. J. Randall (Ed.), *Medieval and renaissance studies: Proceedings of the Southeastern Institute of Medieval and Renaissance Studies,* Summer 1974, Medieval and Renaissance Series No. 6; "Life expectancies for women in medieval society." In Rosemary T. Morewedge (Ed.), *The role of women in the Middle Ages.* Albany: State University of New York Press, 1975; "What we know about medieval marriages," unpublished paper, 1976.

C. Bucher, *Die Frauenfrage im Mittelalter* (Tübingen: Verlag Der H. Laupp'schen Buchhandlung, 1882), provides valuable information about the economic and sexual routes taken by surplus women in the late Middle Ages. Of course, the inferences made on the basis of this work are solely the author's responsibility.

2. David Herlihy, "Alienation in medieval culture and society." In *Alienation: Concept, term and meanings,* New York: Seminar Press, 1973, p. 128.

3. Emily Coleman, "Infanticide in the early Middle Ages." In S. M. Stuard (Ed.), *Women in medieval society.* Philadelphia: University of Pennsylvania Press, 1976, p. 55.

4. Herlihy, 1973, op. cit., p. 128.

5. David Herlihy, "Life expectancies for women in medieval society." In R. T. Morewedge (Ed.), *The role of woman in the Middle Ages.* Albany: State University of New York Press, 1975, p. 6.

6. Coleman, 1976, op. cit., p. 49.

7. Herlihy (1976, op. cit., pp. 10-11) cites *Speculum Naturale.* Graz: Akademische Druck-und Verlagsanstalt, 1964, bk. 24, ch. 67. Also cites *Averrois cordubensis compendia librorum Aristotelis qui Parva naturalia vocantur,* Aelia Ledyard Shields (Ed.), with the assistance of Henry Blumberg. Corpus commentariorum Averrois in Aristotelem 7. Cambridge, MA: Medieval Academy of America, 1949, p. 139.

8. E. G. Jerem, "The late Iron Age cemetery of Szentlorinc." *Acta Archaeologica Academiae Scientiorum Hungaricae,* 1967, 19, 159-208. As cited in Herlihy, 1975, p. 6. Also cites, p. 17, "For a survey of studies of skeletal remains from medieval Hungarian graveyards, see Eric Fugedi, 'Pour une analyse demographique de la Hongrie medievale.' *Annales-Economies-Societés-Civilisations,* 1969, 24, 1299-1312."

9. Herlihy, 1967, op. cit., pp. 10-11.

10. Coleman, op. cit., entire article.

11. Coleman, op. cit., p. 54.

12. Ibid., p. 55

13. Ibid.

14. Coleman (op. cit., p. 57) cites Schmitz, *Die Büssbücher 1: 687, clause 56.*

15. Coleman (op. cit., p. 58) cites *MGH,* scriptores 2, G. H. Pertz (Ed.). Hanover, 1829, p. 406.

16. M. H. Scargill and M. Schlauch, *Three Icelandic sagas.* Princeton, 1950, pp. 11-12; A. B. Kellum, "Infanticide in England in the later Middle Ages." *History of Childhood Quarterly,* 1973-74, 1, 369; R. C. Trexler, "Infanticide in Florence: New sources and first results." *History of Childhood Quarterly,* 1973-74, 6, 98-116; R. R. Trexler, "The foundlings of Florence, 1395-1455." *History of Childhood Quarterly,* 1973-74, 1, 259-284.

17. Herlihy, 1975, op. cit.

18. Herlihy, 1975, op. cit., pp. 8-9.

19. Herlihy, 1975, op. cit., p. 9; *Monumenta Germaniae Historica Leges.*

20. *On Britain and Germany: A translation of the "Agricola" and the "Germania" of Tacitus,* H. Mattingly, transl. Harmondsworth, Middlesex: Penguin Books, 1964, p. 115.

21. Herlihy, 1975, op. cit., p. 9.

22. David Herlihy, "The medieval marriage market," In D. B. J. Randall (Ed.), *Medieval and Renaissance studies: Proceedings of the Southeastern Institute of Medieval and Renaissance Studies,* Summer 1974, Medieval and Renaissance Series No. 6.

23. Ibid., p. 15.

24. Ibid.

25. Ibid., p. 24.

26. See J. Barchewitz, *Von der Wirtschaftstätigkeit der Frau in der vorgeschichtlichen Zeit bis zur Entfaltung der Stadtwirtschaft,* Breslau, 1937; E. Grosse, *Die Formen der Familie und*

die Formen der Wirtschaft, Freiburg-Leipzig, 1896. As cited in David Herlihy, "Land, family and women in Continental Europe, 701-1200." In S. M. Stuard (Ed.), *Women in medieval society.* Philadelphia: University of Pennsylvania Press, 1976, p. 24.

27. Herlihy, 1976, op. cit., p. 24.; Cites *De Germania* 14, 25, C. Halm (Ed.). Leipzig, 1911, pp. 227-228 and 232.
28. Herlihy, 1976, op. cit., pp. 24-25.
29. Herlihy, 1976, op. cit., p. 25. Cites Altonis, *Epistula* 9, PL 134.117 D.
30. Herlihy, 1974, op. cit., p. 15.
31. Herlihy, 1976, op. cit., p. 14.
32. D. Herlihy, "What we know about medieval marriages," unpublished paper, 1976, pp. 12-13.
33. Stuard, op. cit., "Introduction," p. 8.
34. Herlihy, 1976, op. cit., p. 15.
35. Herlihy, 1976, op. cit., p. 12.
36. Ibid.
37. Herlihy, 1976, op. cit., p. 34.
38. C. Bucher, *Die Frauenfrage im Mittelalter.* Tübingen: Verlag Der H. Laupp'schen Buchhandlung, 1882. p. 6.
39. Herlihy, 1975, op. cit., p. 11.
40. Ibid., p. 12.
41. Ibid., pp. 12-13. Also ibid., p. 19, "See Pierre Desportes, La population de Reims au XVe siècle, *Le Moyen Age: Revue d'histoire et de philologie* 74, 1966, p. 486"; *Deutches Städtebuch: Handbuch Städtischer Geschichte,* herausgegeben von Erich Keyser. W. Kohlhammer Verlag, Band III: Nordwest Duetschland. Teil 2. Westfallen: *Westfälisches Städtebuch,* 1954.
42. One can gain an appreciation of how many women were available for the religious life by reviewing the dates of the founding of convents in northern German cities *(Deutsches Städtebuch: Handbuch Städtischer Geschichte,* herausgegeben von Erich Keyser. W. Kohlhammer Verlag, Band III: Nordwest Deutschland. Teil 3. Lanschaftsverband Rheinland: *Rheinisches Städtebuch,* 1956, p. 253).

The *Städtebuch* for Cologne lists the following convents, together with the dates they were founded:

Frauenkloster (ohne die Beginenkonvente), dabei als wichtigste: Benediktinerinnen St. Machabaer (1178, Weihe, 1232, Neubau Anfang 16.Jh., abgebrochen 1808);

St. Mauritius (bei der Pfarrkirche, Kloster zuletzt Rheinishe Musikschule) und St. Agatha (1313 Augustinerinnen, seit 1459 Benediktinerinnen, im 19. Jh. Kaserne, abgebrochen 1865);

Augustinerinnen St. Maxim (??63-72, abgebrochen 1806);

St. Maria Magdalena (Weissfrauen, für Zisterzienserinnen gegr. 1229, seit 1256 Augustinerinnen, abgebrochen, 1809);

Zisterzienserinnen St. Maria-Garten (um 1220, abgebrochen 1803);

St. Maria-Syon (Seyen) oder Maria Spiegel (1246 von Gräfin Mechtildis von Sayn gegr., seit 1613 Brigittiner, abgebrochen 1833);

St. Apern (1474 statt älterer Klause und Kapelle, Neubau 1621, abgebrochen nach 1803);

Dominikanerinnen St. Gertrud (1255, abgebrochen 1808);

Franziskanerinnen St. Clara (1304, abgebrochen 1804);

St. Elisabeth (1312 als Beginenkonvent, seit 1434 Zellitinnenkloster, besteht fort);

Karmeliterinnen St. Maria in der Kupfergasse (1635, Neubau 1705-15, jetzt Pfarrkirche, Kloster jetzt im Besitz der Zellitinnen), und in der Schnurgasse (1637, Neubau 1677 bis 1716, seit 1803 Pfarrkirche, jetzt wieder Karmeliterinnenkloster);

Ursulinerinnen (1639, Neubau der Kirche 1706-12, besteht noch);

Augustinerinnen zum Weiher ("Weyerthal"; 1198, 1474, abgebrochen . . .)

Zisterzienserinnen St. Mechtern (ad martyres; 1180, 1474, abgebrochen . . .)

[*Deutsches Städtebuch: Handbuch Städtischer Geschichte,* herausgegeben von Erich Keyser. W. Kohlhammer Verlag, Band IV: Südwest Deutschland. Teil 1. Land Hessen: *Hessisches Städtebuch,* 1957, pp. 126-127].

In the *Städtebuch* from Frankfurt, one finds similar dates for the founding of convents. Of particular interest are those for reformed prostitutes, namely the ones founded in 1228 and 1313. See also Herlihy, "What we know about medieval marriages," op. cit., p. 24.

43. Herlihy, (1974, op. cit., pp. 7-8) cites Hermann Kantorowicz, *Studies in the glossators of the Roman law: newly discovered writings of the twelfth century.* Cambridge, 1938, p. 261.

44. Ibid.

45. Herlihy (1974, op. cit., pp. 7-8) cites *Il cartolare di Giovanni Scriba,* M. Chiaudano and M. Moresco (Eds.), Regesta chartarum Italiae, 19-20; Rome, 1935. See also Herlihy, 1974, op. cit., p. 24: "According to my count, out of thirty marriage agreements, the dowry is higher than the reverse dowry in ten instances; the reverse dowry is higher in four; and the two are equal in sixteen."

46. Herlihy, 1974, op. cit., pp. 14-19.

47. Ibid., p. 8.

48. Herlihy (1974, op. cit., p. 9) cites *Notai liguri del sec. XII, 5: Giovanni di Guiberto (1200-1211),* M. W. Hall-Cole, H. G. Krueger, R. G. Reinhart, and R. L. Reynolds (Eds.), Documenti e studi per la storia del commercio e del diritto commerciale italiano, 17-18; Turin, 1939-40. See also Herlihy, 1974, op. cit., p. 24: "According to my count, out of forty-one marriage agreements, the dowry is larger than the reverse dowry in twenty-five instances; the reverse dowry is higher in one; and the two are equal in fifteen."

49. *Dante's Paradiso,* L. Binyon, trans. London: MacMillan, 1943, Canto XV, 103-105: "Nor yet did daughter's birth dismay the father; For dowry and nuptial-age did not exceed the measure, upon one side or the other."

50. Stanley Chojnacki, "Dowries and kinsmen in early renaissance Venice." In S. M. Stuard (Ed.), *Women in medieval society.* Philadelphia: University of Pennsylvania Press, 1976, p. 173.

51. Ibid., p. 175.

52. Herlihy, "What we know about medieval marriages," op. cit., p. 23.

53. Herlihy, January 1977, personal communication.

54. Herlihy, "What we know about medieval marriages," op. cit., p. 14. Cites *ASS, Junii I,* pp. 362-363.

55. Ibid., pp. 14-15, also p. 33: "According to C. H. Talbot, Christina was born sometime between 1096 and 1098, and forced into marriage in 1114 or 1115. Her parents were Anglo-Saxon nobles from the county of Huntingdonshire."

56. Ibid., p. 15, cites *ASS, Maii V,* p. 206, also p. 33: "St. Humility, whose baptismal name was Rossana, is described as having entered the convent as a widow at age 24, after 9 years of marriage."

57. Ibid., p. 15, cites *ASS, Aprilis II,* p. 334, also p. 33: "St. Clare came from the prominent Pisan family of Gambacorta."

58. Ibid., p. 34, cites *ASS, Aprilis II,* p. 863, for St. Catherine of Siena; *ASS, Maii V,* p. 224 for St. Rita of Cascia.

59. Ibid., p. 18. Also see D. Herlihy's article, "The generation in medieval history," in *Viator.*

60. Ibid., p. 18.

61. Ibid., p. 19.

62. Herlihy, "What we know about medieval marriages," op. cit., p. 19.

63. Herlihy, 1973, op. cit., p. 132.

64. Stuard, op. cit., "Introduction," p. 8.

65. Herlihy, "What we know about medieval marriages," op. cit., p. 24: "A rewording of the text adds that she did so to escape an unwanted marriage, but this embellishment looks like a pious fiction."

66. Ibid., p. 24, cites *ASS, Junii IV,* pp. 276, 277, 315, 436.

67. Herlihy, 1975, op. cit., p. 15.

68. Herlihy, (1973, op. cit., p. 137) cites G. Volpe, *Movimenti religiose e sette ereticali nella societa medievale italiana* (secoli XI-XIV) 6. Florence: Collana Storica, 1922 "Women now appear in the history of heresy as in no other phase of life."

69. Ibid., p. 136.

70. Ibid., pp. 136-137.

71. Ibid.

72. Ibid., p. 134.

73. Ibid.

74. Ibid., p. 134, cites R. Sacchoni, "Summa de Catharis et Leonistis seu Pauperibus de Lugduno, 1717." In E. Martene and U. Durand (Eds.), *Thesaurus Novus Anecdotorum,* Vol. V. Paris: Montalant, 1717.

75. Ibid.

76. Ibid.

77. Herlihy, 1973, op. cit., p. 134.

78. Ibid., p. 133.

79. Ibid., p. 136, cites G. Koch, *Frauenfrage und Ketzertum im Mittelalter: Die Frauenbewegung im Rahmen des Katharismus und des Waldensertums und ihre sozialen Wurzeln (12-14 Jahrhundert)* 9. Berlin: Forschungen zur Mittelalterlichen Geschichte, 1962.

80. B. M. Bolton, "Muliers Sanctae." In S. M. Stuard (Ed.), *Women in medieval society.* Philadelphia: University of Pennsylvania Press, 1976, pp. 142-43.

81. Ibid., p. 142.

82. Ibid., p. 142, cites J. P. Migne (Ed.), *Patrologiae Cursus Completus* (Latin Series), Vols. 1-222. Paris, 1844-1864.

83. Ibid., p. 143. See also note 17, p. 55, PL 183:1091 (PL refers to *Patrologiae Cursus Completus*, op. cit.).

84. Ibid., p. 143.

85. Ibid., p. 144.

86. E. H. Mizruchi, "On the uses of history in the development of social problems theory." Presented at the annual meetings of the Society for the Study of Social Problems, New York, August 27-30, 1976, Section on Social Problems Theory, p. 5.

87. Bolton, op. cit., p. 145.

88. Mizruchi, op. cit., p. 5, cites E. W. McConnell, *The Beguines and Beghards in medieval culture.* New York: Octagon Books, 1969, p. 140.

89. Bolton, op. cit., p. 237.

90. J. Tarrant, "The Clementine decrees on the Beguines: Conciliar and papal versions," *Archivum Historiae Pontificiae*, Vol. 12, 1974, p. 301.

91. Ibid., p. 305: "Secta quaedam abominabilis . . . quarundam infidelium mulierum."

92. Ibid., p. 308: ". . . the uneducated women who were confusing themselves and others by their unlawful preaching, whom he commanded to disband. . ."

93. Ibid., p. 305

94. Ibid.

95. Ibid.

96. J. Greven, *Die Anfänge der Beginen,* Münster, 1912.

97. D. Phillips, *Beguines in Medieval Strasburg,* Stanford, 1941.

98. Ibid.

99. Ibid., p. 2.

100. Ibid., p. 2.

101. Robert Manz, "Historiography of the Beguine movement," unpublished paper, July 1975, p. 3.

102. Bucher, op. cit., pp. 30-31.

103. Ibid.

104. Ibid., pp. 18-24.

105. Ibid., pp. 4-6.

106. *Deutsches Städtebuch: Handbuch Städtischer Geschichte,* herausgegeben von Erich Keyser. W. Kohlhammer Verlag, Band IV: Südwest Deutschland. Teil 1. Land Hessen: *Hessisches Städtebuch,* 1957, p. 131.

Frankfurt: 1387 population: 2085 men and sons over 12 years
2459 women
3398 children
730 servants
959 maidservants
9632 total population

1440 population: 1863 self-supporting citizens and sons over 14 years
2180 women
3055 children
1621 servants and maidservants
8719 total population

107. *Deutsches Städtebuch: Handbuch Städtischer Geschichte,* herausgegeben von Erich Keyser und Heinz Stoob. W. Kohlhammer Verlag, Band V: Bayern. Teil 1. *Bayerisches Städtebuch.* Teil 1, 1971, p. 391.

Nuremberg: 1449-50 population: 3753 men
                                  4383 women
                                  6173 children
                                  1475 servants
                                  1855 maidservants
                                   446 clergy and nuns
                                   150 Jews
                                  1976 nonresidents, mercenaries, and guests
                                 20,211 total population

108. Ibid.
109. Bucher, op. cit., pp. 10-11.
110. Ibid.
111. Ibid., pp. 15-16.
112. Ibid.
113. Ibid., p. 16.
114. Ibid.
115. Ibid., pp. 43-44.
116. Ibid., pp. 38-39.
117. Ibid.
118. Ibid., p. 44.
119. Ibid., pp. 45-46.
120. Ibid., p. 46.
121. C. C. Willard, "A fifteenth-century view of women's role in medieval society: Christine de Pizan's *Livre des Trois Vertus.*" In R. T. Morewedge (Ed.), *The role of women in the Middle Ages.* Albany: State University of New York Press, 1975, p. 95.
122. Ibid.
123. Ibid., pp. 100-101.
124. Ibid., p. 101.
125. Ibid., p. 110.
126. Ibid., p. 111:
       Sage seroit qui se seroit garder
       Des faulx amans qui ades ont usage
       De dire assex pour les femmes fraudes.
127. Ibid.
128. Ibid.
129. Ibid., p. 47.
130. Ibid., p. 48.
131. Ibid., pp. 48-49.
132. Ibid., pp. 49-50.
133. Ibid., pp. 50-51.
134. Ibid.
135. Ibid., pp. 32-33.
136. Ibid., pp. 33-34.
137. Ibid.
138. Ibid.
139. Ibid.
140. Ibid.
141. Ibid.
142. Ibid.
143. Ibid.
144. Most of this section is based on Herbert Moller's pioneering study, "The social causation of the courtly love complex." *Comparative Studies in Society and History,* 1958-59, 1, 137-163.
145. Ibid., pp. 137-138.
146. Ibid., p. 139. *A book containing the Risala, known as the Dove's Neck-Ring, about love and lovers,* A. R. Nykl, trans. Paris: Librairie Orientaliste Paul Geuthner, 1934, p. 2.
147. Ibid., p. 141.
148. Ibid.
149. Ibid., pp. 142-143.

150. Ibid., p. 140.

151. Ibid., p. 149; ibid., p. 142, cites M. Defourneaux, *Les Français en Espagne aux XIe et XIIe siècles*. Paris: Presses Universitaires des France, 1949, p. 5; C. Verlinden, *L'esclavage dans l'Europe médiévale, I: Peninsule Ibérique—France*. Bruggs, de Tempel, 1955, pp. 181-242; Henri Peres, *La Poésie andalouse en arabe classique au XIe siècle*. Paris: Librairie D'Amérique et d'Orient, 1937, pp. 261-262; Levi-Provençal, *Histoire de l'Espagne musulmane*. Paris: Maisonneuve, 1953, III, pp. 28-31, 130-131; *Ibi 'Abd al-mun'im al-Himyari, Kitab ar-Rawd al-Mi'tar Fi Habar al-Aktar*. E. Levi-Provencal, ed. and trans. Leiden: Brill, 1938, p. 33; Lawrence Ecker, *Arabischer, provenzalischer and deutscher Minnesang*. Bern: Haupt, 1934, pp. 229-231; A. R. Nykl, *Hispano-Arabic and its relations with the old Provençal troubadours*. Baltimore, 1946, pp. 6, 14.

152. Ibid., p. 154, cites J. Buhler, *Die Kultur des Mittelalters*. Leipzig: Kroner, 1931, p. 102: "estimates that there were finally about a hundred *ministeriales* for one old aristocratic family."

153. Ibid., p. 150.

154. Ibid., pp. 152-153.

155. Ibid., p. 153.

156. Ibid., p. 154.

157. Ibid.

158. Ibid., p. 155.

159. Ibid.

160. Ibid.

161. Ibid., p. 156. The daughters of noblemen could even succeed to fiefs if there was no male heir.

162. Ibid., pp. 156-157.

163. Ibid., p. 157.

164. Ibid.

165. Ibid., p. 139.

166. Ibid., p. 140.

167. *The poems of Aimeric de Peguilhan*, W. P. Shepard and F. M. Chambers (Eds.). Evanston, IL: Northwestern University Press, 1950.

168. Moller, op. cit., p. 151.

169. Ibid., p. 146.

170. Ibid.

171. Ibid.; Sidney Painter, *French chivalry: Chivalric ideas and practices in medieval France*. Baltimore, MD: The John Hopkins University Press, 1940, pp. 133-136.

172. C. C. Willard, op. cit.

173. Ibid., pp. 100-101.

174. Ibid., p. 111.

175. Ibid., p. 114.

Chapter Four

1. Traditional Jewish prayer recited by the husband to his wife to open each weekly Sabbath celebration. It was introduced as the opening of the Friday night home Sabbath celebration by the Kabbalists of sixteenth-century Safed.

2. *The Torah*, Genesis 29.18-20, 28-30.

3. Salo W. Baron, *A social and religious history of the Jews*, Vol. 1: *Ancient times, part I.* New York: Columbia University Press, 1952, p. 114.

4. Salo W. Baron, *A social and religious history of the Jews*, Vol. 2: *Ancient times, part 2.* New York: Columbia University Press, 1952, p. 236.

5. *The Torah*, Leviticus 21.13-15.

6. *The Torah*, Deuteronomy 22.13-21.

7. *The Torah*, Numbers 31,14-18.

8. *The Torah*, Deuteronomy 24.5. It may well have been practiced in antiquity. Rabbi Ben Zion Gold, personal communication, 1977; Bernard D. Weinryb, *A social and economic history*

of the Jewish community in Poland from 1100 to 1800. Philadelphia: The Jewish Publication Society of America, 1973, p. 98.

9. *The Torah,* Deuteronomy 25.5-9.

10. Rabbi Ben Zion Gold, personal communication, 1977.

11. Tannaitic is derived from the word Tanna, whose definition is: one of a group of Jewish scholars, active in Palestine during the first and second centuries A.D., whose teachings relating to Jewish law and tradition are found chiefly in the Mishnah; Baron, *Ancient times,* 2, p. 238; *The Holy Bible,* Job 5.24. "You shall know that your tent is safe, and you shall inspect your fold and miss nothing (Yebamot 62b)." *The Torah,* Genesis 12.16. "And because of her, it went well with Abram; he acquired sheep, oxen, asses, male and female slaves, she-asses, and camels."

12. Baron, *Ancient times,* 2, p. 238.

13. Ibid., p. 303.

14. Baron, *Ancient times,* 2, p. 239; *The Torah,* Leviticus 19.3. "You shall each revere his mother and his father, and keep My sabbaths: I the LORD am your God."

15. Baron, *Ancient times,* 2, p. 239; also p. 236.

16. Baron, *Ancient times,* 2, p. 241.

17. Ibid., p. 239.

18. Ibid., p. 237.

19. Ibid., p. 239.

20. Ibid., pp. 239-240.

21. Ibid., p. 222.

22. Ibid.

23. Ibid.

24. Ibid., p. 228.

25. Baron, *Ancient times,* 2, p. 78.

26. Ibid., p. 219.

27. Ibid.

28. Salo W. Baron, *Ancient and medieval Jewish history.* New Brunswick, NJ: Rutgers University Press, 1972, p. 22.

29. Ibid.

30. Baron, *Ancient times,* 2, pp. 240-241.

31. Ibid., p. 241.

32. Salo W. Baron, *A social and religious history of the Jews,* Vol. 3: *High Middle Ages, 500-1200 (Heirs of Rome and Persia).* New York: Columbia University Press, 1952, p. 111.

33. Baron, *Ancient times,* 1, p. 112; Baron, *Ancient and medieval Jewish history,* p. 38.

34. Rabbi Ben Zion Gold, personal communication, 1977.

35. Lecture to the Board of Governors, Hebrew University of Jerusalem, by Yigael Yadin, March 1974.

36. *The Jewish encyclopedia.* New York: Funk & Wagnall, 1903, Vol. 5, p. 639. "About 1,000 (Rabbi Gershom) called a synod which decided the following particulars: (1) prohibition of polygamy . . ."

37. U. O. Schmelz, *Infant and early childhood mortality among Jews of the Diaspora.* The Institute of Contemporary Jewry at the Hebrew University of Jerusalem, 1971, p. 78.

38. M. Finley, "The Greek cities." In W. W. Tarn (Ed.), G. T. Griffin (Rev.), *Hellenistic civilization.* London: 1952, p. 102.

39. *The Torah,* Genesis 36.22-28.

40. *The Torah,* Numbers 1,20-25.

41. *The Torah,* Genesis 35.23-26.

42. Salo W. Baron, *A social and religious history of the Jews,* Vol. 1: *Ancient times, Part I.* New York: Columbia University Press, 1952, p. 114.

43. Adna F. Weber, *The growth of cities in the nineteenth century: A study in Statistics.* New York: MacMillan, 1899, p. 12.

44. A. Rafalovich, "Meditsinskaia Statistika Odessy za 1842 god" (Medical Statistics of Odessa for the year 1842), Zhurnal (Journal), Ministerstvo Vnutrennickh Del (Ministry of Internal Affairs), 1843, no. 4.

45. Ibid., p. 358. Refers to Graffen, "Statistische Uebersicht der Bevölkerung der österreich. Monarchie," in *Jahrbücher der Literatur, Vol. XCVII, XCVIII* (Vienna, 1842), p. 186 for the sex ratio statistics.

46. Ibid., p. 356. In Odessa in 1842, 4662 male Jews and 4641 female Jews of all ages. There were 345 males and 154 females born that year. Sex ratio at birth was 224.

47. Ibid., p. 358 (See n. 4.)

48. Charles Darwin, *The descent of man and selection in relation to sex.* New York: A. L. Burt, 1874, p. 275.

49. *Evreiskoe naselenie Rossii po dannym perepisi 1897 g. i po noveishim istochnikam* (The Jewish Population of Russia according to the date of the 1897 census and according to the latest sources). Petrograd: 1917, p. viii.

50. B. Weinryb, pp. 308-309.

51. For a useful discussion of the inadequacies of medieval Jewish historical censuses, see S. Baron, "Reflections on ancient and medieval Jewish historical demography," in *Ancient and Medieval Jewish History,* pp. 10-22.

52. U. O. Schmelz, *Infant and early childhood mortality among Jews of the Diaspora.* The Institute of Contemporary Jewry, Hebrew University of Jerusalem, 1971.

53. The authors are deeply indebted to Patricia Herlihy, who found these invaluable censuses. They are the only ones that the Widener Library has. The New York Public Library does not have any additional censuses from nineteenth-century Russia.

54. Yehoash and Spivak, *Yiddish dictionary,* Rabbi Ben Zion Gold, trans. New York, 1926, p. 188.

55. Saul M. Ginsburg, *Historical works,* Vol. 3., Rabbi Ben Zion Gold, trans. New York, 1937, p. 183.

56. Mendele Moicher Sphorim, "Autobiographical Sketch," in *Das Mendele Buch,* N. Mayzel (Ed.). New York, 1959, p. 17.

57. Our thanks to Patricia Herlihy both for finding the Odessa census from 1892-1917, and for finding out that the demographers had "corrected" it.

Census is from Y. Leshtsinski, "Geburtn, shtarb-faln, un khasenes ba idn in Odes fun 1892 biz 1919 (Births, Deaths and Marriages among the Jews in Odessa from 1892 to 1919)," in *Bleter far yidishe demografie, statistik un ekonomik,* (Jacob Lestschinsky). Berlin, 1923, Vol. 1., table 1, p. 72.

58. Ibid., p. 71.

59. Irving Howe, *World of our fathers.* New York: Harcourt Brace Jovanovich, 1976.

60. Ibid.

61. Flora Blumberg, personal communication, 1977.

62. Theodore Blau, personal communication, 1976.

63. Herbert Feig, personal communication, Tucson, Arizona, 1976.

64. Leon Shapiro and Joshua Starr, "Recent population data regarding the Jews in Europe." *Jewish Social Studies,* 1946, 8, 82.

65. Ibid.

66. William H. James, "Sex ratios in large sibships, in the presence of twins and in Jewish sibships." *Journal of Biosocial Sciences,* 1975, 7, 1965-1969.

67. Ibid., p. 168.

68. Personal communication, Israeli Consulate.

69. James, 1975, p. 168.

70. Unfortunately, the documentation here has been lost—P.F.S.

71. Survey conducted by Abraham Amran in Shimshon, Ashquelon, Israel, in 1976. We are indebted to Shalom Saar for these data.

72. Louis Rosenberg, "Births, deaths and morbidity among Jews in Montreal in 1950." *Jewish Social Studies,* 1953, 15, 103.

73. Sidney Goldstein, *The Greater Providence Jewish community: A population survey,* 1964.

74. Stanley Bigman, *The Jewish population of Greater Washington in 1956.* Washington, DC: The Jewish Community Council, 1957.

75. Baron, *Ancient times,* 2, p. 241.

76. Patricia Herlihy, "The ethnic composition of the city of Odessa in the nineteenth century." *Harvard Ukranian Studies,* 1977, 1(1), 56.

77. Ibid., p. 57.

78. Ibid., p. 60, n. 16.

79. Ibid., p. 57, n. 7. "Although Jewish immigration into Odessa was substantial, the popula-

tion does now show the bulge of males in the young adult years characteristic of other ethnic groups. Among Jews, the sex ratio of those aged 20 to 29 was 99 men per 100 women. Clearly, Jewish men did not immigrate unaccompanied by women."

80. Ibid., p. 60.

81. Ibid., p. 63.

82. Ibid., p. 68.

83. Ibid., pp. 68-69.

84. Arieh Tartakower, "The Jewish refugees: A sociological survey." *Jewish Social Studies*, 1942, 4, 331.

85. *Maimonides*, Book V, ch. XXI.30.

86. *Maimonides*, Book IV, ch. XXI.11.

87. Ibid., ch. XXI.13.

88. Ibid., ch. XXI.16.

89. Ibid., ch. XXI.17.

90. Schmelz, op. cit.

91. Rosenberg, 1953, p. 105; also p. 111, table V.

92. Ibid., p. 78.

93. Ibid., p. 79.

94. Ibid.

95. Ibid., p. 89.

96. Ibid., pp. 46, 50.

97. Ibid., p. 46.

98. Ibid., p. 50.

99. *Maimonides*, Book V, ch. XXI.11.

100. *Maimonides*, Book V, ch. XXI.18.

101. Rabbi Ben Zion Gold, personal communication, 1977.

102. *The code of Maimonides, book four: The book of women*, treatise I, Isaac Klein, trans. New Haven, CT: Yale University Press, 1972.

103. *Maimonides*, Book IV, ch. IV.1.

104. Ibid., ch. X.12.

105. *Maimonides*, Book IV, ch. XIV.1.

106. Ibid., ch. XV.19.

107. Ibid., ch. XV.17.

108. *Maimonides*, Book V, ch. XXI.12.

109. *Maimonides*, Book IV, ch. XXV.11.

110. Epstein, p. 143.

111. Ibid., p. 146.

112. *Niddah*, p. 217.

113. Ibid.

114. *Maimonides*, Book V, ch. IV.1.

115. Ibid., ch. XI.4.

116. *The Babylonian Talmud: Seder Tohoroth*, Rabbi Dr. I. Epstein (Ed.), Rev. Dr. Israel W. Slotki, trans. London: The Soncino Press, 1948, p. 217.

117. *Maimonides Book V*, Chap. IX.4.

118. Rabbi Ben Zion Gold, personal communication, 1976.

119. Lecture to Board of Governors, Hebrew University of Jerusalem, by Yigael Yadin, March 1974.

120. Baron, *Ancient and medieval history*, p. 38.

121. *Maimonides*, Book IV, ch. XIV.1.

122. Ibid., ch. XIV.2.

123. Ibid., ch. XIV.6.

124. Niddah, p. 219.

125. Ibid., p. 217. "Raba stated: One who desires all his children to be males should cohabit twice in succession."

126. Roald Dahl, New York *Times*, September 14, 1974; H. Bradley and Sons, New York *Times*, December 9, 1976.

127. K. H. Broer, I. Winkhaus, H. Sombroek, and R. Kaiser, "Frequency of Y-chromatic bearing spermatozoa in intracervical and intrauterine postcoital tests." *International Journal of Fertility*, 1976, 21, 181-185.

128. D. M. Rorvik and L. B. Shettles, *Choose your baby's sex.* New York: Dodd, Mead, 1977; R. Guerrero, "Association of the type and time of insemination within the menstrual cycle with the human sex ratio at birth." *New England Journal of Medicine,* 1974, 291, 1056-1059; B. Seguy, "La sélection volontaire du sexe: Point actuel de nos connaissances." *Journal of Gyn. Obst. Biol. Repr.,* 1975, 4, 29-36; "Les méthodes de sélection naturelle et volontaire des sexes: Intérêt dans la prévention des malformations liées au sexe et de certaines interruptions de grosses à répétition." *Journal of Gyn. Obst. Biol. Repr.,* 1975, 4, 145-149.

129. Ibid.

130. M. Freund, "Interrelationships among the characteristics of human semen and factors affecting semen-specimen quality." *Journal of Reproduction and Fertility,* 1962, 4, 143-159.

131. Douglas C. Downing and Donald L. Black, "Equality of survival of X and Y chromosome-bearing human spermatozoa." *Fertility and Sterility,* 1976, 27, 1191-1193.

132. Rorvik and Shettles, op. cit., 1977.

133. Freund, op. cit., 1962, p. 159. "The construction of fertility indices is complicated by the fact that we do not know whether each of the three characteristics, sperm concentration, motility and morphology, is directly related to fertility in a cause and effect relationship or whether only one of the three characteristics is directly related to fertility and the others are only correlated with it and bear no direct relationship to fertility. Finally, there is no definitive evidence that any of the commonly measured semen characteristics is directly related to fertility in a cause and effect relationship."

134. William H. James, "Timing of fertilization and sex ratio of offspring—A review." *Annals of Human Biology,* 1976, 3, 549-556.

135. Ibid., p. 550.

136. W. Crowley, Department of Gynecology at Massachusetts General Hospital, personal communication, 1976.

137. Irving Singer and Josephine Singer, "Periodicity of sexual desire in relation to time of ovulation in women." *Journal of Biosocial Science,* 1972, 4, 471-481.

138. William D. Odell and Dean L. Moyer, *Physiology of reproductiom.* St. Louis: C. V. Mosby, 1971.

139. Ibid., p. 35.

140. Rorvik and Shettles, op. cit.; Guerrero, op. cit.; Seguy, op. cit.

141. John MacLeod and Ruth Gold, "The male factor in fertility and infertility VI: Semen quality and certain other factors in relation to ease of conception." *Fertility and Sterility,* 1953, 4.

142. M. Freund, 1962.

143. Rodrigo Guerrero, "Type and time of insemination within the menstrual cycle and the human sex ratio at birth." *Studies in Family Planning,* 1975, 6, 367-371; S. J. Kleegman, "Therapeutic donor insemination." *Fertility and Sterility,* 1954, 5, 7-31.

144. Seguy, op. cit.

145. Guerrero, op. cit., 1974.

146. Singer and Singer, op. cit.

147. Guerrero, op. cit., 1974.

148. If the probability of male and female conceptions were exactly equal at all times, half of all dizygotic twins would be MF, one-quarter would be MM, and the other quarter FF. But if at times the probability of male conception is greater, and if at other times female conception is favored, the number of like-sex twins (MM and FF) would be slightly larger than half of all dizygotic twins.

149. William H. James, "Cycle day of insemination, coital rate, and sex ratio." *The Lancet,* January 16, 1971.

150. K. S. Moghissi, "Cyclic changes of cervical mucus in normal and progestin-treated women." *Fertility and Sterility,* 1966, 17(5).

151. Ibid.

152. Ibid., Broer et al., 1976; Irving F. Stein and Melvin R. Cohen, "Sperm survival at estimated ovulation time: Prognostic significance." *Fertility and Sterility,* 1950, 1.

153. Rhode et al., 1973; Broer et al., 1976; R. J. Ericsson, C. N. Langevin, and M. Nishino, "Isolation of fractions rich in human Y-sperm." *Nature,* 1973, 246, 421-424; H. Goodall and A. M. Roberts, "Differences in motility of human X- and Y-bearing spermatozoa." *Journal of Reproduction and Fertility,* 1976, 48, 433-436.

154. Rhode et al., 1973; A. M. Roberts, "Gravitational separations of X and Y spermatozoa." *Nature,* 1972, 238.

155. Ericsson et al., 1973; Rhode et al., 1973.

156. Rorvik and Shettles, op. cit.

157. Downing and Black, 1976.

158. Freund, 1962; John MacLeod and Ruth Gold, "The male factor in fertility and infertility." *Fertility and Sterility,* 1952, 3, 297-315.

159. Ibid.

160. Ibid.

161. Ibid.

162. Ibid.

163. Ibid.

164. Ibid.; Broer et al., 1976. "It seems that the motility of spermatozoa has an influence upon the positive or negative result of the Sims-Huhner test (a test indicating numbers of motile sperm) but not upon the percentage of the distribution pattern of the Y-chromatin positive spermatozoa."

165. *Maimonides,* Book IV, ch. XIV.4.

166. Robert C. Bailey, "Variations in the human live-birth sex ratio." Unpublished paper (January, 1977), pp. 16-17.

167. John Whiting, personal communication, 1977.

168. James, 1974, p. 167.

169. John Whiting, personal communication, 1977.

170. James, op. cit., 1976.

171. James, op. cit., 1974.

172. Ibid., p. 167.

173. MacLeod and Gold, 1953; Freund, 1962.

174. Ibid.

175. Alan S. Parkes, "Sexuality and reproduction." *Perspectives in Biology and Medicine,* 1974, Spring.

176. MacLeod and Gold, 1952, p. 150.

177. Freund, 1962 (?).

178. Freund, 1962; MacLeod and Gold, 1952.

179. Freund, 1962.

180. Rorvik and Shettles, op. cit.

181. Moghissi, op. cit.; Robert B. Diasio and Robert H. Glass, "Effects of pH on the migration of X and Y sperm." *Fertility and Sterility,* 1971, 22(5).

182. Diasio and Glass, 1971; Downing and Black, 1976; Broer et al., 1976.

183. William H. Masters and Virginia E. Johnson, "The physiology of the vaginal reproductive function." *West. J. Surg. Obst. and Gyn.,* 1961, March-April, 105-120; C.A. Fox, S. J. Meldrum, and B. W. Watson, "Continuous measurement by radio-telemetry of vaginal pH during human coitus." *Journal of Reproduction and Fertility,* 1973, 22, 69-75.

184. Masters and Johnson, op. cit.

185. Fox et al., 1973; Masters and Johnson, op. cit.

186. Cervical mucus ranges from pH of 7.3-8.4 (Diasio and Glass, op. cit.), and the vagina has a much lower pH range of about 3.5-4.5 (Masters and Johnson, 1961). A pH of 7.0 is neutral; anything above is alkaline and below, acidic.

187. Diasio and Glass, op. cit.

188. C. A. Fox, H. S. Wolff, and J. A. Baker, "Measurement of intravaginal and intrauterine pressures during human coitus by radiotelemetry." *Journal of Reproduction and Fertility,* 1970, 22, 243-251.

189. Ibid.

190. Ibid.

191. William H. Masters and Virginia E. Johnson, *Human sexual response.* Boston: Little, Brown, 1966, pp. 115-116.

192. Parkes, op. cit., pp. 399-410.

193. Ibid., p. 406.

194. Ibid., p. 407.

195. Singer and Singer, op. cit., p. 477.

196. Ibid.

197. Ibid., p. 408.

198. Guerrero, op. cit., 1974; Guerrero, op. cit., 1975.

199. W. H. James, "Coital rate, cycle day of insemination and sex ratio." *Journal of Biosocial Science*, 1977, 9, 183-189.

200. S. Harlap, "Gender of infants conceived on different days of the menstrual cycle." *The New England Journal of Medicine*, 1979, 300, 1445-1448; R. V. Vollman, "Gender of infants conceived on different days of the menstrual cycle." *The New England Journal of Medicine*, 1980, 301, 1125; W. H. James, "Time of fertilization and sex of infants." *The Lancet*, 1980, 1124.

201. Seguy, op. cit.

202. A. M. Roberts, "The origins of fluctuations in the human secondary sex ratio." *Journal of Biosocial Science*, 1978, 10, 169-182.

Chapter Five

1. The preparation of this chapter has been greatly facilitated by the availability of several excellent works. These are: Robert V. Wells, *The population of the British colonies in America before 1776* (Princeton, NJ: Princeton University Press, 1975); Anne Firor Scott, *The southern lady: From pedestal to politics, 1830-1930* (Chicago: University of Chicago Press, 1970); William Forrest Sprague, *Women and the West: A short social history* (Boston: Christopher, 1940); Nancy F. Cott, *The bonds of womanhood: "Woman's Sphere" in New England, 1780-1835* (New Haven, CT: Yale University Press, 1977). Also of great value was Herbert Moller's work on the social effects of sex ratios in colonial times. He was one of the first scholars to grasp the enormous social importance of imbalanced sex ratios in his work, "Sex composition and correlated culture patterns of Colonial America." *The William and Mary Quarterly*, 1945, 2, 113-153. Moller's important work was confirmed in its major conclusions in a study by Robert Thompson, "Seventeenth century English and Colonial sex ratios: A postscript." *Population Studies*, n.d., 28, 1.

2. Sprague, op. cit., 1972, p. 125.

3. Wells, op. cit.

4. Ibid.

5. Ibid.

6. Ibid.

7. Wells, op. cit., p. 85. According to Moller (op. cit.), sex ratios were never extremely high in New England. From 1620 to 1638, 46 ships departed for New England, carrying 1882 men, 1197 women, and 93 persons of unspecified sex. This represents a sex ratio of 157. These passengers accounted for about 17 percent of the immigration to the New England colonies during the period 1620 to 1640. If they may be regarded as representative, then the sex ratio for these colonies, made up almost entirely of immigrants, amounted to about 3 males for every 2 females for the first two decades of New England's history. This compared with a ratio of about 6 to 1 in the Virginia immigration.

8. Wells, op. cit., p. 164. Moller (op. cit.) reports that the first great wave of colonists left England in 1609, in nine ships, and most of them were men. They brought to Virginia about 100 women and 400-500 men. Some idea of the effects of mortality and migration are conveyed by the fact that only seven years later, in 1616, inhabitants of Virginia numbered only 351 and consisted of 205 officers and laborers and 81 farmers—that is, 286 male adults—while women and children taken together numbered only 65. Subsequently, in response to urgent pleas, the Virginia Company of London sent 140 women, 90 in 1620, and 50 in 1621 and 1622. Wells (op. cit.) notes that in 1625, a census of the Virginia Colony indicated a total of 1218 adults. Just over half of the men in this population were between 20 and 29 years of age, as compared with about 38 percent of the women in this bracket. Few people were old; only about 1 percent had reached the age of 50. Aside from the children under 10 years, for whom sex ratios were fairly normal, other ratios were extreme. Males between 16 and 19 outnumbered females by 16 to 1, and above the age of 20 there were about seven men for every woman.

9. Spruill, op. cit.

10. Moller (op. cit.) reports that the years from 1635 to 1705 brought between 1500 and 2000 servants annually, a total of from 100,000 to 140,000. These were predominantly men, although the exact numbers of men and women are unknown. One publication from the ar-

chives of Bristol, England, gives the names of over 10,000 servants to foreign plantations who sailed from that point to America during the years 1654-1686. The sex ratios for these immigrants were 338 for the New England colonies, and for Virginia, 308. About 250,000 indentured servants arrived during the seventeenth and eighteenth centuries. Typically, they were not counted in the census. Also, about 50,000 convicts and Scotch and Irish prisoners of war sent to the colonies were not included in the censuses, which thus considerably underestimated the excess of males. For example, the census of Maryland, taken in 1707, lists 7090 Christian men (free white male adults) and 6325 Christian women, which would mean the sex ratio would be 112. But in addition to the white children and black slaves, there were 3003 white servants, most of whom were male but not counted in the census.

11. Spruill, op. cit.

12. Ibid.

13. Ibid.

14. Ibid., p. 205.

15. Kingsbury, in Moller, p. 130.

16. Spruill, op. cit., 1938.

17. Moller, 1945.

18. Spruill, 1938.

19. Arthur W. Calhoun, *A social history of the American family from Colonial times to the present, vol. 1: Colonial period.* New York: Barnes & Noble, 1945.

20. Ibid.

21. Spruill, 1938, p. 210.

22. Moller, 1945.

23. Calhoun, Vol. I, 1917, p. 249.

24. Ibid., 1917, pp. 250-251.

25. Ibid.

26. Ibid., pp. 264-265.

27. Ibid.

28. Holliday, 1922.

29. Edmund Morgan, *The Puritan family.* New York: Harper & Row, 1944.

30. Moller, 1945, p. 140.

31. Calhoun, Vol. I, 1917.

32. John Demos, "Notes on life in Plymouth Colony." *William and Mary Quarterly,* 1965, 22, 264-286. *A little commonwealth: Family life in Plymouth Colony.* New York: Oxford University Press, 1970.

33. Demos, op. cit., p. 277.

34. Alexander Keyssar, "Widowhood in eighteenth-century Massachusetts: A problem in the history of the family." *Perspectives in American History,* 1974, 8, 83-122.

35. Wells, 1975, p. 77.

36. Ibid., p. 95.

37. Ibid.

38. Ibid., p. 96.

39. Calhoun, Vol. I, 1917.

40. Philip J. Greven, Jr. "Family structure in seventeenth-century Andover, Massachusetts." *William and Mary Quarterly,* 1966, 23, 234-256. *Four generations: Population, land, and family in Colonial Andover, Massachusetts.* Ithaca, NY: Cornell University Press, 1970.

41. Demos, op. cit.

42. Keyssar, op. cit.

43. Wells, op. cit., p. 77.

44. Demos, op. cit.

45. Ibid., p. 279.

46. Moller, op. cit., 1945.

47. Edmund S. Morgan, "The Puritans and sex." *New England Quarterly,* 1942, December, pp. 591-607.

48. Ibid., 1942.

49. Ibid.

50. Ibid.

51. Ibid.

52. John Bargrave, in Sigmund Diamond (Ed.), *The creation of society in the New World.* Chicago: Rand McNally, 1963, p. 33.

53. Ibid.

54. Moller, 1945, p. 140.

55. Robert Horne, in Spruill, op. cit., p. 214.

56. Moller, 1945.

57. Wells, p. 295.

58. Robert V. Wells, "Quaker marriage patterns in a colonial perspective." *William and Mary Quarterly,* 1972, 29, 415-442.

59. W. F. Sprague, op. cit., 1972, p. 27.

60. William S. Greever, *The Bonanza West: The story of western mining rushes, 1848-1900.* Norman: University of Oklahoma Press, 1963.

61. James E. Davis, *Frontier America, 1800 to 1840: A comparative demographic analysis of the settlement process.* Glendale, CA: Arthur C. Clark, 1977.

62. Jack D. Eblen, "An analysis of nineteenth-century frontier populations." *Demography,* 1965, 2, 399-411.

63. Sprague, op. cit., 1972.

64. Sprague, op. cit., 1972, p. 37.

65. Sprague, op. cit., 1940, p. 37.

66. Ibid., p. 43.

67. Ibid., p. 44.

68. Ibid., p. 45.

69. Ibid., p. 39.

70. Ibid., p. 48.

71. Ibid., p. 58.

72. Ibid., p. 68.

73. *The Western Citizen,* Paris, Kentucky, April 10, 1824.

74. Calhoun, 1917, Vol. 2, pp. 103-104.

75. Sprague, op. cit., pp. 192-193.

76. Stanford Lyman, *The Asian in the West.* Social Science and Humanities Publication No. 4, Western Studies Center, Desert Research Institute, University of Nevada, Reno, Nevada, 1970. *Chinese Americans.* New York: Random House, 1974.

77. Lyman, op. cit.

78. Lyman, op. cit.

79. Sprague, op. cit., pp. 121-122.

80. Sprague, p. 131.

81. Greever, p. 171.

82. Greever, p. 64.

83. Ibid.

84. Sprague, p. 129.

85. Wells, pp. 69-109.

86. U.S. Bureau of the Census, *Historical statistics of the United States, Colonial times to 1970, Bicentennial edition, Part I.* Washington, DC: Government Printing Office.

87. Scott, op. cit., 1970, p. xi.

88. Wells, op. cit.

89. Scott, 1970, p. 4.

90. Ibid., pp. 4-5.

91. Ibid., pp. 6-7.

92. Ibid., Chapter 3.

93. Scott, 1970, p. 31.

94. Ibid., 1970, p. 44.

95. Ibid., 1970, Chapter 2.

96. Ibid., p. 51.

97. Ibid., pp. 52-53.

98. Ibid., p. 54.

99. Scott, 1970, Chapter 5.

100. Nancy F. Cott, *The bonds of womanhood: "Woman's Sphere" in New England, 1780-1835.* New Haven, CT: Yale University Press, 1977.

101. Ibid.

102. Ibid.

103. Ibid.

104. Ibid.

105. Ibid., 1977, pp. 36-37.

106. Ibid., 1977, p. 56.

107. Ruth H. Bloch, "Untangling the roots of modern sex roles: A survey of four centuries of change." *Signs: Journal of Women in Culture and Society*, 1978, 4, 237-252.

108. Carroll Smith-Rosenberg, "The female world of love and ritual: Relations between women in nineteenth-century America." *Signs: Journal of Women in Culture and Society*, 1975, 1, pp. 1-30.

109. Nancy F. Cott, "Passionlessness: An interpretation of Victorian sexual ideology, 1790-1850." *Signs: Journal of Women in Culture and Society*, 1978, 4, 219-236.

110. Mark Zborowski and Elizabeth Herzog, *Life is with people: The Jewish little-town of eastern Europe*. New York: International Universities Press, 1952.

111. Ibid.

112. Cott, 1978.

113. Ibid.

114. Barbara Welter, "The cult of true womanhood, 1820-1860." *American Quarterly*, 1966, 18, 151-174.

115. Leslie A. Fiedler, *Love and death in the American novel*. New York: Criterion Books, 1960.

116. Mario Praz, *The romantic agony*. Angus Davidson, trans. 2nd Ed. London: Oxford University Press, 1951.

117. Cott, 1978.

118. Ibid.

119. Ibid., p. 326.

120. Ibid.

121. Ibid., p. 235.

122. Carl N. Degler, "What ought to be and what was: Woman's sexuality in the nineteenth century." *American Historical Review*, 1974, 79, 1467-1490.

123. Ibid.

124. Cott, 1978.

125. Linda Gordon, "Voluntary motherhood: The beginnings of feminist birth control ideas in the United States." *Feminist Studies*, 1973, 1, 5-22. *Woman's body, woman's right: A social history of birth control in America*. New York: Viking Press, 1976.

126. Ibid.

127. Ibid.

128. Ibid.

129. Daniel S. Smith, "Family limitations, sexual control, and domestic feminism in Victorian America." *Feminist Studies*, 1973, 1, pp. 40-57.

130. Daniel S. Smith and M. S. Hindus, "Premarital pregnancy in America, 1640-1971: An overview and interpretation." *Journal of Interdisciplinary History*, 1975, 4, 537-570.

Part II

1. H. Carter and P. C. Glick, *Marriage and divorce: A social and economic study*, rev. ed. Cambridge, MA: Harvard University Press, 1976.

2. Ibid.

Chapter Six

1. Social exchange theory has its origins in social psychology, economics, and sociology. Among the large literature on the topic are the following major works: J. W. Thibaut and H. H. Kelly, *The social psychology of groups*. New York: John Wiley, 1959; P. M. Blau, *Exchange and*

power in social life. New York: John Wiley, 1964; G. C. Homans, *Social behavior: Its elementary forms*, rev. Ed. New York: Harcourt Brace Jovanovich, 1974; G. C. Becker, *The economic approach to human behavior.* Chicago: University of Chicago Press, 1976; H. H. Kelly and J. W. Thibaut, *Interpersonal relations: A theory of interdependence.* New York: John Wiley, 1978.

2. M. Morgan, *Total woman.* New Jersey: Revell, 1973.

3. D. H. Dwyer, *Images and self-images: Male and female in Morocco.* New York: Columbia University Press, 1978.

4. Ibid.

5. Ibid.

6. P. C. Glick and A. J. Norton, "Marrying, divorcing, and living together in the U. S. today." *Population Bulletin,* 1977, 32, No. 5.

7. Ibid.

Chapter Seven

1. Robin Morgan (Ed.) *Sisterhood is powerful: An anthology of writings from the Women's Liberation Movement.* New York: Random House, 1970.

2. Paul C. Glick, David M. Heer, and John C. Beresford, "Family formation and family composition: Trends and prospects." In Marvin B. Sussman (Ed.), 2nd ed. *Sourcebook in marriage and the family.* Boston: Houghton Mifflin, 1963, pp. 30-40.

3. From the 1976 baseline data, we estimate that at that time, slightly less than 2 percent of the men aged 20-24 were overseas in the armed forces; however, a disproportionate number of these would be black. Roughly, only about 1 percent of this white cohort was overseas. About half as many in the 25-29 age bracket and one-quarter as many in the 15-19 and 30-34 age cohorts were overseas. In addition, some of these men would have wives at home. We can conclude that, for the white population at least, the amount of bias accrued by including the armed forces overseas will be less than 1 percent for all age counts (U.S. Bureau of the Census, *Current Population Reports, Projections of the Population of the United States: 1977 to 2050,* Series P-25, No. 704, July 1977, Table J and Table 8, Series II).

4. Henry S. Shryock and Jacob S. Siegel, *The methods and materials of demography* (condensed ed. by Edward G. Stockwell). New York: Academic Press, 1976, Table 15-12.

5. U.S. Bureau of the Census, *Current Population Reports,* Series P-20, No. 349, "Marital status and living arrangements: March 1979." Washington, DC: Government Printing Office, 1980.

6. Ibid.

7. Ibid.

8. Ibid.

9. Ibid.

10. Hugh Carter and Paul C. Glick, *Marriage and Divorce: A Social and Economic Study, Revised Edition.* Cambridge, MA: Harvard University Press, 1976.

11. U.S. Bureau of the Census, *Current Population Reports,* Series P-20, No. 365, "Marital Status and Living Arrangements: March, 1980." Washington, DC: Government Printing Office, 1981.

12. U.S. Bureau of the Census, *Current Population Reports,* Series P-20, No. 349, "Marital Status and Living Arrangements: March, 1979." Washington, DC: Government Printing Office, 1980.

13. Carter and Glick, op. cit.

14. Ibid.

15. Ibid.

16. U.S. Bureau of the Census, *Current Population Reports,* Series P-20, No. 338, "Marital status and living arrangements: March, 1978," Washington, DC: Government Printing Office, 1979.

17. Carter and Glick, op. cit.

18. Mildred, Dickeman, "Demographic consequences of infanticide in man." *Annual Review of Ecology and Systematics,* 1975, 6, 107-137; Mildred Dickeman, "Female infanticide and hypergamy: A neglected relationship," unpublished paper, 1976.

19. Carter and Glick, op. cit., p. 403.

20. U.S. Bureau of the Census, *Current Population Reports*, Series P-20, No. 312, "Marriage, divorce, widowhood, and remarriage by family characteristics: June, 1975." Washington, DC: Government Printing Office, 1977.

21. Carter and Glick, op. cit., p. 403.

22. Ibid.

23. Ibid.

24. U.S. Bureau of the Census, *Current Population Reports*, Series P-20, No. 312, op. cit., 1977.

25. Ibid.

26. Carter and Glick, op. cit., p. 435.

27. U.S. Bureau of the Census, *Current Population Reports*, Series P-20, No. 312, op. cit., 1977, Table G.

28. Carter and Glick, op. cit., p. 229.

29. Carter and Glick, op. cit., p. 404.

30. Ibid.

31. Ibid.

32. Christopher Lasch, *Haven in a heartless world: The family besieged.* New York: Basic Books, 1977.

33. U.S. Bureau of the Census, *Current Population Reports*, Series P-20, Series 338, op. cit., 1979.

34. Paul C. Glick and Arthur J. Norton, "Marrying, divorcing, and living together in the U.S. today." *Population Bulletin*, 1977, 32, No. 5.

35. Ibid.

36. Ibid.

37. U.S. Bureau of the Census, *Current Population Reports*, Series P-20, No. 349, "Marital status and living arrangements: March, 1979." Washington, DC: Government Printing Office, 1980.

38. Ira E. Robinson, Karl King, and Jack O. Balswick, "The premarital sexual revolution among college females." *Family Coordinator*, 1972, 21, 189-194. Melvin Zelnik and John F. Kantner, "The probability of premarital intercourse." *Social Science Research*, 1972, 1, 335-341. Arthur M. Verner and Cyrus S. Steward, "Adolescent sexual behavior in Middle America revisited: 1970-1973." *Journal of Marriage and the Family*, 1974, 36, 728-735. Patricia Y. Miller and William Simon, "Adolescent sexual behavior: Context and change." *Social Problems*, 1974, 22, 58-75. Richard Udry, Karl Bauman, and Naomi M. Morris, "Changes in premarital coital experiences of recent decade-of-birth cohorts of urban American women." *Journal of Marriage and the Family*, 1975, 37, 783-787. Robert A. Lewis and Wesley R. Burr, "Premarital coitus and commitment among college students." *Archives of Sexual Behavior*, 1975, 4, 73-79. Frank W. Finger, "Changes in sex practices and beliefs of male college students: Over 30 years." *Journal of Sex Research*, 1975, 11, 304-317. Jay Roy Hopkins, "Sexual behavior in adolescence." *Journal of Social Issues*, 1977, 33, 67-85. E. R. Mahoney, "Gender and social class differences in changes in attitudes toward premarital coitus." *Sociology and Social Research*, 1978, 62, 279-286. Harold T. Christensen, "Recent data reflecting upon the sexual revolution in America." Presented at the International Sociological Association, 1978.

39. Glick and Norton, op. cit., p. 21.

40. Edward Shorter, *The making of the modern family.* New York: Basic Books, 1975.

41. M. J. Zube, "Changing concepts of morality: 1948-1969." *Social Forces*, 1972, 50, 385-393.

42. R. Hosen, "The influence of sex ratios on the attitudes of men toward women as reflected in popular literature." Ed.D. dissertation, University of Houston, 1981.

Chapter Eight

1. D. P. Moynihan, *The Negro family: Case for national action.* Washington, DC: Government Printing Office, 1965.

2. U.S. Bureau of the Census, *Historical Statistics of the United States: Colonial Times to*

1970, Bicentennial Ed. Washington DC: Government Printing Office.

3. National Academy of Sciences, *America's uncounted people,* 1972.

4. J. S. Siegel, "Estimates of coverage of the population by sex, race, and age in the 1970 Census." Presented at the annual meetings of the Population Association of America, New Orleans, April 1973.

5. Ibid.

6. U.S. Bureau of the Census, "Estimates of the population of the United States, by age, sex, and race: 1970 to 1975." *Current Population Reports,* Series P-25, No. 614. Washington, DC: Government Printing Office, 1975.

7. M. S. Teitelbaum, "Factors associated with the sex ratio in human populations." In G. A. Harrison and A. J. Bower (Eds.), *The structure of human populations.* London: Clarendon Press, 1972.

8. S. Shapiro, E. R. Schlesinger, and R. E. L. Nesbitt, *Infant perinatal, maternal, and childhood mortality, in the United States.* Cambridge, MA: Harvard University Press, 1968: National Center for Health Statistics, "National mortality and infant mortality surveys, 1964-66." *Monthly Vital Statistics Report,* 1971 20(5), Supplement.

9. Ibid.

10. Ibid.

11. Ibid.

12. Ibid.

13. U.S. Bureau of the Census, *Negroes in the United States, 1920 to 1932,* Table 2. Washington, DC: Government Printing Office.

14. National Center for Health Statistics, *Trends in Illegitimacy, United States, 1940 to 1965,* Series 21, No. 15. Washington, DC: Government Printing Office.

15. Ibid.

16. U.S. Bureau of the Census, *Census of the Population, 1960, 1970,* Vol. 1, *Characteristics of the Population,* U.S. Summary Section. Washington, DC: Government Printing Office.

17. Shapiro et. al., op. cit.

18. U.S. Bureau of the Census, *Census of the Population, 1970, Summary Report, Mobility for States and the Nation,* PC(2)-2B. Washington, DC: Government Printing Office.

19. A stepwise regression analysis was performed for the sex ratio and six socioeconomic variables (percent males and percent females in the labor force, rural-urban, education, poverty, and income). The regression coefficient explained about 83.5 percent of the variance in illegitimacy, with 73.7 due to the sex ratio and 9.8 percent to the six socioeconomic variables. When the socioeconomic variables were forced to enter the equation before the sex ratio, they accounted for almost as much variance as the sex ratio (72.0, as compared to 73.7 in the first equation). Of course, this is six variables compared to one.

20. U.S. Bureau of the Census, *Current Population Reports,* Series P-20, No. 312, "Marriage, divorce, widowhood, and remarriage by family characteristics, June, 1975." Washington DC: Government Printing Office, 1977.

21. U.S. Bureau of the Census, *Census of the Population, 1970,* Vols. 2-52, "Household and family characteristics by race," Table 22 in each volume. Washington, DC: Government Printing Office.

22. Ibid.

23. Ibid.

24. U.S. Bureau of the Census, *Current Population Reports,* Series P-20, No. 371, *"Household and family characteristics, March 1981."* Washington, DC: Government Printing Office, 1982.

25. J. J. Jackson, "Black women in a racist society." In C. V. Willie, B. M. Kramer, and B. S. Brown (Eds.), *Racism and mental health.* Pittsburgh: University of Pittsburgh Press, 1973.

26. R. V. Wells, *The population of the British colonies in America before 1776: A survey of census data.* Princeton, NJ: Princeton University Press, 1975.

27. Ibid.

28. S. L. Engerman, R. W. Fogel, E. D. Genovese, and H. Gutman, "A forum symposium on American Negro slavery: New directions in black history." *Forum: A Journal of Social Commentary and the Arts,* 1972, 1(2).

29. Ibid.

30. U.S. Bureau of the Census, *Historical Statistics of the United States, Colonial Times to 1970,* Bicentennial Ed.

31. Ibid.

32. C. D. Goldin, *Urban slavery in the American South, 1820-1860: A quantitative history.* Chicago: University of Chicago Press, 1976. We are indebted to Robert Fogel for showing us this material.

33. H. G. Gutman, *The black family in slavery and freedom,* 1750-1925. New York: Pantheon Books, 1976.

34. Ibid.

35. R. W. Fogel, and S. L. Engerman, *Time on the cross: The economics of American Negro slavery.* Boston: Little, Brown, 1974; H. G. Gutman, op. cit.

36. R. Stekel, personal communication, 1977.

37. Carter and Glick, op. cit.

38. U.S. Bureau of the Census, *Current Population Reports, Special Studies,* Series P-23, No.80. "The social and economic status of the black population in the United States, 1790-1978." Washington, DC: Government Printing Office, 1979.

39. Ibid.

40. C. Safilios-Rothschild, "Dual linkages between the occupational and family systems: A macrosociological analysis." *Signs: Journal of Women in Culture and Society,* 1975, December.

41. "Can population research change history? An interview with Charles Westoff." *Princeton Alumni Weekly,* March 7, 1977, p. 12.

42. C. R. Stone, "Sex differences and sex-role socialization in black children," unpublished paper.

43. W. D. Ten Houten, "The black family: Myth and reality." *Psychiatry,* 1970, 53, 145-173.

44. D. Belle, "Who uses mental health facilities?" In M. Guttentag, S. Salasin, and D. Belle (Eds.), *The Mental Health of Women.* New York: Academic Press, 1980.

45. D. P. Aldridge, "Black female suicide: Is the excitement justified?" In L. F. Rodgers-Rose (Ed.), *The black woman.* Beverly Hills, CA: Sage, 1980.

46. J. Bernard, *Marriage and family among Negroes.* Englewood Cliffs, NJ: Prentice-Hall, 1966.

47. W. H. Wheeler, "Communication between black women and black men as seen by a mental health practitioner." Presented at *The black woman and the Bicentennial,* Arizona State University, June 1976.

48. C. A. Morton, "Mistakes black men make in relating to black women." *Ebony,* December, 1975, p. 172.

49. Wheeler, op. cit., pp. 5-7.

50. Morton, op. cit., p. 174.

51. C. A. Morton, "Mistakes black men make in relating to black women." *Ebony,* January, 1976, p. 30.

52. Ibid, p. 92.

53. R. E. Staples, "Sex and the black middle class." *Ebony,* August, 1973, pp. 106-112.

54. Wheeler, op. cit., pp. 7-8.

55. C. Robinson, "The burdens on black couples: Roles change, strains grow." Detroit Free Press, April 11, 1975.

56. Morton, op. cit., p. 173.

57. N. Shange, *For colored girls who have considered suicide when the rainbow is enuf.* R. A. Inbows, 1976.

58. P. Marshall, "Black-eyed Susans." In M. H. Washington (Ed.), *The black women and the disappointment of romantic love.* Garden City, NY: Anchor Books, 1975.

Chapter Nine

1. L. Tiger and R. Fox, *The imperial animal.* New York: Holt, Rinehart & Winston, 1971. Others have also stressed an evolutionary approach to understanding sex differences; for example, B. A. Hamburg, "The psychobiology of sex differences: An evolutionary perspective." In R. C. Friedman, R. M. Richart, and R. L. Vande Wiele (Eds.), *Sex differences in behavior.* Melbourne, FL: Krieger Press, 1974.

2. S. B. Hrdy, *The woman that never evolved.* Cambridge, MA: Harvard University Press, 1981.

3. We are aware of the exciting and provocative research on the interaction between sex hormones, the nervous system, and behavior, but at this writing findings are too tentative to draw any definitive conclusions.

4. While the menstrual period was once believed to be incapacitating, in contemporary times this appears to apply only to a very small proportion of women.

5. This is not to deny the important role that women played in gathering food and sometimes even in hunting. See M. K. Martin and B. Voorhies, *Female of the species*. New York: Columbia University Press, 1975.

6. U. S. Bureau of the Census, "School enrollment—social and economic characteristics of students: October 1979." *Current Population Reports, Population Characteristics,* Series P-20, No. 360. Washington, DC: Government Printing Office, 1980.

7. R. E. Smith (Ed.), *The subtle revolution: Women at work*. Washington, DC: The Urban Institute, 1979.

8. R. Rapoport and R. N. Rapoport, with J. Bumstead (Eds.), *Working couples*. New York: Harper & Row, 1978; R. Rapoport and R. N. Rapoport, *Dual-career families re-examined: New integrations of work and family*. New York: Harper & Row, 1976; C. Safilios-Rothschild, "Dual linkages between the occupational and family systems: A macrosociological analysis." *Signs: Journal of Women in Culture and Society,* December, 1975; K. Weingarten, "The employment pattern of professional couples and their distribution of involvement in the family." *Psychology of Women Quarterly,* 1978, 3, 43-52.

9. Ibid.

10. Ibid.

11. Ibid.

12. N. F. Cott, "Passionlessness: An interpretation of Victorian sexual ideology, 1790-1850." *Signs: Journal of Women in Culture and Society,* 1978, 4, 219-236.

Index

Biosketches

The late Marcia Guttentag (1932-1977) was Director of the Families and Stress Research Project at Harvard University. A social psychologist with a passion for social action, she identified herself with many causes, including the reduction of poverty and advocacy of women's rights. She was also an active researcher, founder and first President of the Evaluation Research Society of America, and past President of the Society for the Study of Social Psychological Issues and of the Division of Personality and Social Psychology of the American Psychological Association. With Elmer Struening, Marcia Guttentag edited the massive, two-volume *Handbook of Evaluation Research* and was a principal author of *The Mental Health of Women* and of *Undoing Sex Stereotypes*.

Paul F. Secord is Professor of Psychology and Education at the University of Houston. He has long had interdisciplinary interests and expertise. With sociologist Carl W. Backman, he is the author of *Social Psychology*, an internationally famous textbook translated into six languages. His seven books also include the internationally recognized *The Explanation of Social Behavior* (with philosopher Rom Harré). He is General Editor of the international *Journal for the Theory of Social Behavior*, which he founded in 1970 with Rom Harré. Paul Secord has been a Visiting Professor at Princeton, Yale, and Oxford Universities and is past President of the Society for Philosophy and Psychology and of the Division of Personality and Social Psychology of the American Psychological Association. He has twice been awarded a Senior Research Fellowship by the National Institute of Mental Health.